ecpr PRESS

regulation in practice
the de facto independence of regulatory agencies

Martino Maggetti

ecpr PRESS

First published by the ECPR Press in 2012

The ECPR Press is the publishing imprint of the European Consortium for Political Research
(ECPR), a scholarly association, which supports and encourages the training, research
and cross-national cooperation of political scientists in institutions throughout Europe and
beyond. The ECPR's Central Services are located at the University of Essex, Wivenhoe Park,
Colchester, CO4 3SQ, UK

Typeset by ECPR Press
Printed and bound by Lightning Source

British Library Cataloguing in Publication Data
A catalogue record for this book is available from the British Library

Paperback ISBN: 978-1-907301-28-5

www.ecprnet.eu/ecprpress

About the Author

MARTINO MAGGETTI (PhD, University of Lausanne) is a lecturer at the Department of Political Science (University of Zurich) and senior researcher at the Institut d'Etudes Politiques et Internationales (University of Lausanne). He is part of the 'Internationalization, Mediatization, and the Accountability of Regulatory Agencies' project, funded by the Swiss National Science Foundation, and teaches Comparative Regulatory Governance and Public Policy Methodology. His research interests focus on comparative politics, policy analysis and regulatory governance.

His research articles have appeared in various edited books and international journals, including *Business & Society*, *European Political Science Review*, *Journal of European Public Policy*, and *Regulation & Governance*.

ECPR – Monographs

Series Editors:
Dario Castiglione (University of Exeter)
Peter Kennealy (European University Institute)
Alexandra Segerberg (Stockholm University)
Peter Triantafillou (Roskilde University)

contents

List of Figures and Tables   vi

List of Abbreviations   viii

Acknowledgements   ix

Chapter One: Introduction   1

Chapter Two: Theoretical Framework and Analytical Approach   7

Chapter Three: Explaining de facto Independence (I)   33

Chapter Four: The Role of Independent Regulators in Lawmaking (II)   101

Chapter Five: The Media Coverage of Agencies (III)   141

Chapter Six: Conclusive Discussion   169

Appendix: Questionnaires and Data   189

Bibliography   225

Index   253

| list of figures and tables

Figures

Figure 2.1: Structure of the argument   32

Figure 3.1: Cases and conditions   64

Figure 3.2: Threshold setting   65

Figure 3.3: Synthetic view of agencies' de facto independence   75

Figure 4.1: The Explanatory model   109

Figure 4.2: Policy networks   134

Figure 4.3: Graphical representation of the solution   137

Figure 5.1: Typology of democracies (adapted from Lijphart 1999)   150

Figure 5.2: Component plot in rotated space   158

Figure 5.3: Trend of media coverage of the British CC and the Swiss ComCo   160

Figure 5.4: Trend and tone of media coverage   162

Figure 5.5. The tone of the media coverage of the British CC and the Swiss ComCo   163

Figure 5.6: The criteria for credibility and efficiency of the British CC and the Swiss
      ComCo   164

Tables

Table 3.1: Case selection   51

Table 3.2: Calibration versus qualitative coding procedure   54

Table 3.3: Causal conditions   56

Table 3.4: Operationalising the de facto independence of IRAs from the political
      decision makers   72

Table 3.5: Operationalising the de facto independence of IRAs from the regulatees   73

Table 3.6: Coding the de facto independence of IRAs from the politicians   76

Table 3.7: Coding the de facto independence of IRAs from the regulatees   77

Table 3.8: Necessary conditions for de facto independence from politicians   93

Table 3.9: Truth table – de facto independence of IRAs from the politicians   94

Table 3.10: Truth table solution – de facto independence of IRAs from the politicians 95

Table 3.11: Necessary conditions for de facto independence from politicians 96

Table 3.12: Truth table – de facto independence of IRAs from the regulatees 97

Table 3.13: Truth table solution – de facto independence of IRAs from the regulatees 97

Table 4.1: Formal and de facto independence of IRAs 115

Table 4.2: Case selection 119

Table 4.3: The Netbk 126

Table 4.4: The Netco 126

Table 4.5: The Swebk 127

Table 4.6: The Sweco 127

Table 4.7: The Swibk 128

Table 4.8: The Swico 128

Table 4.9: Data 135

Table 4.10: Truth table – remote factors 136

Table 4.11: Truth table – proximate factors 136

Table 5.1: Sample of the coding of the British CC 155

Table 5.2: Sample of the coding of the Swiss ComCo 156

Table 5.3: Principal component matrix 157

Table 5.4: Rotated component matrix 158

Table 5.5: Media favourableness 163

Table 6.1: Summary of the hypotheses (1) 170

Table 6.2: Summary of the hypotheses (2) 171

| list of abbreviations

AFM	*Autoriteit Financiële Markten* (Netherlands)
AGCOM	*Autorità per le Garanzie nelle Comunicazioni* (Italy)
APES	Actor-Process-Event Scheme
BaFin	*Bundesanstalt für Finanzdienstleistungsaufsicht* (Germany)
CBFA	*Commission Bancaire, Financière et des Assurances* (Belgium)
CC	Competition Commission (UK)
CMEs	Coordinated Market Economies
EBK (SFBC)	*Eidgenössische Bankenkommission* (Switzerland)
ERNs	European Regulatory Networks
FI	*Finansinspektionen* (Sweden)
IRAs	Independent Regulatory Agencies
KKV	*Konkurrensverket* (Sweden)
LMEs	Liberal Market Economies
NCA	*Konkurransetilsynet* (Norway)
NMa	*Nederlandse Mededingingsautoriteit* (Netherlands)
NPM	New Public Management
NPT	*Post- Og Teletilsynet* (Norway)
NRAs	National Regulatory Authorities
OECD	Organisation for Economic Co-operation and Development
OPTA	*Onafhankelijke Post en Telecommunicatie Autoritei* (Netherlands)
PA	Principal-Agent
PTS	*Post & Telestyrelsen* (Sweden)
QCA	Qualitative Comparative Analysis
RATA	*Rahoitustarkastus* (Finland)
RTR	*Rundfunk und Telekom Regulierungs* (Austria)
WeKo (Comco)	*Wettbewerbskommission* (Switzerland)

| acknowledgements

Preface and acknowledgments

This book aims to contribute to the study of regulation in three distinct ways. First, it situates the question of regulatory independence within the interdisciplinary agenda on regulatory governance. Second, it expands and develops the empirical analyses of independent regulatory agencies, which were presented in my previous research.[1] Third, it proposes a synthetic account of the de facto independence of regulators and discusses its positive and normative implications for the study of regulation in practice.

The process of writing a book entails unavoidable moments of intellectual loneliness, implying the confrontation with contradictory expectations, the need for dealing with fundamental doubts, and unrelenting anxiety about data availability and the reliability of measurements. Nevertheless, nothing more than writing a monograph gives one the sense of how much science is a collective endeavour and how important are constant exchanges with colleagues and friends. It is not an exaggeration to say that my book, while being an effort to make an original contribution, was forged through constant interaction with several persons whom I would like to thank warmly. According to the conventional formula, the ultimate responsibility for any error or omission is, however, mine.

First, I would like to thank Dietmar Braun for giving me the precious and formative opportunity to work with him and for providing me with intellectual motivation and helpful advice and assurance during the writing of my book. I would also like to thank Fabrizio Gilardi for being a constant source of inspiration and for his accurate evaluation, tireless support, and crucial suggestions in moments of doubt. Additionally, I would like to thank Yannis Papadopoulos for his constant interest, careful reading of previous versions, and many significant comments, and Claudio Radaelli for his warm greeting at the University of Exeter, his constructive advice, and his valuable practical and methodological suggestions. Many thanks are due to David Levi-Faur for his inspiration, kind encouragement, and useful advice. Many thanks must also be given to Dario Castiglione for his crucial suggestions for the final revision of the manuscript and to Mark Kench and the ECPR Press team for their outstanding editorial assistance.

I am grateful to my colleagues and friends at the Department of Political Science at the University of Zurich, at the Institut d'Etudes Politiques et Internationales of the University of Lausanne and at the Centre for European Governance at

---

1.   1. *De Facto Independence After Delegation: a Fuzzy-Set Analysis* (Maggetti 2007); 2. *Delegated Authority: Legitimizing Independent Regulatory Agencies* (Maggetti 2009b); 3. *The Role of Independent Regulatory Agencies in Policy-Making: A Comparative Analysis* (Maggetti 2009c); 4. *Are Regulatory Agencies Delivering What They Promise?* (Maggetti 2009a).

the University of Exeter, and to the doctoral students of the National Centre of Competence in Research (NCCR) Democracy 21 for their careful reading and constructive suggestions, particularly to Charlotte Reinisch and Dominic Senn. I would like to thank Susan Banducci, Jørgen Grønnegaard Christensen, Tom Christensen, Silja Häusermann, Oliver James, Per Laegreid, André Mach, Christine Trampusch, Koen Verhoest, Chantal Vögeli, Claudius Wagemann, Stephen Wilks and Kutsal Yesilkagit for the valuable discussions in which they took part and their helpful comments on earlier versions of the manuscript. Acknowledgments are also made to the Institut d'Etudes Politiques et Internationales of the University of Lausanne, namely to the director Olivier Fillieule, to the Swiss National Science Foundation, and to the NCCR Democracy 21 for their generous financial support and to the Centre for European Governance at the University of Exeter for its great welcome and infrastructure. I also thank all the interlocutors who completed the questionnaires and responded to my questions.

Finally, I give a special thanks to Valentina for always supporting me and to my parents and my brother for their constant encouragement and enduring trust in my work.

chapter one | introduction

The goals of this book

This book focuses on the practices of regulatory governance, throughout the study of the de facto independence of independent regulatory agencies (IRAs). The starting point is the observation that the current version of capitalism corresponds to the golden age of regulation: since the 1980s no government function in OECD countries has grown faster than regulatory activity (Jacobs 1999). Following an apparent paradox, the ongoing dynamics of liberalisation, privatisation, decartelisation, internationalisation, and regional integration hardly led to the crumbling of the state, but instead promoted a wave of regulatory growth in the face of new risks and new opportunities (Vogel 1996). Accordingly, a 'new order of regulatory capitalism' is rising, implying a 'new division of labour' between state and society and entailing the expansion and intensification of regulation (Levi-Faur 2005a). The previous mode of governance, relying on public ownership and direct public intervention, alongside with self-regulation by private actors, is being replaced by a more formalised, expert-based, sector-specific, multi-level, and independently regulated mode of governance.

Independent regulatory agencies (IRAs), that is, formally independent administrative agencies with regulatory powers that benefit from public authority delegated from political decision makers, represent the main institutional feature of regulatory governance (Gilardi 2008). IRAs constitute a relatively new actor in Western Europe, at least for certain domains, and they are increasingly widespread across countries and sectors. For instance, independent regulators have been set up for regulating very diverse issues, such as general competition, banking and finance, telecommunications, civil aviation, railway services, food safety, the pharmaceutical industry, electricity, environmental protection, and personal data privacy. Two attributes of IRAs deserve a special mention. On the one hand, they are formally separated from democratic institutions and from elected politicians, thus raising normative and empirical concerns about their accountability and legitimacy. On the other hand, even though IRAs accumulate executive, rule-making and adjudicatory functions, together with traditional regulatory competencies, some important questions about their role as political actors are still unaddressed.

The argument of the book

The *core argument* of this book is that 'de facto independence' constitutes the key variable for the study of the functioning of formally independent regulatory agencies, and consequently provides the conceptual lenses that offer the greater analytical leverage for the examination of the practices of regulatory governance. De facto independence refers to the effective autonomy of agencies during their day-to-day regulatory action, after the delegation of regulatory competencies. This variable is assumed to be vital for evaluating the effectiveness of the new regulatory order and for appreciating the effects of agencification on the politico-administrative system. However, despite the importance of this variable, few comparative studies examined the de facto independence of agencies across countries and sectors. Plausibly, one of the major reasons for this lack of comparative work is the absence of a suitable method for conceptualising and assessing de facto independence that can be used in cross-case studies. Hence, the primary aim of this research was the development of a systematic measurement of agencies' de facto independence, with clear, precise, and adequately general conceptual foundations. Some appealing theoretical and empirical questions that remain unanswered have then been examined.

To begin with, this book investigates whether IRAs fulfil their mandates after the delegation of competencies and how they use their formal independence. The kind of relationship that they develop with their environment deserves special attention. On the one hand, the analysis aims to determine whether IRAs are operating in the shadow of the administrative hierarchy, are really independent in the exercise of their day-to-day activity, or are deviating from statutory prescriptions. On the other hand, the phenomenon of potential 'capture' by the regulated industries will be discussed. The second step consists of the analysis of the reconfiguration of political power in political systems following the development of regulatory governance and the concomitant phenomenon of delegation of public authority to independent regulators. This implies the assessment of the role of IRAs in policy-making. Finally, the accountability of IRAs will be appreciated with reference to media coverage of their credibility and efficiency, in order to explore the extent to which the news media can provide a means to control agencies that is compatible with their independence.

Concretely, this book proposes an approach for conceptualising, assessing, and explaining agencies' de facto independence in a rigorous way, which is suitable for comparative studies. The relation between formal and de facto independence will be investigated, while political, institutional, and organisational explanatory factors for the variation in de facto independence beyond statutory prescriptions will be considered. Then, the political role of IRAs is examined. As IRAs do not restrain themselves exclusively to the execution of regulatory functions, they may become potentially relevant political actors, which might influence the political decision-making process significantly. The empirical analysis will focus on the impact of de facto independence, together with other organisational and institutional variables, on their 'centrality' in a number of domestic lawmaking processes, following a structural and reputational approach. The last part will concern the media accountability of regulators. Agencies, by design, lack input legitimacy; at the same time, the direct measurement of regulatory results and agencies' performance is conceptually and empirically very demanding. As a second-best strategy, the media could provide an accountability forum for credibility and efficiency. Again, the effect of de facto independence is examined.

Theory, data, and methods

A wide-ranging new institutionalist approach is adopted as the 'middle-range' theoretical framework. This analytical choice implies, on the one hand, that institutional and organisational factors are considered the decisive conditions for explaining political phenomena. On the other hand, it follows the assumption that the 'three new institutionalisms' (Hall and Taylor 1996) – rational choice institutionalism, historical institutionalism, and sociological institutionalism – can be integrated to some extent or at least used in a complementary way, rather than considering them to provide competing explanations. Therefore, specific methodological tools are required, which are in line with the ontological assumptions of the different new institutional theories and with the related need for combining different levels of analysis (Hall 2003).

The data collection procedure followed three steps. The full dataset, which was used for the first empirical part of the book, was selected according to the criteria of comparability between the organisational models and the array of regulatory competencies and consists of sixteen IRAs. Data sources are above all questionnaires, which are improved and validated with interviews, database information, and written first-hand documentation: archive sources, agencies' reports, and official documents from public administrations and parliamentary services. In the second part, in order to ensure the comparability of the politico-administrative systems, the analysis focuses on the six 'most similar' cases, relying on another survey inquiry and enhancing background information with secondary literature, written documentation, and a small number of face-to-face and electronic interviews. In turn, the third part offers an in-depth comparison of two 'most-likely' and 'least-likely' cases, in which the crucial data derive essentially from content analysis of newspapers.

The data analysis techniques are adequate for examining the research questions outlined above with an approach of 'complex causation'. In the first part, a fuzzy-set analysis is executed, that is, a technique where the logic of causal analysis is based on set-theoretic relationships. Cases are seen as configurations of conditions, permitting a diversity-oriented research strategy, which focuses on exploration and discovery, by the examination of singular or deviant cases, while also involving the testing of multiple and conjunctural patterns of causation (Ragin 2000). The second part relies on a two-step qualitative comparative analysis (QCA). In fact, the nature of the selected variables and the reduced number of cases call for the use of 'crisp sets', applying a Boolean logic with simple dichotomised values that account for the presence/absence of a given condition (Rihoux

2006). Finally, the third part presents a 'most different' comparison, where the potential effects of the conditions under investigation are explored by means of the discussion of a 'most likely' and 'least likely' cases (Mahoney 2007).

Main findings

The main empirical findings can be summarised as follows. The first empirical part demonstrates that formal independence is neither a necessary nor a sufficient condition for explaining variations in IRAs' de facto independence from political decision makers and regulatees; instead, their life cycle, their inclusion in networks or regulators, and the presence of veto players have a crucial positive impact. The role of agencies in policy making is investigated in the second part, showing that IRAs are the most central actors in policy making related to their area of competence, more than expert commissions, organised interest representatives, and ordinary agencies subordinated to the ministerial level; in addition, results suggest that de facto independence from political decision makers is necessary for explaining the maximal centrality of agencies in lawmaking and that the combination of the non-professionalisation of the legislature and low independence from regulatees is a sufficient condition. Finally, the third empirical part shows that the media provides quite consistent coverage of IRAs' activities and constitute a potential 'accountability forum' for independent regulators.

A number of consequences of these findings can be mentioned. First, the disjuncture between formal and de facto independence appears critical for the study of the consequences of agencification, because the democratic deficit may become unsustainable; this problem is complicated by the fact that actors other than elected politicians, that is, the representatives of the regulated sector, may have an influence on agencies' factual independence. Nonetheless, it appears that regulators are neither under direct political control nor systematically captured by the regulated industries, challenging, in this way, the core argument of the economic theory of regulation (Stigler 1971; Pelzman *et al.* 1989). Second, following a structural and reputational perspective, IRAs have a central role in lawmaking. This point supports arguments about the rise of an age of 'regulocracy' (Levi-Faur 2005a) and 'agencification' (Christensen and Lægreid 2005), while also suggesting that the activity of formally independent regulators is not limited to the implementation of the delegated regulatory competencies (i.e. market supervision and technical regulatory functions), but that they may also exert significant political power. The third point relates to the fact that the news media compose a 'multi-pronged' system of control, which, when effective, can make agencies accountable without hindering their factual independence.

In conclusion, the degree of de facto independence, after delegation of regulatory competencies, varies according to institutional and organisational variables. In turn, it helps to explain, on the one hand, the influence of agencies in policy making and, on the other hand, their media accountability. These results provide quite a different picture of the regulatory state and regulatory capitalism than what is commonly assumed. Not only are IRAs' statutory prescriptions not always directly implemented in practice, possibly challenging the effectiveness of the new regulatory order and thus raising substantial concerns about the scientific and societal fascination for fancy notions such 'best practices', and 'benchmarking', but also, in practice, the crucial role of IRAs does not lie only in their regulatory functions, but rather in the execution of policy-making tasks in their domain of competencies. Therefore, the study of agencies' political power, accountability, and legitimacy should be considered paramount for the research agenda on regulation, as in general for the study of political institutions (Moe 2005).

Structure of the book

The structure of the book is as follows. The next chapter will offer a literature review, before presenting the theoretical framework and the research design. Chapter Three consists of the first empirical part, that is, the analysis of the de facto independence of IRAs. The role of agencies in policy making is analysed in Chapter Four. The third empirical part will be discussed in Chapter Five, concerning IRAs' media accountability as regards credibility and efficiency. Chapter Six summarises the main findings, offers a sketch of the synthetic model, and, after a section on the normative consequences of independence and a very brief gloss about the recent trends of regulatory capitalism, presents some perspectives for further research.

chapter two | theoretical framework and analytical approach

Defining regulation and regulatory functions

This research study on independent regulatory agencies (IRAs) is embedded in the broader interdisciplinary research agenda on *regulation*. This term requires some clarification. Three traditional meanings should be distinguished, which are situated at different levels of generality (Baldwin *et al.* 1998; Jordana and Levi-Faur 2004). In the widest sense, regulation refers to all rules and mechanisms of social control, including non-intended actions and non-state processes. The second meaning is related to regulation as public governance, that is, state intervention in the 'private sphere', with the purpose of steering the economy and supporting a number of goals that promote the 'public interest'. In this sense, state intervention encompasses a variety of measures, such as taxation, subsidies, redistribution, and public ownership, in addition to rulemaking and implementation. Following the narrowest concept, which is the one adopted in this book, regulation can be defined as a specific form of governance that is operating through the promulgation of authoritative sets of rules, while setting up mechanisms for monitoring, scrutinising, and promoting compliance with these rules. This form of regulation is typically accomplished through the work of IRAs.

Regulation is said to go in tandem with agencification, and the two phenomena are even mutually reinforcing (Christensen and Lægreid 2005). The political decisions leading to liberalisation, privatisation, and deregulation in the last two decades implied the need for re-regulating the markets, while the promulgation of new rules required the creation of independent regulators (Vogel 1996). In turn, the establishment of regulatory bodies fostered the development of new technologies of regulation, promoting regulatory governance by the state, inside the state and from outside the state. In this context, crucial regulatory functions were delegated to IRAs: goal formulation, rule making, and standard setting; monitoring and control, information gathering, scrutiny, supervision, inspection, audit, and evaluation; enforcement, behaviour modification, adjudication, and the application of rewards and sanctions (Christensen and Lægreid 2001; Hood *et al.* 2001). Agencification also involved a complexification of the vertical and horizontal inter-organisational tasks of the public administration, combining, for instance, performance assessment, compliance appraisal, government audit, contractualisation, and oversight (Power 1997; James 2000; Radaelli 2004). As a result, independent regulatory agencies are cumulating an increasing number of competencies and exerting – at least potentially – a considerable amount of public authority. The fusion of different competencies and regulatory powers typifies IRAs as a very peculiar and remarkable type of public sector organisation.

Governance by independent regulatory agencies

The development of regulatory governance in Western Europe is visibly epitomised by the macroscopic phenomenon of agencification of the civil service and the establishment or reform of regulatory authorities at the level of individual countries and EU institutions. From a very general perspective, the term 'agencies' refers to a variety of non-autonomous, semi-autonomous, and largely autonomous organisations, without clear distinction between their statutory independence, managerial or organisational autonomy, and other forms of bureaucratic autonomy. Pollitt and colleagues defined agencies simply as public organisations that have 'some extra degree of autonomy', in comparison to normal division and directorates in the core of the ministries (Pollitt *et al.* 2004). Agencies defined as such represent a very heterogeneous type of public sector organisation, which is increasingly common. As an illustration, public agencies, when broadly defined, employ more than 75 per cent of all the civil servants in the United Kingdom and 95 per cent of the employees in the Swedish central government (Jordana and Levi-Faur 2004). According to a worldwide comparative study covering sixteen sectors and forty-nine countries over thirty-nine years (1964–2002), more than twenty agencies were created per year from the 1990s to 2002, and, by the end of 2002, regulatory agencies were identified in about 60 per cent of the possible cases (Jordana *et al.* 2007). Using more aggregate data, agencies account for approximately 50-75 per cent of public expenditure and public employment at the OECD level (OECD 2003).

This study has a more specific focus: it examines IRAs, those agencies that possess regulatory competencies, have a specific organisational model, which comprises a chairperson, board and own secretariat, and benefit from formal independence from elected politicians. Not all agencies are in fact regulatory agencies: some have only executive tasks; others are simple consultative organisations for policy makers. Moreover, not all agencies are formally independent: some are in subordinate relationships with public administration and ministries or are structurally integrated into the ordinary civil service. Instead, IRAs are defined as 'governmental entities that possess and exercise some grant of specialized public authority, [constitutionally] separate from that of other institutions, but (...) neither directly elected by the people, nor directly managed by elected officials' (Thatcher and Stone Sweet 2002). This definition approximately corresponds to the 'fourth' type of organisation identified by Verschuere and colleagues, that is, 'externally autonomous public organisations with their own budget, defined as legal entity under public law, and with a governing board' (Verschuere *et al.* 2006).

Western European IRAs comprise a relatively uniform universe of cases, which is particularly interesting for the study of the consequences of the delegation of public authority, given the scope and the extension of their regulatory competences, i.e. rule making, monitoring and supervision, and adjudication and sanctioning. What is more, the impressive spread of IRAs across European countries implies a major institutional change (Levi-Faur 2005a; Gilardi 2008) that deserves careful attention for its potentially significant consequences on the distribution of power in political systems at domestic, supranational and global level. Finally, as IRAs represent a constitutional anomaly, due to their formal separateness from democratic institutions, they are also raising a number of normative concerns. Therefore, after the consolidation of the new regulatory order, it is crucial to develop a comprehensive analytical approach to examine the practices of regulatory governance by IRAs.

The next section reviews the literature on agencification, with a special focus on the functioning of IRAs in Western Europe. The review is more thematically ordered than chronological. The first part covers research studies that illustrate the rationales for delegating regulatory competencies to IRAs and elucidate their worldwide diffusion. Second, a number of studies are presented concerning the implementation of regulatory governance, as well as the theoretical perspectives that are adopted for conceptualising and analysing the functioning of regulators. In the third part, the consequences of agencification are discussed with respect to democratic legitimacy, reconsidering the principles for securing accountability. By way of conclusion, the examination of some open questions is provided. Please note that each review is necessarily selective: here, the emphasis is on European empirical studies and comparative political science approaches. In addition, the interpretation of the contribution of some research studies may appear to be presented in an over-simplified manner. However, a certain grant of schematisation is useful to depict the broad picture of an interdisciplinary, complex, heterogeneous, and ever-evolving field; finally, the classification of different streams of literature has to be considered a meta-analytical tool for systematisation purposes, as those categories largely overlap in practice.

Origins and diffusion of the regulatory state and regulatory capitalism

Origins of the American regulatory state

The United States of America led the way early on in establishing specialised agencies to supervise and control the business sector and, afterwards, to implement social regulations (Carpenter 2001b). To put it simply, the development of the American regulatory state followed three steps: the first was related to the 'Progressive Movement', from the 1890s to the 1920s; the second was a consequence of the 'New Deal' during the 1930s; and the third emerged in accordance with the 'New Era' of social regulation in the 1960s (Moran 2002). The creation of autonomous regulatory bodies first followed a tendency towards the depoliticisation and proceduralisation of the political process, promoting 'the values and ideals of professionalism, scientific and technical expertise, administrative competence and neutrality, and efficiency [...]' (Vogel 1986). Then, the priority of regulation over public ownership was affirmed, with the aim of minimising market failures and promoting virtuous competition between business actors. The third step corresponded to the broadening of the scope of the regulatory state, from its initial economic focus to the creation of new agencies, which started to endorse concerns that fall beyond the functioning of markets, namely social and environmental regulation.

Origins of the European regulatory state

The concept of regulatory state re-emerged in another context. It has proven to be particularly helpful to defining the style of policy making exerted by the supranational institutions of the European Union (EU), namely the European Commission (Majone 1994b, 1996a, 1997a, 2001c). Majone argued that regulation, defined as 'the development of rules and regulation by independent agencies', is the most important mode of policy making in Europe, with the purpose of increasing the allocative efficiency of markets and correcting market failures. In fact, while the growth of regulation at the national level must be understood primarily as a reorientation of public priorities, following the 'post-Keynesian' shift of states' functions from direct interventionism in the economy to a more indirect approach, at the EU level, this phenomenon derives from the inherent lack of modes of command at the disposal of European institutions in front of policy implementation in member states. Specifically, the strong prominence of regulation at the European level is due to two main characteristics of the European political system (Moran 2002). On the one hand, the tight budget limits the capacity of positive policy making. On the other hand, regulation is a political strategy adopted in the absence of an administrative means to implement European policies. Therefore, the Commission followed the so-called principle of subsidiarity, by expanding European regulation, while delegating the competencies of implementing new policies to member states in a number of economic and social domains, which are predominantly regulated through the so-called non-majoritarian institutions, consisting above all of independent regulatory agencies. This kind of policy-making approach, which appears to be very common in practice, despite the diversity of actors' interests and the consensus-oriented nature of European institutions, has been interpreted as part of a political strategy of 'subterfuge' adopted by the Commission and the Courts of Justice to prevent political impasse and promote innovative regulatory processes (Héritier 1997).

Origins of the hyper-regulatory state

The British regulatory state originates from the American experience and recovers some elements of the EU 'negative' regulatory state, but presents a number of distinctive features (Moran 2003). The model of regulatory governance that emerged in Britain from the 1970s corresponds to an innovative redefinition of state's functions in Europe, while also presenting, quite surprisingly from the perspective of common sense, a quite proactive style of governance. To begin with, delegation to independent agencies in the UK represented the solution to the new challenges with which policy makers needed to cope, following the crisis of the Keynesian welfare state and the subsequent political decisions of privatising and liberalising the markets, and in line with the momentum for a reorganisation of the government usually designated as 'new public management', or 'NPM' (Moran 2003). The command-and-control bureaucracy has been thus largely transformed into a more fragmented set of public bodies, which function in a multi-level mode and benefit from a certain degree of bureaucratic autonomy. These agencies received several brand new regulatory competencies, leading to a phase of 'regulatory hyper-innovation' (Moran 2003). They were tasked with re-regulating areas where policy makers had decided to withdraw direct public interventionism, so as to prevent market failures and to sustain the 'public interest'. In addition, quite unexpectedly, agencies started to colonise and administrate some vital sectors that were previously uniquely self-regulated, such as universities and financial markets (Moran 2002). At the end of the day, though the state abandoned most of its interventionist ambitions, it also acquired new responsibilities; accordingly, the boundaries between the public and the private were deeply redefined, or, more precisely, they became more and more indistinct.

The diffusion of the regulatory state in Western Europe

Regulatory governance by IRAs proliferated across Western Europe, in a wide range of sectors: finance, pharmaceutical products, electricity, telecommunications, environmental protection, and so forth. Gilardi examined these phenomena of diffusion, suggesting at first that governments have two distinct types of rational incentives to delegate competencies to IRAs (Gilardi 2002a, 2005c, 2008). Governments may decide to tie their own hands in order to create credible commitments and to deal with the problem of political uncertainty by securing their political choices for the future. However, he explained, phenomena of delegation are also shaped by non-functional factors. The diffusion of IRAs across Europe followed a process of emulation, where governments adopted such an institutional model of regulatory authority, as it was socially valued and represented the 'taken-for-granted' solution to a given problem. These insights improved the theoretical foundations for the study of delegation and regulation. In fact, new institutionalist approaches were increasingly endorsed for explaining delegation emerged, referring principally to two streams of literature (that partially overlap). On the one hand, following a sociological research tradition, drawing from organisational theory (DiMaggio and Powell 1983), phenomena of policy learning and institutional isomorphism are highlighted for explaining the interdependent decisions of delegating public authority to IRAs (Gilardi 2008). On the other hand, the focus on historical legacies and patterns of national and sectoral regulation permitted the explanation of the adoption of different regulatory models, despite being confronted with similar functional pressures (Thelen 1999).

The globalisation of regulatory capitalism

Levi-Faur and Jordana expanded the approach of the regulatory state by identifying the phenomena of agencification as part of a global structural transformation towards a new form of governance beyond the state, that is, regulatory
capitalism (Levi-Faur and Jordana 2005). The emerging regulatory order, which
is characterised by 'a new division of labour between state and society', points
to the proliferation and the growing heterogeneity of the institutional forms and
the technologies of regulation. Accordingly, regulation seems to increase despite
efforts in the opposite direction, given that the rationale for the creation of IRAs
seems stronger than the rationale for privatisation and deregulation. Furthermore,
regulatory governance by independent agencies is diffusing worldwide, beyond
OECD countries, namely in Central and South America and in South Asian countries (Jayasuriya 1999) and in a number of developing countries (Cook 2004). In
particular, Jordana, Levi-Faur and Fernandez drew attention to the restructuring
of the state in Latin America through the ongoing creation and reform of regulatory agencies (Jordana *et al.* 2007). Their results confirm that this process follows
a contagious diffusion pattern, which is driven more by (social) emulation than
(rational) learning. The authors further distinguished between national patterns of
diffusion and sectoral diffusion. On the one hand, the number of previously established regulatory agencies predicts the probability of establishing a new one in that
country. On the other hand, the number of regulatory authorities in the same sector
in other countries influences the probability of the establishment of new regulatory
authorities in that sector.

Global and multi-level regulatory governance

Agencification and standard-setting

Besides agencification at domestic level, another trend towards the consolidation
of a transnational form of regulatory governance is identified by some scholars of
international relations (IR) and international political economy (IPE), in which
regulatory bodies are regarded essentially as promoters of 'soft law' and standard
setters. Their goals and tasks are varied, as they combine different degrees of private and public powers at different levels of governance – national, regional or
global – according to the policy issue and the institutional capacity (Abbott and
Snidal 2003). As a result, agencification at the transnational level redefines the
patterns of global authority and blurs the boundaries between states and markets.
The provision and distribution of public goods is highly affected by a regulatory
context that is simultaneously shaped by private and public actors. International
agencies typically differ from domestic regulators because they consist of non-
governmental or multi-stakeholder organisations that function as global networks
through the so-called technical committees, which usually involve experts that
represent the industry at the national level, and various types of officials, namely

representing the most powerful states (Mattli and Büthe 2003; Mattli and Büthe 2005). One should note that certain political systems display institutional features that easily accommodate the new international standards, while others exhibit low complementarities, generating competitive disadvantages and limited representation at the international level. Moreover, the global landscape of standardisation agencies is portrayed as heterogeneous and highly complex, with overlapping jurisdictions. As a consequence, for instance, large companies can choose the most suitable organisation and then switch from one organisation to another or proceed in parallel in different organisations so as to facilitate the adoption of a certain standard (Werle 2001). Following a similar argument, the standard-setting process is used by firms as a competitive tool when seeking to establish their technology or a standard that promotes their technology as a global standard, by selecting those organisations that provide them with a higher level of influence either through the exclusion of rivals or by beneficial decision-making mechanisms (Austin and Milner 2001).

Networks governance

The literature on 'multi-level' governance recently examined the creation of EU networks of regulatory authorities, such as the Committee of European Securities Regulators, the European Regulators Group, and the European Platform of Regulatory Authorities (Héritier *et al.* 2001; Eberlein and Grande 2005; Coen and Thatcher 2008; Eberlein and Newman 2008). These developments are in line with the new style of network governance promoted by the European Commission (Kohler-Koch 2002). National IRAs are progressively included in various transnational regulatory networks (Coen and Thatcher 2008) – together with scientific experts, business actors and representatives of member states, the Commission, and the European Parliament – ideally contributing to 'harmonisation', 'convergence', and the promotion of 'best practices' through the diffusion of norms and policy learning. Indeed, on the one hand, networks should provide 'as a more or less unintended by-product' (Majone 2000) incentives and means to agencies for the development of a more effective regulatory process, given the long-term dynamic of cooperation among agencies and the requirement of international reputation. On the other hand, networks might configure a system of reciprocal controls that make agencies more accountable to their peers (Moe 1985). Eberlein and Grande examined the emergence of the European regulatory regime constituted by transnational regulatory networks as an informal way to support the Europeanisation of member states' regulation (Eberlein and Grande 2005). The point is that even weak supranational institutions can be influential through the adoption of decision-making processes that are informal, horizontal, multi-layered and 'experimentalist' (Slaughter 2004; Sabel and Zeitlin 2010). The articulation among the levels remains an open question, but some preliminary evidence shows that the network of European national competition authorities may offer advantages to both the Commission and national regulators (Wilks 2005; 2007). It allows the Commission to reduce its workload and obtain greater freedom on the use of resources; on the other hand, national regulators gain potential 'horizontal' partners and vertical allies in front of national governments and regulatees. Moreover, it has been observed that European networks have a decisive impact on the domestic adoption of standards, for which the most central actors within the network are the early adopters (Maggetti and Gilardi 2011).

IRAs after delegation

Public and private interest theories

The early approaches to the functioning of IRAs were essentially normative, following two broad research agendas: public interest theories and private interest approaches. In the first case, the positive effects of delegation to IRAs were taken for granted, as regulation was seen as the solution required to correct a number of fundamental market failures, specifically in order to neutralise the oligopolistic-monopolistic tendencies of an open economy; cut down any potential negative externalities; ensure the universal supply of public goods; compensate for the asymmetry of information that may pervert market operations; counteract moral hazard phenomena implying increased collective costs; and reduce transaction costs by providing shared standards (Mitnick 1980; Jordana and Levi-Faur 2004). In an effort to extend the theory, Bernstein argued, in his seminal study, that regulatory agencies might follow a life cycle from initial activism to gradual devitalisation and progressive inertia and bureaucratisation (Bernstein 1955). Private interest tenants, on the contrary, conceive free markets as the best solution for maximising social and economic welfare, thus postulating negative effects of delegating regulatory competencies to agencies. The economic theory of regulation (ET) of the Chicago school, based on microeconomic assumptions drawn from classic rational choice theory, offered the general theoretical framework of this approach (Stigler 1971; Pelzman et al. 1989). The central argument is that regulators and regulatory processes are unavoidably shaped by the regulated industries. Narrow and well-organised private interest groups, who detain crucial pieces of information, are able to 'capture' regulatory agencies and obtain regulation in line with their interests, at the expense of the more dispersed interest of consumers. Elected politicians and civil servants are conceived as purely strategic self-interested agents that are relentlessly pursuing their rent-seeking goals. According to Stigler, government officials and bureaucrats will seek to maximise their wealth by adopting collusive behaviour with the regulated firms, in exchange for some valuable goods, such as campaign contributions, rewarding employment perspectives, and even cash incentives. As a consequence, it is assumed that 'as a rule, regulation is acquired by the industry and is designed and operated primarily for its benefit' (Stigler 1971: 3). To sum up, both public and private interest approaches conceive the independence of regulatory agencies (or, respectively, their non-independence) as a constant that is directly derived from their postulates about the virtuous or kleptomaniac nature of agents, and their behaviour is seen as functionally predetermined, without any explicit discussion of the factors that may produce unintentional phenomena. Public interest theories of regulation have been criticised because of their somewhat idealised assumptions about the neutral and disinterested behaviour of supposed competent experts who populate agencies (McLean and Foster 1992; Feintuck 2004). Moreover, it has been noted that they fail to address the question of the inherent conflicts around the societal definition of public interest (Francis 1993). Similarly, as regards private interest theories, three other flaws can be identified. It has been noted that this approach is built on unrealistic assumptions on the exaggerated rationality of actors and fails to recognise the critical role of organisational and institutional factors. From an empirical point of view, the ET suffers from a lack of systematic evidence; finally, it can hardly explain the beginning of an era of deregulation, even if Pelzman partially reframed the argument (Pelzman *et al.* 1989), trying to accommodate with limited success the developments of the regulatory state since 1980.

Institutional design

Historically, the phenomena of deregulation offered substance to a new academic literature that focused on the – alleged – crisis of the American regulatory state, starting from the works of public lawyers who pointed out the risky expansion from economic to social regulation, potentially leading to implementation failures and control problems (Moran 2002). The answer has been a renewed focus on institutional design (Goodin 1996) in order to depict the appropriate mechanisms of control over bureaucracy and regulatory agencies, often proposing models that are made operational with insights from game theory. For instance, the process of policy execution has been illustrated as a game among legislators, the chief executive, and bureaucratic agents to whom authority is delegated, by studying the trade-off between administrative discretion and opportunities for oversight and political control (Calvert *et al.* 1989). Snyder and Weingast studied how elected officials may influence regulation through the appointment of agency leaders (Snyder and Weingast 2000). Spiller investigated the strategic interactions between agencies and courts using a three-level game (Spiller 1998). Huber and Shipan showed how elected politicians can still steer the policy-making process in a context where electoral laws, the structure of the legal system, and the professionalism of the legislature shape bureaucratic autonomy and their relation with agencies, using a transaction cost approach (Huber and Shipan 2002). In general, the principal-agent (PA) framework was considered suitable for defining the relationships between elected politicians and bureaucracies and for analysing the rationale for delegating public authority to agencies. Yet these models have been criticised for their inaccuracy in portraying the functioning of those particular bodies that benefit from formal independence: IRAs. Indeed, following Majone, the regulatory action of independent agencies should not be understood in terms of a PA relation (Majone 1997a, 2001c). The PA model, drawing from the theory of the firm, was conceived for portraying a relationship in a structure where the principal should minimise any possibility of an agent's shirking. Instead, the need for credibility, a core element of the rationale for delegating public authority to IRAs, requires that the agency will benefit from a factual independence in their day-to-day activities. In other words, according to a fiduciary mode of delegation, the principal's powers and competencies are substantially delegated to the independent body – the trustee –that is, the IRAs.

Similar models, diverging patterns

The expansion of regulatory governance and the development of IRAs at the domestic level do not follow linear and constant patterns, illustrating rather the diversity of the actors, mechanisms, and principles that are concerned (Levi-Faur 2005a; Levi-Faur and Jordana 2005). Considerable cross-national and cross-sectoral variation in the extent of liberalisation and re-regulation has been noted, highlighting the importance of domestic politics in shaping regulatory reform, which were usually promoted by government ministries and supported or opposed by sectoral interest groups (Vogel 1996). Braithwaite and Drahos offered a synthesis of the globalisation of regulatory capitalism through the creation of international regimes in thirteen sectors worldwide (Braithwaite and Drahos 2000; Levi-Faur 2006a). They identified and investigated several mechanisms driving global regulation, such as coercion, reward, modelling, adjustment, coordination, and capacity building, and they distinguish the role of states, international organisations, corporations, individual actors, and epistemic communities. The result is a picture of the dynamic of globalisation that follows very diverse patterns in different countries and different areas of business regulation, showing that many forms of regulatory governance can emerge from the interaction between the markets, firms, and states in a global environment and that the globalisation of regulatory governance has been successful in some cases and has been resisted in others. They have also indicated within the general trend the existence of diverse local patterns through which some states have become rule takers rather than rule makers. In a similar vein, scholars of public policy and public administration argue that the dynamic of regulatory change is shaped by cultural and institutional norms, stressing the role of country-specific and sector-specific path dependence. First, some authors insist on national factors, maintaining that regulatory policies are best explained with reference to the action of national interest groups and showing how historical legacies matter when adopting specific regulatory regimes (Hood *et al.* 2001; Pollitt *et al.* 2004). Following a similar line of reasoning, scholars who adopt a sociological organisational approach show that analogous statutory prescriptions can mean different things in different institutional contexts (Christensen and Yesilkagit 2005). In fact, while formal rules and institutional design are important to illustrating the choice of an organisational model (Egeberg 1999), informal norms play a crucial role in determining their implementation (Peters 2001). As an illustration, Christensen and Lægreid demonstrated the limits of implementing NPM reforms by showing that administrative reforms are generally incremental and often symbolic, although they agree on the existence of a general trend indicating that authority is progressively decentralised from ministries to agencies (Christensen and Lægreid 2002). They also maintained that the development of the new agency model – more autonomous, more horizontal, and more formalised – is mainly driven by international isomorphism, but it varies across and within countries in the balance between these three characteristics (Christensen and Lægreid 2005). Finally, regulatory competencies are said to overlap between regulatory agencies, ministries, legislative bodies and courts, in the context of a movement from a state-centric approach to a multi-level perspective.

Unintended consequences

The delegation of regulatory competencies to IRAs raised serious concerns about the possible unanticipated outcomes of regulatory governance. First, the study of EU regulation as an instrument of policy making revealed the existence of a number of problems related to potential regulatory capture and implementation failures (McGowan and Wallace 1996). A similar argument emerged from the cross-country comparative analysis of public management reforms, involving IRAs and other semi-autonomous public bodies (Pollitt and Bouckaert 2004). Concretely, it appears that the results of regulatory reforms may form only a loose relationship with the initial intentions of the decision makers, which, in turn, has to be understood not as the coherent product of a single policy maker, but rather as the side-effect of a series of partial, plural, and localised attempts. Therefore, not only institutional design but also cognitive limits, the diversity of political strategies, and institutional inertia should indeed be taken into account to explain the regulatory outcomes. Wilks and Bartle's case study of a number of competition policy agencies in Europe showed that agencies were created essentially for their symbolic significance and were not expected to be factually active for rule making or implementation (Wilks and Bartle 2002). However, this policy area has been populated with powerful actors that possess great technical expertise and can exert significant influence, imposing their policy priorities and regulatory interpretations. As a result, agencies have redefined their roles so as to have a real impact on the economy: specifically, according to the authors, the investigated competition agencies were able to reorient their regulatory action from a narrower technocratic focus on market freedoms, both escaping from business capture and replacing the broader criteria of public interest. In parallel, the political concerns about the implementation of regulatory governance pushed the development of a European agenda on meta-regulation. Following the Lisbon agenda, the emphasis on 'best practices' that emerged in the OECD context was translated into the European programme on 'better regulation' (Radaelli and De Francesco 2007). Regulatory impact assessment (RIA) became a central concern of the member states of the EU, however still without producing actual convergence (Radaelli 2005). In fact, even the development of meta-regulation seems to produce some unintended consequences. For instance, due to differences in political contexts, specifically in some crucial elements such as institutions, territory, policy process, and legitimacy requirements, the introduction of instruments that are labelled 'impact assessment' does not always actually correspond to proper RIA practices (Radaelli 2004).

Legitimising regulatory governance by IRAs

The democratic deficit of the regulatory state

Besides unintended consequences, several scholars pointed to the so-called democratic deficit of regulatory governance by IRAs. The argument goes as follows. Democratic systems can be conceptualised as chains of delegation from voters, to parliament (in parliamentary systems), to government, to ministers, to administration (Strom *et al.* 2003). Delegation to IRAs constitutes an additional step, which is, however, qualitatively different, as IRAs are not directly accountable to voters or to elected officials (Gilardi 2008). IRAs are indeed, by definition, non-majoritarian and unelected bodies. As a consequence, in the regulatory state, the role of elected representatives is becoming less relevant, in favour of influence connected to specialised experts (Papadopoulos 2003), while the significance of democratic participation is undermined (Lodge 2004), leading to a 'net loss' of democratic legitimacy (Majone 1999; Scott 2000b). In order to compensate for this deficit, the legitimacy of regulatory governance by independent agencies – in the Weberian sense of social acceptance of the regulatory order – is supposed to derive from (1) the separateness of IRAs from politics and organised interests; (2) the expected high credibility and efficiency of IRAs, based on the assumption that they are more proficient in producing qualitatively better policy output than democratic institutions; and (3) the expected high procedural accountability of IRAs, i.e. the assumption that they operate in a law-baked, transparent, open, and fair way, more than democratic institutions can do. Hereafter, these options are briefly presented.

A Madisonian state

The intrinsic absolute value of agencies' independence is a critical point in the theory of delegation to IRAs (Majone 1996a; Spence 1997). Administrative bureaucracies in general and regulatory agencies in particular have been described as the fourth branch of government. In this sense, the legitimacy of the new regulatory order derives from the separation of powers, a concept that has enjoyed a long history since Montesquieu and the French Enlightenment to typify the modern constitutional state (Manin 1997; Maravall and Przeworski 2003). The separation of powers, that is, a system of government with the appropriate checks and balances, helps to prevent the abuse of power and guarantees the rule of law (Persson *et al.* 1997). This view of legitimacy is consistent with the Madisonian model of democracy (Hamilton and Madison 1788), prescribing the fragmentation and limitation of the political power in order to impede the tyranny of the majority (Riker 1982). IRAs can be considered institutions protecting some pre-established 'basic principles' from the 'populist' component of democracy and from the possibly arbitrary use of power by the political decision makers. However, the effective separation of powers cannot be simply deduced from the formal independence of regulators. Hence, in order to endorse this form of legitimacy, even before discussing its relevance, we should primarily assess whether independence, as prescribed in agencies' statutes, really corresponds to effective independence from political decision makers (see Chapter Three). Otherwise, in the case of a systematic discrepancy, the legitimacy of the regulatory order would risk being contested, reducing the 'social sustainability' of regulatory governance by IRAs (Costanza 1992; Kemp and Rotmans 2005; Knoepfel *et al.* 2007), because when they miss the 'non-majoritarian standards of legitimacy', the democratic deficit would be considered unjustified (Majone 2002).

Output-oriented legitimacy

The traditional argument to counteract the democratic deficit consists in the claim that a lack of 'inputs-oriented legitimacy' might be compensated by a positive evaluation of results by citizens (Scharpf 2000a). Accordingly, the legitimacy of IRAs could rely on the capacity of producing regulatory outcomes considered satisfactory: this is the substantive component of IRAs' legitimacy (Majone 2001a). After all, regulatory agencies are cut off from the chain of democratic delegation precisely with the purpose of obtaining 'better' results from regulatory action because, on the one hand, a certain amount of autonomy is supposed to be necessary for credible regulation. Particularly in sensitive, unpredictable, and globalised economic sectors, such as the financial markets (Baker 2005), the enhanced credibility derived from the expected time-consistency of independent regulatory policies is considered such a crucial stake for the functioning of the system that the choice of an independent regulator could be considered per se legitimate. On the other hand, specialised agencies are expected to possess the expert-based knowledge that politicians and bureaucrats lack, which is indispensable to perform some tasks in a complex society, increasing the efficiency of decision making (Majone 2001a, c). Nevertheless, two major drawbacks are challenging this form of legitimacy pertaining to IRAs. The first scepticism is about empirical evidence: there is still no clear-cut evidence concerning the results of the regulatory action performed by IRAs. Moreover, it is not even certain that a deficit of 'inputs legitimacy' could be perfectly compensated thanks to a 'better' quality of the outcomes. Indeed, ex-post legitimacy can hardly be conceptually separated from input legitimacy because the positive evaluation of results by political actors depends primarily on the previous agreement about the existence and the framing of a specific problem, which is rare in practice, and because scientific expertise and political interests are often firmly intertwined (Papadopoulos and Benz 2006).

Procedural accountability

The literature on regulatory governance proposes a way to solve the legitimisation dilemma by providing the belief in legitimacy through enhanced procedural accountability of the regulatory process, namely with reference to independent regulators (Baldwin *et al.* 1998; Flinders and Buller 2006). The basic idea is as follows. Political actors, even if they disagree with a decision, should accept it as legitimate if it was made in a way considered fair, namely if it originated from an open and inclusive political process, ideally based on openness, transparency, equal access, and deliberation. Therefore, one can compensate for the democratic deficit if the regulatory agencies in charge engender the belief among the relevant actors that procedures are appropriate. Indeed, according to some scholars – this solution is generally adopted by IRAs' professionals as well – it is eventually possible to legitimise regulation by independent agencies thanks to a 'legitimacy by the throughputs', whatever the costs the decisions may entail (Stern 1997; Stern and Holder 1999; Lodge 2004). This corresponds to the procedural component of IRAs' legitimacy (Majone 2001a). Nonetheless, once again, a double-side criticism to this form of IRAs' legitimacy has to be considered. On the one hand, accountability and efficiency may conflict, undermining the underlying assumption that justifies the delegation to IRAs. Indeed, it has been argued that a participative and deliberative process would weaken the efficiency of the regulatory action (Majone 1994b, 2001a), as such a process would increase the political transaction costs of the process significantly. On the other hand, a minimal version of accountability probably cannot grant the legitimacy of the IRA to the relevant political actors. In fact, when participation is reduced, and legitimacy is only based on procedural correctness, the regulatory order will risk being considered scarcely legitimised, likewise a 'weak democracy' (Barber 2004). This puzzle is inherent to all scenarios in terms of procedural accountability, as stated by Sosay (Sosay 2006). In the participatory scenario, the diffusion of power is emphasised, and the public involvement is improved. The management of the social complexity is accomplished by decentralising power and opening channels of access to decision. This scenario appears roughly in line with the Habermasian ideal of communicative and collective deliberation. Nevertheless, apart from the criticisms about the idealisation of that assumption – the prospect that only certain powerful interest groups are actually able to influence the process, thus excluding ordinary citizens and looser organisation, such as consumer associations (Olson 1971) – it is plausible that the participation of an increasing number of actors does undermine the decision-making capacity of the agency, reducing its efficiency (Majone 1999), i.e. its raison d'être. Conversely, the technocratic scenario presents the merely procedural way to legitimise IRAs. The instrument is the implementation of a strict rule-based system providing expertise in order to maximise the efficiency of the regulatory action. It corresponds to the Weberian process of rationalisation and bureaucratisation that follows the development of a complex and differentiated society. This scenario implies the minimisation of the involvement of political representatives and public participation, generating the supremacy of the technocratic rule over democracy.

In conclusion, regulatory governance by independent agencies, although uncontested at present, can hardly rely on a strong stock of legitimacy. Delegation and depoliticisation are thus quite fragile political strategies, and the new regulatory order is likely to be quite easily challenged, especially in the case of a paradigm shift. Yet some recent trends entail new perspectives for legitimising IRAs. On the one hand, the emergence and ongoing consolidation of transnational networks of regulators might configure a new potential source of legitimacy of regulatory policies, if these institutional arrangements are effective (Eberlein and Grande 2005). For instance, European networks (Coen and Thatcher 2008) – where domestic IRAs, scientific committees, member states, the Commission, and the European parliament are involved – could provide, 'as a more or less unintended by-product' (Majone 2000), incentives and means to agencies for the development of an independent and efficient regulatory process, given the lasting cooperation among agencies and the requirements of international reputation, ideally also making the agencies reciprocally accountable (Moe 1985). On the other hand, the media could provide an 'accountability forum' which is particularly suitable for IRAs, as it will be discussed at length in Chapter Five.

Studying the functioning of regulators: regulation in practice

The question of the functioning of regulatory agencies is becoming a central concern for a number of scholars in the fields of public policy, comparative politics, public administration, public management, and political economy, leading to the emergence of a series of empirically oriented case studies and comparative analysis. For instance, Thatcher and Stone Sweet focused on delegation to agencies as a distinctive instrument of public governance and explored the behaviour of IRAs after delegation in Britain, France, Germany, and Italy (2002). It is confirmed that functional explanations are insufficient: for instance, Britain has delegated the most, despite facing less problems of credible commitment than Italy or France. Some contextual variables, such as state traditions and political leadership, help to explain the diverse responses to pressures for delegation, by influencing the choice of the institutional model and the form of delegation (Thatcher 2002c). In another research study, Thatcher showed that, on the one hand, in the cases under study, elected officials have rarely used their formal powers to overturn IRAs' decisions. On the other hand, little IRA activity against the regulatees is found, reflecting the idea that regulators may partially act in favour of the interest of the regulated industries (Thatcher 2002d).

Nonetheless, in spite of these progresses in the literature, the study of the implementation of regulatory reforms remains rather underdeveloped. Specifically, the literature on the behaviour of independent regulatory agencies in practice and their role in regulatory reforms has been described as 'characterized by weak theoretical development, an absence of comparable data, little comparative analysis, and few empirical studies' (Christensen and Lægreid 2005). In particular 'the effects of administrative reforms are often promised or assumed but seldom well documented'. Indeed, a number of major issues in the study of the effects of regulatory reforms are intensely debated; three points can be considered crucial. First, as Verhoest and colleagues argues, contemporary research on the consequences of organisational autonomy of public agencies usually adopts too heterogeneous definitions of autonomy and, at the same time, a too restrictive conceptualisation and operationalisation of it (Verhoest et al. 2004). They called for a more integrated approach to autonomy that should also reach a higher level of abstraction, generalisation, and applicability. Accordingly, the priority consists of investigating the distinction between the de jure (or formal) independence of agencies and their de facto (or informal) independence, which may be considerable, thus triggering the assumption of depoliticisation and neutrality of regulatory governance by independent agencies. Second, the functioning of autonomous agencies must also be analysed from the point of view of the redistribution of power within the political system, wherein the role of agencies in policy making deserves more attention, as specialised agencies possess the technocratic competencies to deal with complex issues that may constitute valuable political capital and benefit from an increasing separateness from democratic institutions (Christensen and Lægreid 2005). Third, the new forms of accountability should be investigated further, that is, those composing a 'multi-pronged system of controls', which can make agencies accountable without hindering their independence (Majone 1996b). The main themes of this research study derive precisely from these three empirical issues, as I will illustrate in detail in the subsequent chapters.

To tackle these three issues, a scientific inquiry into the practice of regulation by IRAs has three main broader theoretical focal points that will be considered through the next chapters. This study first endeavours to extend the study of regulation, as a hybrid, multi-level form of governance (Marsh and Stoker 1995; Jordana and Levi-Faur 2004) to the appreciation of those elusive, slippery, informal aspects that have been neglected but are nonetheless crucial for a full understanding of the functioning of regulators. In this sense, the causes and main consequences of the key variable for the study of regulation in practice – IRAs' de facto independence – will be investigated. This implies examining whether IRAs fulfil their mandates after the delegation of competencies, how they actually use their formal independence, and what kind of informal relationship they develop with their environment. Second, when conceiving regulation as a public policy executed by IRAs (Wilson 1980), the aim of this book is to contribute to the literature on policy formulation and implementation by discussing the conditions that shape not only the execution of regulatory policies but also the role of agencies in the political process. The related questions refer to participation in policy making, and the strength of different actors in the regulatory state. The third question concerns the examination of the impact of the news media, as an increasingly autonomous actor, which can crucially shape the conduct of policy making and regulatory governance, in a context of 'mediatisation', and specifically the extent to which they can act as 'accountability forum' for independent regulatory agencies (Bovens 2007).

An institutional approach to regulatory governance

New institutionalisms and organisation theory

Before presenting the empirical analyses, it is time to briefly depict the general theoretical framework. A specific analytic perspective is adopted, that is, a comprehensive new institutionalist approach. New institutionalism is a compound theoretical framework – a collection of interrelated theories, concepts, and hypotheses – for the study of the relations between institutional features, political agency, performance, and change (March and Olsen 1984). The 'new' institutionalism(s) (or neo-institutionalism) differs from the 'old' because of its focus on empirical research, its analytical orientation, and its concern with methods and methodology (Peters 2005). It constitutes a relatively composite approach that stresses the substantially greater leverage for explaining political and social phenomena through an understanding of the institutional framework. The central concern of scholars from new institutionalism is not only the impact of institutions on politics, policies, and political choices but also the explanation of where institutions come from and how they change. Actors' interests, strategies and ideas also matter, while agents and structure should be understood as necessarily intertwined, as two sides of the same coin (Giddens 1986; Giddens and Turner 1987). However, the distinctive feature of this approach is to start from an analysis of the structures and then eventually focus on the 'independent' impact of agents, while institutional and organisational factors also shape the preferences and behaviour of those actors. Accordingly, actors' preferences and strategies are usually conceived, not as postulates about the immanent nature of agents, but as open empirical questions, and are expected to be influenced by structural (endogenous and exogenous) factors and contextual variables.

How should institutions be defined? The answer depends mostly on the 'variety' of new institutionalist theory that is adopted. However, it is possible to note a shared set of fundamental assumptions concerning the operational definition of this concept. Following a classic argument (Berger and Luckmann 1966), institutions can be conceived at the most abstract level as structures that create 'desire-independent' reasons for action, through collectively accepted systems of rules (Searle 2005). Therefore, a minimal definition of the term 'institution' should include the persistence of a collectively accepted and relatively durable set of rules that can be more or less formalised; the prospect of a partially autonomous impact on the political system and the political process; and the possibility of predetermining the actors' behaviour to a certain extent.

It is crucial to distinguish between the terms 'organisations' and 'institutions'. As North stated, the term 'organisation' refers to the players, whereas the term 'institutions' denotes the (more or less formalised) rules of the game (North 1990). To put it differently, the former term consists of levels of groups as actors, and the latter term consists of grades of conventions or constitutions (Khalil 1995). Of course, the categories forming this conceptual distinction may occasionally overlap, namely because organisations are irremediably enmeshed in the broader institutional framework. However, at an analytical level, organisations are said to be collective entities that are both distinguishable from institutions, on the one hand, and from (the behaviour of) individual actors, on the other hand (Scott 2001). Last but not least, it should be noted that the focus on institutional factors is also relevant for political decision makers and society at large, since it can potentially enlighten political reforms and offer solid evidence for enhancing constitutional design, legal frameworks, and implementation provisions.

Varieties of new institutional theories: towards an unified framework

Three types of new institutionalisms can be identified: rational choice institutionalism, historical institutionalism, and sociological institutionalism (Hall and Taylor 1996). Here it is argued that the articulation of the three new institutionalisms may configure a quite consistent analytical approach, which can fruitfully guide the empirical analysis, by offering the most advanced and comprehensive overarching theoretical framework, which is appropriate for this research study, both in terms of theoretical development and analytical leverage. In fact, much common ground exists.

To begin with, the three new institutionalisms share similar theoretical foundations. At the heuristic level, four main commonalities can be highlighted (Peters 2005). First, all the new institutional perspectives share the goal of overcoming both the old institutionalism and behaviouralist theories, with a more analytically oriented and methodologically sound approach and with a focus on structures of interactions, formal rules, norms, and beliefs. Second, the three approaches are based on the assumption that institutions are the central component of political life and that they represent the main explanatory factor in policy analysis. Third, all new institutionalisms postulate that institutions create regularities in political behaviour. Fourth, they treat a set of common empirical questions, for instance, concerning the implementation of policies, the forming and functioning of executives, parliaments, and bureaucracies, and the effectiveness of political decisions. At an analytical level, another four characteristics of the 'unified core' of new institutionalism can be mentioned (Immergut 1998). First, one of the new institutionalism's main goals is to illustrate the discrepancy between actors' potential interests and those expressed in their empirical behaviour. Second, according to the tenants of new institutionalism, the aggregation of individual preferences cannot easily be translated into collective phenomena. Third, new institutional theories often focus on institutional biases to explain unintended outcomes. Fourth, a major common research interest is to open the black box of political demands and outcomes. To sum up, the three new institutionalisms originate from similar foundations and share several fundamental assumptions and scientific goals.

In fact, they have been often implicitly or explicitly integrated in many well-known theoretical and empirical studies. At least three distinctive sets of attempts can be identified. (1) Mayntz' and Scharpf's 'actor-centered institutionalism' offers a good example of this kind of flexible approach (Mayntz and Scharpf 1995;

Scharpf 1997), insofar as they treat actor orientations as a 'theoretically distinct category influenced but not determined by the institutional framework within which interactions occur'. In their view, the preferences of relatively autonomous rational actors, which are embedded in institutional arrangements and societal structures, are shaped by 'individual and organizational self-interest on one hand and (internalised) normative obligations and aspirations on the other' (Scharpf 2000b). Likewise, the neo-corporatist approach (Lehmbruch and Schmitter 1982) shares similar principles of explanation (Schneider 2003). The basic assumption is that the institutional framework shapes the action of participants in policy bargaining in a way that they also integrate group or public concerns in their strategic interaction. That is, they combine instrumental and normative commitments. The complementary use of rational choice institutionalism and sociological institutionalism is even more evident in March and Olsen's (1989) approach, as noted among others by Elinor Ostrom (Ostrom 1991). According to the authors, the institutional setting may enable the dominance or promote the interaction between a 'logic of appropriateness' (i.e. human action driven by rules and practices prescribing appropriate behaviour for actors in specific situations) and a 'logic of consequentiality' (i.e. the rational and instrumental action motivated by incentives and personal advantage); in short, political institutions deploy rules of appropriateness that subsequently shape the calculus and actions of rational actors (March and Olsen 2004; March and Olsen 2005). (2) Rational choice institutionalism has been used in combination with historical institutionalism as well. To begin with, the analytic narrative project (Levi 1997; Bates *et al.* 1998) endeavours to transcend the traditional 'Methodenstreit' between rationalists and historicists (Blyth 2006), by extending rational choice assumptions and tools to institutional historical research. The purpose of this approach is to explain singular crucial events, by adopting a combination of inductive case studies of historical processes and deductive formal modelling, in order to generate hypotheses applicable to a larger set of cases and generalise conclusions to some extent (Bates *et al.* 1998). Correspondingly, Pierson's well-known notion of 'increasing returns' is intended to 'provide a more rigorous framework for developing some of the key claims of recent scholarship in historical institutionalism', with reference to the concept of 'path dependence' (Pierson 2000; Pierson 2004). This concept, which operationalises the idea that 'history matters', is framed in rational choice terms, that is, as a self-reinforcing process where the costs of switching to other policy alternatives increase over time. Finally, Katznelson and Weingast focus on 'the deployment of institutions as middle-level mediations between large-scale processes and the microdynamics of agency and action' so as to study the intersections between historical and rational choice institutionalism (Weingast and Katznelson 2007). In particular, they argue that 'many of the putative differences separating historical institutionalism and rational choice institutionalism diminish, or even disappear, when (we) ask how institutional situations shape and help constitute and induce preferences people use to make judgements and choices about the present and the future at particular moments in time'. (3) Concerning the cross-fertilisation between historical institutionalism and sociological institutionalism, the literature is somewhat sparser, but still important. Thelen quotes Katzenstein's approach as an example of a comprehensive and dynamic view of institutions, considered 'not just as strategic context but as a set of shared understandings that affect the way problems are perceived and solutions are sought' over time (Thelen 1999). For instance, Katzenstein studied the historical evolution of international relations through the institutionalisation of collective norms that define the appropriateness of actors' behaviour and shape their identities (Katzenstein 1996). In addition, Mahoney and Rueschemeyer employ an open comparative methodology situated at the intersection of historical sociology and historical institutionalism, derived from the claim that the two research traditions display common concerns for causal analysis, the study of processes over time and the use of systematic and contextualised comparisons (Mahoney and Rueschemeyer 2003). They conceive comparative historical analysis as a potential mediator between rival paradigms, such as rational and cultural approaches, because the former constitutes a middle position between the two 'extremes' of a purely speculative subjective understanding and the ambition of deductive, universally valid theories.

After this short review (which could be easily extended), one should recognise the convergence of the scope, the aim and several postulates of (comparative) new institutional analyses, and the concomitant use of different new institutionalist approaches in empirical research. However, instead of building bridges to unify these complementary paradigms, the most common objective still appears to be the accommodation of the core assumptions of a specific research tradition with insights and criticisms coming from competing approaches (Sil 2000, 2004). Indeed, hardly a single theory of action will meet the requirements for analysing and interpreting complex political phenomena (Olsen 2001), and hardly a parsimonious theory may explain everything focusing on a particular (set of) explanatory conditions (Hirschman 1997; Katzenstein and Sil 2005). The search for theoretical purity may lead to an investigation of a world that just does not exist, making comparative political science look like 'an odd anthropological sect that imagines, theorises, and measures a world that is not there, and spends its time predicting the unpredictable, rather than being a progressive intellectual discipline' (Blyth 2006). A more realistic approach would presume, for instance, that strategic-oriented and rule-driven action would both occur concurrently, consecutively, or, to some degree, simultaneously and that unintended consequences may arise from the implementation of a certain policy design.

Therefore, in a problem-oriented perspective, it is helpful to 'give peace a chance' (Schmidt 2006) by adopting a comprehensive approach, without prioritising any research tradition, instead of choosing in advance one paradigm following non-verifiable ontological assumptions. Following Eckstein's call for an end to the 'war of paradigms' (Eckstein 1998), this goal implies an effort to bridge old divisions – between interests and norms, agency and structure, qualitative and quantitative methods (Goodin and Klingemann 1996) – and at the same time to link the common ground to more general questions of social theory, such as the interrelationship between institutions, interests and ideas (Jachtenfuchs 2006), in order to recognise interesting questions and test alternative and complementary explanations, instead of engaging in grand meta-theoretical debates (Katzenstein and Okawara 2001). A moderate 'analytical eclecticism' is thus adopted in this research study, heading for the integration of the three new institutionalisms, conceived as three parallel research traditions displaying a certain degree of prior compatibility and relative coherence (Sil 2000, 2004; Katzenstein and Sil 2005). Analytical eclecticism is a fruitful middle path between the ambition for a synthesis moving beyond existing approaches (i.e. the convergence upon a new, unified framework of assumptions, concepts, methods, and interpretive logics) and, on the other side, the mere juxtaposition of competing paradigms. Rather, it consists in the – quite inductive – integration of different research traditions into a single explanatory framework; at the same time, they can continue to evolve on relatively separate tracks in order to portray the complexity and contingency of the social world and human agency (Hirschman 1997). To do that, the distinct epistemological postulates underlying each research tradition should be adjusted, relaxed, or even suspended. Following Katzenstein, the analytical advantages of eclecticism are numerous: it enhances analytical leverage through the study of power, interest, and norms; it highlights different connections that parsimonious explanations dismiss; it protects researchers from taking as natural paradigmatic assumptions about the world; it offers a safeguard from the unavoidable failings of any one paradigm; and it helps making sense of empirical anomalies (Katzenstein and Okawara 2001).

Therefore, the three approaches can be used in a complementary way so as to model and explain complex political phenomena, by bringing into being a framework, wherein the three new institutionalisms are each expected to portray one analytically distinct facet of the investigated phenomena. For instance, hypotheses derived from rational choice institutionalism can be adopted to draw attention to the effect of actors' strategic behaviour, and namely to 'reveal how intentional and rational actors generate collective outcomes and aggregate behaviour' (Levi 1997). Hypotheses derived from sociological institutionalism can be used to give an account of the relevance of organisational factors for policy outcomes and the importance of symbolic action for the understanding of politics (March and Olsen 1984). Finally, hypotheses derived from historical institutionalism can help to conceptualise the impact of contextual variables, showing how institutions mediate through time the way political actors structure the power relations among them and shape the goals they pursue (Steinmo et al. 1992). All three levels constitute a component of a comprehensive explanation in social science: according to the individualist-structuralist 'bath-tub' model of causal explanation in social science (Coleman 1990), the social, cultural, and institutional context influences the micro level of individual perceptions, values, and subsequent intentional actions, which, in turn, influence the meso level through a process of aggregation, arbitration, and mediation in particular organisations and groups, leading, finally, to the explanandum at the macro level (Berg-Schlosser 2003). The unity of analysis of this research study is localised at the organisational level (the IRAs), whereas the independent and dependent variables are located at the micro, meso, and macro levels. It remains to determine, following the empirical analysis, to what extent which level(s) is (are) significant to explain a particular facet of the investigated phenomena investigation, and under which scope conditions causal relations empirically hold.

At a methodological level, connecting the new institutionalisms requires a set of methods and techniques that is not only coincident with the complex structure of contemporary political science theories but also allows the researcher to integrate different explanatory factors in a compound explanatory model with a unified view of causation, while keeping the analytical levels distinct. The next section will discuss this point.

The possible alignment of ontology and methodology

This research study is built on the explicit choice of a 'diversity-oriented' qualitative comparative analytical framework, which focuses on combinations of explanatory conditions (instead of individually independent variables), multiple causal paths (and not to average effects of single variables), and discovery (in opposition to rigorous test of pre-established hypotheses). This analytical choice also stem from a number of more practical limitations concerning the medium-small universe of cases here represented, for reasons of feasibility and given the availability of reliable datasets and data sources. To this aim, Ragin developed the qualitative comparative analysis (QCA), a configurational analytical technique based on Boolean algebra (Ragin 1987) and its extension in terms of fuzzy sets (Ragin 2000, 2006b; Rihoux 2006; Ragin 2008b; Rihoux and Ragin 2008). QCA assumes that the research environment of political science is extremely rich and that the connections between variables are better described in terms of multiple and conjunctural causation (Ragin 2000). Accordingly, in-depth knowledge of cases and attention to multiple, singular, or deviant patterns of causation could be combined with analytical precision, transparency, and systematic accuracy (Rihoux 2006). This research strategy attempts to underscore heterogeneity and difference in kind and degree, using a configurational approach to social phenomena that allows researchers to conceive each case as a combination of necessary and/or sufficient causal conditions (i.e. set memberships) (Smithson and Verkuilen 2006).

Specifically, following this framework of complex causation, causal relations are decomposed in set theoretic terms (Ragin 1987, 2000). Causation can be multiple because different causal paths can lead to the same outcome. Causation can be conjunctural because single explanatory factors can be jointly necessary and/or jointly sufficient for a given outcome. Within this kind of comparative analysis, necessity means that the presence of the outcome B always involves the condition A, and sufficiency means that the condition A always implies the presence of the outcome B. This technique will be discussed for the specific details of its application in the methodological section of each empirical part of the dissertation.

The analytical framework

Research design and methodology

This study takes seriously the need for aligning ontology and methodology (Hall 2003). Following the paradigm of 'unity amid diversity' (Gerring 2001), this book does not oppose case-oriented and variable-oriented research. Rather, it combines different techniques within a single logic of complex causation, in line with the conceptual foundations of the theoretical framework. As regards data collection, the present research relies upon survey inquiries, face-to-face semi-directed interviews, archives and electronic databases. Pertaining to data analysis, different techniques are employed in a complementary manner: crisp-set QCA analysis, fuzzy-set analysis, social network analysis, the actor-process-event scheme, and content analysis. Empirically, this book sheds light on the practices of regulation through a focal point: the de facto independence of IRAs from elected politicians and regulated industries. This question appears to be essential not only for the understanding of the implications of the recent spread of regulatory capitalism but also for the study of the dynamics of the global political economy and the challenges to democracy these transformations entail. In addition to the academic interest of this research, the improvement of the understanding of the functioning of IRAs may be relevant for the public at large. Indeed, political decision makers are delegating a number of crucial competences to independent regulators, which benefit from public authority without being elected by the people or directly managed by elected representatives. In this context, the practices and performance of agencies are still obscure and little known. With reference to these developments, elected politicians, their representatives in international and supranational organisations, and, above all, citizens would benefit from a more precise understanding of these evolutions, which refer to the substance of democracy and the signification of political representation.

Research questions

To endorse the concerns outlined above, this book starts from a series of 'problem-driven' questions about the functioning of IRAs, which will be translated into a set of middle-range theoretical questions in the form of testable hypotheses.

- Do IRAs fulfil their mandates after the delegation of competencies?
- Which factors shape the implementation of their formal independence?
- How do IRAs use their independence?
- What kind of relationship do they develop with their environment?
- Are they really independent in their routine?
- Or are they operating in the shadow of the administrative hierarchy?
- Are they deviating from the statutory prescriptions?

- Are they captured by the regulated industries?
- Who is involved in the regulatory process?
- Which are the key political actors in the regulatory state?
- How far do agencies influence the political decision-making processes?
- What are the outcomes of the activity of regulation?
- Do IRAs improve decision making?
- Can IRAs be(come) accountable?

All these questions are crucial to understand the meaning, significance, and implications of the new order of regulatory capitalism. To tackle this question, the line of attack developed in this book is the study of the distinctive characteristic of IRAs, that is, their factual independence. Specifically, the main goal of the present inquiry is to discover what is shaping the de facto independence of regulatory agencies and investigate its consequences on their role in policy making and accountability. It is worth noting that a crucial point that has received, until now, little systematic attention in the European literature on regulation will be specifically examined, that is, the relationship between IRAs and actors other than the political decision makers, and namely those being regulated.

The structure of the empirical analysis

The structure of the empirical analysis is threefold. The first part illustrates and explains the variation of de facto independence of IRAs, beyond statutory prescriptions. The second studies the role of IRAs in the domestic policy-making processes, according to different levels of de facto independence and controlling for a set of contextual variables. The third examines the accountability of IRAs by investigating the link between their factual independence and their media evaluation, in terms of credibility and efficiency. It follows that de facto independence, the key variable of the dissertation, is the 'dependent variable' in the first part of my research, while it is one of the 'independent variables' of the second and third parts (see Figure 2.1).

(i) *Explaining de facto independence.* There are arguments according to which de facto independence could be different from statutory prescriptions. Indeed, while formal rules are important, they only partially portray the functioning of agencies, and the institutional framework allows them a certain amount of discretion. More precisely, prescriptions concerning independence, which are written in the constitutions of agencies, represent the intentions of the political decision makers, in the context of the structural, functional, and strategic pressures for developing a formally independent organisational model of agencies. On the contrary, the notion of de facto independence characterises the effective independence of agencies during their day-to-day regulatory action. The complex relations between de facto and formal independence are examined with a cross-national, cross-sectoral comparison of sixteen Western European IRAs using fuzzy-set analysis. Organisational and institutional explanations are discussed.

(ii)   *The effect of de facto independence on the role of agencies in policy making.* IRAs are relatively new powerful actors intervening in the political process at different stages, specifically rule making, monitoring, adjudication and sanctioning. In addition, they often initiate national legislative procedures, participate in pre-parliamentary consultations, and are integrated into parliamentary commissions. However, the impact of agencies on domestic policy making has hardly been studied. The role that IRAs play in a number of political decision-making processes is thus made operational and then examined, with special attention to the impact of de facto independence.

(iii) *The media accountability of agencies.* IRAs were officially established as the instruments of a technocratic approach, which lacks democratic legitimacy, in order to reconcile the credibility of the regulatory order with the efficiency of policy making. Here, the focal point is to see to what extent can the news media function as an accountability forum, eventually enhancing IRAs' legitimacy, by providing a consistent evaluation of their official goals in terms of credibility and efficiency.

Analytical scope and levels of analysis

As this research study is built on a comprehensive theoretical framework, it is necessary to develop a model for connecting the levels of analysis, whereby the three new institutionalisms play a complementary role in explaining social phenomena. Accordingly, rational choice institutionalism, sociological institutionalism, and historical institutionalism should not be considered competing theories, but as partially overlapping research traditions that could bring into being a multifaceted explanatory model, wherein each one ideally portrays a distinctive component. Before presenting the model, it is worth reminding that the present research starts from organisations as units of analysis (the IRAs), while the crucial variable (the agencies' de facto independence) is epistemologically located at the meso level, and other explanatory variables are situated at the micro, meso, and macro levels.

Part I concerns the examination of the (micro-meso-macro) causes of a certain effect at the meso level (i.e. the causes of the de facto independence). This necessitates the following: the specification of the context shaping actors' perceptions/ beliefs/preferences; the identification of the strategies driving actors' behaviour; and the examination of the logic of aggregation of actions at the meso level of the organisation. Parts II and III consist of the investigation of the (macro) consequences of a certain cause at the meso level (i.e. the consequences of the de facto independence). This requires the study of how this variable interacts with other meso factors, aggregating actors' strategic decisions, which are, in turn, mediated by their perceptions/ beliefs/ preferences, within the contextual structure that offers them a range of opportunities and constraints, while accounting for implementation problems and unintended consequences for the outcomes. The thorough application of this 'bathtub-like' explanation (Coleman 1990; Berg-Schlosser 2003) entails the matching of all the three new institutionalisms by adopting a configurational approach where the explanatory factors may be regarded as complementary.

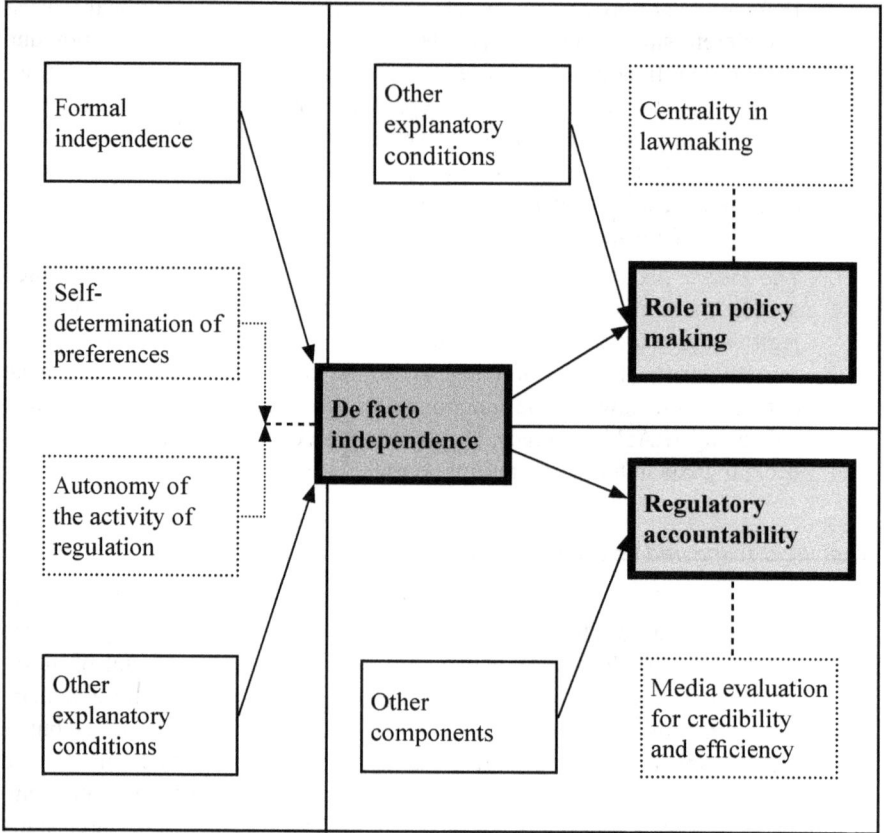

Figure 2.1: Structure of the argument

chapter three | explaining de facto independence (part i)

Summary

The delegation of public authority and regulatory competencies from governments, ministries and public administrations to formally independent regulatory agencies (IRAs) entails a pressing question regarding the effectiveness of their independence. This chapter examines the relation between formal independence, as prescribed in the constitutions of agencies, and de facto independence, as exerted in practice in their day-to-day regulatory routine. To this end, it conceptualises and assesses the de facto independence of IRAs, and discusses organisational, institutional, and political factors for explaining its possible divergence from formal independence. The complex relations between these two conditions are examined with a cross-national, cross-sectoral comparison of sixteen Western European IRAs, using fuzzy-set analysis. The results show that formal independence is neither a necessary nor a sufficient condition for explaining variations in the de facto independence of IRAs. Other factors, such as the life cycle of agencies, veto players, and networks of agencies, have a decisive impact.

Towards the study of de facto independence

The tasks of political decision makers are being profoundly reshaped in Western countries. Governments and bureaucracies are increasingly delegating regulatory competencies to formally independent regulatory agencies (IRAs), which now represent the main institutional feature of the 'new global order of regulatory capitalism' (Levi-Faur 2005a; Levi-Faur and Jordana 2005). The shift of power in favour of these bodies is quantitatively impressive and qualitatively relevant. They have proliferated across countries and sectors, becoming the taken-for-granted, preformatted answer to a wide range of regulatory problems (Gilardi 2005b). IRAs are officially designed to improve the credibility and efficiency of policy making by insulating it from the short-term pressures of the political cycle, while also providing specialised, supposedly neutral technical expertise to policy makers. In this sense, the phenomenon of delegation to IRAs is conceptualised by new public management (NPM) tenants as a technocratic procedure for managing 'complex' political systems through depoliticisation and the use of technical knowledge. However, a number of fundamental questions about the consequences of delegation to IRAs are still unanswered, first and foremost concerning the *ef-*

fectiveness of their independence.[1] To be precise, we still lack clear, comparative, systematic evidence concerning the factual independence of IRAs.

Are IRAs truly independent? In theory, delegation to factually independent regulators is the precondition for reliable, high-quality regulation. Therefore, the transfer to IRAs of 'political property rights' – regulatory competencies and regulatory powers – is required, according to a 'fiduciary mode of delegation' (Majone 2001c). In fact, delegation to an 'agent' who simply executes the orders of the 'principal' cannot enhance decision-making credibility. At the same time, the 'trustor' can transfer its powers to the 'trustee' but not its democratic legitimacy, locating the process of delegation to IRAs outside the chain of democratic delegation (Strom *et al.* 2003). As a consequence, regulatory governance by IRAs involves a 'net loss of legitimacy' for the political system (Majone 2005). In this context, the question of the effective implementation of this mode of delegation is particularly relevant and should constitute the first step of an inquiry into the practices of regulatory governance, before any investigation of the consequences of delegation. Any prospective lack of IRAs' factual independence from elected politicians is likely to be contested by those being regulated, especially in the case of outcomes perceived as adverse by the stakeholders, reducing the social sustainability of regulatory governance. It is also possible that some political actors will challenge the extant regulatory order because its 'democratic deficit' would be perceived as unjustified. Conversely, in the case of unanticipated higher independence and lower accountability, uncontrolled agencies may develop their own strategies and reroute the mandated goals of delegation, overruling the will of elected politicians, reframing the definition of 'public interest' according to their organisational logic, and risking being captured by the regulated industries (Braun 2002).

Endorsing these analytical and normative concerns, this chapter explores the conceptual and empirical relations between formal independence, as prescribed in the constitutions of agencies, and de facto independence, as exerted in practice, and examines whether, to what extent, and under which conditions the two types of independence may diverge from each other. The structure of the chapter is as follows. First, I propose a way to conceptualise the distinction between formal and de facto independence. Then, I present a theoretical discussion of factors that may influence agencies' de facto independence, and I develop hypotheses about variations in de facto independence, illustrating why it can be expected to differ from formal independence. Next, I discuss data and methods before testing my theoretical expectations on sixteen Western European regulators using a fuzzy-set analysis technique. Results and conclusions follow. The main insight is that formal independence is neither a necessary nor a sufficient condition for explaining the de facto independence of agencies, and the divergence from statutory prescriptions reflects a significant range of organisational and institutional conditions.

---

1   The criterion of effectiveness assesses the extent to which a process (here, the delegation of competencies to IRAs profiting from formal independence) actually delivers its intended result (i.e. the implementation of a regulatory order that is factually independent from the elected politicians and from those being regulated) (Blühdorn 2006).

Conceptualising the de facto independence of IRAs

There are several definitions of organisational 'autonomy' (Verhoest *et al.* 2004), but not many concern the more precise notion of 'independence', and very few specifically treat the problem of its effectiveness. It is worth noting that a certain degree of vertical and/or horizontal organisational separation and bureaucratic discretion is a characteristic of all branches of government and civil service, that is, ministerial departments, executive agencies, expert committees, advisory boards, extra-parliamentary commissions, street-level services, and so forth. In fact, the study of bureaucratic autonomy is an old concern for political scientists, especially for US students of bureaucracy and the Congress. The autonomy of executive agencies from elected officials has been depicted by rational choice institutionalists as a strategic game, which includes decisions over the initial delegation of authority, the range of choices of policy alternatives, and the opportunities for oversight and control (Calvert *et al.* 1989). Typically, bureaucratic autonomy can emerge from dynamic systems in which imperfectly informed participants – the agency board, its staff, the legislature, the executive, the courts, and the stakeholders – adapt to one another's decisions over time, accommodating thus a heterogeneous array of results (Moe 1985). In addition, the importance of agencies' autonomy was emphasised when investigating the balance of power between the parliament and the bureaucracies, indicating that politicians concede less policy discretion when the level of conflict increases or their legislative capacity grows (Huber and Shipan 2002).

On the other hand, following a historical-organisational perspective, executive agencies' autonomy can be conceived as a social relation shaped by reputational factors (Carpenter 2001b). Accordingly, public sector organisations gain supplementary autonomy when they are able to develop politics of legitimacy, which are socially rooted, politically forged, and grounded in agencies' capacity, involving networking and coalition building. In this context, autonomous bureaucracies are expected to be able to materially reorient and command public policies designed by elected authorities (Carpenter 2002a). However, in both cases, the conceptual foundations of effective autonomy remained quite implicit. At a later stage, European scholars of public administration and public management adopted several typologies to systematise the multiple definitions of organisational autonomy, proposing different conceptualisations, operationalisations, and measurements (Verhoest *et al.* 2004). In their extensive review, Verhoest and colleagues drew inspiration from previous research to pinpoint six basic alternative and complementary conceptions of autonomy (Verhoest *et al.* 2004).

Managerial autonomy occurs when agencies possess important decision-making competencies concerning the choice and use of their financial, human, and organisational resources. *Policy autonomy* relates to the extent to which agencies can make decisions about the procedures to reach external goals, policy implementation instruments, target groups and, at the higher level of autonomy, the social aims of regulation. *Structural autonomy* indicates how far the agency is separated from hierarchical governmental pressures, for which relevant factors are the appointment procedure, accountability requirements, and the direct political influence of government on board members. *Financial autonomy* derives from the agencies' funding procedure, namely distinguishing between government sources and internal sources, and between fixed or variable revenues. *Legal autonomy* is conceived as the degree to which statutory prescriptions can prevent the government from changing agencies' decisions or reallocating agencies competencies. Finally, *interventional autonomy*, according to the authors cited above, refers to the extent to which the agency is bounded or not by accountability requirements, performance evaluation, impact assessment, and audit duties with respect to regulatory outcomes and to (the lack of) restrictions concerning possible sanctions and external interventions. Three further, partially overlapping, distinctions should be added: first, internal autonomy referring to the organisational structure should be distinguished from external autonomy towards its environment (Bouckaert and Verhoest 1999). Second, organisational and managerial autonomy could be combined into a single notion, while the latter could be defined separately from financial autonomy (Pollitt *et al.* 2004). Finally, Lægreid and colleagues conceived strategic autonomy as the possibility for agencies to formulate their own goals and objectives, while operational autonomy represents the room for manoeuvring when determining the use of policy instruments and resources (Lægreid *et al.* 2006b). However, once again, as Pollitt and Bouckaert maintained in their very widely cited textbook, the effects and implications of the formal structures for guaranteeing autonomy are still poorly understood (Pollitt and Bouckaert 2004).

To begin with, the recurrent problem when using these kinds of typologies is 'conceptual stretching' (Sartori 1970): The approaches for defining organisational autonomy become more and more multidimensional and sparse, while, at the same time, they tend to adopt a too narrow focus, leading to a mislaying of analytical leverage and inconvenience associated with inappropriate comparative logic (Sartori 1991). The study of organisational autonomy is producing quite inconclusive evidence (Verhoest *et al.* 2004; Verhoest 2005). Instead, I propose to use the term 'independence' in a more specific way, in order to define those bodies that, possessing the highest level of institutional and organisational disaggregation, also hold a formal status granting separateness from elected politicians, i.e. independent regulatory agencies (IRAs). The scientific study of this specific type of public sector organisation is vital because they enjoy a considerable deal of public authority when developing, adopting and implementing crucial regulatory competencies without possessing democratic responsiveness. Formally independent agencies with regulatory functions correspond to the 'fourth type' of public sector organisation identified by Verschuere and colleagues (Verschuere *et al.* 2006), that is:

> Externally autonomous public organisations with their own budget, defined as legal entities by public law, and with a governing board.

The concept of organisational independence as such was originally adopted to characterise the institutional status of central banks (Rogoff 1985). In its most encompassing version, the measure of central bank independence comprises two elements (Alesina and Summers 1993): political independence, defined as the ability to select policy objectives without influence from the government, and economic independence, that is, the ability to use instruments of monetary policy without restrictions. The various existing indices of central banks' independence are usually based on statutory prescriptions, such as the procedure of appointment of the members of the board, the approval requirements for monetary policy decisions, the prior definition of monetary objectives in the central bank statute, and the budgetary control mechanisms (Bade and Parkin 1982; Grilli *et al.* 1991; Cukierman *et al.* 1992; Alesina and Summers 1993). The seminal work of Gilardi drew inspiration from this approach to assess the formal independence of IRAs, with reference to a series of prescriptions, enshrined in the constitutions of agencies, which are intended to guarantee independence from elected politicians (Gilardi 2002a, 2005a, 2008). Formal independence is the key factor to be considered when investigating the decision of delegating power to IRAs because it corresponds to the intentions of the decision makers about the need for providing time consistency and knowledge-based advice to regulatory policies. Here, an extension of this approach is proposed, by the means of the concept of de facto independence, to appraise the regulatory action of IRAs after delegation. Indeed, factual independence cannot be taken for granted but depends on both mechanisms for granting independence and the use of those mechanisms (Moe 1985).

To this end, Yesilkagit and Van Thiel proposed a relational conception of 'actual autonomy', suggesting that agencies shall develop ties with all actors in the politico-administrative system and with societal actors at large: pressure groups, interest groups, consultants, public opinion, clients, target groups, the media, and so forth (Yesilkagit and Van Thiel 2008). The authors developed thus a measure of autonomy based on the level of financial and policy autonomy of the investigated public sector organisations. This innovative and ambitious approach presents three main shortcomings that make it difficult to apply as such to the present book for the study of IRAs' functioning. First, it presents a wide-ranging, horizontal view of autonomy, *vis-à-vis* a large number of institutional, political, and societal actors, instead of focusing on the hierarchical relationship between agencies and elected politicians and its mirror image with those being regulated. Here I argue instead that, while all relationships can be relevant for studying the reconfiguration of power in the political system, nonetheless, only those with politicians and regulatees are crucial for measuring the effective independence of regulators in the execution of their regulatory competencies. The latter relationships display indeed qualitative differences in comparison to informal ties that agencies may develop with other actors, as IRAs, politicians and regulatees, 'the three forces in regulation' (Thatcher 2005a), that might have contradictory interests in the practice of regulatory governance. Second, their approach focuses on all types of bureaucratic agencies, without pinpointing the specific features of IRAs, so that, given the need for very detailed contextual evidence, it entails feasibility problems for extensive, systematic, comparative cross-national and cross-sectoral studies.

Another attractive and original approach consists of interviewing agencies' managers about the degree of autonomy they perceive themselves to have (Lægreid *et al.* 2006a; Lægreid *et al.* 2008). It is argued that even if this measure might not accurately reflect the actual level of autonomy, managers' perceptions matter, as they guide agencies' regulatory action and have important symbolic functions. This perspective is indeed very useful for the sociology of administration and for the examination of the legitimising effects of independence. As regards its application in the present book, however, the major problem is that what is measured might not really correspond to the managers' opinions concerning their autonomy, but rather to their perceptions about the degree of autonomy that has to be considered appropriate, given the institutional context. The interviewed managers may behave strategically, constructing their answers so as to try to gain external and internal legitimacy. In addition, and above all, this approach is not suitable for fully capturing the more structural, sometimes even unconscious, or at least rationally bounded features of factual independence, which also have an impact on the political role of agencies and on their regulatory performance. For instance, no external pressure is perceived if agencies' preferences are 'organically' in line with those of the politicians or the regulatees, e.g. when the representatives of one of the two groups of external actors are 'naturally' populating agencies' boards. Nonetheless, it would be hard to qualify these agencies as truly autonomous. In addition, agencies' managers may perceive themselves as very autonomous, in the sense of not being subject to any explicit external pressures, but actually they may not dispose from the capacity of implementing their own decisions. Instead, to paraphrase a famous dictum, it seems more judicious to consider that 'only those remain *independent* who use their *independence*'. Hence, I propose to conceive the de facto independence characterising IRAs in a more abstract, general, and comprehensive way, starting from a very simple proposition:

> *De facto independence* characterises the effective independence of agencies as they manage day-to-day regulatory actions.

To move towards a definition, one can conceptualise de facto independence drawing from Majone's seminal paper (Majone 1997a), in which he identified IRAs as 'highly specialized organisations enjoying considerable autonomy in decision-making.' Autonomy means, above all, to be able to translate (1) one's own preferences (2) into (authoritative) actions, without external constraints (Nordlinger 1981).[2] Therefore, I suggest that the de facto independence of formally independent regulatory agencies can be seen as a synthesis of two necessary components:

---

2. Please note that I adopt Nordlinger's (1981) abstract definition of autonomy, leaving aside his conception of independence that refers to his typology of states' self-rule and strength. Rather, following Majone (2001), I use the term 'independence' in the sense of separateness, developing the concept of de facto independence as a way to assess the independence of the agencies' day-to-day regulatory action and operationalising it through the two components derived from the abstract definition of autonomy.

(1) *The self-determination of agencies' preferences,* and

(2) *The agencies' autonomy throughout the use of regulatory competen-cies,* that is, during the activity of regulation.

According to this conception, factually independent agencies should be able to carry on their regulatory action without constraints within the limits of their mandate. In that regard, not only has the informal aspect of independence been somewhat neglected in the literature, but also the role of actors other than the politicians has been underestimated.[3] Yet in view of the process of the delega-tion of regulatory competencies to agencies, it is plausible to consider IRAs as 'intermediary organisations' that act as mediators between the elected politicians and the regulatees, i.e. the representatives of the sectors targeted by regulation (Braun 1993). Indeed, even if agencies enjoy operational autonomy in order to promote the 'public interest' as defined in their constitutions, they have to interact regularly with those being regulated to gather relevant information and ensure the implementation of their decisions. In turn, those being regulated have incentives to obtain the more favourable regulation, making the most of their material and in-formational resources. Accordingly, the 'three forces' in regulation are represented by three distinct sets of actors: elected politicians, IRAs and regulatees (Thatcher 2005a). Therefore, *elected politicians* and *regulatees* are the relevant external ac-tors, which may be able to mould the regulatory action of agencies and should be considered particularly relevant in assessing the independence of IRAs in practice.

To examine the relationship between IRAs and the regulated industries, and especially the possibility of 'capture', three indirect indicators are usually adopted (Thatcher 2002d). First, the extent to which there is a 'revolving door' is consid-ered, i.e. the number of staff members moving from regulated industries to IRAs and then back. The underlying assumption is that the occurrence of revolving door phenomena from agencies provides them with material incentives favouring pro-regulatees regulation, while revolving door from agencies may shape their cogni-tive framing of regulatory issues and alter their hierarchy of values and policy beliefs in favour of the interests of the regulated industries. The second indicator is the number of sanctioning decisions that are made against the regulated industries, illustrating agencies' operational functioning and the degree of their activism. Third, the number of legal challenges to the decisions of IRAs offers a measure of conflict between regulatees and IRAs, which could be interpreted as an indica-tor of independence. According to this perspective, a comparison of regulators in Britain, France, Germany, and Italy showed that agencies are generally free from capture, with, however, some exceptions, as the author observed that IRAs have not broken decisively with prior regulatory traditions. In several cases, they favour

---

3. Pedersen scrutinised agencies' independence from the perspective of stakeholders and regulated industries, but she does so only dealing with formal rules (Pedersen 2006). Thatcher examined the relationships between agencies and the regulatees, but focused only on indirect indicators (Thatcher 2002d).

suppliers, and, in crucial areas, such as merger control, IRAs have undertaken little activity (Thatcher 2002d).

This approach represents a very useful starting point, but as such it has two limitations. On the one hand, the extent to which there exists a revolving door cannot be considered alone, but should be combined with additional information on phenomena with similar effects on actors' cognitive and strategic processes, such as regular meetings, exchanges of expertise, and ad hoc contacts between agencies, political decision makers, and regulatees. On the other hand, it is difficult to interpret unambiguously the number of decisions, sanctions, and challenges to agencies' decisions. For instance, given the absence of sanctions, can we conclude that regulators act in the interests of regulatees or rather that there is little IRAs' activity because the regulated firms are already thoroughly respecting the applicable rules?

My operationalisation of the notion of de facto independence will be presented in the methodological section. At this point, it is worth noting that the approach in terms of de facto independence is useful only when we expect that agencies' de facto independence cannot be directly derived from formal independence. Therefore, in the next section, I will illustrate my theoretical expectations starting from the possible disjunction between formal independence, as prescribed in the constitutions of agencies, and their de facto independence. Then, a set of organisational, institutional, and political explanations for the variation of de facto independence is offered.

Theoretical expectations

Analytical framework

The present study relies upon a fuzzy-set analysis (fs/QCA), which is particularly suitable for the extant research goals. First, this technique permits the discovery of all the configurations that explain the outcome of interest, so as to portray the complex relationship between agencies' formal and de facto independence in a comprehensive manner. Accordingly, a variety of conditions can be examined, leading to the assessment of multiple causal paths, according to the notion of 'equifinality' (Bennett and Elman 2006)). Second, this research strategy attempts to underscore heterogeneity and difference in kind and degree, instead of estimating the average 'net effect' of independent variables. Each case is conceived as a combination of necessary and sufficient causal conditions, defined by their 'set memberships' in the outcome (Smithson and Verkuilen 2006). In fact, given my research question, I am more interested in subtly examining the causal connections between variables in terms of necessary and sufficient conditions than in studying the general patterns of covariation of two variables. Third, fuzzy set QCA is particularly helpful when dealing with a small-to-medium number of cases, balancing intensive and extensive investigation, while focusing on exploration and discovery (Ragin 2000). Fuzzy set QCA combines the advantages of case-oriented (qualitative) studies in terms of in-depth knowledge of cases and attention to multiple, singular, or deviant patterns of causation, and the precision, transparency, and systematic accuracy of a variable-oriented (quantitative) approach (Rihoux 2006).

Following this approach, the present research is built on a comprehensive new institutional perspective. Therefore, a number of joint combinations of variables are offered, which are expected to lead to the different types of outcomes. Hypothesis 1.1 and Hypothesis 1.5 depict two non-causal relationships. Hypothesis 1.2 mixes historical and rational institutionalist explanations for high de facto independence from elected politicians. Hypothesis 1.3 combines historical and sociological explanatory factors of low de facto independence from elected politicians, and, respectively, of low de facto independence from regulatees. Hypothesis 1.4 offers a rational-sociological perspective for explaining high de facto independence from regulatees. What is more, it is recognised that, following a partially inductive approach (Schneider and Wagemann 2003), the empirical analysis also permits the discovery of other configurations and causal patterns.[4]

Hypotheses

Outline of the hypotheses:

H 1.1   *High formal independence is expected to be neither necessary nor sufficient for agencies' high de facto independence from elected politicians*

H 1.2   *The combination of the old age of agencies and the presence of many veto players should lead to high de facto independence from elected politicians*

H 1.3   *The joint effect of highly coordinated economy and sectoral path dependency should be sufficient to predict low de facto independence from the politicians and the regulatees*

H 1.4   *The intense participation of agencies in European networks and the organisational weakness of regulatees are expected to lead to high de facto independence from regulatees*

H 1.5   *High de facto independence from politicians should imply scarce independence vis-à-vis the regulatees*

---

4.   To be precise, the development of middle-range theories is necessary for guiding the selection of the causal conditions and it is useful for identifying theoretically meaningful combinations that deserve special attention; yet the methodological approach that is embraced – looking for the potential combination of necessary and sufficient conditions – permits the discovery of different causal patterns, implying a constant interaction between theory-testing and theory-building, which shall lead to a cumulative process of theory refinement and development of new empirical questions.

The first hypothesis regards the disjuncture between formal and de facto independence. Prescriptions concerning independence, which are enshrined in the constitutions of IRAs, correspond to the official goals of the decision makers who delegated regulatory competencies to agencies, in line with functional pressures and political strategies for creating formally independent regulatory bodies. The formal structure of organisations constrains choices, and, at the same time, it creates and enhances capacity in certain directions; therefore, the presence of a formally independent model should have a certain impact on the effective independence of IRAs (Egeberg 1999). However, earlier empirical research on organisations has concluded that there is a gap between formal and informal structures, and even that the latter may have a greater impact than the former on organisational outcomes (Downs 1967; Dalton 2004).

On the one hand, formal rules are constantly reinterpreted and adapted by the organisation *vis-à-vis* its environment. In fact, no rule can escape a certain degree of indeterminacy, as its meaning is always interpretatively flexible (Wittgenstein 1958). They tend to function as symbolic elements that organisations incorporate to gain legitimacy, resources, stability, and enhanced survival prospects (Meyer and Rowan 1977). In particular, the process of delegating public authority from political decision makers (the 'trustor') to independent agencies (the 'trustee'), though law-backed and highly formalised, invariably relies upon an incomplete contract, since it is impossible to spell out in explicit details all the precise obligations of the agent throughout the life of the contract, and the cost of monitoring the whole process would be prohibitive (Williamson 1985, 1993). Therefore, any organisational framework allows a certain amount of discretion (March and Simon 1958; Friedberg 1997). In this context, diverse actors have incentives to sway the formal prescriptions of independence, by taking advantage of the existing leeway. For instance, following their internal organisational logic, agencies might develop their own 'self-centred' strategies, for developing further their role in regulatory regimes, and for gaining distinctive political power (Bendor *et al.* 2001). Similarly, elected politicians and civil servants are likely to try to retain controls over IRAs after delegation, so as to informally steer agencies as they desire, in order to reduce agencies' discretion 'by stealth' and promote their political and economic goals, while avoiding public blame in the case of unpopular decisions (Egan 1998; Braun 2002). Finally, the regulated industries may seek to capture the regulatory agencies to obtain the most favourable regulation for their economic activities and competitive advantages in front of their internal and external business competitors (Stigler 1971).

In fact, a number of research studies suggested that the diversity of statutory prescriptions corresponds only partially to the variations in actual practices of IRAs (Stern 1997; Stern and Holder 1999; Thatcher 2002c, d; Wilks and Bartle 2002). For instance, as regards utility regulation, Stern (1997) argued that a formally independent regulator might not act impartially in practice, and that following the US experience the introduction of formally independent regulators does not guarantee the development of effective regulation. As a consequence, informal regulatory arrangements – namely related to the understanding of the custom and practice of regulation – appear to be at least as important as legal prescriptions. Similarly, Wilks and Bartle (2002) showed that European competition authorities that were created essentially for constitutional and symbolic purposes were nonetheless able to reshape their design and redefine their mission over time, so as to exert an increasingly important impact on the regulation of market economies. In addition, it seems that, whereas several formal controls on agencies exist, such as the appointment of directors, the possibility of forcing early departures of IRA members, the overturn of IRA decisions, and the reduction of IRA budgets and powers, these powers are mostly unused to limit 'agency losses' in practice (Thatcher 2005a).

Therefore, we expect a disjuncture between formal and de facto independence of IRAs, while a number of organisational and institutional conditions should affect the 'repertoire of action' at disposal to the relevant actors – IRAs, political decision makers and regulatees – by determining their structure of opportunities and constraints and shaping their preferences and behaviour (Tilly 1975, 2006), having thus critical consequences for the effectiveness of delegation and the implementation of regulatory governance.

H 1.1   High formal independence should be neither a necessary nor a sufficient condition for a high level of de facto independence from politicians.

The second hypothesis pertains to the degree of de facto independence from politicians. First of all, one would expect de facto independence to be time dependent. Indeed, following an historical institutionalist argument, institutions are embedded in temporal processes that shape their development and their role, highlighting the causal relevance of origins, 'critical junctures', sequences, and positive and negative feedback effects (Thelen 1999). Therefore, the impact of the 'rules of the game' may become visible only when we account for temporal variables, instead of paying attention only at slices of time or short-term phenomena (Pierson and Skocpol 2002). Accordingly, IRAs, probably even more than other public sector organisations, enjoy an incremental institutional development that permits the evolution of their relationships with elected politicians and with regulatees beyond the constitutional design that was set up at the time of their establishment. To begin with, the influence of interest groups is said to increase over time, producing the accumulation of collusions that are detrimental to the 'public interest' (Olson 1982). Regulatory agencies are indeed expected to go through a life cycle, setting out as protagonists of the 'public interest' and then gradually becoming routinised and increasingly bureaucratised (Martimort 1999) and protective of the interests of the actors they are supposed to regulate (Kahn 1988). In that sense, agencies' functioning should be understood as a dynamic game in which politicians, interest groups, and IRAs interact repeatedly within regulatory regimes. Collusion might be self-enforcing, as the two partners, who share information that is not available to the political principals, may prefer the future benefits derived from continuing to cooperate to the current gains derived from non-collusive behaviour. In fact, when examining different regulatory styles in Europe, it seems that the role of regulators has frequently diverged from initial prescriptions; in particular, the relation between regulators and stakeholders evolved over time, following both functional market developments and organisational learning processes (Coen 2005).

These arguments would lead us to suppose that an older IRA will be more de facto independent from politicians and less independent from regulatees than will be a younger one. Agencies are indeed expected to benefit from a process of autonomisation from their principal, due to the accumulation of informational, material and symbolic resources in the course of the repeated interactions with the regulated sector. At the same time, they are expected to develop a possible collusive behaviour, in the form of a structural dependency, or at least to undertake a socialisation process in front of those being regulated that reduces progressively their factual independence. Furthermore, I consider that another condition could be jointly relevant for explaining the outcome of interest, by applying the notion of 'multiple and conjunctural causation' (Ragin 2000). Following a rational choice institutionalist argument, the presence of veto players should be a factor enabling the occurrence of the higher level of de facto independence of agencies.

To begin with, it is worth noting that the concept of veto players permits to summarise and operationalise many institutional characteristics of the political systems under investigation, such as the regime type, the legislature type and the party system. Veto players are individual or collective actors whose agreement is necessary to make political decisions and change the status quo. The presence of many veto players indicates a political and institutional context where changes are difficult to make. On the one hand, institutional veto points are constituted, for instance, by presidential vetoing prerogatives, by the composition of parliamentary bicameralism, and by the existence of federalist representative arrangements. On the other hand, the number and ideological distance between partisan veto players, who are populating these veto points, depending on the different configurations of political coalitions, determine the eventual potential for policy change (Tsebelis 2002). The consequences of veto players for the process of delegation are still empirically indefinite. According to prior research, this variable has an opposite effect on the formal independence of central banks and on that of IRAs, although the main theoretical rationale of delegation is supposedly identical: the creation of credible commitments to reduce the expected time-inconsistency of policies (Gilardi 2007). Following the empirical analysis of Gilardi, in the former case, veto players have a facilitating effect on formal independence (the more veto players, the more independence); in the latter, they are the functional equivalent of formal independence (the less veto players, the more independence). In other words, veto players constitute a necessary precondition for credible delegation to central banks (if delegation can be easily reverted, it is useless for improving credibility), while this does not hold for IRAs (delegation to formally independent IRAs is especially needed when credibility is not provided by the existence of veto players). The crucial point is that, instead, the effect of veto players on agencies' de facto independence is expected to be univocal. The number (and, implicitly, distance) of veto players in the political system makes it more difficult for the political decision makers to find an agreement and adapt their strategies to changing situations, producing a reduction in the steering capacity of the elected politicians over independent regulators (Tsebelis 2002). This condition leads to a situation where those agencies, which are the object of competing control by multiple, and possibly conflicting, political principals, may become able to exert increased discretion in their day-to-day regulatory routine (Epstein and O'Halloran 1999; Whitford 2005). To sum up, multiple or divided principals should be less capable of monitoring, controlling, and influencing the agent, allowing agencies to develop more de facto independence.

H 1.2   The combination of conditions that might give rise to high de facto independence from politicians is expected to be the old age of agencies and the presence of many veto players.

The third hypothesis is about predictors of low de facto independence of IRAs. Theoretical expectations concerning low de facto independence cannot be simply deduced from the reverse of those that regard high de facto independence. In fact, the presence of the preceding combination of conditions is expected to be sufficient for the positive outcome, but its absence, although necessary, is not directly sufficient for predicting the occurrence of the negative outcome. Other explanatory factors must be mentioned. A frequent argument in comparative political science is that institutional reforms, when they occur, tend to produce different effects across countries according to their 'fit' or 'misfit' with the domestic institutional context. In fact, even if powerful cross-national pressures can drive exogenous, homogenising institutional changes, producing formal convergence across nations (Thatcher 2005b), nevertheless the implementation and outcomes of the new institutional arrangements could vary from country to country (Crouch and Streeck 1997; Hall and Gingerich 2004), and be affected by the behaviour the institutional context itself generates (Streeck and Thelen 2005). Therefore, the study of the effect of a single institutional reform implies considering the 'embeddedness' of political organisations in political economies and political systems (Polanyi 1983), requiring a methodological framework which allows the researcher to adopt a comprehensive view of institutions, economy and society (Gemici 2008).

The 'varieties of capitalism' approach (VoC) makes these insights operational (Hall and Gingerich 2004). The starting point is the observation that several models of capitalism exist in advanced industrialised democracies. To put it simply, the literature distinguishes between two basic ideal types of institutional models concerning the organisation of the political economy: the coordinated market economies (CMEs), based on extra-market coordination between economic and political actors, and the liberal market economies (LMEs), in which the architecture of markets is expected to ensure coordination (Hall and Gingerich 2004). The German case represents the paradigmatic example of CME. As an illustration, the German financial system traditionally provides firms with access to credit according to criteria that are not entirely dependent from immediate returns. This makes it possible for firms to engage in long-term projects, while the monitoring of firms is achieved through the presence of banking managers on their boards of directors. At the same time, since the pursuit of long-term profitability may limit the maximisation of the shareholder value, the corporate strategies generally entail a number of regulations that are designed to prevent mergers and acquisitions, so as to avoid the prospect of hostile takeovers. Long-term development strategies also require the employment of a highly skilled, loyal labour force, that necessitates, on the one hand, setting wages through industry-level bargains and, on the other, the existence of an education system capable of providing high industry-specific skills. As this system also fosters the stability of the firm's personnel, innovation and technology transfers tend to diffuse through dense inter-company networks. Conversely, the USA displays a typical LME, where firms rely more on competitive markets. The organisation of US financial markets induces US firms to pay attention to the current price of their shares on equity markets. Investors' behaviour depends largely on public information on the performance of the firm. The labour market is weakly regulated, and firms can quickly adapt their strategies to macroeconomic conditions, by implementing flexible hiring policies. Consequently, the labour force has incentives to develop general, transferable skills. The constant relocation of professionals also ensures technology transfer from one firm to another. Finally, inter-firm relations are mostly based on market relationships and are mediated through a highly formalised legal system, which should provide certainty and transparency.

The concept of institutional complementarities underlines the fact that institutions must be analysed in a relational manner, and it operationalises a comprehensive view of institutions: Two institutions are complementary if the presence of one increases the 'returns' (i.e. positive outcomes) from the other. Thus, a system deploying a particular type of coordination in one sphere should tend to develop complementary coordination devices in other spheres. As a result, political dynamics and adaptation strategies to global phenomena tend to differ across countries, reflecting the overall influence of the domestic institutional settings. According to a sociological institutionalist interpretation of this approach, these considerations might imply that IRAs created with very similar formal competencies across countries could nevertheless function in different ways, as the role they play depends on the relationships they develop with other domestic organisations and institutions (Deeg and Jackson 2007). For instance, Deeg and Jackson show that the German system of co-determination, while displaying remarkable formal institutional continuity, has experienced in fact numerous substantial transformations that have converted it to different purposes. Here, we can expect that the web of intertwined relationships among the decision makers, the regulators and those being regulated should be denser in CMEs than in LMEs because of the need for extra-market coordination, relying on more informal devices for organising the national political economy. Hence, ceteris paribus, agencies in CMEs might be expected to have less de facto independence from politicians and regulatees than agencies in LMEs.

At the same time, IRAs' functioning could also be shaped by sector-specific regulatory patterns.[5] Indeed, (regulatory) capitalism varies not only across nations but also across sectors, with significant effects on institutional outcomes. Accordingly, the focus on sectoral patterns should provide a great deal of intranational variation, while regulatory policy making in similar sectors is expected to exhibit strong international commonalities (Levi-Faur 2006b, c). In fact, political phenomena and organisational trajectories are frequently described as sectorally path dependent by historical institutionalists (Pierson 2000). The underlying assumption is that the cost of switching from one alternative to another grows over time. In addition, adherents of this approach maintain not only that the probability of further steps along the same path increases with each move down that path, but also that early events are more important than later ones and that the temporal sequence could be causally relevant. The application of this argument to the study of institutions and organisations can, for instance, explain unrelenting divergences of Western market economies (North 1990), while also leading some scholars to affirm that organisations have a strong tendency to persist once institutionalised (Skocpol and Fiorina 1999). This approach is helpful in the context of the examination of the functioning of IRAs, wherein one considers that an earlier sector-specific mode of regulation is likely to continue operating to a certain extent, namely because of the persistence of informal linkages among the relevant actors, constituting a durable policy community. Therefore, we may suppose that when IRAs are created (or reformed), the old regulatory arrangement will still partly determine their functioning. For instance, we can suppose that when IRAs are created in a former public sector, they will be less de facto independent from elected politicians than agencies regulating long-term privatised sectors.

H 1.3   *A highly coordinated economy and sectoral path dependency will be two concomitant conditions for the low de facto independence of agencies from both the politicians and the regulatees.*

The fourth hypothesis pertains to causal paths leading to high de facto independence from regulatees. The incorporation in agencies' networks is the first condition that is expected to explain the outcome of high de facto independence from the regulated industries. Indeed, following a sociological institutionalist line of reasoning, it is plausible that organisations gain autonomy when they are able to legitimise their policies through their ability to locate themselves in multiple networks (Carpenter 2002a). For instance, previous research has shown that agencies' integration in regulatory networks largely explains the decisive institutional changes in the American postal system that occurred between 1890 and World War I (Carpenter 2001a). By taking advantage of their position, network-embedded agencies can enhance their independence by building a supporting coalition for

---

5. It is worth noting that these two conditions correspond also to the pertinent features of the concept of 'bureaucratic culture' that are plausibly expected to influence the de facto independence of regulators.

their policies and programmes, and providing the belief in their superior organisational capacity (Carpenter 2001b). In addition, agencies' networks are said to sustain the technical skills and the effective exercise of delegated competencies, while also allowing wide discretionary power to independent regulatory agencies (Majone 2001b).

For the present study, the pertinent networks are those created following the expansion of EU regulation and governance, after the establishment of the single market in the European Union and the liberalisation of the European financial markets and utilities (Coen and Thatcher 2006). Specifically, the European Commission has set out to coordinate the implementation of regulatory arrangements in member states and to harmonise regulatory governance through agencies' networks, such as the Committee of European Securities Regulators (CESR) (Coen and Thatcher 2008). This strategy was developed as a reaction to member states' unwillingness to dismantle national IRAs in favour of prospected European regulatory bodies, following their strong concerns for sovereignty and control over their political economies (Coen and Thatcher 2007). At the same time, bottom-up networks emerged, such as the Council of European Energy Regulators (CEER) and the Independent Regulators Group (IRG), which are voluntary associations of national regulatory authorities, with the aim of facilitating consultation, coordination, cooperation, information exchange and assistance amongst regulators (Maggetti and Gilardi 2011). As a consequence, a hybrid, multiple and intertwined set of European regulatory networks, federating national independent regulatory agencies, was created and institutionalised, regulating some crucial sectors, such as energy, telecommunications, railways, and financial services (Eberlein 2003; Coen and Héritier 2005). The network of European national competition authorities (ECN) offers a good example of the potential consequences for national regulators. According to some exploratory evidence, it offers greater implementation choices and additional resources to the domestic authorities, and, above all, it provides them with potential allies in front of domestic governments and regulatees (Majone 1996a; Wilks 2005).

Here, we shall expect that networks of regulators reinforce national agencies by providing them with a range of resources in terms of technical expertise, relevant information, and legitimacy, altering thus the balance of power between IRAs, elected politicians, and regulatees. Specifically, weak national agencies should be empowered by a process of diffusion of information, policy learning and coalition building. In this sense, agencies' networks may function as transnational epistemic communities – expertise-based networks – that dispose from considerable power and could promote policy coordination and influence in specific issues (Haas 1992). As a result, the incorporation of agencies into multiple networks is expected to enhance their independence from those they are regulating. It is worth noting that this condition should display a good deal of variation, as the degree of institutionalisation of these networks differs greatly across countries and sectors.

However, the de facto independence of agencies should also depend on the organisational strength of the regulatees. Following the classic argument of the rational choice version of the capture theory, which is incidentally analogous on this point to some neo-Marxist views on firms' strategies (Posner 1974), the regulatees have strong incentives for actively challenging agencies' independence, and vice versa IRAs' staff may anticipate the individual gains of capture (Stigler 1971; Pelzman *et al.* 1989). Accordingly, the regulated industries are expected to lobby policy-makers and agencies for obtaining the most favourable regulation, for instance in order to be able to close their markets to new potential competitors or raise prices artificially; at the same time, regulators who might benefit from the expansion of their activities and are said to employ their regulatory powers to relocate wealth from less organised to more organised groups (James 2000). These privileged groups correspond to business sector interests, at the expense of the more disperse and less organised interests, such as consumers. Conversely, small and cohesive groups, such as coalitions of producers or employers, have greater incentives to form lobbies and influence regulatory policies in their favour, as they will face relatively low costs and anticipate high and concentrated benefits when they attempt to organise for collective action (Olson 1982). Here, a good indicator of the organisational strength of the regulatees is whether the regulatory target of IRAs is sector-specific rather than oriented towards general competition.

The former type of regulation (regulation-for-competition) concerns a narrow set of regulated industries that faces relatively homogenous problems and generally disposes from institutionalised representatives, such as peak organisations, professional associations, lobbyists, think tanks, and other intermediation devices. The latter (regulation-of-competition) relates to a vast and heterogeneous universe of small firms, medium business and large companies, displaying conflicting interests, for instance between export-oriented firms and those oriented toward the internal market, and no unique or coherent voice, favouring free-riding tendencies (Olson 1982). In the first case, highly organised regulatees are expected to be able to make a collective effort to reduce the de facto independence of agencies, unlike the second scenario, where incentives for lobbying are lower and collective action is more difficult.

H 1.4   Intense participation of agencies in European networks and the organisational weakness of those being regulated are expected to lead to high de facto independence from regulatees.

The final hypothesis regards the interplay between independence from political decision makers and from regulatees. When IRAs are conceived as intermediary organisations (Braun 1993), we might suppose that their de facto independence from politicians and their de facto independence from regulatees should be directly related. On the one hand, when an agency is scarcely de facto independent from political decision makers, it is expected to be de facto independent from regulatees: It is indeed implausible that an agency could be the servant of two distinct masters.[6] In theory, agencies cannot be devoted to two principals with

---

6.   'No one can serve two masters. Either he will hate the one and love the other, or he will be

conflicting regulatory aims at the same time: elected politicians look for efficient regulation following their conception of the 'public interest' and/or their prospects for re-election in front of their broader constituency; regulatees seek to obtain the most favourable regulation according to their narrower private interest concerns. Similarly, a high level of de facto independence from political decision makers should imply low de facto independence from regulatees. Moreover, following Bernstein, we might suppose that a lack of political intervention is the reflection of political disinterest in regulation and that, as a result, the agency could not rely upon its political principals for support *vis-à-vis* the regulated industries, thus favouring a capture process (Bernstein 1955). Finally, the existence of regulators that are factually independent both from elected politicians and regulatees is logically possible, and even desirable, as it constitutes the equilibrium that could allow agencies to develop organisational legitimacy at both sides (Braun 1993, Braun 1997).

H 1.5   In cases of high de facto independence from politicians, a 'footloose' agency could become scarcely independent vis-à-vis the regulatees.

Methodology

Case selection

According to the theoretical expectations, two distinct analyses are applied. First, I test explanations about the de facto independence of agencies from political decision makers ('defindpdm'), using the following as explanatory conditions: the formal independence of IRAs, the regulatory life cycle, the presence of veto players in the political system, the type of coordination of the domestic political economy, the path dependence from the prior mode of regulation, and the inclusion in agencies' regulatory networks. Second, I test hypotheses regarding the variation of de facto independence from regulatees ('defindreg'). This time, I use de facto independence from politicians as an additional explanatory condition, whereas I exclude formal independence and veto players, which refer only to the relationship with politicians. I also add another variable, namely, the organisational strength of regulatees.[7] The investigated cases are sixteen IRAs, selected in ten Western European countries and three sectors according to the criteria for case selection outlined below and following the availability of data (see Table 3.1).

The purpose of case selection is to obtain a relatively homogeneous sample with a consistent internal variety concerning the relevant variables. The main

---

devoted to the one and despise the other' (Matthew 6:24).

7.   Please note that this model is slightly different from that used in my previous empirical work on the same topic (Maggetti 2007). Here, I employ the new and more precise algorithm for the fuzzy-set analysis (Ragin 2006a). Data are, therefore, recoded due to small differences in the application of the analytical procedure (namely following the need for minimising the occurrence of the .5 coding in the causal conditions). Results are nonetheless very similar.

Table 3.1: Case selection

Sector	Country	Label	Official names of the investigated IRAs
	Belgium	belbk	*Commission Bancaire, Financière et des Assurances*
	Germany	gerbk	*Bundesanstalt für Finanzdienstleistungaufsicht*
Banking and Financial sector	Finland	finbk	*Rahoitustarkastus*
	Netherlands	netbk	*Autoriteit Financiële Markten*
	Sweden	swebk	*Finansinspektionen*
	Switzerland	swibk	*Eidgenössische Bankenkommission*
	Netherlands	netco	*Nederlandse Mededingingsautoriteit*
	Norway	norco	*Konkurransetilsynet*
Competition	Sweden	sweco	*Konkurrensverhet*
	Switzerland	swico	*Wettbewerbskommission*
	United Kingdom	ukico	*Competition Commission*
	Austria	austc	*Rundfunk und Telekom Regulierungs*
	Italy	itatc	*Autorità per le Garanzie nelle Comunicazioni*
Telecommunications	Netherlands	nettc	*Onafhankelijke Post en Telecommunicatie Autoritei*
	Norway	nortc	*Post- Og Teletilsynet*
	Sweden	swetc	*Sweden Post & Telestyrelsen*

criterion for including a case in the dataset is the comparability within the agencies' organisational models: the presence of a structurally disaggregated formally autonomous public organisation with a chairperson or director, a governing board or similar body and its own secretariat. The other crucial criterion is the focus on the most institutionalised agencies, those that benefit from the greatest powers and the broadest array of regulatory competencies, concerning rule making, decision making, adjudication and sanctioning. Concretely, I started from Gilardi's

(Gilardi 2002b, 2008) dataset on the formal independence of agencies focusing on three sectors: a long-standing privatised sector (banking and finance), a former public sector (telecommunications), and general regulation (competition). I sent a detailed questionnaire to all selected agencies' chairpersons; I refined data with written and electronic documentation and interpreted it with the help of electronic and telephone interviews with the agency personnel.[8]

The operationalisation of the causal conditions

The next step is the operationalisation of explanatory variables, that is, causal conditions using QCA terminology. The formal independence of agencies ('hformalind') is measured with Gilardi's index (Gilardi 2002b, 2005a, c, 2008).[9] In order to keep the richness and significance of this causal condition almost intact, the data were coded on a 6-point ordinal scale with the value '0' for cases scarcely independent and '1' for the highly independent cases.[10] In this regard, a brief digression about the coding procedure is required, as regards 'calibration' and the standard qualitative coding. In fact, the procedure of calibration has been developed for the precise adjustment of interval-scale measures in fuzzy-sets (Ragin 2008a), extending the standard procedure, based on the qualitative appraisal of set membership (Ragin 2000). I applied the new procedure to Gilardi's index of formal independence, using the 'indirect method' described by Ragin, in order to calibrate the interval scales for the fuzzy-set analysis, along a standard 6-point scale. Two possible qualitative 'benchmark codings' are tested: the one being very conservative (i) and the other using more relaxed parameters (ii). Data were coded as presented in Table 3.2. At the end of the day, however, the decision about the definition of the benchmark values as required by the procedure of calibration came out to be difficult. The consequences of this choice are not intuitively straightforward, and they appear quite arbitrary, while at the same time results seem excessively determined by the technical procedure.[11] For instance, according to my substantive knowledge about the cases under investigation, the first coding (i) underestimates the relative independence of some cases, such as the Belgian *Commission Bancaire, Financière et des Assurances*, and the German *Bundesanstalt für Finanzdienstleistungaufsicht*. Conversely, using the second

---

8.   The response rate was very high (80 per cent), with, however, the notable exception of the British Financial Services Authority (for the details, see the appendix).

9.   This index summarises many different statutory features, such as the formal status of the agency head, the formal status of the members of the board, the formal relationship with government and parliament, the statutory financial and organisational autonomy, and the constitutional extent of regulatory competencies (Gilardi 2002b).

10. For information about the construction of a fuzzy set-scale, see Ragin *et al.* (2006).

11. Anyhow, it is worth noting that in the present research study, the results of the fuzzy set QCA change only modestly for de facto independence from political decision makers, no matter what scale is adopted.

coding (ii), the independence of other cases is comparatively overrated, for instance the *Sweden Post & Telestyrelsen*. In conclusion, I decided to continue with the standard qualitative procedure, by defining six clusters of agencies. This procedure is more transparent and it captures better the distinction between relevant and irrelevant variations of formal independence, so as to avoid the degreeism fallacy (Sartori 1991; Radaelli 2000c).[12] Figure 3.2 presents a graphical illustration of the coding procedure. Raw values for continuous variables are ordered with the 'threshold setter' function of the Tosmana package (Cronqvist 2007).

Then, the measurement related to the age of agencies (oldage), with reference to agencies' life cycle, was constructed by simply subtracting the year of the creation of the agency from the year of the data collection (i.e. 2006). Sources are agencies' Web sites and official archive documents. Seven clusters are identified, ranging from recently established regulators (less than 5 years old) to elderly IRAs (more than 50 years). Please note that one category remains empty (0.87), as no agency was created 30-40 years before data collection. The number of veto players (manyveto) was determined by using the Tsebelis dataset on number and distance (Tsebelis 2002), using a 3-point scale: few veto players (less than 2), some veto players (from 2.1 to 3.9), and several veto players (more than 4). Concerning the degree of coordination of the political economy, I adopted the index created by Hall and Gingerich (Hall and Gingerich 2004). This index extends the quite rough distinction between LMEs and CMEs by devising and combining several indicators for the central concepts of the variety of capitalism approach, so as to measure the overall logic of coordination – the crucial dimension – in the key spheres of the political economy: shareholder power, dispersion of corporate governance control, size of stock market, level of wage coordination, labour turnover, and degree of wage coordination. Here, the degree of coordination of the national economies (coordeco) is appreciated on a 6-point scale that also relies upon substantive knowledge of each case (Hall and Soskice 2001; Hall and Gingerich 2004).

The operationalisation of the mode of regulation that was applied before the establishment or reform of the investigated agencies led to a distinction between general regulation, regulators of long-standing privatised sectors, and agencies regulating former public sector monopolies. I used '1' to code prior public ownership of the regulated industries (sectorpubl); otherwise, I used '0' (Conway and Nicoletti 2006). Then, the variable 'network' was coded '0' when the agency did not participate in European networks, '0.4' in the case of partial membership (e.g. as observer), '0.6' in the case of participation with one, and '0.8' in the case of inclusion in two official networks. The organisational strength of those being regulated (orgreg) was roughly approximated by a distinction between sectoral ('1') and general ('0') regulators. Finally, the operationalisation of de facto independence

---

12. According to Sartori, 'degreeism' occurs when, instead of recognising qualitative differences among observations, the researcher insists on differences of degree. This conceptual mistake is nicely illustrated by the famous 'cat-dog' example: if we cannot conceptualise the difference between a cat and a dog, we see various degrees of cat-dogs.

Table 3.2: Calibration versus qualitative coding procedure

Case	Gilardi's index	Qualitative benchmark coding		Predicted coding		Degree of membership		Degree of membership as qualitatively coded
		i)	ii)	i)	ii)	i)	ii)	
belbk	0.47	-0.5	0.5	-0.95214	-0.06049	0.278454654	0.48488109	0.4
gerbk	0.34	-5.0	-2.0	-4.84960	-1.49826	0.007770654	0.18268518	0.0
finbk	0.48	-0.5	0.5	-0.68547	0.07272	0.335041551	0.518171993	0.4
netbk	0.53	0.5	0.5	0.57691	0.79444	0.640356088	0.688783889	0.6
swebk	0.54	0.5	0.5	0.81518	0.95043	0.693212231	0.721201646	0.6
swibk	0.48	-0.5	0.5	-0.68547	0.07272	0.335041551	0.518171993	0.4
netco	0.46	-0.5	0.5	-1.22355	-0.19018	0.227312320	0.452597786	0.4
norco	0.39	-5.0	-2.0	-3.25592	-1.00540	0.037114742	0.267881043	0.0
sweco	0.41	-2.0	-0.5	-2.65158	-0.78826	0.065891694	0.312542403	0.2
swico	0.45	-0.5	0.5	-1.49969	-0.31641	0.182471764	0.421550907	0.4
ukico	0.66	2.0	2.0	3.30532	3.16039	0.964610868	0.959316170	0.8
austc	0.71	5.0	5.0	4.14173	4.28456	0.984353379	0.986407616	1.0
itatc	0.71	5.0	5.0	4.14173	4.28456	0.984353379	0.986407616	1.0
nettc	0.62	2.0	2.0	2.55100	2.35078	0.927640667	0.912996206	0.8
nortc	0.52	0.5	0.5	0.33390	0.64243	0.582708003	0.655302559	0.6
swetc	0.64	2.0	2.0	2.93763	2.74597	0.949675581	0.939685347	0.8

from politicians, which is conceived as a causal condition in the second model, is discussed in the next section (where the outcome conditions are presented). Table 3.3 displays raw data and the coding scale for each causal condition; the characteristics of each case are summarised in Figure 3.1.

Descriptive outlook

A quick outlook to cases and conditions (see Figure 3.1) illustrates a good deal of variation within and across cases. To begin with, the degree of formal independence ranges from 0.34 of the German *Bundesanstalt für Finanzdienstleistungaufsicht* to 0.71 of the Austrian *Rundfunk und Telekom Regulierungs*, while the age of IRAs is situated on an interval between 72 years of the Swiss *Eidgenössische Bankenkommission* and 4 years of the Dutch *Autoriteit Financiële Markten*. It is interesting to observe that there is also considerable intranational variation. When we compare the *Autoriteit Financiële Markten*, the *Mededingingsautoriteit* and the *Onafhankelijke Post en Telecommunicatie Autoritei* in The Netherlands, we can see that the crucial sector-specific conditions, namely, the former public regulation, the organisational force and the regulatees and, above all, the participation in networks, display very dissimilar values. What is more, it seems that IRAs' participation in European networks is more intense as regards competition than in banking and finance in The Netherlands, while the reverse is true in Sweden.

Table 3.3: Causal conditions

Sector	Country	Case acronym	Formal independence data	scale	Old age data	scale	Veto players† data	scale	Coordination of the economy data	scale	Former public sector data	scale	Networks data	scale	Org. force of regulatees data	scale
Banking and Financial sector	Bel	belbk	0.47	0.4	72	1	4.47	1	0.74	0.6	Priv	0	2	0.8	Spec	1
	Ger	gerbk	0.34	0	4	0.17	2.23	0.66	0.95	1	Priv	0	2	0.8	Spec	1
	Fin	finbk	0.48	0.4	13	0.5	4.39	1	0.72	0.6	Priv	0	2	0.8	Spec	1
	Net	netbk	0.53	0.6	4	0.17	2.58	0.66	0.66	0.4	Priv	0	1‡	0.4	Spec	1
	Swe	swebk	0.54	0.6	15	0.5	1.82	0.33	0.69	0.4	Priv	0	2	0.8	Spec	1
	Swi	swibk	0.48	0.4	72	1	4	1	0.51	0.2	Priv	0	0	0	Spec	1
Competition	Net	netco	0.46	0.4	9	0.33	2.58	0.66	0.66	0.4	Gen	0	1	0.6	Gen	0
	Nor	norco	0.39	0	12	0.5	1.28	0.33	0.76	0.6	Gen	0	0	0	Gen	0
	Swe	sweco	0.41	0.2	15	0.5	1.82	0.33	0.69	0.4	Gen	0	1	0.6	Gen	0
	Swi	swico	0.45	0.4	11	0.5	4	1	0.51	0.2	Gen	0	0	0	Gen	0
	Uki	ukico	0.66	0.8	8	0.33	1	0.33	0.07	0	Gen	0	1	0.6	Gen	0
Telecommunications	Aus	austc	0.71	1	9	0.33	2	0.33	1	1	Ex-p	1	2	0.8	Spec	1
	Ita	itatc	0.71	1	9	0.33	4.94	1	0.87	0.8	Ex-p	1	2	0.8	Spec	1
	Net	nettc	0.62	0.8	9	0.33	2.58	0.66	0.66	0.4	Ex-p	1	1§	0.4	Spec	1
	Nor	nortc	0.52	0.6	20	0.67	1.28	0.33	0.76	0.6	Ex-p	1	0	0	Spec	1
	Swe	swetc	0.64	0.8	14	0.5	1.82	0.33	0.69	0.4	Ex-p	1	1§	0.4	Spec	1

† Average years 1990–2000 ‡ Only securities § Only telecommunications

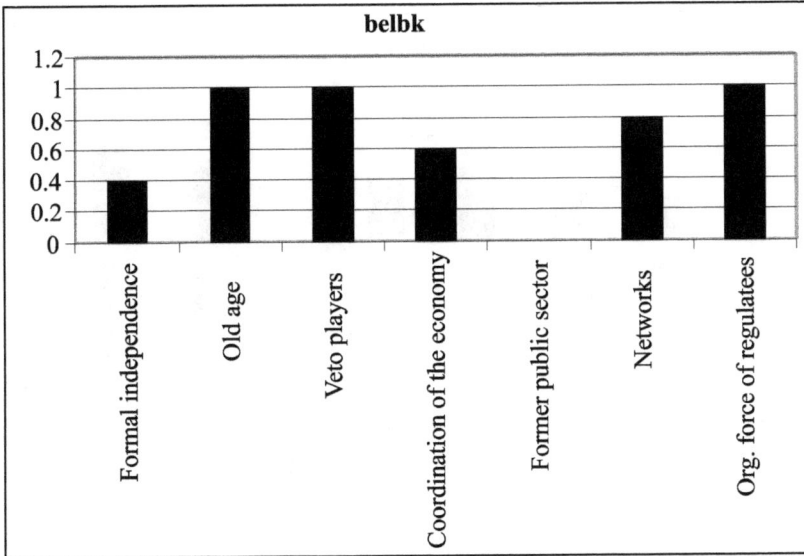

Figure 3.1a

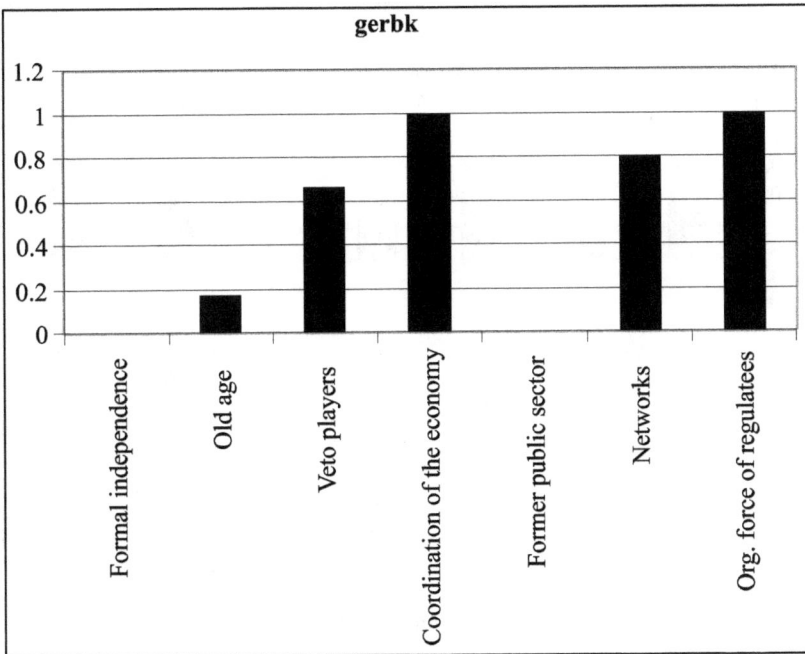

Figure 3.1b

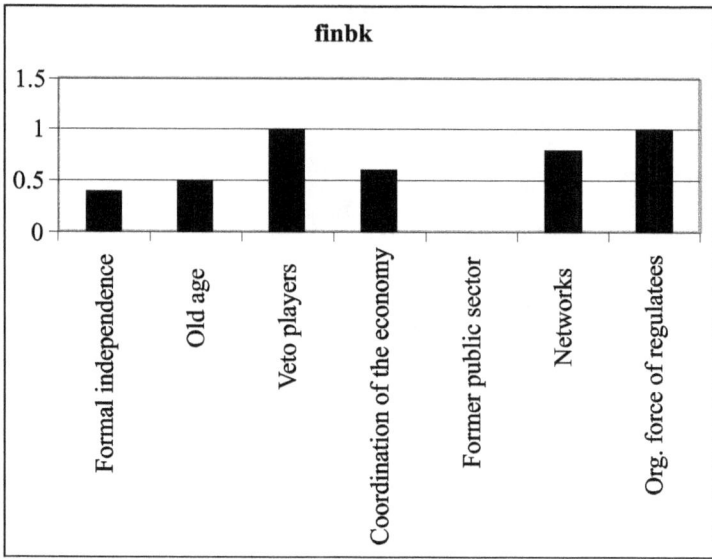

Figure 3.1c

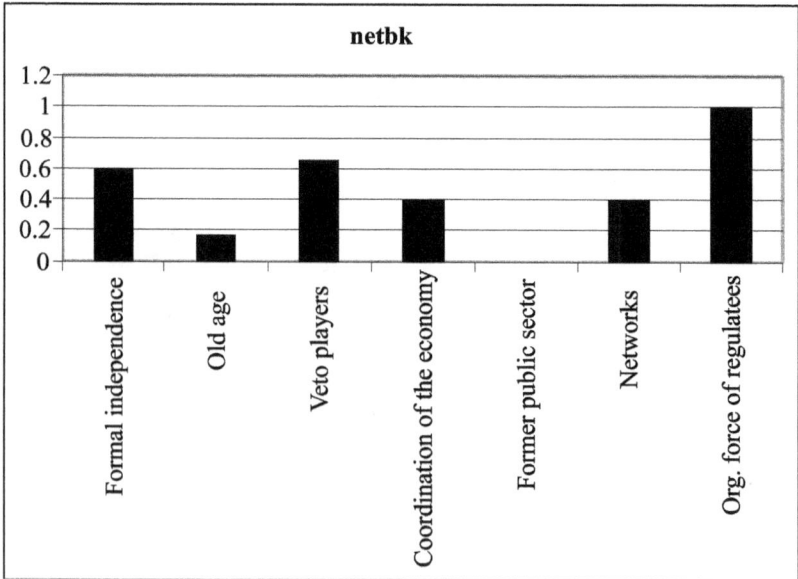

Figure 3.1d

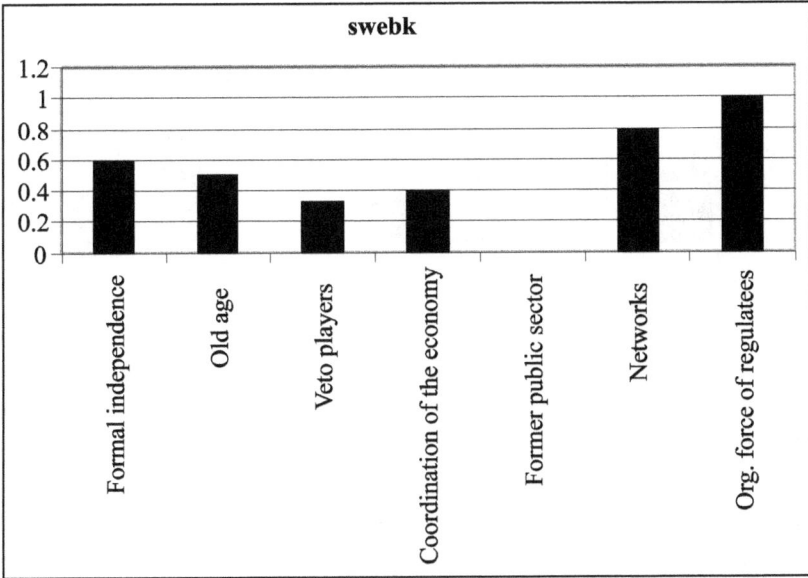

Figure 3.1e

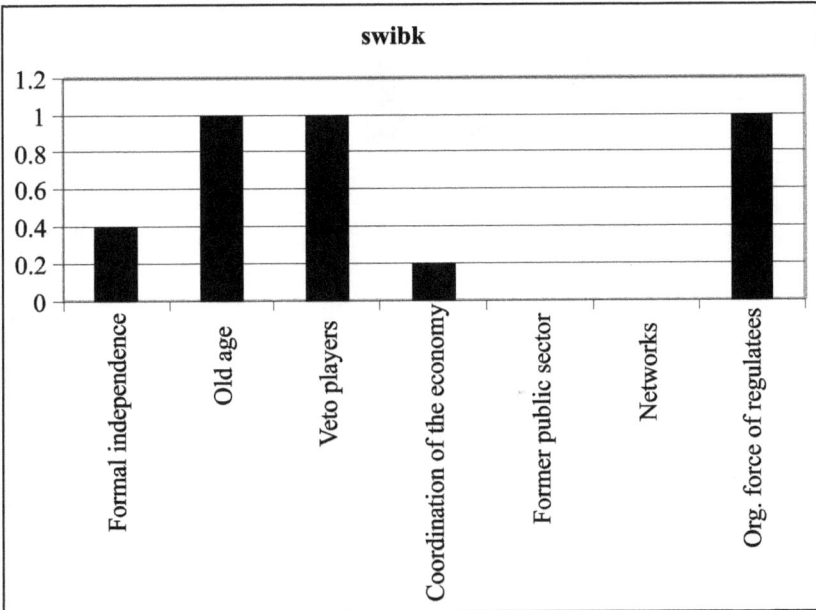

Figure 3.1f

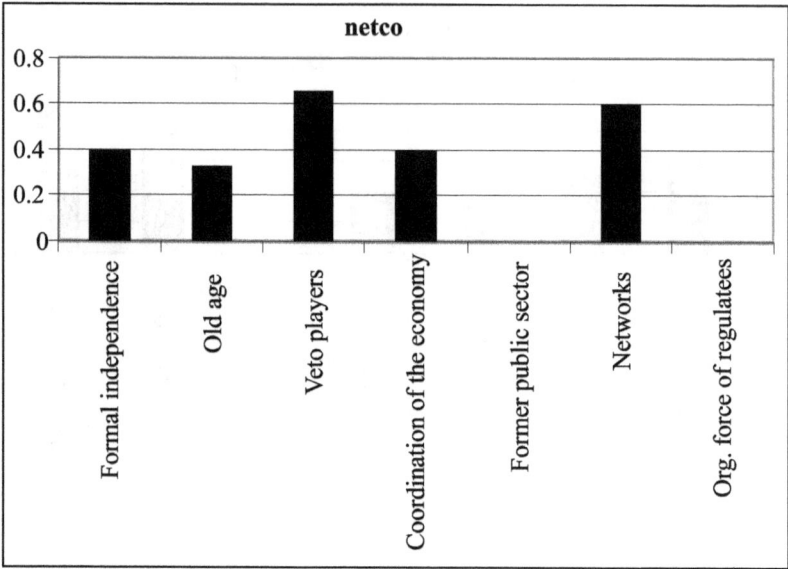

Figure 3.1g

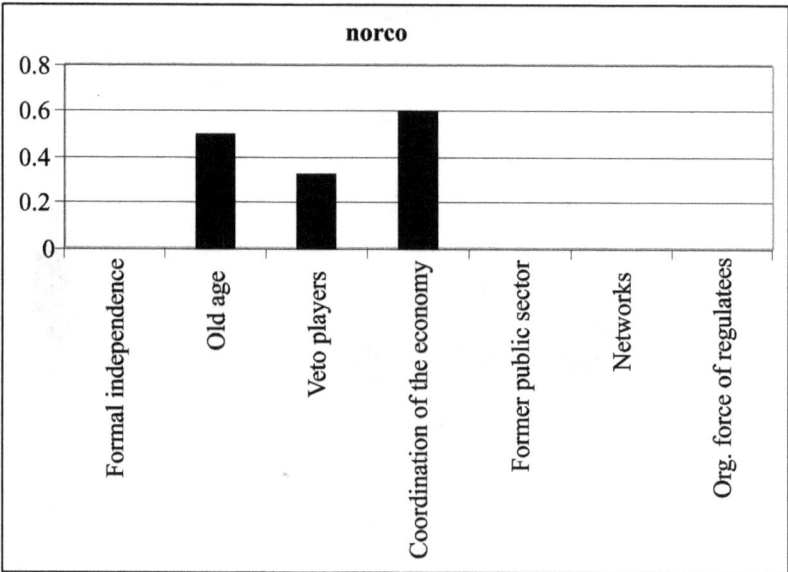

Figure 3.1h

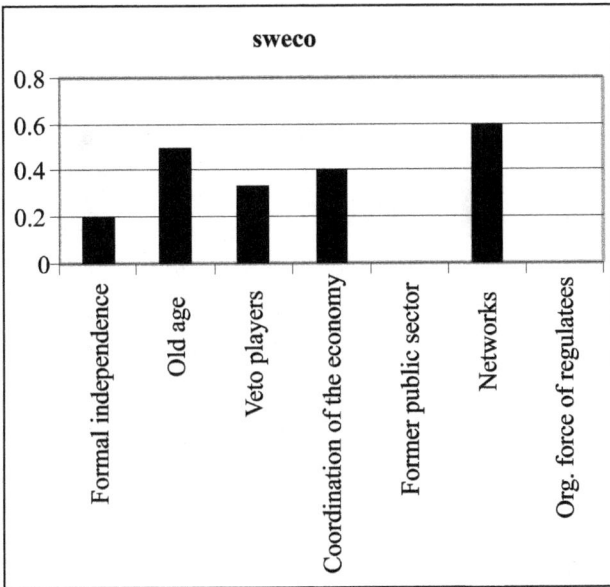

Figure 3.1i

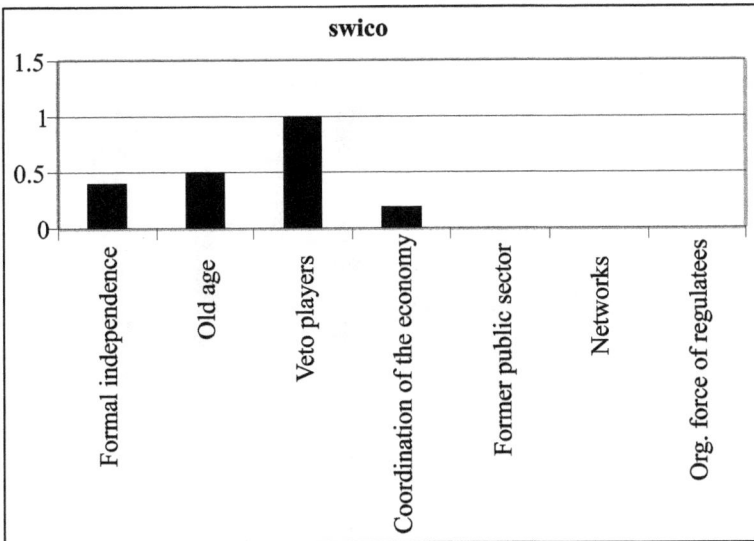

Figure 3.1j

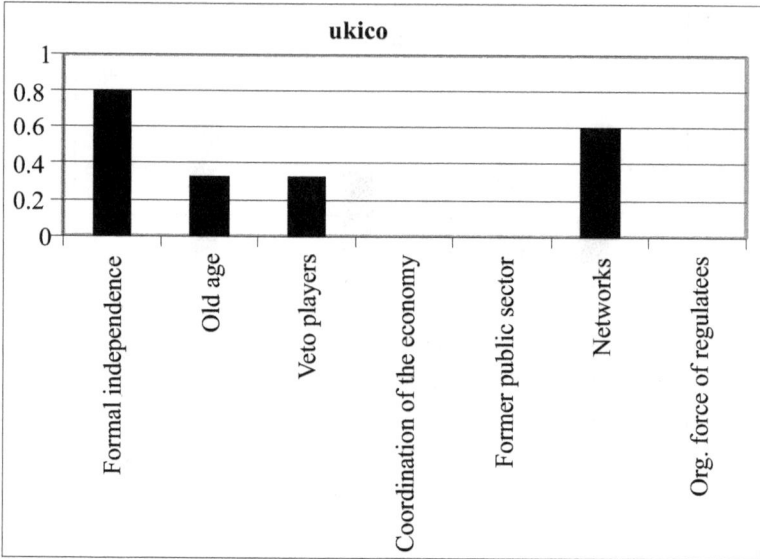

Figure 3.1k

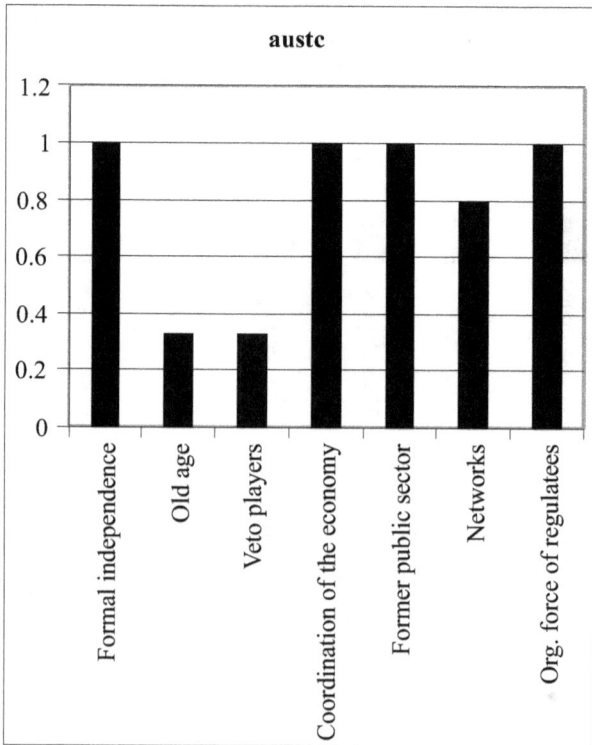

Figure 3.1l

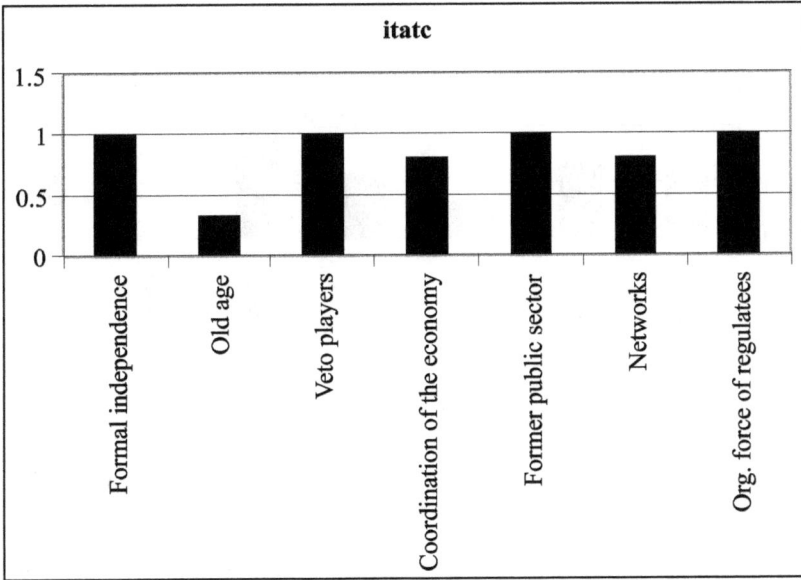

Figure 3.1m

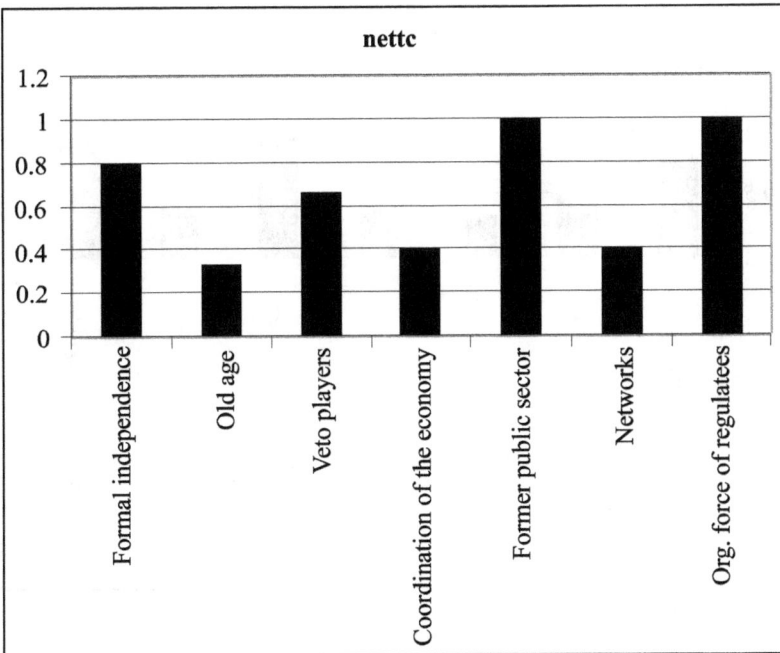

Figure 3.1n

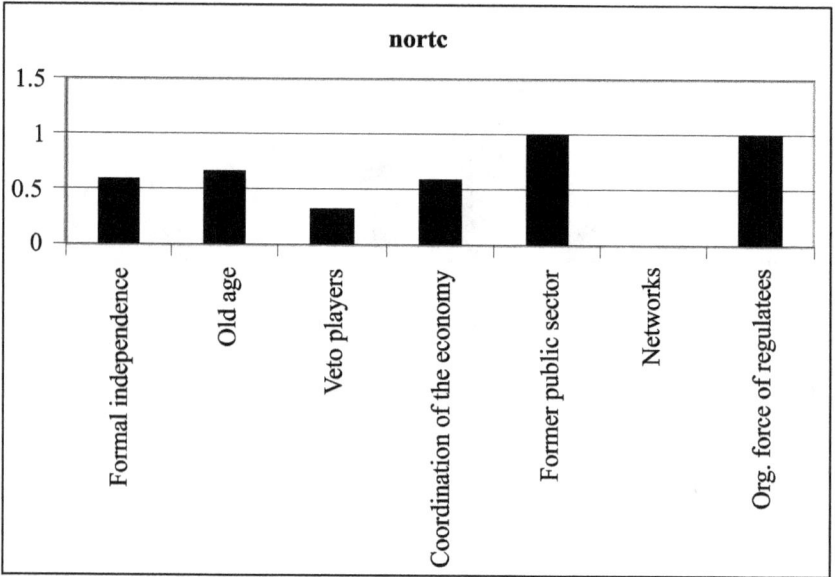

Figure 3.1o

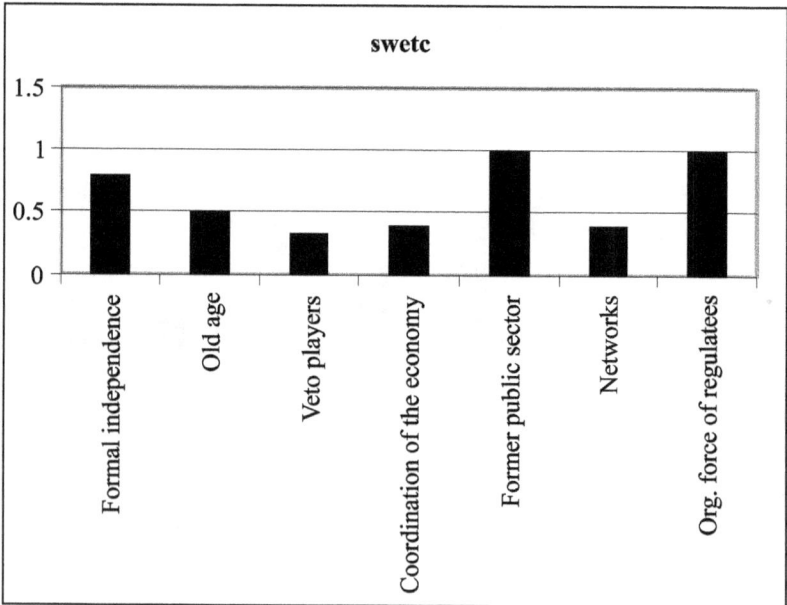

Figure 3.1p

Figure 3.1: Cases and conditions

Formalind

Oldage

Manyveto

Coordeco

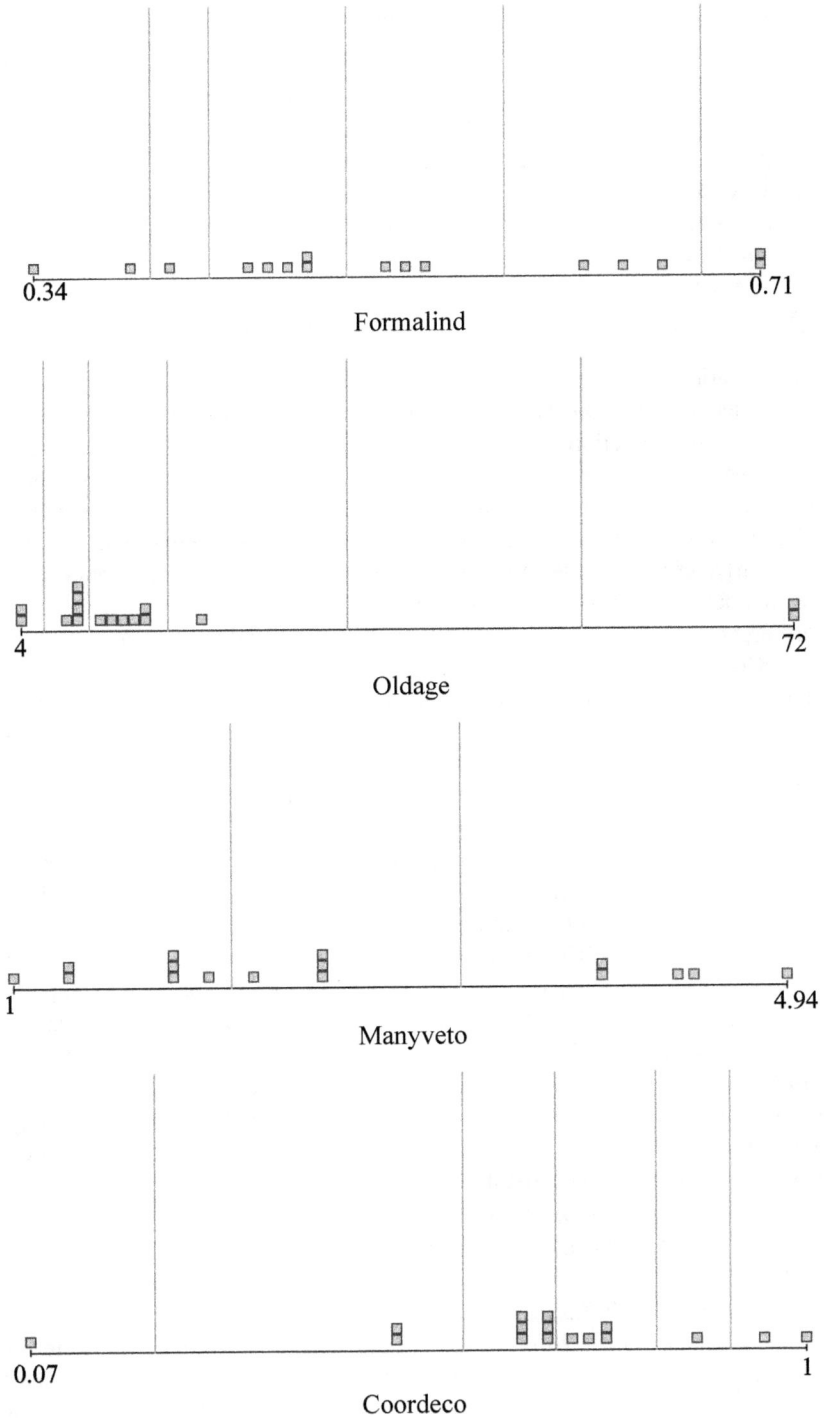

Figure 3.2: Threshold setting

The operationalisation of the outcome conditions

Starting from the prior conceptualisation of IRAs as intermediary agencies, two distinct measurements of the de facto independence of agencies are offered: one concerning the relationship with elected politicians and one concerning the relationship with those being regulated. Within each dimension, as stated above, the level of de facto independence can be assessed through the aggregation of two components: the self-determination of preferences and the autonomy of the activity of regulation.

i) The self-determination of preferences

As organisations are open systems, agencies are neither fully independent from nor fully dependent on their environment, and their preferences are always shaped by their social interaction with other actors. Yet the present conceptualisation of independence points out the extent to which preferences are mostly internally formed or, conversely, externally affected. The underlying assumption is that these – relative – levels, situated on a continuum between the two extremes, may vary significantly across agencies, but are never absolute. Accordingly, agencies are de facto independent if their preferences are endogenous, that is, when the process of preferences formation is mostly determined by the internal organisational dynamic. Conversely, the minimum level of independence occurs when agencies' preferences are predefined by the fundamental interests of external actors, beyond the official goals of delegation. This is the case when the investigated agency is *ex ante* decisively colonised by those external actors, which are able to promote their contingent and particularistic interests, instead of the 'public interest' (Pelzman *et al.* 1989; Buchanan *et al.* 2004). Thus, to ascertain the indicators of IRAs' self-determination of preferences, the organisation's 'black box' must be unpacked. For this purpose, I have drawn inspiration from different research fields, specifically from the literature on the independence of central banks (Barro and Gordon 1983; Grilli *et al.* 1991; Cukierman *et al.* 1992; Alesina and Summers 1993); the regulation after delegation to IRAs (Thatcher 2002c, d); the role of experts in public policy (Peters 2001; Papadopoulos 2003); the independence of courts of justice (Breton and Fraschini 2003); the capture theory (Stigler 1971; Pelzman *et al.* 1989); and the independence requirements in corporate governance (IOSCO 2002; OECD 2004). As a result, the nature of the relationships between IRA and elected politicians can be qualified by six indicators, which will be aggregated at the component level. First, I list indicators of staff independence.

1) *The proportion of revolving door.* This indicator measures the 'relational distance' between IRAs' personnel and the civil service under the direct responsibility of the ministry in charge. A reduced 'relational distance' indicates low independence (Thatcher 2002d; Thatcher and Stone Sweet 2002). Indeed, revolving doors provide agencies with material incentives and, respectively, shared cultural assumptions and mindsets of external actors. On the one hand, IRAs' personnel who anticipate a future career in the ordinary civil service have incentives

to adopt similar regulatory frameworks and follow the directives of ministries and high-level civil officials. On the other hand, IRA's employees who have spent a career in the public administration are likely to continue to some extent to store up administrative routines and the cognitive framework that they constituted in the past. In the case of the lack of any apparent perceived distinction between the day-to-day work of the civil service under ministerial responsibility and the regulatory task of independent regulatory agencies, then the factual independence of the latter has to be considered to be the lowest according to that aspect.

2) *The frequency of contacts*. This indicator refers to the occurrence of ad hoc interactions, information exchanges, regular meetings, internships, and stable collaborations between the agency and the ordinary civil service. Close, durable and regular contacts of agencies' staff and board members with elected politicians and the ordinary civil service can be considered functional equivalents of revolving doors. In fact, constant proximity and exchange favour the development of 'epistemic' communities of experts exchanging information, ideas, solutions and arguments, eventually sharing similar regulatory goals and co-producing regulatory arrangements (Haas 1992; van Waarden and Drahos 2002). Below, I list indicators about resources' independence.

3) *Influence over IRAs' budget*. Elected politicians that can directly control agencies' budget are crucially able to reduce the manoeuvring room of regulators (Carpenter 1996). Not only the effective manipulation but also the threat of budgetary cuts or shifts gives powerful signals to the agency and is likely to influence IRAs' preferences and behaviour, constituting an important form of latent power (Bachrach and Baratz 1962). Conversely, when the agency budget is fixed, neither subjected to the approval of elected politicians through governmental or parliamentary decisions, nor dependent from other unsecured sources, then the potential discretional power of agencies *vis-à-vis* elected politicians increases.

4) *Influence over internal organisation*. The leeway for elected politicians to determine the organisational structure of regulatory bodies can have crucial effects on agencies' preferences and behaviour (Wilson 1989; Egeberg 1999). In fact, politicians can influence agencies' autonomous workflow by manipulating their internal organisation and bureaucratic hierarchy, namely their inter- and intra-organisational division of labour, the career plans of agencies' personnel and board members, and the balance of power between the chairperson, the board and the secretariat. Then, the third category involves the individual and collective independence of the board members, and specifically, their political exposure.

5) The weight of partisan membership in nominations. The possibil-

ity of political appointments by the government and parliament is an important instrument of political control over the bureaucracy; this point is consistent both with a perspective that focuses on the struggle for political power, and with the managerial conception of policy monitoring (Wood and Waterman 1991). Two elements should be considered. First, if board members are nominated according to a partisan logic, they are expected to be more inclined to follow the instructions of (some) elected politicians. Second, the existence of a balance of power between board members may mitigate the weight of partisan membership (Breton and Fraschini 2003). Finally, the last indicator concerns:

6) *The political vulnerability of IRAs* as it is related to early departures of board members. The prospect of forcing early departures of IRA members constitutes another important means of political control (Goodsell and Gayo 1970; Thatcher 2005a). Therefore, the frequency of the replacement of board members due to a decision by elected politicians in ministries and/or parliaments before the ordinary end of their statutory mandate is a good, although quite indirect, indicator of their material capacity of influencing agencies' behaviour and preferences (obviously, when excluding any contingent or personal reason for departures).

For the relationship between the IRA and the regulatees, I identify another six indicators of de facto independence. The indicators used for studying the first relation are, after some simple adjustments, once again useful in regard to the first category.

1) *The proportion of revolving door.* As mentioned above, this indicator refers to the phenomenon of agencies' staff moving to the regulated industries and back, offering an indication of the 'relational distance' between IRAs and regulatees (Thatcher 2002d; Thatcher and Stone Sweet 2002). On the one hand, IRAs' employees who anticipate the possibility of being hired in the regulated industries have incentives to favour regulatees, by anticipating enhanced prospects for employment, or higher salary benefits. On the other hand, staff members who are enrolled in agencies after a career in the regulated industries are expected to bring in not only their technical competencies but also their social ties, shared cultural assumptions, and set of mindsets (at least partially) in line with those of the regulatees.

2) *The frequency of contacts*, such as ad hoc interactions, information exchanges, regular meetings, internships, and ongoing collaborations between the agency and the regulatees. The close proximity between regulators and those being regulated do not only favour a process of rational learning to improve regulatory quality through the exchange of essential pieces of information and the improvement of technical skills. Plausibly, it also induces a socialisation process and the cre-

ation of powerful coalitions of interests, which may try to reorient the official regulatory policies, in line with their own goals (Haas 1992; van Waarden and Drahos 2002). Then I consider:

3) *The adequacy of agency's budget* with respect to their regulatory tasks. Agencies' decision-making effectiveness depends largely on financial resources (Spiller 1990; Olson 1995). An inadequate budget invariably involves a reduced manoeuvring room when preparing and executing the required regulatory tasks. In the case of scarce resources, agencies are, for instance, obliged to rely on information and technical expertise directly provided by the regulated industries, producing a situation that can critically influence agencies' preferences and behaviour and reduce their autonomous decision-making capacity.

4) *The adequacy of the organisational resources* in relation to those of the regulated industries must also be discussed. Human resources are crucial to sustain organisational performance and agency independence (Brudney and Hebert 1987; Perry 1993). The management of human resources is indeed a decisive element, not only in quantitative terms but also as regards employees' education and technical skills and with reference to agencies' ability to apply their competencies of supervision and sanctioning. After that, the third category relates to the autonomy of the agency's board, taking into consideration, first,

5) *The closeness of the professional activity of board members* as regards the regulatees. To begin with, one should determine if board members are full-time or part-time hired, considering that full-time professionals are usually more trained and skilled with respect to the execution of their day-to-day regulatory tasks, and less dependent on the potential influence of external actors through the prospect of additional remuneration. On the other hand, the occurrence of possible conflicts of interests between the professional activity of board members and their regulatory duties should be considered (IOSCO 2002). The second element refers to:

6) *Personal affairs and relationships.* The so-called OECD principles of 'good governance' mention the existence of personal affairs or personal relations between regulators and regulatees as a factor reducing the independence of the former (OECD 2004). Specifically, this indicator concerns the existence of informal ties between board members and the regulated industries. However, given the practical difficulties of assessing this kind of relationship, only the noticeable, public, freely available information over these linkages can be taken into account, probably leading to an underestimation of the impact of these linkages.

All indicators of this first component are summarised in Tables 3.4–3.5, while the related survey questions are presented in the appendix of this chapter. Each indicator is appreciated on a 7-point ordinal scale from 0 (lowest level of de facto independence) to 1 (highest level). Next, the second component of agencies' de facto independence corresponds to their independence when executing their activity of regulation, namely concerning their autonomous capacity to produce regulations (ordinances, directives, resolutions, recommendations, and so on) and make individual decisions (pieces of advice, authorisations, sanctions, etc.) (see again Tables 3.4-3.5 and the appendix).

ii) The autonomy of the activity of regulation

The second component of agencies' de facto independence is the autonomous conduct of their activity of regulation. In this view, we have a reduction of de facto independence of IRAs when external actors – the political decision makers and, respectively, the regulatees – whose preferences diverge from agencies', can ex-post crucially manipulate their activity of regulation in order to override the will of the relatable IRA. From this point of view, the agency has to be considered a black box, and then one shall try to determine whether these external actors can exogenously sway the regulatory process. Unfortunately, there is neither empirical feasibility nor any theoretical basis for measuring the agency's independence directly during the process of supervising and possibly sanctioning the target sector.

Indeed, it is impracticable to highlight the informal pressures potentially exerted by the elected politicians, or by those being regulated, with reference to any particular decision, as no suitable trace of such pressures exist. Unlike a full judiciary inquiry, a scientific research study cannot rely upon authoritative means or pervasive instruments to collect supplementary evidence, and does not allow the researcher to gain access to undisclosed documentation. These differences stem from not only obvious practical limitations or from ethical and deontological concerns but also the need for guaranteeing, as far as possible, the replication of the empirical tests and the falsifiability of the argument (Popper 2002). Given these limitations, it is very difficult to establish the influence of external actors on specific decisions, following the inherent contingency of singular political phenomena, while, at the same time, the significance of a specific decision or non-decision cannot be easily deductively appreciated, as it entails serious difficulties of interpretation. In fact, the boundaries between 'nonpositive' negative cases and 'nonpositive' irrelevant cases are extremely difficult to distinguish when examining non-decisions (Mahoney and Goertz 2004). A case of non-decision could suggest the non-occurrence of the investigated phenomenon, or it may constitute a deliberate decision not to act, such as decisions of non-sanctioning certain infractions. In this sense, a non-decision can favour some regulated industries or produce nuisances to other stakeholders, representing a form of latent power, while the rationale for non-deciding is necessarily undetermined (Lukes 1974; Bachrach and Baratz 1994).

However, the burden of proof still lies with the researcher who is formulating new hypotheses. Therefore, I decided to assess the independence of regulators during their activity of regulation in a slightly more indirect manner, namely, through the study of independent regulatory agencies' inner policy cycle (Howlett and Ramesh 2003). Specifically, I propose to examine the active participation of external actors in the IRAs' rule-making process in order to assess the extent to which these external actors affect the regulatory outputs, such as agencies' ordinances, directives, pieces of advice and recommendations. The basic idea is that the most prominent external actors in the inner rule-making process are then able, by this means, to crucially influence the activity of the IRAs in charge, at least during the investigated period. Conversely, the more exclusive the process is, the more factually independent the agency. Concretely, I divide the inner policy cycle of independent regulatory agencies into six events, which are not necessarily sequential, by adopting a quite inductive reasoning, based on my exploratory face-to-face and electronic interviews and preliminary investigation of the written documentation:

(1)   Impulsion

(2)   Preparation of the draft of the regulation

(3)   Consultation

(4)   Final decision and adoption

(5)   Monitoring

(6)   Sanctioning of infringements

Then, I assess the de facto independence of IRAs from elected politicians during the activity of regulation through the examination of their active participation in these six events, which are regarded as analytically distinct, considering involvement in no event as a proxy of very high independence ('7' on a 7-point scale) and active participation in all events as a proxy of very low independence ('1'). Respectively, I examine the active participation of those being regulated in the agencies' rule-making process in a similar manner. If the regulatees participate actively in several events of the inner policy cycle, the relevant agency is then considered scarcely independent from them, and vice versa; if they participate hardly at all, the agency is considered highly independent.

Finally, results concerning (i) the self-determination of preferences and (ii) the autonomy of the activity of regulation, which, as illustrated above, are derived from the aggregation of the indicators measured and adjusted on the 7-point scale adopted in the questionnaire, can be once more aggregated by simply calculating the mean value of the two components to obtain one single measurement of agencies' de facto independence from elected politicians ('defindpdm') and one single measurement of agencies' de facto independence from regulatees ('defindreg') on another 7-point ordinal scale.[13] So I obtain two 'dependent' variables that will be tested separately with the comparative design.

---

13. From this scale, a simpler dichotomous coding can be derived to be used for the standard QCA crisp-set analysis, by considering that the presence of the condition of 'high de facto independence', that is, the dichotomous code 1 corresponds to a value of ^{3} 0.5 on the 7-point ordinal scale, ranging from 0 to 1.

Table 3.4: Operationalising the de facto independence of IRAs from the political decision makers

(1) Relationship IRA – Political decision-makers		
Indicators of self-determination of IRA preferences	• Frequency of revolving door	– Proportion of the current employees of the agency's secretariat that have previously worked in the public administration – Proportion of the former employees of the agency's secretariat that will work in the public administration
	• Frequency of ad hoc contacts	– Participation of the employees of the agency's secretariat in internships related to the public administration – Frequency of the requests for support of agencies' expertise to the public administration – Frequency of meetings between the agency and the public administration
	• Influence on budget	– Influence of the government on the budget of the agency – Influence of the parliament on the budget of the agency – Influence of the public administration on the budget of the agency
	• Influence on organisational setting	– Influence of the government on the internal organisation of the agency – Influence of the parliament on the internal organisation of the agency – Influence of the public administration on the internal organisation of the agency
	• Weight of partisan membership on board members' nominations	– Role of political parties when deciding who should become a member of the agency's management board – Homogeneity of the representatives of the political parties in the board – Distribution of powers among board members
	• Political vulnerability	– Earlier departures of members of the management board before the end of its mandate – Replacements of the management board's director (or chair of the agency)
Autonomy of the activity of reg.	• Active participation in the IRA's rule-making process	– External influence on the main regulations issued by the agency to which the supervised institutions should conform 1) Inspiration of the basic principles of the main regulations that the supervised institutions should satisfy 2) Working out the draft of the regulations 3) Consultations during the draft preparation of the regulations 4) Decision and adoption of the regulations 5) Monitoring the respect of the regulations by the supervised institutions 6) Sanctions in case of non-respect of regulations by the supervised institutions

Table 3.5: Operationalising the de facto independence of IRAs from the regulatees

(2) Relationship IRA – Regulatees		
Indicators of self-determination of IRA preferences	• Frequency of revolving door	– Proportion of the current employees of the agency's secretariat that have previously worked in the private sector – Proportion of the former employees of the agency's secretariat that will work in the private sector
	• Frequency of ad hoc contacts	– Participation of the employees of the agency's secretariat in internships related to the private sector – Frequency of the requests for support of agencies' expertise to the private sector – Frequency of meetings between the agency and the private sector
	• Budget dimension	– Influence of the private sector on the budget of the agency – Adequacy of the budgetary resources of the agency in relation with the private sector
	• Organisational dimension	– Influence of the private sector on the organisation of the agency – Adequacy of the human resources of the agency in relation with the private sector

	• Proximity of the former or current professional activity of board members	– Full-time or part-time position of the agency's board director/chairperson
		  – Current occupation of the director
		  – Former occupation of the director
		– Full-time or part-time position of the agency's board members
		  – Current occupations of the board members
		  – Former occupations of the board members
		  – Conflicts of interest

	• Personal relations	– Informal ties
Autonomy of the activity of the reg	• Active participation in the IRA's rule-making process	– External influence on the main regulations issued by the agency to which the supervised institutions should conform 1) Inspiration of the basic principles of the main regulations that the supervised institutions should satisfy 2) Working out the draft of the regulations 3) Consultations during the draft preparation of the regulations 4) Decision and adoption of the regulations 5) Monitoring the respect of the regulations by the supervised institutions 6) Sanctions in case of non-respect of regulations by the supervised institutions

The empirical analysis

The assessment of the de facto independence of IRAs

The results of the survey inquiry concerning the outcome conditions (i.e. the 'dependent variables') are presented below, with the corresponding degree of de facto independence: Table 3.6, concerning the relationship with the elected politicians, and Table 3.7, concerning the relationship with the regulatees (see the appendix of the chapter for the details of the questionnaire). After case names and data labels, the third column of the tables presents the aggregated results concerning the indicators of the self-determination of preferences, and, respectively, the autonomy of the activity of regulation (on 7-point scales); the fourth column specifies the level of de facto independence derived from these measures; and the fifth column displays the corresponding coding for the fuzzy-set analysis. Figure 3.3 offers a synthetic view of agencies' de facto independence from the politicians and from the regulatees. This information, which is used for the fuzzy set analysis, has been collected with detailed questionnaires sent to the chairpersons of the investigated agencies, received between June 2006 and March 2007. It has been completed and refined with other data: semi-directive interviews with agencies' board members between August 2005 and June 2006; and written and electronic documentation, namely annual agency reports and agencies' Web sites, as briefly summarised in the following mini-case studies (sections 3.6.1.1 and 3.6.1.2), so as to produce a 'thicker' description of each case, to verify the validity of previous information and improve the interpretation of results.[14]

Figure 3.3 presents the description of the two outcomes. It is apparent that factual independence varies greatly across agencies, especially when considered in front of elected politicians. Furthermore, the relation between factual independence from politicians and from regulatees seems quite intricate: the two outcomes do not co-vary in any visible manner nor do they configure any straightforward trade-off. Therefore, one can plausibly assume that they are determined by different sets of explanatory conditions. Before the analysis, the following mini-case studies summarise the empirical assessment of the de facto independence of IRAs from politicians, and, subsequently, their de facto independence from the regulated industries, as reported in Tables 3.6 and 3.7, according to the two dimensions

---

14. This procedure guarantees higher robustness. For instance, in the case of the swico, the information about the proportion of the 'revolving door' has been checked and confirmed with interviews and written documentation. As an illustration, I quote three excerpts: 'Le secrétariat de la Comco aura perdu (…) 25 per cent de son personnel scientifique par rapport à fin 2004' (Rapport annuel Comco 2005); 'Es kamen laufend frische Kräfte, direkt von der Uni, mit viel Dynamik. Die blieben zwei bis drei Jahre' (Tages Anzeiger, 3 January 2007); 'C'est difficile de retenir de personnes qui se voient offrir une situation plus intéressante dans le privé (…)' (Interview) (this item generated an indicator that varies from '2' in the case of the belbk to '6' in the case of the netbk).

outlined above, (i) the self-determination of preferences and (ii) the autonomy of the activity of regulation.

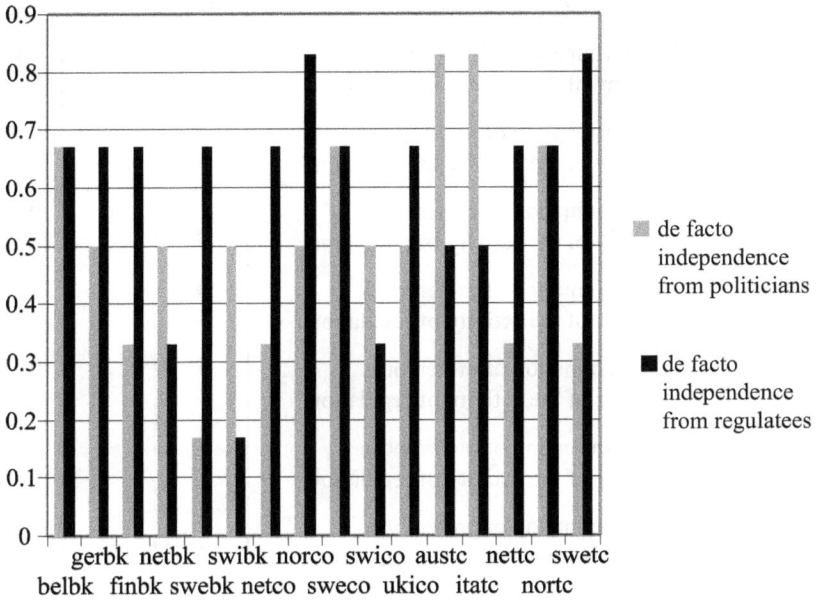

Figure 3.3: Synthetic view of agencies' de facto independence

Table 3.6: Coding the de facto independence of IRAs from the politicians

Case	Data (1): defindpdm	Scale:	Total:	Coded as:
belbk	(i) Self-determination of preferences (ii) Autonomy of the activity of regulation	4 6	5	0.67
gerbk	(i) Self-determination of preferences (ii) Autonomy of the activity of regulation	5 4	4	0.5
finbk	(i) Self-determination of preferences (ii) Autonomy of the activity of regulation	4 3	3	0.33
netbk	(i) Self-determination of preferences (ii) Autonomy of the activity of regulation	4 4	4	0.5
swebk	(i) Self-determination of preferences (ii) Autonomy of the activity of regulation	1 4	2	0.17
swibk	(i) Self-determination of preferences (ii) Autonomy of the activity of regulation	4 4	4	0.5
netco	(i) Self-determination of preferences (ii) Autonomy of the activity of regulation	1 6	3	0.33
norco	(i) Self-determination of preferences (ii) Autonomy of the activity of regulation	5 3	4	0.5
sweco	(i) Self-determination of preferences (ii) Autonomy of the activity of regulation	4 7	5	0.67
swico	(i) Self-determination of preferences (ii) Autonomy of the activity of regulation	3 6	4	0.5
ukico	(i) Self-determination of preferences (ii) Autonomy of the activity of regulation	4 5	4	0.5
austc	(i) Self-determination of preferences (ii) Autonomy of the activity of regulation	7 5	6	0.83
itatc	(i) Self-determination of preferences (ii) Autonomy of the activity of regulation	6 6	6	0.83
nettc	(i) Self-determination of preferences (ii) Autonomy of the activity of regulation	4 3	3	0.33
nortc	(i) Self-determination of preferences (ii) Autonomy of the activity of regulation	5 5	5	0.67
swetc	(i) Self-determination of preferences (ii) Autonomy of the activity of regulation	1 6	3	0.33

Table 3.7: Coding the de facto independence of IRAs from the regulatees

Case	Data (2): defindreg	Scale:	Total:	Coded as:
belbk	(i) Self-determination of preferences (ii) Autonomy of the activity of regulation	5 6	5	0.67
gerbk	(i) Self-determination of preferences (ii) Autonomy of the activity of regulation	5 6	5	0.67
finbk	(i) Self-determination of preferences (ii) Autonomy of the activity of regulation	5 6	5	0.67
netbk	(i) Self-determination of preferences (ii) Autonomy of the activity of regulation	3 4	3	0.33
swebk	(i) Self-determination of preferences (ii) Autonomy of the activity of regulation	5 6	5	0.67
swibk	(i) Self-determination of preferences (ii) Autonomy of the activity of regulation	2 3	2	0.17
netco	(i) Self-determination of preferences (ii) Autonomy of the activity of regulation	5 6	5	0.67
norco	(i) Self-determination of preferences (ii) Autonomy of the activity of regulation	5 7	6	0.83
sweco	(i) Self-determination of preferences (ii) Autonomy of the activity of regulation	5 6	5	0.67
swico	(i) Self-determination of preferences (ii) Autonomy of the activity of regulation	2 5	3	0.33
ukico	(i) Self-determination of preferences (ii) Autonomy of the activity of regulation	5 5	5	0.67
austc	(i) Self-determination of preferences (ii) Autonomy of the activity of regulation	2 7	4	0.5
itatc	(i) Self-determination of preferences (ii) Autonomy of the activity of regulation	3 6	4	0.5
nettc	(i) Self-determination of preferences (ii) Autonomy of the activity of regulation	4 7	5	0.67
nortc	(i) Self-determination of preferences (ii) Autonomy of the activity of regulation	5 6	5	0.67
swetc	(i) Self-determination of preferences (ii) Autonomy of the activity of regulation	6 6	6	0.83

De facto independence of IRAs from politicians

Commission Bancaire, Financière et des Assurances (Belgium)

(i) The revolving door phenomenon is less frequent than on average. In particular, former employees of the secretariat of this agency will rarely work in the ordinary services of the public administration in the future. Contacts and meetings between the agency and the public administration are also infrequent, except for reciprocal exchanges of expertise. The influence of government, parliament and ordinary public administration on agency's budget is very low, while the government can determine the internal organisation of the agency to some extent. The overall weight of partisan membership on board members' nominations is considered to be fairly high. However, political parties are homogenously represented in the board, and members enjoy equal powers. In addition, forced early departures of board members, before the end of their mandates, are rare. Lastly, the board functions according to a quite consensual mode, and decisions are made by deliberation, with some votes.

(ii) The agency's rule-making activity regards above all the implementing provisions for the minimal standards to which the supervised institutions must conform, and the promulgation of detailed technical circulars. Most regulation is initiated by the agency secretariat and the agency board itself. The drafts of the regulations are then prepared by the secretariat, and, after consultation, submitted to the government, who yields to parliament if applicable. The interventions of politicians during the rule-making activity are very infrequent and they are related only to the final step of the process when adopting them as pieces of legislation. Then, the secretariat is in charge of monitoring and supervising the regulated industries, while the board decides upon the individual actions to be taken where necessary. Namely, the board can adjudicate administrative sanctions in the applicable fields.

Bundesanstalt für Finanzdienstleistungaufsicht (Germany)

(i) The employees of the secretariat of this agency will frequently work in the public administration in the future, but the reverse is not true. Informal contacts and meetings between the agency's staff and the public administration are rare. The government can partly influence the budget of the agency and it usually decides upon the structure of its internal organisation. Political parties, though, do not play an important role when deciding who should become a member of the agency board. The powers of board members are not homogenously distributed, as this agency is headed by a president, who holds the ultimate responsibility for the execution of the regulatory process, despite the fact that she/he actually often delegates some tasks to her/his deputy or to other members of the management. Early departures of members and chair replacements are very rare.

(ii) During the activity of regulation, the *Bundesanstalt für Finanzdienstle-istungaufsicht* ensures the application and supplies the implementation provisions for the legislation on banking, insurance and securities supervision, the secondary legislation and the supervisory minimum requirements. Government and parliament generally inspire the basic principles of the requirements that the regulated industries must satisfy. The agency, in collaboration with the ministry of finance, normally works out the draft of the regulations, making use of its specialised knowledge. The interventions of elected politicians are rather important for the approval of regulations. Then, however, monitoring, supervision, and sanctioning competencies are mostly delegated to the agency.

Rahoitustarkastu (Finland)

(i) The revolving door phenomenon is very common for the employees of this agency's secretariat, especially in the direction of the ordinary public administration. Ad hoc contacts, regular meetings, and exchanges of expertise between the agency and the public administration are also very frequent and are considered very important for the agency. However, the government, the parliament and the public administration cannot control the agency's budget, and their influence on its internal organisation is low. The weight of partisan membership is also low. Departures of members of the management board before the end of the mandate are rare, but the chairperson was quite often replaced during the investigated period. Finally, it is worth noting that decisions of the board are made by a majority vote.

(ii) The crucial regulations issued by *Rahoitustarkastus* concern the prudential standards to which supervised institutions must conform, according to the capital requirements, risk management and internal control systems. The agency has the responsibility of the initiation of new regulations and it is in charge of the subsequent procedure of draft preparation, in addition to its common attributions concerning monitoring and sanctioning. The elected politicians participate actively in several phases of the inner rule-making process: impulsion, draft preparation, consultations, and final decision making about the adoption of the new regulations.

Autoriteit Financiële Markten (Netherlands)

(i) The occurrence of the revolving door phenomenon for the personnel between the agency and the ordinary public administration is not very common. However, contacts with the public administration, and regular meetings, especially for expertise exchanges are quite frequent. Then, the ministry of finance must approve the final sum of the agency's budget, and the parliament can also have an indirect influence, through questions and pressures to the ministry of finance. The public administration has a certain influence on the budget of the agency, too. Conversely, neither the government nor the parliament can determine its internal organisation. The weight of political parties when deciding who should become a member of the board of the agency is considered to be low. Decisions of the board are usually made by consensus. Early departures of members are rare, but the chairperson was replaced quite frequently during the investigated time-period.

(ii)   Concerning the activity of regulation, this agency is in charge of the business conduct of the supervised institutions, whereas the responsibility for prudential supervision is with the central bank. The elected politicians participate in some phases of the inner rule-making process, especially in the initiation phase and when deciding the adoption of regulations as pieces of legislation.

Finansinspektionen (Sweden)

(i)   Employees of the secretariat of this agency have frequently worked in the ordinary public administration under ministerial responsibility, and they will often work there again in the future. Very frequently, different services of the public administration ask for the support of the agency for expertise purposes. Regular meetings between the agency and the public administration are constant. It is worth noting that, despite the formal prescriptions of structural disaggregation, the *Finansinspectionen* is considered to be actually incorporated into the structure of the ordinary public administration, as with other public sector agencies. In addition, the influence of government and parliament on the agency's budget and on its internal organisation is very high. Similarly, political parties are very influential on board member nominations. Normally, one half of the representatives are directly appointed by the government, and the other half by the opposition. The board is homogeneous in composition and in power. Early departures of the members of the board are rare, and decisions are made by consensus.

(ii)   The main regulations concern the prudential specifications of minimum capital requirements, internal controls, risk management systems, and compliance issues. These regulations are often prepared by specific commissions and then submitted to consultations. The agency is the crucial actor for monitoring and sanctioning, while the inner rule-making processes are to a certain extent influenced by the elected politicians, for example with reference to their initiation, in the course of draft preparation, and when finally deciding to adopt them.

Eidgenössische Bankenkommission (Switzerland)

(i) The revolving door phenomenon between this agency and the ordinary public administration is rare, while ad hoc contacts and regular meetings are quite common. Specifically, the public administration frequently asks for the support of the agency for expertise purposes. The government, the parliament and the public administration can partly influence the agency's budget, and they can also determine the agency's internal organisation to some extent. Political parties have a moderate impact when deciding who should become a member of the board. Political parties are not homogenously represented, while board members enjoy equal powers, except from the president, which can be considered a *primus inter pares*. Decisions are generally made by a majority vote. The frequency of early departures of board members is average, and the chairperson's position is stable over time.

(ii) Rule-making processes include the provisions for the application of the legislation, regulatory circulars and ordinances. The *Eidgenössische Bankenkommission* usually provides inputs for new regulations and works out the drafts and propositions. In collaboration with other bodies, it also ensures the supervision and sanctioning of the regulated industries. The elected politicians participate in some phases of the inner rule-making process, such as the initiation, the draft preparation, and the adoption of new regulations.

Nederlandse Mededingingsautoriteit (Netherlands)

(i) The occurrence of the revolving door phenomenon between the agency's personnel and the public administration is common. Ad hoc contacts and meetings are also very frequent, especially for expertise purposes. Moreover, the influence of the government and the parliament over the size of agency's budget and its internal organisation is very high. Partisan membership is considered crucial for board member nominations. In addition, the representatives of political parties are not homogenously represented in the board, while they enjoy equal powers. The deliberations and the related decisions of the board are generally quite consensual.

(ii) The regulations issued by the agency consist of administrative law guidelines, recommendations and advice, and opinions on request of the regulated companies. The *Nederlandse Mededingingsautoriteit* initiates the development of regulations, works out the draft and then also detains the competencies of monitoring and sanctioning. The elected politicians participate sporadically, specifically in consultations for the preparation and adoption of new regulations.

Konkurransetilsynet (Norway)

(i)   The frequency of the revolving door phenomenon for employees between the agency's secretariat and the public administration is moderate. Ad hoc contacts are not very frequent. The government can to some extent influence the budget of the agency, but it has almost no chance of determining its internal organisation. Parliamentary influence on budget and organisation is, overall, modest. Political parties do not play any important role when deciding who should be nominated as a member of the agency board. The director general was replaced only once during the investigated time period, and early departures of members are also rare.

(ii)   Regulations comprise circulars, recommendations, and regulatory guidelines. The agency is in charge of the preparation of the drafts, monitoring respect for the regulations, and sanctioning, in the case of non-compliance. Elected politicians affect quite intensively the regulatory activity: they participate actively in the initiation, the draft preparation, the consultation, and the adoption of new regulations.

Konkurrensverhet (Sweden)

(i)   The occurrence of the revolving door phenomenon for the agency's staff in the direction of the public administration is on average. The public administration asks quite frequently for the support of this agency for expertise purposes. Regular meetings between the agency and the public administration are also quite frequent. The influence of government and parliament on the budget of the agency is fairly high, but their influence on its internal organisation is very low. Political parties do not play an important role in the procedure of nomination of the board. Early departures of members are rare, and the director general also enjoys a stable position.

(ii)   The activity of regulation, namely, the inner rule-making process, specifically concerns directives and guidelines for the interpretation of the competition rules. It appears to be autonomously executed by the *Konkurrensverhet*. Elected politicians intervene rarely, above all during the initial consultation phase.

Wettbewerbskommission (Switzerland)

(i)   The phenomenon of the revolving door between the agency's secretariat and the ordinary public administration is moderate. Conversely, ad hoc contacts and regular meetings are rather frequent. The public administration quite often asks the support of the agency for expertise purposes. The government can determine the budget of the agency, but its actual influence on the internal organisation is considered quite low. The parliament has almost no weight concerning budget and organisation. However, partisan membership is fairly important for board members nominations. The representatives of political parties are not homogeneously represented in the board, while members possess equal powers. Board discussions are quite consensual, but most decisions are made by a majority vote. Early departures of board members are moderately common, and the chairperson was replaced quite frequently.

(ii) The main regulations issued by the *Wettbewerbskommission* comprise circulars, directives and communications. The agency normally initiates, prepares and ensures the implementation of regulations. The elected politicians do not significantly affect the regulatory activity, except during the phase of consultations.

Competition Commission (United Kingdom)

(i) The occurrence of the revolving door phenomenon for the personnel between the agency and the public administration is rather frequent. Regular meetings and ad hoc contacts are also quite common. The budget of the agency is entirely determined by the government, while governmental influence on its internal organisation is low. The parliament has almost no importance as regards budget and organisation. Partisan membership is also irrelevant for nominations. Powers are equally distributed, but the chairperson has the final decision. Decisions are, however, generally made by consensus. Early departures of deputies and directors are very rare, but the replacement of the chairperson is rather frequent in the investigated period.

(ii) Regulations principally include rules of procedures, guidelines, advice, reports and documents on individual inquiries. These texts are normally drafted internally and circulated to third parties for consultation before being finalised. The agency has the competence of inquiry in the case of non-compliance and can impose sanctions. The political decision makers are able to participate in the initiation and the adoption of regulations.

Rundfunk und Telekom Regulierungs (Austria)

(i) The occurrence of the revolving door phenomenon between the agency and the public administration is rare in both directions. Ad hoc contacts and regular meetings are moderate, whereas the public administration occasionally asks the agency's support for expertise purposes. The influence of government and parliament on budget is low and, similarly, their influence on the internal organisation is very small. Political parties do not play any role when deciding who should become a member of the board of the agency. Powers are equally distributed among board members, and their discussions and decisions are generally consensual. Early departures of board members and the replacement of the chairperson are both very infrequent.

(ii)   The *Rundfunk und Telekom Regulierungs* issues a number of regulations and communications for the regulated industries. The board inspires the basic principles of the regulations, together with other independent agencies, and the involved actors. The agency also works out the drafts and makes decisions about the adoption of regulations. The relevant services of the public administration participate in some later phases of the activity of regulation, that is, in monitoring and sanctioning.

Autorità per le Garanzie nelle Comunicazioni (Italy)

(i)   Employees of the secretariat of this agency have not frequently worked in the public sector beforehand, nor they will work for the public administration in the future. Ad hoc contacts for expertise purposes between the agency and the public administration are moderate, and so are regular meetings. The influence of government and parliament on the budget of the agency is considered quite low at this time, and it is very low concerning its internal organisation. The influence of political parties when deciding who should become a member of the board is also considered quite low. Powers are equally distributed, and decisions are made by consensus after deliberation. Early departures of members or departures of the chairperson are very rare, and the latter's position is rather stable.

(ii)   The activity of regulation usually unfolds as follows. The secretariat of the agency is in charge for drafting regulation, doing preliminary inquiries and adopting regulations. Operational services supervise and refer to the board, which is in charge of final decisions. The elected politicians do not significantly affect the regulatory activity, apart from participating in the initiation of the inner rule-making process.

Onafhankelijke Post en Telecommunicatie Autoritei (Netherlands)

(i)   Employees of the secretariat of this agency have quite frequently worked in the ordinary public administration beforehand, and they will often return there in the future. Regular meetings between the agency and the public administration are common, and the latter frequently asks for the support of the agency for expertise purposes. The influence of the government on the agency's budget is quite high, while it is quite low concerning the structure of its internal organisation. However, the parliament has no prerogatives on the *Onafhankelijke Post en Telecommunicatie Autoritei*. Political parties have a certain influence on nominations of the members of the board, while their representatives are not homogeneously represented in the board and powers are unequally distributed. Decisions are, however, generally consensual. Early departures of board members are very rare, whilst the chairperson was occasionally replaced during the investigated period.

(ii)   The most important regulations issued by the agency consist of guidelines, circulars and communications about decisions and sanctions. The agency works out the draft and adjudicates sanctions in the case of non-respect to the supervised institutions. The elected politicians significantly affect the activity of regulation: they participate actively in the initiation, draft preparation, consultation, and adoption of regulations.

Post- Og Teletilsynet (Norway)

(i)   The occurrence of the revolving door phenomenon between the agency and the public administration is quite frequent in both directions. Ad hoc contacts and regular meetings are rather rare, even if the public administration relies frequently on this agency for expertise purposes. Governments and parliaments have a certain influence on the budget of the agency, but they cannot determine its internal organisation. The weight of partisan membership on nominations is very low. The director enjoyed a stable position during the investigated time period.

(ii)   The regulations developed by the *Post- Og Teletilsynet* concern, in essence, the implementing provisions for national legislation and secondary law. This agency prepares drafts and organises consultations, makes decisions, also ensuring supervision and adjudication. The elected politicians participate in some phases of the rule-making process, namely initiation and monitoring.

Sweden Post & Telestyrelsen (Sweden)

(i)   Agency's staff frequently worked in the public administration in the past, and will return there in the future. Ad hoc contacts, regular meetings and exchanges of expertise are continuous. The government and the parliament can entirely determine the budget of the agency. Concerning the internal organisation, this agency is perceived as a branch of the ordinary public administration. Political parties play a quite important role when deciding who should become a member of the board of the agency. They are homogeneously represented, and members possess the same competencies. Discussions in the board are generally consensual. Early departures are quite rare.

(ii)   Regulations issued by this agency concern specific regulations, guidelines, and communications about decisions. The agency initiates the procedure, works out the drafts, adopts the regulations, and ensures supervision and sanctioning. The intervention of elected politicians during the activity of regulation is moderate and focused on the initiation of the rule-making process.

De facto independence of IRAs from regulatees

Commission Bancaire, Financière et des Assurances (Belgium)

(i)   The revolving door phenomenon between this agency and the regulated industries is moderate in both directions. In particular, former employees of the secretariat of the agency will rarely work for the regulated industries in the future. Ad hoc contacts and expertise exchanges with the regulatees are not very frequent, and the frequency of regular meetings is on average. The regulated industries cannot influence the budget of the agency. Budgetary and human resources are regarded as satisfactory. The chairperson, a former professor, was hired full-time. Four members of the board out of seven were hired full-time (two former employees of the secretariat of the agency and two former professors) and three are not full-time, as they work as directors of the central bank.

(ii)   Those being regulated do not intervene significantly during the rule-making process, apart from consultations before adopting the new regulations.

Bundesanstalt für Finanzdienstleistungaufsicht (Germany)

(i)   The employees of the secretariat of this agency occasionally worked in the private sector beforehand, while the agency's staff will rarely work in the regulated industries in the future. The exchanges of expertise and ad hoc contacts are moderate, but informal meetings are regular and frequent. The private sector can partly determine the budget of the agency. Budgetary resources are, however, satisfactory, and human resources are regarded as largely sufficient. The president was hired as the head of the former federal banking supervisory authority, which was merged with the insurance and securities supervisor in 2002. He is now full-time. The board members were also hired full-time, and they held former positions as public officials of the ministry of finance (50 per cent), employees of the secretariat of the agency (25 per cent), and employees of foreign supervisory authorities (25 per cent).

(ii)   The regulatees usually take part in a single phase of the activity of regulation: namely, the peak association representing the supervised institutions is consulted during the draft preparation of the new regulations.

Rahoitustarkastus (Finland)

(i)   The employees of the secretariat of this agency occasionally worked in the private sector beforehand. They will rarely work in the regulated industries in the future. The number of ad hoc contacts is average, while regular meetings are frequent. The private sector sometimes asks for the support of the

Rahoitustarkastus for expertise purposes. It has no influence on the budget of the agency, and financial and human resources are considered abundant. The chairperson and the members of the board were not hired full-time, as they are simultaneously enrolled in the ordinary civil service.

(ii)   Those being regulated do not intervene significantly during the activity of regulation, apart from consultations when preparing the draft of the regulations on minimal prudential standards.

Autoriteit Financiële Markten (Netherlands)

(i)   The revolving door phenomenon between the agency's secretariat and the private sector is frequent in both directions. Ad hoc contacts are recurrent and regular meetings with the representatives of the private sector are rather frequent. The budget is always discussed with the representatives of the banking and financial sector. The quantity of financial and human resources appears satisfactory. The chairperson, a former public official, was hired full-time. Board members are also hired full-time, and they consist of 50 per cent of former civil servants and 50 per cent of former managers in the private sector.

(ii)   Those being regulated intervene moderately in the activity of regulation of the *Autoriteit Financiële Markten*. Specifically, they participate actively in the preliminary discussions for the new regulations, and they are consulted for the preparation of all the secondary legislation drafted by the agency.

Finansinspektionen (Sweden)

(i)   The occurrence of the revolving door phenomenon between this agency and the regulated industries is moderate. The number of regular meetings, expertise exchanges, and ad hoc contacts is average. The private sector can hardly influence the budget of the agency. Budgetary resources are considered to be largely sufficient, and human resources are adequate. The chairperson, a former civil servant, was hired full-time. Board members are not hired full-time; the majority of them have positions as public officials (55 per cent), while 11 per cent are employees, executives, and managers in the private sector, 11 per cent are liberal professionals (namely lawyers) and 22 per cent are members of the parliament.

(ii)   The regulatees do not have significant influence over the inner rule-making process of *Finansinspektionen*. They intervene only in consultations during the draft preparation of the new regulations.

Eidgenössische Bankenkommission (Switzerland)

(i)   The employees of the secretariat of this agency have quite frequently worked in the private sector in the past, and they will work for the regulated industries in the future remarkably often. The agency regularly asks for the support of the regulated industries and their representatives for expertise purposes, and regular meetings are common. The private sector has a limited influence of the budget, but the financial and human resources are regarded as barely sufficient. The chairperson, a former executive in the private sector, was hired full-time. Members are not full-time, and the board composition is as follows: 50 per cent of employees, executives and managers from the banking and financial sector, 17 per cent of liberal professionals, 33 per cent of professors.

(ii)   The regulatees intervene intensively during several phases of the activity of regulation, namely through their peak association. They inspire the basic principles of the regulations, and participate in the consultation process concerning the draft preparation of regulations. They are also very active in monitoring and sanctioning.

Nederlandse Mededingingsautoriteit (Netherlands)

(i)   The occurrence of the revolving door phenomenon between the secretariat of this agency and the regulated industries is on average. Regular meetings and ad hoc contacts involving personnel of the *Nederlandse Mededingingsautoriteit* are fairly frequent. Those being regulated can hardly influence the budget of the agency. Financial and human resources are considered to be barely sufficient. The chairperson, a former judge, was hired full-time. Members of the board are full-time, and they are all former public officials.

(ii)   The regulatees do not influence significantly the activity of regulation. Producers' peak associations intervene only during the phase of open consultation and during the draft preparation of the regulations issued by the agency.

Konkurransetilsynet (Norway)

(i)   The revolving door phenomenon between the agency and the regulatees is not very common. Ad hoc contacts, regular meetings and exchanges of expertise between this agency and the regulated industries are moderately frequent. The private sector cannot influence the budget of the agency. Financial and human resources are considered abundant. The director general, a former public official, was hired full-time and so were the deputies.

(ii)   The activity of regulation of the *Konkurransetilsynet* is autonomous from those being regulated. They do not participate in the development of regulations issued by the agency.

Konkurrensverhet (Sweden)

(i)   The occurrence of the revolving door phenomenon between the agency and the regulated industries is on average. Expertise exchanges and ad hoc contacts with the private sector are rare, except for some customary meetings between the agency and the representatives of the private sector. The regulated industries have almost no influence on the budget of the agency, and financial and human resources are regarded as abundant. The director general, a former public official and director of another agency, was hired full-time.

(ii)   The regulatees do not intervene significantly during the activity of regulation. They only participate in the consultations for the draft preparation of the regulations issued by the agency.

Wettbewerbskommission (Switzerland)

(i)   The occurrence of the revolving door phenomenon between the agency and the regulated industries is high in both directions. Contacts and exchanges of expertise are also frequent, and so are regular meetings with the representatives of the private sector. Even though the private sector has a limited influence on the budget of the agency, financial resources are considered to be insufficient, and human resources are considered to be barely sufficient. The chairperson, a professor and former liberal professional, was not hired full-time. Board members are not full-time, either: 6 per cent are public officials, 22 per cent are representatives of producer associations, 6 per cent are representatives of consumers associations, and 66 per cent are professors.

(ii)   The regulatees intervene in some stages of the activity of regulation of the *Wettbewerbskommission*. They are especially influential as regards the initiation of rule-making processes and during the procedure of consultation about the draft of the new regulations issued by the agency.

Competition Commission (United Kingdom)

(i)   A number of this agency's staff members have previously worked in the private sector and may work in the regulated industries in the future. The number of ad hoc contacts and regular meetings is average. Financial resources are considered to be abundant and are not influenced by those being regulated. Human resources are also adequate. The chairperson, a former member of the board and liberal professional, was hired full-time. The deputy chairs work four days per week, so are considered part-time. They are public officials, employees of the secretariat, employees in the private sector, liberal professionals, and professors. The non-executive directors sit on the council for one day every two months, but the chief executive is a full-time employee.

(ii) Concerning the activity of regulation of the *Competition Commission*, the regulatees participate in the preparation of the draft of new regulations issued by the agency and are involved in public consultations.

Rundfunk und Telekom Regulierungs (Austria)

(i) The occurrence of the revolving door phenomenon is common, especially in the direction of the private sector. Ad hoc contacts for expertise purposes and regular meetings between the agency and the representatives of the regulated industries are very frequent. The regulatees have a limited influence on the budget of the agency. Financial and human resources are considered adequate. The chairperson and the members of the board are all former employees, executives, and managers in the private sector, and they are now full-time.

(ii) The regulatees are not involved in the development of regulations issued by the *Rundfunk und Telekom Regulierungs*; therefore, the activity of regulation is essentially autonomous.

Autorità per le Garanzie nelle Comunicazioni (Italy)

(i) Former employees of the secretariat of this agency will quite frequently work in the private sector in the future. The exchanges of expertise are modest, but informal meetings are very frequent. The budget of the agency is strongly determined by those being regulated and it is considered to be barely adequate. Human resources are regarded as insufficient. The chairperson, a former administrative judge, was hired full-time. Members are also full-time. The 80 per cent comes from the public sector, 10 per cent are former employees, executives and managers in the private sector, and 10 per cent are professors.

(ii) The regulatees do not significantly influence the regulatory activity of the Autorità per le Garanzie nelle Comunicazioni, apart from their active participation in consultations concerning the regulations issued by the agency.

Onafhankelijke Post en Telecommunicatie Autoritei (Netherlands)

(i) The occurrence of the revolving door phenomenon between the agency and the private sector is proportionally medium. Ad hoc contacts, expertise exchanges and regular meetings are moderately frequent. The regulated industries can influence the budget of the agency to a good extent, while financial resources and human resources are considered to be sufficient. The chairperson, a former liberal professional, was hired full-time. Members of the board are not full-time: 50 per cent of them come from the private sector, 25 per cent from a liberal profession, and 25 per cent are professors.

(ii)   The activity of regulation of this agency is autonomous as regards the influence of those being regulated. They do not intervene in the inner rule-making process.

Post- Og Teletilsynet (Norway)

(i)   The occurrence of the revolving door phenomenon between the agency and the public administration is on average. Ad hoc contacts, expertise exchanges and regular meeting are quite frequent. The private sector has a limited influence on the budget of the agency. Financial and human resources are regarded as largely sufficient. The director, a former employee of the secretariat of the agency, was hired full-time.

(ii)   The regulatees do not have a significant influence on the regulations issued by the *Post- Og Teletilsynet*. They are integrated in the process only during consultations concerning the preparation of the drafts.

Sweden Post & Telestyrelsen (Sweden)

(i)   The occurrence of the revolving door phenomenon between the agency and the private sector is moderate. Ad hoc contacts and expertise exchange are modest, but regular meetings are fairly common. The regulated industries have hardly any influence on the budget of the agency. Financial and human resources are adequate. The chairperson, a public official and former professor, was not hired full-time. Board members are not full-time, either, and the board is composed as follows: 60 per cent consists of public officials, 10 per cent of employees of the secretariat of the agency, and 30 per cent of professors.

(ii)   The intervention of the regulatees during the activity of regulation is moderate, basically limited to the participation in consultations for the development of the draft of the new regulations issued by the *Sweden Post & Telestyrelsen*.

Fuzzy-set analysis and discussion

(i)   The fuzzy-set analysis is used to assess the necessity and sufficiency of each combination of causal conditions for the two distinct outcomes: agencies' de facto independence from the political decision-makers, and agencies' de facto independence from the regulatees.[15] I am especially interested in the analysis of sufficiency (that is, the identification of the combinations of causal conditions that constitute a subset of the outcome),

---

15. The second version of the 'Quine - McCluskey' algorithm included in the fs/QCA software is applied (Ragin *et al.* 2006).

while I will employ very restrictive criteria for the test of necessity (that is, the examination of whether instances of the outcome represent a subset of a specific cause) (Ragin and Giesel 2006).[16] According to Ragin, a fuzzy set can be considered a variable that has been 'purposefully calibrated' to indicate the degree of membership in a specified set.[17] Researchers can adjust partial membership in sets using interval scales between 0 (non-membership) and 1 (full membership) (Braumoeller and Goertz 2000; Ragin 2008b). Then, the fuzzy subset relation is assessed using the fuzzy set algebra implemented in software packages such as the above mentioned fs/QCA, as follows. After coding raw data, the first analytical step is to discover all causal conditions (i.e. 'independent variables') with membership scores that are consistently greater than or equal to outcome ('dependent variable') membership scores, in order to determine the possible necessary conditions (Jackson 2005). The second step is to examine the sufficient conditions by means of the comparison of membership scores in the outcome with the scores of all possible combinations of conditions.[18] Then, I use the procedure described by Ragin for the assessment of consistency and coverage, respectively indicating reliability, that is, how closely the subset relation is approximated (i.e. the degree to which the cases sharing a given combination of conditions agree in displaying the outcome), and validity, that is, the empirical relevance of a consistent subset (i.e. the proportion of cases following a specific path) (Ragin 2006a).[19]

---

16. In set-theoretic terms, the examination of causes shared by cases with the same outcome is appropriate for the examination of necessary conditions, while a condition (or combination of conditions) is considered sufficient for the outcome if the former is a subset of the latter, i.e. the membership score in the cause is less than or equal to the membership score in the outcome (Ragin 2008b). The study of set relations, which are asymmetrical by nature, permits to decompose the information that is normally pooled and conflated in symmetrical correlations, in order to fill the gap between theory and empirical testing of real-world phenomena that are potentially set theoretic (Braumoeller and Goertz 2000; Ragin 2008b).

17. A fuzzy set is a 'class of objects with a continuum of grades of memberships', characterised by 'a membership function that assigns to each objects a grade of membership between zero and one', which extends and generalises the Boolean logic grounded in the examination of the presence/absence of a given condition (Zadeh 1965). In dichotomic Boolean algebra a case is either in or out of a set, with 1 indicating the presence and 0 the absence of the condition, while when using fuzzy-set theory the membership in sets can be partial, with membership ranging from 1 indicating full membership and 0 indicating non-membership (Ragin 2000). Using Ragin's example, an Eastern European country might have a membership score of .68 in the fuzzy set of "rich countries", whereas this attribute (richness) can be less easily translated in mere dichotomous terms.

18. Sufficient combinations of causal conditions are substantially relevant both for case-oriented and population-oriented research, because independent variables that exert partial mean effects in well-specified statistical models are in fact INUS causes (Mahoney 2008).

19. Consistency and coverage are 'descriptive measures for evaluating the strength of the empirical support for arguments specifying set-theoretic connections' (Ragin 2008b). The procedure for

Results: Agencies' de facto independence from elected politicians

Results of the fuzzy set analysis of necessary conditions are reported in Table 3.8 and presented below.[20] The most consistent condition is the 'high coordination of the economy' (0.87). This is a quite important score, but it almost certainly does not fulfil the very stringent conditions for the assessment of necessity (i.e. an absolute value that is strictly major than 0.95) (Ragin 2006a). Moreover, it makes little theoretical sense. No necessary causes are then retained for high de facto independence from the elected politicians.

Table 3.8: Necessary conditions for de facto independence from politicians

Outcome: high de facto independence from the politicians	
Condition	*Consistency*
manyveto	0.74
oldage	0.75
hformalind	0.86
coordeco	0.88
networks	0.65
sectorpubl	0.36

Afterwards, the fuzzy-set/QCA analysis generates two combinations of conditions, which jointly possess an adequate score of consistency (i.e. an absolute value that is strictly major than 0.8) and significant coverage for the test of suffi-

---

calculating consistency, implemented in the fuzzy-truth table algorithm of fs/QCA (Ragin *et al.* 2006), is the following: first, the consistent cases are differentiated from the inconsistent ones when their membership score in the causal condition is less or equal to membership in the outcome; then, the sum of the consistent membership scores in a (combination of) causal condition(s) divided by the sum of all membership scores of the (combination of) causal condition(s) produces the final measure of set-theoretic consistency (that can be refined further with credit for near misses and penalties for scores that largely exceed their mark) (Ragin 2006a). The set-theoretic measurement of coverage corresponds to the number of cases that display the outcome following a specific path divided by the total number of instances of the outcome in crisp-set analysis ; and, similarly, to the proportion of the sum of the membership scores in the outcome in the case of fuzzy-set analysis (Ragin 2008b).

20. The standard terminology of the Boolean algebra and fuzzy set theory is adopted. The logical AND (set intersection) is represented by the * symbol (multiplication). The logical OR (set union) is represented by the + symbol (addition). The à symbol (arrow) indicates the causal connection between the conditions and the outcome. An upper case letter represents the value 1 for a given variable (presence for binary variables, respectively strong membership for interval-scale variables). A lower case letter represents the value 0 for a given variable (absence for binary variables, respectively weak membership for interval-scale variables) (Rihoux and Ragin 2008).

ciency, using the following model (see Table 3.9 for the truth table and Table 3.10 for the solution): [21]

DEFINDPDM = SECTORPUBL + MANYVETO + HFORMALIND + COORDECO + NETWORKS + OLDAGE:

> OLDAGE+
>
> MANYVETO*HFORMALIND
>
> → DEFINDPDM

The coverage score of the overall solution is excellent (0.92). However, two unique solutions must be discarded, as they display a null empirical relevance: SECTORPUBL and HFORMALIND*COORDECO. The two remaining combinations of conditions can be retained (OLDAGE and MANYVETO*HFORMALIND), given their consistency score, (0.80 and respectively 0.85), that is, above the benchmark level 0.8 (Ragin 2006a).

Table 3.9: Truth table – de facto independence of IRAs from the politicians

sector- publ	many- veto	hfor- malind	coor- deco	net- works	oldage	n	defind- pdm	Consis- tency
0	0	1	0	1	0	1	0	0.77
0	1	0	0	0	1	1	1	0.96
0	1	0	0	1	0	1	0	0.78
0	1	0	1	1	0	1	0	0.79
0	1	0	1	1	1	1	1	0.86
0	1	1	0	0	0	1	1	0.91
1	0	1	1	0	1	1	1	0.95
1	0	1	1	1	0	1	1	0.94
1	1	1	0	0	0	1	1	0.81
1	1	1	1	1	0	1	1	0.96

---

21. The procedure for obtaining a crisp table from fuzzy sets is recommended, in order to improve transparency and to consent the computation of the measures of consistency and coverage (Ragin 2005b). Table 3.9 is a fuzzy-set truth table (Ragin 2008b).

Table 3.10: Truth table solution – de facto independence of IRAs from the politicians

	Raw coverage	Unique coverage	Consistency
OLDAGE+	0.75	0.18	0.80
MANYVETO*HFORMALIND+	0.64	0.01	0.85
SECTORPUBL+	0.36	0.00	0.59
HFORMALIND*COORDECO	0.63	0.00	0.88

Solution coverage: 0.92
Solution consistency: 0.68

The results of the fuzzy set analysis can be interpreted as follows. As high formal independence is neither a necessary nor a single sufficient condition for high de facto independence, we can confirm Hypothesis 1.1 about the causal disjuncture between formal and de facto independence. Indeed, agencies can enjoy a high level of de facto independence even without regard to formal independence. See, for example, the *Bundesanstalt für Finanzdienstleistungaufsicht* in Germany, the Norwegian *Konkurransetilsynet*, and the *Konkurrensverhet* in Sweden.

Crucial conditions in both expressions leading to high de facto independence are the old age of IRAs and the presence of many veto players, the latter in combination with high formal independence. Therefore, agencies are highly de facto independent when they are old and when the politicians have to cope with several veto players. This means that the presence of multiple veto players fosters the formal independence of agencies, as it becomes more difficult for divided principals to sway the regulatory action. Moreover, agencies may benefit from a process of autonomisation when ageing. This finding is clearly in line with Hypothesis 1.2 about the positive effect of veto players and old age of agencies. This is the case, for instance, of the Belgian *Commission Bancaire, Financière et des Assurances*.

The third sufficient combination (HFORMALIND + COORDECO) presents poor coverage, therefore it should be interpreted with some care. However, it is interesting to note that, quite surprisingly, the presence of highly coordinated economies turns out to be a jointly sufficient condition for independence. My theoretical expectations on this point are thus not confirmed. In contrast to Hypothesis 1.3, the presence of a coordinated economy comes out as a condition leading to high de facto independence from politicians, likewise the case of the *Rundfunk und Telekom Regulierungs* in Austria and the Italian *Autorità per le Garanzie nelle Comunicazioni*. This is quite unexpected, as we may reasonably suppose that in a coordinated economy, the network of relationships among the politicians, the regulators, and the private actors will be denser, suggesting a lower de facto independence of agencies. However, an alternative explanation could be that the need for coordination among the relevant stakeholders may favour a sort of horizontal control, implying that the elected politicians cannot critically sway the agencies. Incidentally, note that the path dependence from the prior mode of sectoral regulation has no effect. In that regard, it is worth noting that there is no apparent sector-specific or country-specific pattern, suggesting thereby the limited significance of explanations in terms of 'bureaucratic culture' (as predicted by my exploratory studies based on different model specifications, too).

Results: De facto independence from the regulatees

Pertaining to explanations for high de facto independence from the regulatees, again, no necessary causes are included in the analysis, given the restrictive conditions for the assessment of necessity (see Table 3.11).

Table 3.11: Necessary conditions for de facto independence from politicians

Outcome: high de facto independence from the regulatees	
Condition	*Consistency*
networks	0.65
sectpubl	0.33
oldage	0.66
coordeco	0.81
orgreg	0.68
defindpdm	0.72

Nevertheless, we obtain two significant combinations of jointly sufficient conditions (according to Tables 3.12 and 3.13), for the model:

DEFINDREG = COORDECO + NETWORKS + OLDAGE + DEFINDPDM + ORGREG:

The solution coverage score is very satisfactory (0.88), indicating a very high empirical relevance of the subset relations under examination. Concerning the level of consistency, three combinations of conditions present a sufficient consistency score to be considered, that is, above the benchmark value of 0.8: OLDAGE (0.83), NETWORKS*defindpdm (0.96), and coordeco*NETWORKS (0.98). The latter, however, can be discarded, as it displays a null unique coverage.

Table 3.12: Truth table – de facto independence of IRAs from the regulatees

coordeco	networks	oldage	defindpdm	orgreg	n	defindreg	Consist
1	1	0	1	1	2	0	0.88
0	0	0	0	1	1	0	0.93
0	1	0	0	0	1	1	1
1	0	1	1	1	1	1	0.98
1	1	1	1	1	1	1	1

Table 3.13: Truth table solution – de facto independence of IRAs from the regulatees

	Raw coverage	Unique coverage	Consistency
OLDAGE+	0.66	0.16	0.83
orgreg+	0.33	0.06	0.63
NETWORKS*defindpdm+	0.53	0.06	0.96
coordeco*NETWORKS	0.48	-0.00	0.98

Solution coverage: 0.88
Solution consistency: 0.72

NETWORKS appears to be a sufficient causal condition for agencies' de facto independence in combination with low de facto independence from the politicians (or, respectively, coordeco, even if this latter solution possess a poor coverage). To begin with, the fact that agencies are highly de facto independent from regulatees when they participate in European networks of agencies confirms the pertinence of Hypothesis 1.4. See, in this regard, the cases of the German *Bundesanstalt für Finanzdienstleistungaufsicht*, the Finnish *Rahoitustarkastus*, the Swedish *Finansinspektionen*, and the Dutch *Mededingingsautoriteit*. Plausibly these agencies are reinforced by the diffusion of expertise and information coming from other regulators, while gaining potential allies in front of third parts. In other words, networks seem to offer a range of technical and symbolic resources to IRAs that enhance their emancipation from the regulatees. Furthermore, the concomitant presence of the condition 'defindpdm' is in line with the conceptualisation of IRAs as intermediary agencies: the relationship between agencies and politicians and, respectively, the relationship between agencies and those being regulated are mutually related, in line with Hypothesis 1.5. To be precise, it appears that an agency cannot be a servant of two masters: if it is scarcely independent from the politicians, it should be highly independent from those being regulated. Moreover, interestingly, and against some pessimistic insights of the theory of agencies' life-cycle, OLDAGE seems also to support their independence *vis-à-vis* the regulatees.

Conclusion

The primary aim of this chapter was to develop a sound approach for conceptualising and assessing the de facto independence of IRAs from elected politicians and, respectively, from regulatees, so as to explore the complex causal relations between formal independence, as prescribed in the constitutions of agencies, and de facto independence, as it is effectively implemented in practice. To this end, organisational, institutional, and political explanations were examined with a cross-national and cross-sectoral comparison of sixteen Western European IRAs using fuzzy-set analysis. The heuristic power of this technique was illustrated by the empirical analysis, pointing to the advantages of applying a framework of complex causation on a small-to-medium number of cases. The results demonstrate that formal independence is neither a necessary nor a sufficient condition for explaining variations in the de facto independence of agencies. Other factors have a decisive impact.

The high level of agencies' de facto independence from elected politicians can be explained with two combinations of jointly sufficient conditions. First, formal independence combined with the presence of many veto players leads to high de facto independence. Second, agencies can enjoy a high level of de facto independence, even regardless formal independence, when they are in place for a long time. The high de facto independence from regulatees can also be explained by two combinations of causal conditions. Agencies are highly de facto independent from those being regulated when they are old and when they are part of official networks of agencies at European level. This is the case when agencies are scarcely de facto independent from elected politicians, corroborating the hypothesis about the conceptualisation of IRAs as intermediary agencies: an agency cannot be the servant of two masters.

To sum up, with a quite robust and parsimonious empirical analysis, this chapter showed that de facto independence matters and divergence from formal independence reflect a significant range of causal conditions. Three main theoretical insights can be derived from this research study. First, it suggests that formal independence alone is insufficient for explaining variations in the de facto independence of IRAs. This point is critical for the study of the consequences of agencification, as the disjuncture between statutory and effective independence will render the structural disaggregation and consequent separateness from the representative institutions problematical, making the democratic deficit even more questionable (Majone 2002). Similarly, the delegation of public authority to IRAs could be challenged, as their capacity to deliver 'better' regulatory outputs would be potentially reduced in relation to the expectations, given that the effective implementation of formal independence is seen as the precondition for high-quality regulation. Thus, special attention should be given to factors that enable the proper implementation of statutory prescriptions; otherwise, the accountability structure of the regulatory regime could become unintelligible and hardly lead to legitimacy gains (Majone 1999).

Two explanatory conditions have special theoretical relevance. On the one hand, the impact of agencies' networks: the embeddedness of IRAs into international networks promotes de facto independence, while ideally also producing a situation where 'no one controls the agency, yet the agency is under control' through 'peer pressures' and reputational mechanisms (this state of affairs being still an open empirical question) (Moe 1985; Majone 1994a, 1996a, 1997b). On the other hand, the role of veto players: As mentioned before, the theory of delegation seems incomplete on this point, because veto players are a precondition for delegation according to the literature on central banks while they can be a functional equivalent of delegation in the case of IRAs (Gilardi 2007). Following the empirical analysis, the findings of this chapter would suggest that the political strategies before delegation differ in the two cases: elected politicians might anticipate that they will be able to informally steer agencies to some extent, whereas the same would be more difficult in the case of central banks. In fact, the mandate of central banks is clearer, simpler and more difficult to reorient than the complex mix of overlapping tasks that is usually attributed to IRAs. Therefore, politicians, when they can choose, are comparatively more eager to delegate competencies to IRAs that enjoy high formal independence, in order to enhance regulatory credibility, while in the case of central banks a broad delegation of powers is more likely in the case of the presence of many veto players that prevent further policy changes. Above all, the results of this empirical analysis are also relevant because it appears that the presence of veto players is a crucial condition for effectively translating high formal independence into factual independence. This implies a possible dilemma: countries with less veto players are said to give agencies more formal independence, but veto players constitute one of the (sufficient but not necessary) conditions for implementing high formal independence in practice.

Second, it appears that actors other than the elected politicians, namely the representatives of the regulated sector, may have a decisive influence on agencies' de facto independence. This finding sustains the conceptualisation of IRAs as intermediary organisations, which are involved in a double relationship with the political decision makers and with those being regulated, whereby the two double relations are significantly influencing each other (Braun 1993). This finding is particularly relevant because an agency can hardly survive in the long run if it is not capable of avoiding the trap of being captured by the elected politicians or the regulatees (Braun 1997). Third, in that regard, the analysis shows that regulators are neither constantly under direct political control nor are they systematically captured by the regulated industries, challenging thus a crucial argument of the economic theory of regulation (Stigler 1971; Pelzman *et al.* 1989). Rather, they constitute a relatively new, important player of regulatory governance, that, more often than not, enjoy a considerable level of de facto independence, while cumulating competencies of rule-making, monitoring, sanctioning and adjudication, even if, under some circumstances, external actors may be occasionally able to influence the agencies' conduct of regulatory tasks.

chapter four | the role of independent regulators in lawmaking (part ii)

Summary

This chapter examines the role of IRAs in policy making, focusing on six cases concerning the revision of crucial laws related to the competencies of independent regulators. These cases were selected from three small European countries (The Netherlands, Sweden, Switzerland) and two policy areas (banking/finance and competition). After collecting survey and documental information on the participation and weight of each actor, the actor-process-event scheme (APES) was used to obtain a synthetic measure of agencies' centrality in the course of each policy process. My hypotheses on the centrality of agencies are then tested with a 'two-step' qualitative comparative analysis (QCA). Results suggest that de facto independence from political decision makers is a necessary condition for the maximal centrality of agencies in policy making, whilst non-professionalisation of the legislature and low independence from regulatees are jointly sufficient for explaining this outcome.

Introduction: IRAs and policy making

This chapter focuses on the role of independent agencies in policy making beyond their regulatory competencies. It should be noted that not all public sector organisations that participate in policy making are regulatory agencies: some have executive tasks; others are simple consultative organisations for policy makers. Not all agencies are formally independent; some are in subordinate relationships with ministries and the ordinary public administration. The most institutionalised IRAs are those promoting market regulation: general competition authorities, utility regulators, and banking and financial commissions (Thatcher 2002d, 2005a). The political decision makers delegated to those IRAs several regulatory competencies, for instance, the issuing and enforcement of licenses for operating in the market; the regulation of important market operations, such as mergers and takeovers; the prevention of anti-competitive behaviour of the regulated firms; the prudential supervision of the financial institutions; the setting of minimal quality standards to which those being regulated should conform; the elaboration of directives, circulars, and guidelines; and the prospect for imposing fines and other measures to sanction the infringements of the rules they issue (Majone 1994b; Gilardi 2002b; Coen and Thatcher 2005; Levi-Faur 2005a; Levi-Faur and Jordana 2005).

However, beyond their regulatory attributions, agencies also represent a new type of political actor in Western Europe. Following the process of delegation, they obtain not only considerable public authority for executing their regulatory tasks, but they also gain exclusive competencies involving material and symbolic resources, constituting valuable political capital (Sørensen 2002; Sørensen and Torfing 2003). In fact, IRAs should not be considered neutral technocratic devices, but institutions that are created through a process of collective choice among the 'insiders' and imposed on society as a whole, hence also to the 'losers' of the coordination games, being thus directly involved in political struggles for attaining a number of political goals (Moe 2005). In this context, IRAs have incentives for involving themselves in policy making. On the one hand, they are likely to look for institutional legitimacy as a major resource for securing their survival within the social and economic environment (DiMaggio and Powell 1983). On the other hand, once they are in place, according to their organisational logic, agencies are expected to seek political power, defined at the most basic level of signification, that is, instrumental participation in decision making for the resolution of political issues (Bachrach and Baratz 1962). Accordingly, one shall expect that agencies play an important role in policy making. First, agencies can be included in decision processes in order to legitimise a preformatted solution developed by the political actors in favour of a given reform. Second, they should possess the technical expertise and exclusive pieces of information that can be considered useful for developing the 'best solution' to a given problem. Third, their agreement can be considered necessary by the political decision makers in order to ensure the proper implementation of the new laws.

The empirical literature in political science typically deals with the question of the governmental and parliamentary influence on agencies, and the balance between control and discretion over executive bureaucracies (Weingast and Moran 1983; Weingast 1984; McCubbins et al. 1987; Bawn 1995; Epstein and O'Halloran 1996; Hammond and Knott 1996; Epstein and O'Halloran 1999; Huber et al. 2001; Huber and Shipan 2002). The question about the policy discretion of agencies is considered particularly relevant, as delegating powers involves a constant tension between effectiveness and responsiveness, and the place where policy is actually made may have significant impact on policy outcomes (Epstein and O'Halloran 1999). The role of IRAs in the core of the policy process, namely, lawmaking, has been less intensively investigated. However, some general insights can be mentioned, starting from the radical position of Lowi who argued that delegation to unelected regulatory agencies corresponds to the abdication of the parliament's policy-making role, resulting in an opaque process where the particular interests are gaining power at the expense of the legislature (Lowi 1969). The counterarguments are numerous; first of all, several authors suggested that delegation to agencies is politically efficient (Epstein and O'Halloran 1999). Accordingly, the process of delegation, in theory, is scattered by a series of control mechanisms, such as opportunities for oversight, parliamentary hearings and reports requirements (McCubbins et al. 1987; Kiewiet and McCubbins 1991). At the same time, according to Calvert, McCubbins, and Weingast, bureaucrats are active participants in the (American) policy-making process, conceptualised as a strategic game, where legislators, the chief executive, and bureaucratic agents to whom authority is delegated interact constantly and develop durable relationships (Calvert *et al.* 1989). Other scholars came to similar conclusions, applying a principal-agent transaction cost approach to study the relations among the elected politicians and autonomous agencies in policy making (Huber and Shipan 2002).

After the development of the regulatory state in Europe (Majone 1997a; Moran 2002) and the transformation of West European policy styles (Richardson 2000) a new wave of research on the impact of agencification on political systems emerged. A common finding is that the expansion of regulatory governance may lead to unintended consequences as regards the hierarchy and the relationships among political actors (McGowan and Wallace 1996; Gehring 2004; Pollitt and Bouckaert 2004). Wilks and Bartle (2002) argued that competition agencies, although created essentially for symbolic purposes and not expected to be active in rulemaking or implementation, have gradually redefined their roles so as to exert a material impact on market economies. There is also evidence showing that contextual factors shape the functioning of agencies and imply potential implementation problems (Hood *et al.* 2001; Peters 2001; Pollitt *et al.* 2004; Christensen and Yesilkagit 2005; Christensen and Lægreid 2005). Similarly, some studies emphasised the changes introduced by IRAs in decision-making processes, which have dramatically opened up, in contrast to closed processes before delegation (Thatcher 2002d; Coen and Thatcher 2005). As a consequence, it appears that independent regulatory agencies have become the 'third force' in regulation, constituting a set of political actors that is more or less differentiated from elected politicians and regulatees (Thatcher 2005a).

Nonetheless, a number of crucial questions are still on the table, namely concerning the factors explaining the role of IRAs in policy making, from a systematic comparative perspective that entails an investigation of the whole policy process. The research questions guiding this chapter can be summarised as follows:

1. *Are IRAs more central in the policy-making process than other actors?*

2. *In which stages of the policy-making process are IRAs the most central?*

3. *What explains the expected variations in the centrality of IRAs in policy making?*

Plausibly, one of the major reasons of these research gaps is the absence of a way of conceptualising the role of agencies that can be used in cross-national and cross-sectoral studies. In an effort to address these issues, the role of agencies will be made operational in this chapter with a measure of agencies' centrality in policy making.

The measure developed here combines a structural perspective with a reputational approach, assuming that the aggregated information on the 'participation' and 'perceived importance' of actors indicates their overall influence in policy making. To be precise, central actors are considered to hold a key role in the lawmaking process. The rest of this chapter is structured as follows: first, I will present five theoretical expectations to explain variations in the centrality of agencies in policy making. Second, I will present the logic of the comparison. After discussing how to compare different decision-making processes and case selection, I will operationalise the 'dependent' variable—the centrality of IRAs in the course of the decision-making processes—with the actor-process-event scheme (APES). The qualitative comparative analysis (QCA) follows. According to the analysis, de facto independence from political decision makers is a necessary condition for the maximal centrality of agencies in policy making, and the combination of non-professionalisation of the legislature and low independence from the representative of the regulated sector is jointly sufficient for explaining this outcome.

Theoretical expectations

Analytical framework

This first step is to seek to identify the explanatory factors for the higher centrality of IRAs in policy making. As for the first empirical part, I will use a configurational method to discern the different combinations of competing or complementary conditions leading to the outcome, assuming that causal complexity is the rule instead than the exception (Rihoux and Ragin 2008). Here, due to the nature of the causal conditions, which can be dichotomised, and to the number of cases, which is limited to six for reasons of feasibility and comparability of the policy-making processes, the crisp sets version of QCA is adopted (Ragin 1987, 2005a, b). This time, hypotheses about each explanatory factor are presented separately. In fact, the main aim of this chapter is to discern the effect of de facto independence of IRAs on their role in lawmaking, and not to fully explain agencies' centrality in policy making. Nonetheless, the possibility of finding other complex causal patterns is open, in line with the partially inductive focus of the QCA technique, oriented towards exploration and discovery (Schneider and Wagemann 2003). Hypothesis 1, as outlined below, does not refer to a particular causal relation but it is essentially descriptive; Hypotheses 2 and 3 relate to 'remote' explanatory factors (i.e. structural or contextual factors that enable the occurrence of the outcome); and Hypotheses 4 and 5 refer to 'proximate factors' (i.e. factors closely linked to the outcome that connote the causal relationship) (Schneider and Wagemann 2006) (see Figure 4.1).

Outline of the hypotheses:

H 2.1   IRAs hold the most central role in policy making.

H 2.2   Monocratic system → higher centrality of IRAs.

H 2.3   Non-professionalised legislature → higher centrality of IRAs.

H 2.4   Sector-specific expertise → higher centrality of IRAs.

H 2.5   *a)* High de facto independence from political decision-makers → higher centrality of IRAs.
         b) Low de facto independence from regulatees → higher centrality of IRAs.

Hypotheses

The overall centrality of IRAs in policy making

The literature on agencies and policy making typically examines the ability of elected politicians to control agencies and shape the regulatory outcomes, and, respectively, the discretion of agencies when carrying out their regulatory duties in front of their political principals (Bernstein 1977; Weingast 1984; McCubbins *et al.* 1987; Calvert *et al.* 1989; Spiller 1990; Kiewiet and McCubbins 1991; Hammond and Knott 1996; Spence 1997; Epstein and O'Halloran 1999; Gerber and Teske 2000; Bendor *et al.* 2001; Carpenter 2001b; Peters 2001; Moran 2002). However, it is worth looking at the question also from the reverse angle, starting from the observation that the capacity of independent regulatory agencies to take part in policy making and influence lawmaking has been much less investigated. This is a crucial question for policy analysis, when presuming that regulatory agencies, even though they are formally independent – and perhaps precisely because of their high independence from elected politicians – should play a key role in policy making as well. In fact, as mentioned in the introduction, besides the execution of regulatory tasks in a narrow sense, the delegation of public authority led to the establishment of a new, distinct and apparently powerful kind of political actor. The study of post-delegation relationships showed that IRAs hold distinctive functions in regulatory policies, hence representing a crucial actor in regulatory governance, along with governments and regulatees (Thatcher 2005a). IRAs are likely to initiate new legislative procedures, offer their expertise to the decision makers, and ensure implementation of the new rules. IRAs dispose from essential resources for policy making in terms of technical expertise, and they benefit from a unique acquaintance with the regulated sector that is critical for collecting relevant information and gaining political support (Majone 2001a). As a consequence, IRAs are expected to be integrated extensively in the political processes, more than extra-parliamentary commissions, in which experts and interest groups participate mainly for consultative purposes, and more than ordinary agencies, which are subordinated to the ministry in charge, being determinant in the course of policy making.

H 2.1   IRAs are expected to hold the most central role in the course of the political decision-making processes in their area of competence.

The political-administrative culture

This study concentrates on agencies that enjoy formal independence from elected officials, that is, those that benefit from statutory prescriptions of separateness. The formal structure of bureaucracies has well-known consequences on their relations with the government and other political actors (Egeberg 1999). However, not only formal rules but also informal norms are expected to affect the role of agencies in substantive policy making, following the so-called political-administrative culture (Peters 2001). The sociological institutionalist literature shows that institutions function as routines and procedures that entail taken-for-granted norms for action (Berger and Luckmann 1966; March and Olsen 1989; DiMaggio and Powell 1991). According to a 'logic of appropriateness', political actors go through a socialisation process and follow rules that associate particular identities to specific situations, whereby ideational factors shape the appropriate rule for a given situation (March and Olsen 2004). In this sense, the perceptions of the appropriate role of organisations are encapsulated in the institutional ethos, practices, and expectations about the proper behaviour of actors at individual and collective level. These shared understandings influence the way actors define their goals and what they perceive as rational action, and redefine their interests and identities accordingly (Börzel and Risse 2000). It follows that similar organisations may function differently in practice, according to the 'logic of appropriateness' surrounding their respective institutional framework. The official organisational means and ends could be reinterpreted and incorporated into the institutional norms, ideas, meanings, and practices. Concretely, we can distinguish between a vertically integrated system, called 'monocratic', and a dual model in which a strict separation between political decision making and administrative implementation exists. In the former case, no 'cultural' limitation to the inclusion of IRAs in the policy-making process exists. Conversely, we may expect that in the latter case, equally formally independent agencies have fewer opportunities to influence the policy-making process because of a different logic of appropriateness, which characterises the decision-making process as an exclusive competence of ministerial departments and executive agencies.

H 2.2   The presence of a 'monocratic' system is expected to lead to the higher centrality of IRAs in policy making, unlike a dual model.

The professionalisation of the legislature and public administration

According to the core assumption of rational choice institutionalism, institutions represent structures of incentives that enable and constrain actors' behaviour, which can be in turn modelled as strategic games eventually leading to 'structure-induced' equilibria (Ostrom 1986; Shepsle 1995; North 1998). In this context, policy makers have two types of rational incentives for integrating regulatory agencies in policy making, in line with the notion of epistemic communities, that is, 'networks of professionals with recognised expertise and competence in a particular domain and an authoritative claim to policy relevant knowledge within that domain or issue-area' (Haas 1992). On the one hand, following a problem-solving perspective, agencies' expertise can be considered crucial to find the 'best' solution to a given problem; on the other hand, from a strategic point of view, the role of agencies in policy making may depend on the varying need for legitimising the solution preferred by policy-makers in a number of policy issues. In both cases, the relevant institutional feature that shall determine the magnitude of the pressures for including agencies in policy making is the degree of professionalisation of the legislature and the ordinary civil service.

Concretely, we can distinguish between specialised, professionalised legislatures and a less professionalised parliamentary model in terms of resources and staff (Huber and Shipan 2002). In countries where the legislature is more professionalised, legislators should have the capacities, resources and ability to write detailed, policy-specific legislation. This also depends on the extent to which political decision makers can directly rely on civil servants for dealing with technical issues on the political agenda. On the contrary, if members of parliaments only have part-time positions that are relatively low paying, independent agencies should be intensively included in the course of the decision-making processes because of the constant need for expertise or technocratic legitimacy. Agencies are indeed highly specialised bodies that possess a distinctive expertise capacity in the field due to their vast resources, their technical competencies, and their regular interaction with the regulated sector.

H 2.3   IRAs are expected to be highly central in policy making where the legislature is non-professionalised.

Sector-specific expertise

Following a crucial argument of historical institutionalism, policy-making processes are largely determined by specific historical trajectories. This phenomenon is due, on the one hand, to the self-reinforcing effect of existing structures and patterns of behaviour; on the other, to the distributional effects of institutions that reproduce the existing allocation of power in specific time junctures (Thelen 1999; Pierson 2000; Pierson and Skocpol 2002). According to this view, regulators are likely to develop different policy-making roles over time, as processes of political feedback may occur, reinforcing the political functions of those agencies that already enjoy important tasks in regulation. In other words, the relative 'force' of IRAs in regulation should also foster their influence in lawmaking. Given the differential levels of institutionalisation across regulatory fields, the magnitude of this phenomenon is expected to vary from sector to sector.

The starting point is the consideration that legislatures, governments and ordinary bureaucracies rarely dispose from the resources required to make effective responses to specific policy problems (Papadopoulos 2003), so they must increasingly rely on presumably independent experts to shape public policy (Majone 2001a; Pollack 2002; Héritier and Eckert 2008). Accordingly, the need for expertise that results from a state of imperfect information and scarce resources of the political decision makers, and the related lack of capacity to perform crucial tasks, is an important justification for delegation to IRAs (Pollack 2002; Pollack 2003). Agencies are expected to develop and employ expertise in order to produce, or help their 'principals' to produce, appropriate public policies (Thatcher and Stone Sweet 2002). According to the argument developed above, one can distinguish between sector-specific regulation and general regulation. In the first case, namely in areas perceived as technically complex, agencies enjoy a structurally important position, due to their unique expertise in regulation that may, in turn, affect their role in policy making. One might suppose that sector-specific IRAs are the taken-for-granted technocratic tool for developing the 'best' regulatory policy by providing reliable pieces of advice to decision makers, due to the prior experience in regulation. Conversely, the second case, that is, general competition regulation, is considered a more politically salient and a less technical issue, for which agencies' participation should be less important. These IRAs are thus expected to be less involved in the development of new legislation. To sum up, we can expect that the agencies' centrality in policy making should be higher in a very technical sector, such as finance, than in general competition regulation.

H 2.4   IRAs possessing sector-specific expertise are expected to play a very central role in policy making, unlike general regulators.

De facto independence

De facto independence characterises the effective autonomy of agencies during their day-to-day regulatory action (Maggetti 2007). This variable, which is determined not only by formal prescriptions for independence but, above all, from organisational and institutional factors, constitutes in turn a critical resource for regulators that is expected to influence their role in policy making. To be precise, factually independent IRAs should also be key political actors. Rational choice institutionalist and sociological institutionalist logics are expected to be complementarily or alternatively present, depending from whether efficiency-driven or legitimacy-driven behaviour can be considered prevalent. First, a high level of de facto independence from political decision makers should be related to an instrumental argument for including agencies in the policy process, as independent agencies are considered to retain crucial pieces of information that are seen as essential for policymakers. Instead, non-independent agencies should not necessarily be integrated in policy making because due to the permanent contacts and structural commonalities with the political decision makers, the latter would previously possess the relevant information. What is more, when IRAs are included in policy-making processes in order to legitimate the prior position of the political actors that are in favour of a given reform, they are not expected to be truly influential to the development of the new law. Finally, a low level of de facto independence from regulatees is also expected to lead to the inclusion of agencies in the decision-making process, in order to overcome ex-ante their potential veto in later stages of policy making. Indeed, the political decision makers will plausibly perceive those agencies, which are 'captured' by regulatees' interests, as credible veto players (Tsebelis 2002) that might challenge the implementation of the new rules.

H 2.5 a) *High de facto independent IRAs from political decision makers should be central actors in policy making.*

b) *Low de facto independent IRAs from regulatees should be central actors in policy making.*

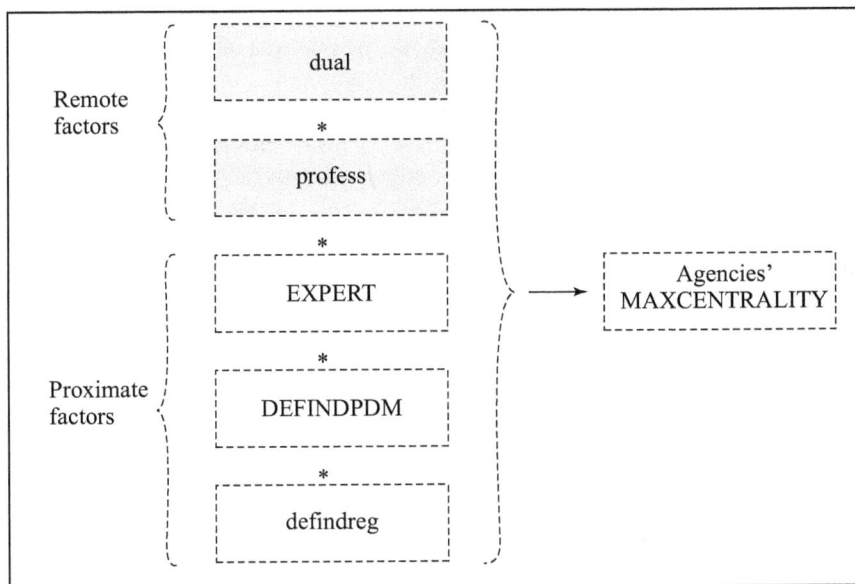

Figure 4.1: The Explanatory model

Methodology

First, a comparative logic close to a 'most similar system design' (Przeworski and Teune 1970) is adopted to select a set of countries by comparing cases as similar as possible, those that differ only in those 'independent' variables ('causal conditions,' in QCA terms), which could explain the variation of the 'dependent' variable ('outcome condition'). This method, combined with a qualitative comparative analysis (QCA) (Ragin 1987), can be used to identify necessary and sufficient causes leading to the outcome (Mahoney 2007). Here, the causal conditions derived from the above mentioned hypotheses refer to the existence of a dual/monocratic political-administrative system; the professionalisation of the legislature; the sector-specific expertise of the agency in charge; the de facto independence from elected politicians; and the de facto independence from regulatees. The (positive) outcome is the maximal centrality of the investigated agency, compared to the centrality of the other actors involved in lawmaking.

The crisp set QCA technique relying on Boolean algebra is used to perform a diversity-oriented systematic comparison. Each case is conceived as a combination of dichotomised (present/absent) causal conditions that lead to the outcome. Given the number of cases and the nature of variables, this method is particularly suitable for the present study. Following the approach developed by Schneider and Wagemann (2006), a two-step QCA analysis will be executed. This implies first the identification of contextual conditions (remote factors) that enable the occurrence of the outcome. Second, the remote factors are combined with more specific conditions (proximate factors) in a more precise analysis in order to find out necessary and sufficient combinations leading to the outcome. The goal is to reduce complexity so as to mitigate the problem of limited diversity and accurately model the causal structure of the argument (Schneider and Wagemann 2006). Here, the remote factors are the conditions related to the structure of the political-administrative system (*dual, profess*), while the proximate factors are the conditions that refer to the characteristics of the investigated agency (*expert, defindpdm, defindreg*).

Next, the analysis requires a number of policy-making processes 'as similar as possible' in which a relevant indepependent regulatory agency is expected to be steadily included.

Modelling and comparing the decision-making processes

Here, policy making is conceived in its core dimension as lawmaking and conceptualised as the entire decision-making process of adopting/revising a new law in the domain of the related IRA, from the agenda setting to the policy implementation. How can we compare different political decision-making processes? A cross-country and cross-sectoral comparison of decision-making processes is considered feasible. However, this enterprise is not straightforward because the existent models of decision making are extremely heterogeneous (Peters 1998). What is more, when comparing the role of public sector organisations in decision making, three additional difficulties exist: the first is the absence of a shared theoretical language, which is useful for the comparison of public administrations; the second refers to the absence of precise indicators for the behaviour of public sector organisations. The third relates to the fact that small structural differences appear to make a great deal of difference in practice (Peters 1990).

In particular, it has been noted that any notion defining processes or institutions can hardly be applied as such to different cases because its meaning is decisively contingent to the context in that processes and institutions are embedded (Rose and Mackenzie 1991). When thinking about research design for comparative analysis it is thus essential, at the most basic level, to avoid any 'trap of nominalism' that would induce to attribute similar implications to processes or institutions that actually perform very different functions (Petiteville and Smith 2006). Notions and concepts should be precise and abstract enough to 'travel' across countries and policy sectors (Radaelli 2000b), as the literature on policy transfer specifically underscores (Dolowitz and Marsh 1996; Dolowitz and Marsh 2000; Radaelli 2000a). Similarly, we should be aware of the risk of 'conceptual stretching,' which Sartori derived from the inherent trade-off between the number of cases to which a concept can be applied and the precision of the categorisation (Sartori 1970). The excessive 'intension' would imply a limited generalisation of the typology and the impossibility of reaching broader knowledge; the excess of 'extension' would reduce the number of attributes defining the category hence the accuracy of the conceptualisation.

It is possible to deal with these shortcomings. First, we shall start from a number of decision-making processes that are structurally 'as similar as possible' across and within countries in order to distinguish the relevant variations due to the pertinent variables from 'background' phenomena (Przeworski and Teune 1970). This reserve is crucial to avoid any 'scientific colonialism' that would impose a unifying theoretical framework to non-suitable cases, resulting in 'seeking, examining and comparing non-existing phenomena' (Allardt 1990). Similarly, in order to exclude any endogenous selection bias, we need to focus on some comparable pieces of legislation. Legislation coming from different jurisdictions should be selected to be formally and substantially similar, while the application of a number of reasonable simplifying assumptions can be useful to keep things manageable (Boer *et al.* 2003). Third, we have to compare processes by dividing them into a number of events, which can be considered functional equivalents across cases (Collier and Mahon 1993). Therefore, the policy cycle can be divided into a number of stages, which are not necessarily sequential (Howlett and Ramesh 2003); for instance, the formulation of a solution does not always follow the emergence of a specific problem (Olsen 2001). This way, it is possible to adopt a self-conscious thinking in terms of ideal-types, by using a system-specific contextual approach involving analytical techniques that do not assume that all members of a category share a full set of attributes (e.g. QCA) (Collier and Mahon 1993). Fourth, we must compare our findings with the empirical literature in the field in order to benefit from previous knowledge so as to distinguish trivial from relevant explanatory factors. To be precise, non-trivial conditions are those that invoke factors that may vary across the values of the dependent variable and that are potentially sufficient for the outcome (Goertz 2006a).[1] Finally, it should be noted that several biases could be avoided when data are generated directly by

---

1. Following Goertz, the most trivial necessary conditions are those that are invariably present (such as 'oxygen' for predicting the success of revolutions), while the most trivial sufficient conditions are those that never occur (such as 'alien invasion' for predicting the occurrence of wars) (examples are mine).

the researcher, as it is the case in the present research study (Przeworski 2007).

As a result, this study focuses on a peculiar type of decision-making process, that is, those in small corporatist European states. Here, many shared characteristics among models of policy making ensure a high level of comparability. These countries display an open economy to international trade associated with developed welfare states (Katzenstein 1985). They also show a constant cooperation between the government and administration, the representatives of economic and social interest groups, and political parties, in many crucial policy areas (Lehmbruch and Schmitter 1982). It should be noted that even if corporatist arrangements have to face tensions generated by several political developments, such as economic internationalisation and European integration, some studies emphasise the 'greater not lesser reliance on previous structures of national intermediation' in these countries (Schmitter and Grote 1997). Specifically, the need to re-coordinate policies across policy fields implies a renewed importance of 'tripartite concertation' and similar arrangements in many cases (Ebbinghaus and Hassel 1999, 2000).

Beyond their political economies, these countries tend to be associated with political systems presenting different forms of power-sharing arrangements (Lijphart 1999). In these countries, an ideology of 'perceived vulnerability' together with a number of structural factors – such as the existence of multiple cultural and social cleavages, the political need for grand coalitions, the presence of geographically concentrated minorities – lead to some kind of consensus democracy (Rae and Taylor 1970; Rogowski 1987; Katzenstein 2003). In this context, the 'pre-parliamentary' phase of consultation, discussion and negotiation among the representatives of the main political and economic actors is traditionally considered crucial, as it predefines, to some extent, the scope of any possible decision made by the more politicised parliamentary arena (Kriesi 1994; Papadopoulos 1997).

Case selection and causal conditions

Hence, a number of small corporatist countries are identified, with a similar ideal-type of decision-making process. Three countries are selected, which fulfil these criteria: The Netherlands, Sweden, and Switzerland.[2] The three countries can be considered political regimes characterised by collegial governments indirectly elected by the parliamentary assembly (Siaroff 2003), while also displaying a similar economic structure (Schnyder 2008). We can assume that the political

---

2. There are some important differences not to be neglected—on the one hand, the varieties of corporatism (Falkner *et al.* 2004) and, on the other, the ongoing reconfiguration of national decision-making structures in consensus democracies (Häusermann, Mach and Papadopoulos 2004). However, beyond these important developments, concertation and social partnership in the policy-making processes seems still very much alive (Schmitter and Grote 1997; Baccaro 2003).

decision-making process in Sweden, Switzerland, and The Netherlands is, on the whole, corporatist-oriented and consensual (Lijphart 1984, 1999). On the one hand, a specific 'institutionalised pattern of policy-formation' (Schmitter and Lehmbruch 1979) is present, as the political decision making in all the selected countries is traditionally open and includes administrative actors and representatives of organised interests, according to a logic of dialogue and social partnership. On the other hand, the three countries present the fundamental characteristics of a consensus democracy, where cooperation between political parties and groups is institutionalised in order to simultaneously achieve a number of goals relating to economic and social policy (Armingeon 2002).

As required by Hypothesis 2.1, The Netherlands, Sweden, and Switzerland have a long tradition of extra-parliamentary commissions and expert committees that detain crucial tasks in the course of the decision-making processes. Appointed economic and legal experts are consulted when formulating policy reforms and drafting the initial bills; they act as norm entrepreneurs, together with administrative actors, and often follow interest groups concerns (Papadopoulos and Benz 2006). These procedures are crucial coordination devices, also leading to the constitution of sectoral policy communities in particular policy areas. In *The Netherlands*, associations, representatives of organised interests and experts committees are usually involved in parliamentary policy making and policy implementation (Compston 1994; Andeweg and Irwin 2005). In *Sweden*, administrative agencies hold crucial expertise capacities that empower them not only in implementation but also in prior stages of policy making (Pierre 1993; Svensson and Oberg 2002); at the same time, the government traditionally integrates experts in commissions to draft law proposals (Lindvall and Rothstein 2006). In *Switzerland*, new pieces of legislation are typically prepared in expert committees and submitted to consultation before they reach the parliamentary discussions (Kriesi 1995; Häusermann *et al.* 2004).

The type of the political-administrative culture (Hypothesis 2.2) is made operational through the following distinction. The *Dutch* civil service is habitually presented as relatively depoliticised and shaped by a high level of formalism and legalism. It is comparatively quite small and fragmented (Andeweg and Irwin 2005). While agencies normally enjoy a high level of formal autonomy, the system is described as 'monocratic,' that is, the public administration is subordinated to ministers, who are political executives with strong decision-making powers within their portfolio (Christensen and Yesilkagit 2005). In *Sweden*, the system is characterised by a principle of dual functioning that implies a strict separation between policy formulation, relying on ministries, and policy implementation. Agencies are perceived as autonomous, and often they are performing semi-judicial functions, even if informal linkages with politicians exist (Peters 2001; Pierre 2004). In *Switzerland*, many implementation competencies are delegated to the cantonal level, but they often overlap with the central administration, which is under the political responsibility of the federal government (Kriesi 1995). The civil service, even if relatively depoliticised, is subordinated to the relevant departments and enjoys an important role in ordinary legislative processes (Ruffieux 1975).

Hypothesis 2.3 refers to the professionalisation of the legislatures. In *The Netherlands*, the Second Chamber is composed of full-time members who enjoy a high level of professionalisation. Specifically, the parliamentary committees are composed of parliamentary members that are considered valid policy specialists. Concerning the public administration, the recruitment is based on a position principle, which implies a high level of specialisation (Andeweg and Irwin 2005). In *Sweden*, the parliament is strong (Colomer 1996) and disposes from considerable resources and overall professionalism (Copeland and Patterson 1994). The public administration is centralised, professionalised, and coherent (Kriesi 1994). Conversely, the *Swiss* parliament is a semi-professional institution where each legislator combines their professional activity with parliamentary duties and disposes from limited resources and staff.[3] According to Kriesi, this weakens the assembly that lacks time, information, and competences (Kriesi 2001). Public administration is small and decentralised, frequently relying on extra-parliamentary commissions and quasi-state implementation agencies (Varone 2007).

Next, two different policy areas are selected so as to introduce more variation in the dataset and precisely to test Hypothesis 2.4. The need for relying on agencies' expertise in policy making is expected to follow the level of technicality attributed to the related regulatory domain, no matter how effectual or politically constructed. It can be assessed through the distinction between highly technical sector-specific regulation and general regulation (Maggetti 2007). Therefore, two different kinds of IRAs are chosen, which are comparable pertaining to their organisational model and statutory competencies (Thatcher 2002c; Gilardi 2008), that is, sector-specific banking and financial commissions and general competition authorities. The former are regulating a sector perceived as highly technical, requiring sector-specific experts and the use of detailed knowledge. The latter, conversely, are regulating a more politically salient and a less technical issue.

The selected agencies must also possess a similar level of formal independence – to avoid any potential problem of exogenous influence of this variable – (Gilardi 2002b, 2005a), for which they should display a consistent variation concerning de facto independence from political decision makers and, respectively, from the representative of the regulated industries (see Table 4.1). For the operationalisation of this latter condition, which is needed to test Hypotheses 2.5a and 2.5b, data derived from the survey-based dataset on de facto independence presented in the previous chapter is used, in which de facto independence is seen as a synthesis of two components: the self-determination of agencies' preferences and their autonomy during the activity of regulation. Following the standard procedure of the qualitative comparative analysis, a dichotomous coding is proposed (Ragin 1987, 1994), where '1' corresponds to the condition of agencies' de facto independence from elected politicians, while '0' denotes agencies that cannot be considered strictly speaking as highly factually independent.

---

3. Comparatively, this argument seems to hold even in the face of recent trends towards a modestly increased professionalisation.

Table 4.1: Formal and de facto independence of IRAs

IRA	Label	Formal independence	De facto independence from the politicians	De facto independence from the regulatees
Konkurrensverhet	sweco	0.41	1	1
Wettbewerbskommission	swico	0.45	1	0
Nederlandse Mededingingsautoriteit	netco	0.46	0	1
Eidgenössische Bankenkommission	swibk	0.48	1	0
Autoriteit Financiële Markten	netbk	0.53	1	0
Finansinspektionen	swebk	0.54	0	1

Selected pieces of legislation

Each one of the six cases corresponds to a decision-making process that refers to the development of a crucial piece of legislation in the range of competencies of the related IRA in the years 2000–2006 (see Table 4.2). Three pieces of legislation concern IRAs regulating the banking and financial sector in each country. First, the act on the disclosure of major holdings and capital interests, issued in The Netherlands in 2006 (Wmz 2006).[4] The Wmz 2006 replaced the act on disclosure of major holdings in listed companies of 1996 (Wet melding zeggenschap in ter beurze genoteerde vennootschappen), which the *Autoriteit Financiële Markten* (AFM) has employed since 1996 as the basis for its supervision of the disclosure and registration of major holdings and capital interests, and since 2002 as the basis for its supervision of disclosures by directors and supervisory board members.

---

4. Sources: Act of 28th September 2006, on rules relating to the financial markets and their supervision (Financial Supervision Act); AFM, the most important amendments to the supervision of conduct following the introduction of the Act on Financial Supervision (Wft) 2006; AFM, Act on the disclosure of major holdings and capital interests in securities-issuing institutions - Information brochure for securities-issuing institutions, directors and supervisory board members 2006; Staatsblad van het Koninkrijk der Nederlanden Besluit van 25 augustus 2006, houdende vaststelling van het tijdstip van inwerkingtreding van de Wet melding zeggenschap en kapitaalbelang in effectenuitgevende instellingen; Staatsblad van het Koninkrijk der Nederlanden, Wet van 5 juli 2006, houdende regels betreffende de melding van zeggenschap en kapitaalbelang in, alsmede de melding van het geplaatste kapitaal van effectenuitgevende instellingen (Wet melding zeggenschap en kapitaalbelang in effectenuitgevende instellingen); Eerste Kamer der Staten-Generaal, Regels betreffende de melding van zeggenschap en kapitaalbelang in, alsmede de melding van het geplaatste kapitaal van effectenuitgevende instellingen (Wet melding zeggenschap en kapitaalbelang in ter beurze genoteerde vennootschappen), 23 mei, 23, 26, 27 juni 2006.

The aim of the new act is to increase transparency regarding major holdings and capital interests in securities-issuing institutions and to simplify the disclosure and registration process for the regulated industries. Namely, the Wmz 2006 imposes a duty to disclose on all parties that acquire or lose shares in a company, and the obligation to disclose ownership of shares with special controlling rights. The AFM was given the competencies of implementation of the Wmz 2006, and almost all tasks and powers of the Minister of Finance under the Wmz 2006 have been ultimately delegated to the agency.

Second, the *banking and finance business act*, promulgated in Sweden on 2004 (Banking Act 2004).[5] This new piece of legislation is part of the large-scale reform of the regulations concerning banking and financial business in Sweden, which were drafted with the goal of contributing to the overall stability and efficiency of the financial system. On the one hand, new pieces of legislation deregulated further banking and financial operation. For instance, the activity of credit provision, without financing by the means of deposits, no longer requires a licence. On the other, hand, the new banking and financing business act redefined and extend the competencies of the *Finansinspektionen* (FI). To begin with, the notification requirements to this IRAs are made stricter. Not only bank institutions, but also unlicensed activities where the principal activity is to provide financial advice should have to be notified to the agency, and any changes in relation to owners and management of the supervised institutions must be notified as well. In addition, the *Finansinspektionen* reinforces its statutory responsibility to directly supervise the individual institutions operating in the financial market, and acquire the competence of issuing general guidelines, while also being in charge of investigating whether the requirements are fulfilled on a regular basis.

Third, the *stock exchange and securities traders act*, revised in Switzerland in 2006 (Stock Exchange Act 2006).[6] This law extends the regulatory competencies of the Swiss Federal Banking Commission (SFBC/EBK – *Eidgenössische*

---

5.   Sources: Swedish Chambers of Commerce, 'An overview of the Swedish securities market 2006'; Banks in Sweden – 'Facts about the Swedish banking market', Swedish Bankers' Association 2004; Ministry/Agency: Ministry of Finance, 'The Banking and Finance Business Act' 2004:297, promulgated on 19 May 2004; 'Supervisory developments in Sweden', *Finansinpektionen* 2006.

6.   Sources: 'Loi sur les bourses: entrée en vigueur de la disposition révisée sur l'assistance administrative', Département fédéral des finances DFF, novembre 2005; 'La CFB souhaite une modification des reègles relatives à l'entraide boursière', EBK, 23 janvier 2002; 'Loi fédérale sur les bourses et le commerce des valeurs mobilières (Loi sur les bourses, LBVM) Modification du 7 octobre 2005; 'Bulletin officiel, Conseil des Etats, Loi fédérale sur les bourses et le commerce des valeurs mobilières (…)'; 'Bulletin officiel, Conseil National, Loi fédérale sur les bourses et le commerce des valeurs mobilières (…)'; 'Message concernant la modification de la disposition sur l'assistance administrative internationale de la loi fédérale sur les bourses et le commerce des valeurs mobilières du 10 novembre 2004'; 'Révision de la loi sur les bourses: résultats de la consultation et message du Conseil fédéral, DFF, 10 novembre 2004'; 'Rapport concernant la modification de la disposition sur l'assistance administrative internationale dans la loi fédérale sur les bourses et le commerce des valeurs mobilières', DFF, janvier 2004; 'Révision des modalités de l'assistance administrative dans la loi sur les bourses' (archives), DFF, 09 fevrier 2007.

Bankenkommission) concerning the supervision of stock exchange and securities, and it simplifies the procedures for information exchange and administrative assistance. Before the revision of the law, this agency could not provide administrative assistance to foreign authorities if they used the information requested exclusively for direct supervision of stock exchanges and trade in securities. It followed that the applicant supervisory authority could not provide information to another authority before the Swiss Federal Banking Commission had given his consent. In this context, information could be transmitted only when the crime was punishable in both the country of the foreign agency and Switzerland, which was typically not the case for certain types of fiscal fraud. The revision relaxes the principle of confidentiality and permits the transmission of information to a second foreign authority provided that it is responsible for enforcing regulations on stock exchanges, securities trading and securities dealers. Moreover, the requirements of double criminality are lifted. Finally, the procedure relating to clients of traders is simplified and accelerated. The cooperation with foreign authorities is thus considerably improved, following the increasing pressures coming from several governments, international institutions and foreign regulatory authorities for improving the international cooperation, and to promote the transparency and disclosure of the Swiss banking and financial regulatory framework.

Then, three other laws relate to general competition regulation. First, the *competition act*, revised in The Netherlands in 2005 (Competition Act 2005).[7] This law enhances the statutory independence and competences of the *Nederlandse Mededingingsautoriteit* (NMa). According to the previous status, the NMa was not fully independent. The minister for economic affairs detained powers to set policy lines and give specific instructions in individual cases, while the NMa had the organisational form of a specialised administrative body, which was exclusively responsible for enforcement under the Competition Act. The primary aim of the new law is to make NMa decisions in individual cases fully independent. The board is given the responsibility for the running of the NMa with discretion in day-to-day decision making. The position of director-general is replaced by a three-person board, which is responsible for the running of the NMa. Above all, independence is reinforced as the Ministry lose the power to give instructions in individual cases, although remaining responsible for the broad lines of competition policy.

Second, the *competition act*, revised in Sweden in 2004 (Competition Act 2004).[8] Conventionally, the Swedish Competition Act prohibits cooperation

---

7. Sources: International Competition Network, *Implementation Handbook, Examples of Legislative Text, Rules, and Practices that Conform to Selected ICN Guiding Principles and Recommended Practices for Merger Notification and Review Procedures*, April 2006; 'Competition ExtraNews', De Brauw Blackstone Westbroek, 4/4, July 2005; 'More Power for Dutch Competition Authority', Press release, Ministry of Economic Affairs, 23 October 2003; 'Wijziging Mededingingswet om oneerlijke concurrentie te voorkomen', Ministerie van Economische Zachen, 17 February 2006; 'De Voorzitter van de Tweede Kamer', Aanbieding van de onderzoeksrapportages evaluatie Mededingingswet, 31 mei 2002.

8. Sources: The Swedish Competition Act, Kkv, 075/03; OECD Competition Committee, Annual

between companies that significantly limits or distorts competition, such as price collaboration, market sharing between competing companies, and abuse of dominant market positions, and it also includes provisions on the control of mergers. This revision of the competition act deeply redefines the competencies of the independent regulatory agency in charge of its implementation, the *Konkurrensverhet* (KKV). For instance, undertakings can no longer apply for so-called negative clearance and exemption from the Competition Authority decisions. This revision also enhances the capacity of the agency: it increases the resources for ensuring supervision and improves the competencies of raids and investigations, while also permitting the issuance of new general guidelines for regulation-of-competition.

Third, the *act on cartels*, revised in Switzerland in 2003 (Cartels Act 2003).[9] The act on cartels of 1995 has been considered quite ineffective in practice by the political decision-makers, as the Competition Commission was only enabled to detect the infringements to the law, and sanctions were possible only in the case of repeated offence to the law. The preventive effect of the regulatory action of the agency was thus considered very feeble. With the revision of the act on cartels, a number of incentives against cartels have been introduced, so as to favour companies that disclose illicit behaviour of cartels. In addition, the so-called vertical cartels have been prohibited, whereas a number of clarification clauses have been introduced to improve the effectiveness of ComCo. At the same time, the attributions and the capacity of the Swiss Competition Commission are strengthened. On the one hand, the new act reinforced the means and resources at disposal for supervising the activities of the supervised firms. On the other, direct sanctioning capacities were attributed to the agency, which constitute crucial pre-emptive regulatory instruments, in line with the majority of OECD countries.

Report on Competition Policy Developments in Sweden – 2003; Directorate For Financial And Enterprise Affairs Competition Committee Annual Report On Competition Policy Developments In Sweden 2004, 10 May 2005; Motion Till Riksdagen 2003/04:N14, Med Anledning Av Prop. 2003/04:80 Moderniserad Konkurrensövervaknin; Motion 2004/05:N413 Näringspolitik; Betänkande 2003/04:Nu13; Näringsutskottets Betänkande 2003/04:Nu13mer Information, Moderniserad Konkurrensövervakning.

9. Sources: 'Révision de la loi sur les cartels: Le résultat des débats parlementaires, La Vie Economique, Revue de politique économique' octobre 2003; 'Révision de la loi sur les cartels et révision totale de la loi sur la banque nationale: la commission a achevé l'examen dans les délais impartis', Commission de l'économie et des redevances du Conseil des Etats (CER-E), 28 février 2003; 'La révision de la loi sur les cartels est en cours', 'Modification de la loi sur les cartels' Résultats de la consultation et suite de la procédure, Communiqué de presse, Berne, 4 avril 2001; Messagerelatif à la révision de la loi sur, les cartels du 7 novembre 2001; Commission de l'économie et des redevances du Conseil des Etats, La commission préconise la lutte contre les cartels et les abus en matière de biens immatériels, 31 janvier, 2003; Bulletin officiel, Conseil National, 'Loi fédérale sur les cartels et autres restrictions à la concurrence (…)'; Bulletin officiel, Conseil des Etats, 'Loi fédérale sur les cartels et autres restrictions à la concurrence (…)'; 'Loi fédérale sur les cartels et autres restrictions à la concurrence' (Loi sur les cartels, LCart) Modification du 20 juin 2003; 'Révision de la loi sur les cartels: entrée en vigueur' 1 avril 2004, Commission de la concurrence.

Table 4.2: Case selection

Sector	Country	Piece of legislation	IRA	Label
Banking and financial sector	Netherlands	*Act on the Disclosure of Major Holdings and Capital Interests in Securities-Issuing Institutions, of 2006*	*Autoriteit Financiële Markten* (AFM)	netbk
	Sweden	*Banking and Finance Business Act, promulgated on 2004*	*Finans-inspektionen* (FI)	swebk
	Switzerland	*Stock Exchange and Securities Traders Act, revised in 2006*	*Eidgenössische Bankenkom-mission* (EBK)	swibk
Competition	Netherlands	*Competition Act, revised in 2005*	*Nederlandse Mededingings-autoriteit* (NMa)	netco
	Sweden	*Competition Act, revised in 2004*	*Konkurrens-verhet* (KKV)	sweco
	Switzerland	*Act on Cartels, revised in 2003*	*Wettbewerbs-kommission* (WeKo)	swico

Conceptualising the outcome condition

The 'explanandum' of this chapter is the specific role of IRAs during the political decision-making processes under investigation. In order to obtain a single measure, a structural and a reputational approach are combined by asking the crucial actors the following questions:

(1) Which actor participated in a given phase of the decision-making process?
(2) What was the (political) weight of each actor?

The derived synthetic measure, aggregating *participation* and *weight*, represents *the centrality of IRAs* in the course of the selected decision-making processes. Concretely, the centrality of the political actors in the course of each decision-making process will be systematised and compared with the actor-process-event scheme (APES) (Serdült and Hirschi 2004; Serdült *et al.* 2005), an analytical tool that allows transforming process information from case studies into structural data in order to execute some simple operations of social networks analysis (SNA). The APES is a two-dimensional graph that links the participating actors with the different stages of the lawmaking process under investigation. In the process axis, we need to select the crucial events that comprise one or more stages of a policy cycle (Howlett and Ramesh 2003).[10] In the actor axis, we can distinguish whether an actor participates in an event and places a value on the weight of his participation. The second step is the transformation of the APES into a policy network.

The APES gives us information allowing us to create a data matrix containing data about event participation (two mode actor-event matrix). This first matrix is built by filling the cells with a zero (0) in case an actor did not participate in an event or with a value (e.g. 1) if an actor participated. Then, we have to transform this matrix into an actor-actor one, with the adequate procedure in UCINET (Borgatti et al. 2002), to obtain the symmetric relations between all pairs of actors (excluding the diagonal, which is meaningless here). The result should represent the policy network derived by process data. We then have a matrix that provides parsimonious, clear, and comparable data that we can analyse using the classical social network analysis tools. Here the centrality degrees of all participating actors are calculated to compare the range of values as ordinal categories within each policy network, with the aim of discovering which ones play a crucial role in each decision-making process.

Degree centrality is a measure of 'local popularity' that can be used to highlight the relative prominence of focal points, so as to identify the most important actors within the network (Everett and Borgatti 2005). This measure of centrality was chosen, among other possible, more structural, options because we cannot assume that the actors' participation in different phases of policy-making processes constitute a relational network possessing holistic properties. Therefore, the analysis focuses on the so-called ego-networks of participants, that is, concerning nodes that are directly connected to each participant, in order to ensure the validity of the measurement, even if this choice may imply a loss of accuracy. In addition, the assessment of local centrality is helpful, as it does not imply the existence of a single central point in the network (Scott 2000b). Instead, several local centres may emerge from the APES, according to the idea that different actors can hold central positions in the different events of the political decision-making process. Finally, the degrees of actors' centrality can be compared, by bearing in mind one limitation: the comparison of centrality scores are meaningful only among the members of the same graph, or between graphs of similar size, since the degree of a point depends also on the size of the graph. A simple solution for comparing the actors' degrees across networks is to analyse not their absolute values but the relative scores of the participants when situated on an ordinal scale of centrality.

In addition, it is worth stressing that, in the current application of the APES,

---

10. The definition of these events depends on the parameters of the political system and on the peculiar characteristic of the process under investigation.

an encompassing conceptualisation of centrality is adopted, which is not only structural but also reputational. Both actors' 'participation' and 'weight' are taken into account (Adam and Kriesi 2007). According to a structural approach, central individuals are those that dispose from positional power, so that they are the able to shape the policy process. For instance, they control the essential information, they perform key integrative and coordinating activities, and they represent the best functional partner for any subsystem. Following a reputational perspective, a reputation for influence indicates a latent capacity to affect the outcome of events in which the actor has an interest or stake (Knoke 1990; Diani 2003). Finally, the measurement of actors' centrality can be further interpreted thanks to detailed contextual information on the participation and weight during any phase of the processes, which is synthesised in the APES graphs.

The assessment of the outcome condition

To assess the outcome condition, which refers to the centrality of each agency, every actor who participated in the decision-making process is examined, using both theoretical literature and existing documentation about the specific cases, namely: the government, first chamber of the parliament, second chamber (if any), parliamentary committee of the first chamber, parliamentary committee of the second chamber (if any), public administration, IRA, other agencies and courts, employers and producers peak associations, consumer associations, liberal professionals, academic experts, trade unions, supervised institutions, the EU, and other actors (expert committees, individual companies, international organisations, etc.), as presented in Tables 4.3 - 4.8. The next step is the partition of the policy process into a series of discrete events. The mapping procedure starts with the existing literature over each type of decision-making process: (Colomer 2002; Andeweg and Irwin 2005) for The Netherlands; (Kriesi 1994; Peters 2001) for Sweden; (Kriesi 1994; Papadopoulos 1997; Sciarini 2002; Sciarini *et al.* 2002) for Switzerland. Then, the reading of the story is improved by information given by the actors themselves in a short series of electronic interviews, and with archive documents. The functional sequence of events is as follows:

1) agenda-setting
2) preliminary investigations
3) working out the draft
4) consultation
5) draft modification
6) decision
7) monitoring/implementation
8) sanctioning/evaluation

Then, for each process, an exploratory empirical investigation was executed, starting from a small number of electronic and telephone interviews, and written documentation.[11] In that way, it was possible to identify a number of crucial ministerial officials, civil servants, elected politicians, and agency board and staff members in the course of the investigated decision-making processes. Then, different categories of those crucial actors were interviewed by survey inquiry in order to gain knowledge about the 'participation' and 'weight' of each actor: The relevant services within the investigated agency; the offices in charge in the public administration; the chancellor/chairperson/members of the parliamentary commissions in charge.[12] Non-participation in a given event is coded 0. According to the reputational data, participation is coded 1 when the actor is in a merely passive phase (e.g. consultations) and when the actor is considered scarcely influential on the event (i.e. an average value of 1, 2, or 3 on the aggregated 7-point weight scale from the survey inquiry). Participation is coded 2 when the actor is considered influential to a certain extent (4, 5), and it is coded 3 when the actor is considered to be strongly influential (6, 7) with respect to the process.

Individual answers are aggregated first at the level of each category and then among categories. Concerning 'participation', any actor is taken into account even if only one interlocutor mentions him. Concerning 'weight', the simple average is calculated at the higher value. If a respondent does not mention an actor who is, however, mentioned by others, we consider that the former gives him the lowest weight. In the case of a huge discrepancy among answers, those cases would have needed a deeper examination with semi-directed interviews,

---

11. Written sources are annual agencies' reports; agencies', public administration's, and parliaments' Websites; drafts of the new pieces of legislation; expert commissions' reports; parliamentary debate documentation; and specialised press articles; agencies', public administration's, and parliaments' press releases.

12. Sources of data concerning the outcome conditions are as follows: Netbk: three questionnaires to the relevant services within the agency in charge; three questionnaires to the offices in charge in the public administration/ministry; two questionnaires to the chancellor/chairperson/members of the parliamentary commissions in charge; received between 22 May–14 June 2007; Swebk: two questionnaires to the relevant services within the agency in charge; two questionnaires to the offices in charge in the public administration/ministry; two questionnaires to the chancellor/ chairperson/members of the parliamentary commissions in charge; received between 18 May–19 June 2007; Swibk: two questionnaires to the relevant services within the agency in charge; two questionnaires to the offices in charge in the public administration/ministry; two questionnaires to the chancellor/chairperson/members of the parliamentary commissions in charge; received between 29 May–30 July 2007; Netco: three questionnaires to the relevant services within the agency in charge; three questionnaires to the offices in charge in the public administration/ ministry; two questionnaires to the chancellor/chairperson/members of the parliamentary commissions in charge; received between 22 May–24 July 2007; Sweco: two questionnaires to the relevant services within the agency in charge; three questionnaires to the offices in charge in the public administration/ministry; two questionnaires to the chancellor/chairperson/members of the parliamentary commissions in charge; received between 8 June–19 July 2007; Swico: two questionnaires to the relevant services within the agency in charge; two questionnaires to the offices in charge in the public administration/ministry; three questionnaires to the chancellor/ chairperson/members of the parliamentary commissions in charge; received between 26 April–9 July 2007.

but that was not the case. Questionnaires were precise and case-specific, non-anonymous, accompanied by electronic interviews, prepared and confirmed with written documentation, and without any reference to a research interest in the role of IRAs. Therefore, the information can be considered reliable (see the appendix for the details). [13]

The Analysis

Assessing centrality

The APES software was employed (Serdült *et al.* 2005) to draw the actor-process-event schemes (Tables 4.3 to 4.8) and derive the corresponding data matrices (reported in the appendix). The centrality degrees of participating actors were then calculated using the appropriate procedure in UCINET (Borgatti *et al.* 2002) so as to compare the relative centrality of actors within each policy network (as illustrated in Figure 4.2 and by the corresponding centrality values). As a result, we obtain the following typology concerning the agency's centrality in the investigated decision-making process:[14]

1.	*The agency is clearly the unique central actor (maxcentral).*	→	*Eidgenössische Bankenkommission*	(swibk)
		→	*Wettbewerbskommission*	(swico)
2.	*The agency is a central actor together with another actor (normally, the government).*	→	*Nederlandse Mededingingsautoriteit*	(netco)
		→	*Finansinspektionen*	(swebk)
		→	*Autoriteit Financiële Markten*	(netbk)
3.	*The agency is still important, but it is definitely not the central actor.*	→	*Konkurrensverhet*	(sweco)

---

13. The overall rate response was about 62 per cent (almost entirely due to a high non-response rate of members of parliaments, nearly equally distributed across countries and sectors).

14. The typology comprises three qualitatively different degrees of centrality. The QCA analysis focuses on the outcome of 'maximum centrality', because of the theoretical relevance of this result, and following a deliberate methodological choice: the output 'centrality with another actor' would be difficult to interpret; the outputs 'maximum centrality + centrality with another actor' and 'not the central actor' display a single negative outcome for the former, and respectively, a single positive outcome for the latter, both not corresponding to ideal situations in terms of the required variety of configurations.

Each agency holds an important position in the investigated decision-making processes, thus supporting Hypothesis 2.1. To be precise, it appears from the detailed information summarised in the APES that IRAs are not only central in the ordinary phase of policy implementation through the application of their regulatory competencies, but they are extensively included during lawmaking processes.

The Dutch act on the disclosure of major holdings and capital interests of 2006 (Wmz) was initiated by several actors, among which the most influential were the EU and the *Autoriteit Financiële Markten*. The centrality of the EU is not surprising, as the Wmz 2006 partly implements the European directive 2004/109/EC of 15 December 2004 on the harmonisation of transparency requirements in relation to information about issuers whose securities are admitted to trading on a regulated market. The agency was the other key player during the preliminary investigations for preparing the draft, and when working out the new bill. The government and the relevant offices of the public administration were able to modify the draft before adopting the new law, with the aim of increasing transparency and simplify the disclosure process. Professionals, independent experts and the supervised institutions were extensively consulted throughout the policy-making process. Finally, the agency was given the competencies of implementation, and sanctions in the case of non-respect of the new law are delegated to the agency together with courts.

The Dutch competition act of 2005 concerns above all the transition of the regulatory agency to an autonomous body. This revision was inspired by the *Nederlandse Mededingingsautoriteit*, the parliament, and the minister of economic affairs, following the existing EU model. The initial draft was also prepared with the support of this agency and subsequently modified by the government. It was decided that initially the agency should not be fully independent, but the bill was heavily amended in parliament and then put on hold while a more pressing bill was dealt with, the aim to bring the Competition Act in line with EC competition law. The parliamentary committees held several hearings and a number of academic experts was consulted, which influenced the new act through the report in the evaluation of the Competition Act 2002. Monitoring and sanctioning were ultimately established as shared competencies among the agency, the parliament, and the government, while appeals to the agency's decisions are possible in administrative tribunals.

The banking law committee promoted the development of the Swedish banking and finance business act of 2004, to reform financial and banking regulation and achieve uniformity with EU regulations. To this aim, an independent committee was charged with drafting a preliminary proposal for the new law. The ministry of finance worked out the draft, which had been circulated to interested parties for comments. The most important actors that modified the draft of the new law were the parliamentary committee of finance and a number of major Swedish companies. At the end of the day, the *Finansinspektionen* was given the responsibility for adopting the suitable regulations in order to implement the new framework, and it is in charge of the procedure of authorisation and notification and the day-to-day supervision of the regulated industries.

Concerning the Swedish competition act of 2004, we observe that the *Konkurrensverket* participate in several events of the decision-making process, but it seems truly important only in the phase of implementation and monitoring. The EU was crucial for inspiring the basic principles of the new law, that is, prohibiting companies from anti-competitive cooperation, concerning for instance prices and market sharing arrangements. Specifically, the act provides the Swedish Competition Authority with the power to carry out investigations and inspection of companies in order to collect evidence of practices contravening these prohibitions. The agency can order infringements of the prohibitions of the Act to be terminated, with the attachment of a fine. The government, namely through an executive committee of inquiry, is the most important actor in several crucial events, such as draft preparation and adoption, together with a number of independent experts. Courts are involved in competition law enforcement and can impose sanctions, the city court in first instance and the market court in final instance.

The *Eidgenössische Bankenkommission* was very important in setting the new act on the political agenda of banking regulation in Switzerland. The basic principles of the legal framework were inspired in accordance with key international organisations, namely the International Organisation of Securities Commissions (IOSCO) and the International Monetary Fund (IMF), following the internationalisation of financial markets. The crucial point was the necessity to improve the exchange of information with foreign authorities, for instance concerning insider trading crimes and other markets infringements. The agency was the most influential actor in draft preparation and when working out the draft of the Swiss stock exchange and securities traders act of 2006, in collaboration with the department of finance, academic experts and representatives of the regulated industries. After extensive external consultations, the government and parliament guided the phases of draft modification and adoption of the bill. The agency is the crucial actor for monitoring the respect of the new law, whilst the supervised institutions detain still important competencies of self-regulation. Sanctions in the case of non-respect can be decided by the agency and by courts.

The Swiss act on cartels of 2003 was largely determined by the *Wettbewerbskommission*, namely in its early stages: agenda-setting, preliminary investigations, consultations, and implementation and monitoring. The goal of the reform was to avoid any market distortion by extending the range of application of the act on cartels to each firm whatever its legal status, specifically by enhancing the competencies of the agency, through the possibility of new direct sanctions and more effective investigation capacities. Foreign experts invited by the extra-parliamentary committee, the public administration (notably the state secretariat for economic affairs – SECO) and the representatives of the regulated industries (through their peak association, *Economiesuisse*) had as well a certain impact in inspiring the principles of the new law. The offices of the public administration participated in the preparation and working out of the draft of the new law, with the help of external actors, such as the academic experts. The government participates extensively in the course of the decision-making process, but at the end of the day it appears hardly influential. Finally, the draft was quite importantly modified by the parliamentary committees, before the definite adoption and promulgation.

Tables 4.3–4.8 summarise each lawmaking process in great detail, with the help of the Actor-Process-Event Schemes. The policy networks derived from the APES are plotted in Figure 4.2, with corresponding centrality degrees of participating actors.

Table 4.3: The Netbk

Time / Actors	06
Political-administrative actors	
Government	1 ● 2 ● 3 ● 5 ● 6 ▲ 7 ◉
Parliament	◉ ◉ ▲
Parliamentary Committee(s)	◉ ●
Public Administration	● ● ● ◉
Independent bodies	
Independent Regulatory Agency	● ▲ ● 4 ◉ ▲ 8 ▲
Other Agencies or Courts	◉ ▲
Societal actors	
Employers' Associations	◉ ◉
Liberal Professionals	◉ ◉
Academic Experts	● ◉
Supervised Institutions	● ◉
Supranational actors	
European Union	● ◉ ◉

Table 4.4: The Netco

Time / Actors	05
Political-administrative actors	
Government	1 ● 2 ▲ 3 ▲ 4 ◉ 5 ◉ 6 ▲ 7 ◉ 8 ●
Parliament	▲ ◉ ▲ ◉
Independent bodies	
Independent Regulatory Agency	▲ ▲ ● ◉ ▲ ●
Other Agencies or Courts	● ◉
Societal actors	
Employers' Associations	◉ ◉
Consumers' Associations	◉
Liberal Professionals	◉
Academic Experts	▲ ●
Trade Unions	◉
Supranational actors	
European Union	●

Tables 4.3 – 4.8: APES Legend	
◉	Low weight (1, 2, 3) / passive participation
●	Medium weight (4, 5)
▲	High weight (6, 7) → maxcentral

Table 4.5: The Swebk

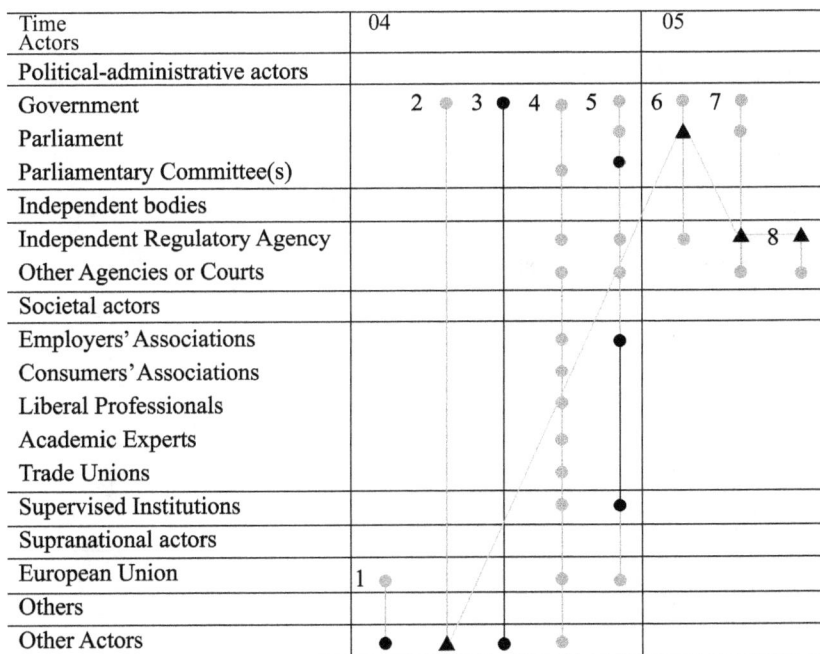

Time / Actors	04	05
Political-administrative actors		
Government	2 3 ● 4 5	6 7
Parliament		▲
Parliamentary Committee(s)	●	
Independent bodies		
Independent Regulatory Agency		▲ 8 ▲
Other Agencies or Courts		
Societal actors		
Employers' Associations	●	
Consumers' Associations		
Liberal Professionals		
Academic Experts		
Trade Unions		
Supervised Institutions	●	
Supranational actors		
European Union	1	
Others		
Other Actors	● ▲ ●	

Table 4.6: The Sweco

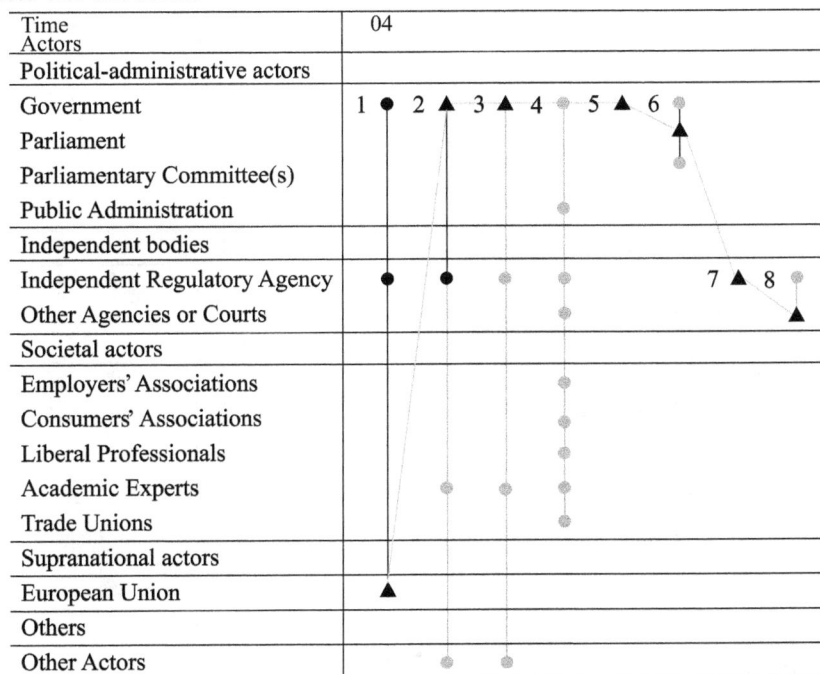

Time / Actors	04
Political-administrative actors	
Government	1 ● 2 ▲ 3 ▲ 4 5 ▲ 6
Parliament	▲
Parliamentary Committee(s)	
Public Administration	
Independent bodies	
Independent Regulatory Agency	● ● 7 ▲ 8
Other Agencies or Courts	▲
Societal actors	
Employers' Associations	
Consumers' Associations	
Liberal Professionals	
Academic Experts	
Trade Unions	
Supranational actors	
European Union	▲
Others	
Other Actors	

Table 4.7: The Swibk

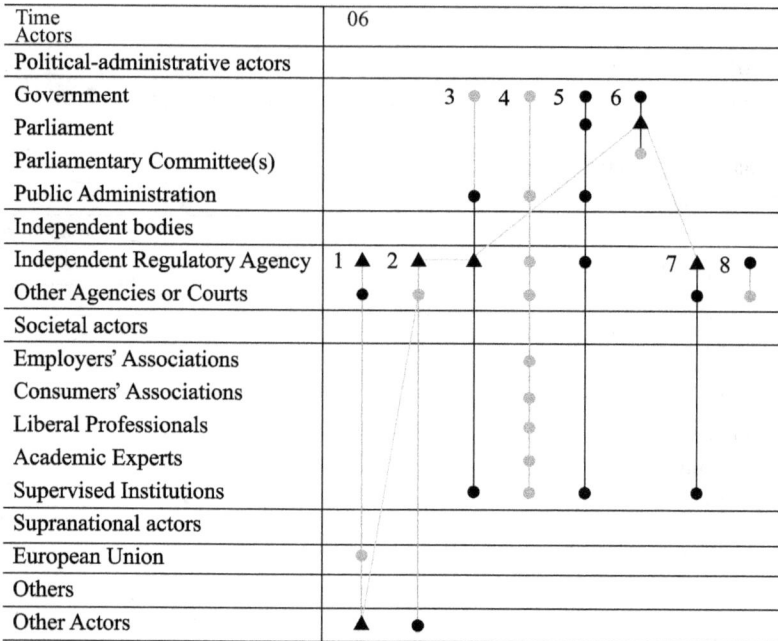

Time / Actors	06
Political-administrative actors	
Government	3 ● 4 ● 5 ● 6 ●
Parliament	● ▲
Parliamentary Committee(s)	●
Public Administration	● ● ●
Independent bodies	
Independent Regulatory Agency	1 ▲ 2 ▲ ▲ ● 7 ▲ 8 ●
Other Agencies or Courts	● ● ●
Societal actors	
Employers' Associations	●
Consumers' Associations	●
Liberal Professionals	●
Academic Experts	●
Supervised Institutions	● ● ● ●
Supranational actors	
European Union	●
Others	
Other Actors	▲ ●

Table 4.8: The Swico

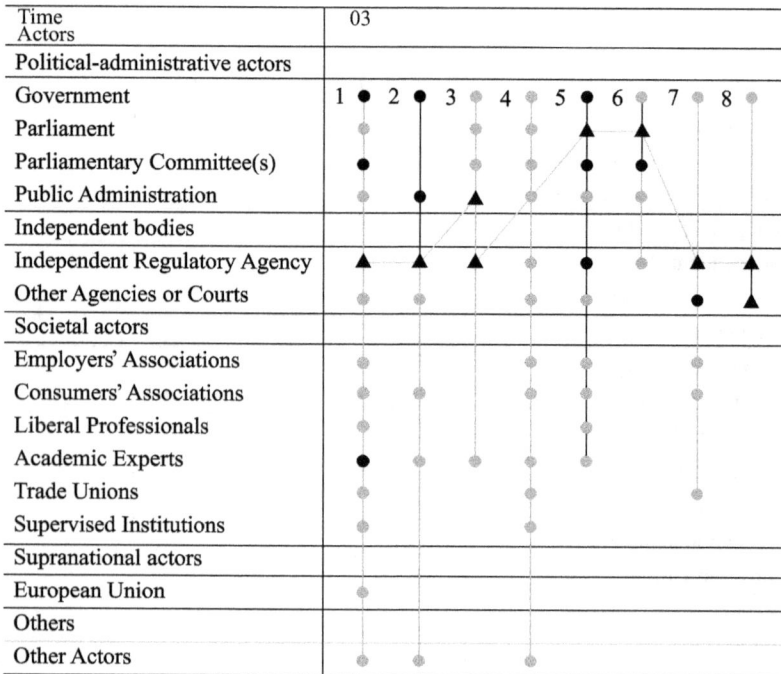

Time / Actors	03
Political-administrative actors	
Government	1 ● 2 ● 3 ● 4 ● 5 ● 6 ● 7 ● 8 ●
Parliament	● ▲ ▲
Parliamentary Committee(s)	● ● ●
Public Administration	● ▲
Independent bodies	
Independent Regulatory Agency	▲ ▲ ▲ ● ▲ ▲
Other Agencies or Courts	● ▲
Societal actors	
Employers' Associations	● ● ●
Consumers' Associations	● ● ● ● ●
Liberal Professionals	● ●
Academic Experts	● ● ● ●
Trade Unions	● ●
Supervised Institutions	● ●
Supranational actors	
European Union	●
Others	
Other Actors	● ● ●

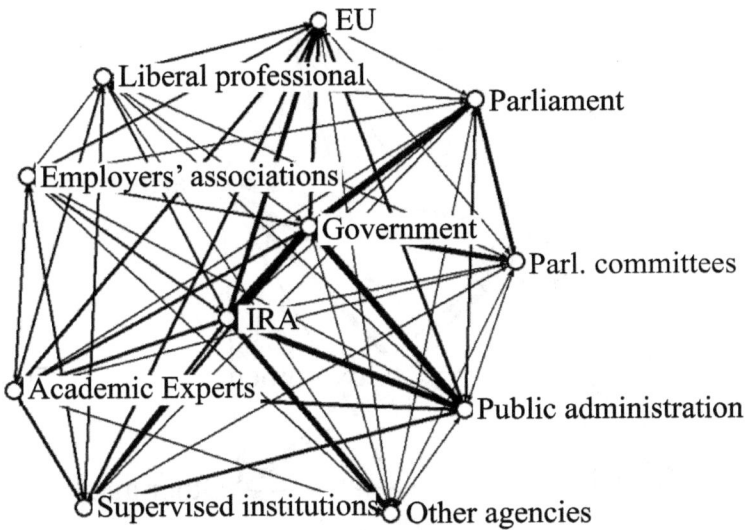

	Actors	Centrality
1.	Government	72
2.	IRA	70
3.	Public Administration	53
4.	European Union	42
5.	Academic Experts	35
6.	Supervised Institutions	35
7.	Parliament	34
8.	Parliamentary Comm.	28
9.	Other Agencies or Courts	25
10.	Liberal Professionals	21
11.	Empl./Prod. Associations	21

4.2a The Netbk

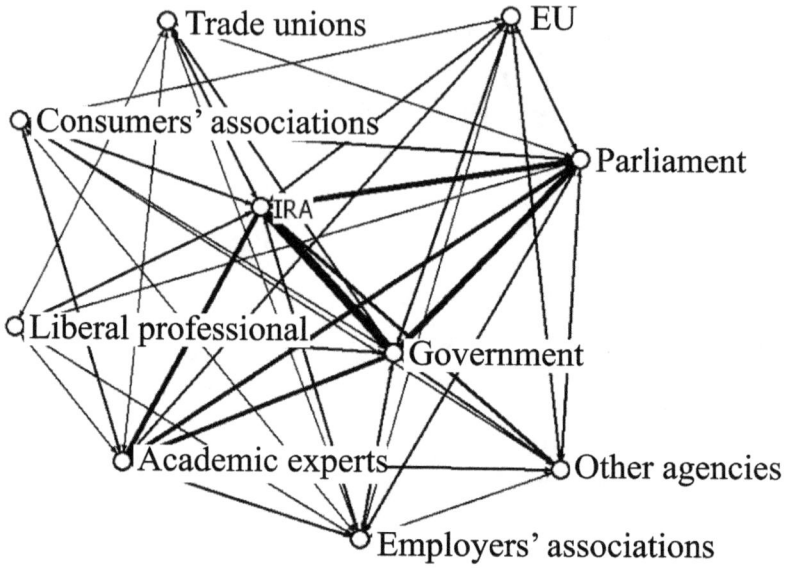

	Actors	Centrality
1.	IRA	90
2.	Government	87
3.	Parliament	68
4.	Academic Experts	62
5.	Other Agencies or Courts	32
6.	European Union	30
7.	Empl./Prod. Associations	27
8.	Consumers Associations	16
9.	Liberal Professionals	11
10.	Trade Unions	11

4.2b The Netco

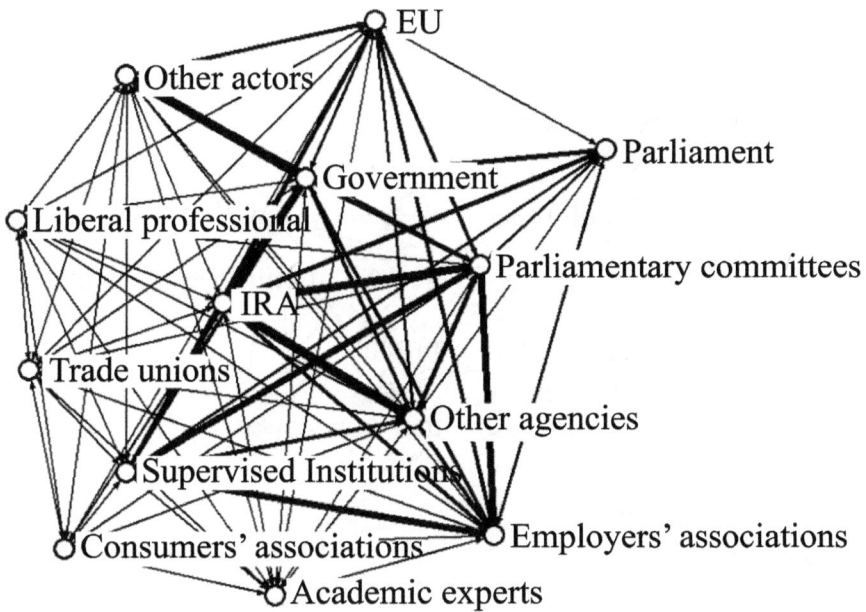

	Actors	Centrality
1.	Government	37
2.	IRA	37
3.	Parliamentary Comm.	34
4.	Other Agencies or Courts	29
5.	Supervised Institutions	29
6.	Empl./Prod. Associations	29
7.	European Union	23
8.	Other Actors	20
9.	Parliament	16
10.	Trade Unions	11
11.	Liberal Professionals	11
12.	Academic Experts	11
13.	Consumers Associations	11

4.2c The Swebk

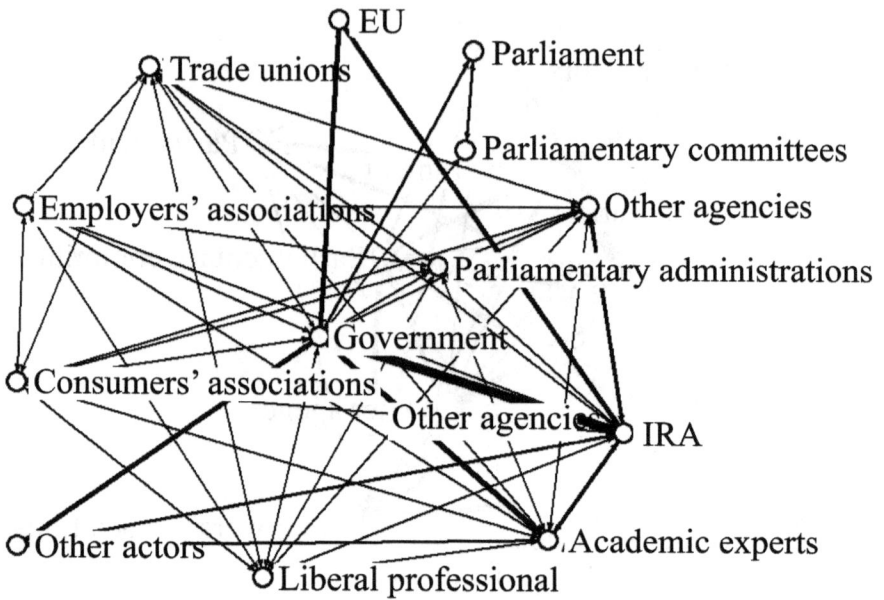

	Actors	Centrality
1.	Government	43
2.	IRA	36
3.	Academic Experts	19
4.	European Union	12
5.	Other Agencies or Courts	11
6.	Other Actors	11
7.	Consumers Associations	8
8.	Trade Unions	8
9.	Liberal Professionals	8
10.	Public Administration	8
11.	Empl./Prod. Associations	8
12.	Parliament	6
13.	Parliamentary Comm.	4

4.2d The Sweco

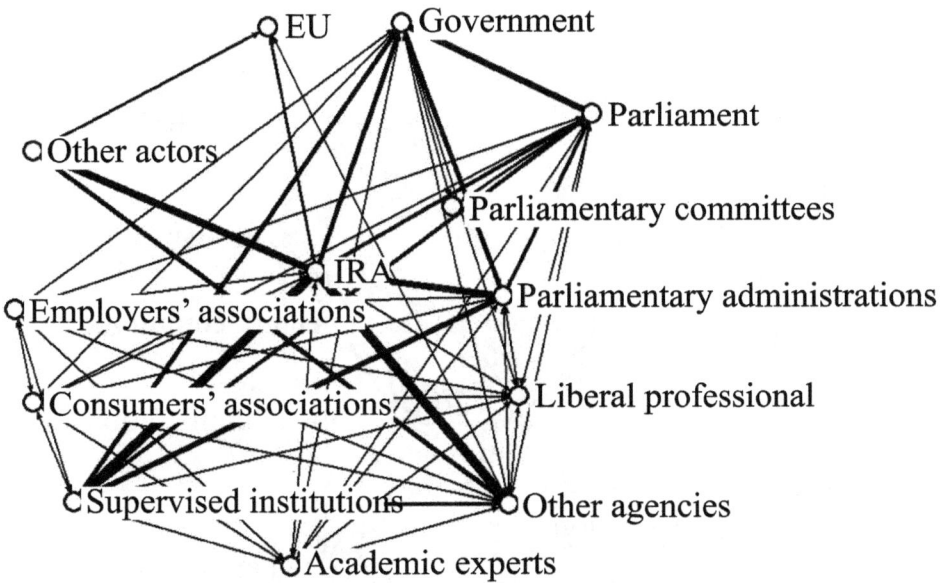

	Actors	Centrality
1.	IRA	81
2.	Supervised Institutions	47
3.	Government	40
4.	Other Agencies or Courts	40
5.	Public Administration	37
6.	Parliament	34
7.	Other Actors	26
8.	Liberal Professionals	9
9.	Academic Experts	9
10.	Consumers Associations	9
11.	Empl./Prod. Associations	9
12.	European Union	8
13.	Parliamentary Comm.	5

4.2e The Swibk

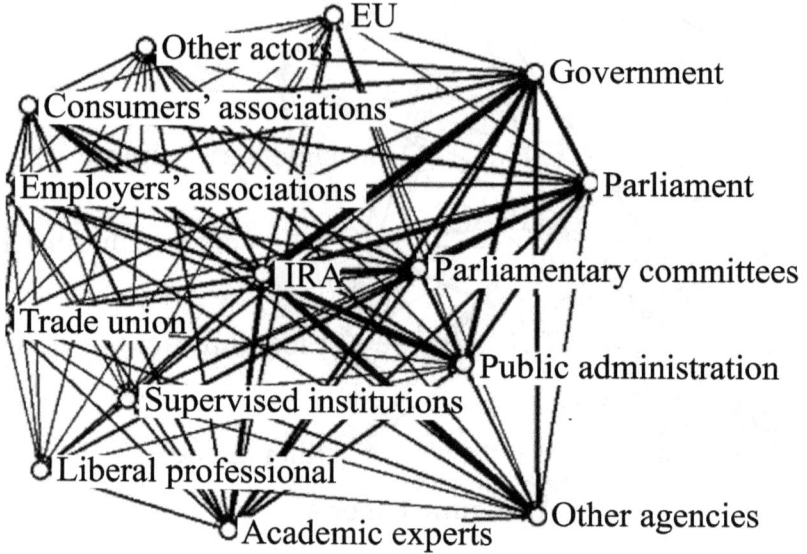

	Actors	Centrality
1.	IRA	168
2.	Government	120
3.	Parliamentary Comm.	94
4.	Public Administration	93
5.	Parliament	91
6.	Academic Experts	80
7.	Other Agencies or Courts	73
8.	Consumers Associations	71
9.	Empl./Prod. Associations	51
10.	Other Actors	40
11.	Trade Unions	37
12.	Liberal Professionals	32
13.	Supervised Institutions	30
14.	European Union	30

4.2f The Swico

Figure 4.2: Policy networks

QCA and results

Data, as prepared for the QCA analysis, are presented in Table 4.9. The explanatory conditions are coded as follows. For the first condition, the Swedish case is coded 1, as agencies are incorporated in a dualist system, while the code 0 corresponds to the Dutch and Swiss 'monocratic' models. The Netherlands and Sweden have specialised and professionalised legislatures; hence the second condition is coded 1 for these countries. Switzerland, conversely, which has a semi-professional parliament, is coded 0. The agencies regulating the banking and financial sector, where the need for technical expertise is expected to be the higher, are coded 1 for the third condition, while general competition agencies are coded 0. Finally, agencies possessing a medium/high level of de facto independence from the elected politicians and, respectively, from the regulatees are coded 1, whereas agencies possessing a lower level of de facto independence are coded 0. Concerning the outcome conditions, the code 1 corresponds to the maximal centrality of the agency.

Table 4.9: Data

case	Remote conditions		Proximate conditions			Outcome
	dual	profess	expert	defindpdm	defindreg	maxcentral
sweco	1	1	0	1	1	0
swico	0	0	0	1	0	1
netco	0	1	0	0	1	0
swibk	0	0	1	1	0	1
netbk	0	1	1	1	0	0
swebk	1	1	1	0	1	0

Then, the results of the analysis for remote factors and proximate factors are presented, using the Quine-McCluskey algorithm included in the Fs/QCA software (Ragin *et al.* 2006). As suggested by Schneider and Wagemann (2006), a two-step analysis is executed in order to reduce complexity so as to mitigate the problem of limited diversity and accurately model the causal structure of the argument. First, we discover remote factors that enable the occurrence of the outcome (see Table 4.10). Second, we combine proximate factors with the remote conditions in a more precise analysis in order to find out necessary and sufficient combinations of conditions (see Table 4.11).

Remote Factors

In this step, outcome 1 is explained, while outcome 0 is set as 'false'; remainders are set as 'don't care' in order to obtain a parsimonious statement on outcome-fostering context (Schneider and Wagemann 2006). At this stage, no *necessary* conditions are discovered. However, the analysis shows that a single remote condition is *potentially sufficient* for the outcome of maxcentral: *'profess,'* that is, the non-professionalisation of the legislature. Following Schneider and

Wagemann, this condition is then included into the dataset for analysing proximate factors.

Table 4.10: Truth table – remote factors

	Remote conditions		Outcome
case	dual	profess	maxcentral
sweco, swebk	1	1	0
swico, swibk	0	0	1
netco, netbk	0	1	0

Proximate Factors

In this second step, we explain outcome 1; outcome 0 is set as 'false,' and remainders are also set as 'false' (which means that no simplifying assumptions are allowed on the logical remainders), applying stricter analytical criteria and parameters in order to obtain the more complex and precise solution (Schneider and Wagemann 2006). The QCA solution shows that a single *sufficient combination* of conditions leads to the outcome of maximal centrality of IRAs. Specifically, the combination of conditions that (in the population here represented) jointly explains the maximal centrality of agencies in policy making is: the non-professionalisation of the legislature, coupled with scarce de facto independence from the regulatees and agencies' high de facto independence from the political decision makers. This result is very robust, because I tested in the first step 3 of the 4 possible combinations (the unique non-observed combination being theoretically implausible and empirically very rare). In the second step, I tested 6 of the 16 possible combinations. However, when the necessary condition (defindpdm) is excluded from the dataset, I obtain the combination profess*defindreg, which is virtually identical to the one offered above and is based on 6 observed cases out of 8. In addition, the non-observed cases refer mainly to a number of combinations that are, as said, not empirically plausible (or irrelevant) (e.g. a low de facto independence from both the political decision makers and the regulatees) (Maggetti 2007).

Table 4.11: Truth table – proximate factors

	Remote c.	Proximate conditions			Outcome
case	profess	expert	defindpdm	defindreg	maxcentral
sweco	1	0	1	1	0
swico	0	0	1	0	1
netco	1	0	0	1	0
swibk	0	1	1	0	1
netbk	1	1	1	0	0
swebk	1	1	0	1	0

The latter condition (*DEFINDPDM*) also appears to be individually *necessary* for the outcome. This point is consistent with prior knowledge, because the two latter conditions could be mutually constitutive (Maggetti 2007). In other words, a low de facto independence from the regulatees usually implies a high de facto independence from the political decision makers. This is the case of the swibk and the swico, in opposition to the sweco, where both conditions are present.

The solution can be summarised with the following expression:

$$profess * defindreg * DEFINDPDM \rightarrow MAXCENTRAL \ (swico+swibk)$$

Discussion

This solution must be interpreted as a causal whole. The non-professionalisation of the legislature, the scarce de facto independence from the regulatees and the high de facto independence from the political decision makers are to be considered as individually necessary parts of the unique sufficient combination (X) that leads to the maximal centrality of agencies in policy making (Y). Adopting a more formalised QCA terminology, X is a sufficient condition of Y when X is a subset of Y (Goertz 2003), where X = *profess * defindreg * DEFINDPDM*, and Y = MAXCENTRAL (see Figure 4.3). Here, X can also be considered as a relevant condition. We demonstrated indeed that this combination occurs quite frequently in the real world (2 instances out of 6), while, conversely, trivial sufficient conditions are those where X tends to 0 for all the possible cases.

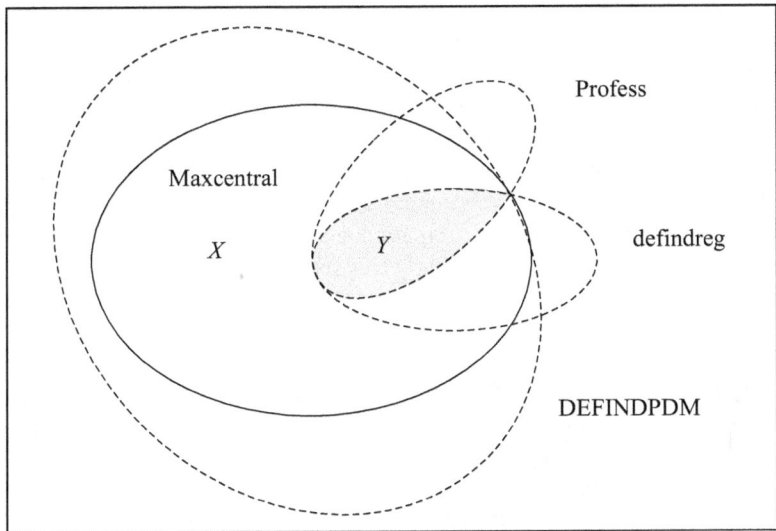

Figure 4.3: Graphical representation of the solution

Before concluding, it is worth discussing the individual role of each single condition in relation with the theoretical expectations. The results of the QCA analysis do not support Hypothesis 2.2; the presence of a monocratic system does not lead to higher agencies' centrality. Hence, the organisational logic of appropriateness, with reference to the political-administrative culture, is not helpful for explaining the outcome of maximal centrality of agencies. Similarly, there is no data to maintain the idea that sector-specific IRAs regulating technical issues are more central in political decision making than general regulators. This means that sectoral patterns of regulation are not decisive for including IRAs in policy making, disconfirming our Hypothesis 2.4. Conversely, evidence corroborates Hypothesis 2.3, showing that a non-professionalised parliamentary system, which is a characteristic of the Swiss political system, seems to lead to higher centrality of agencies in lawmaking. The other condition that is jointly sufficient to explain the outcome of maximal agencies' centrality is the low de facto independence from the regulatees, and the related necessary presence of high de facto independence from the political decision makers, which is in line with our expectations with reference to Hypotheses 2.5a and 2.5b. Those agencies are plausibly perceived as credible veto players by the political decision-makers. This is the case of the swibk, the swico, and to a certain extent, the netbk.

This result can be interpreted as follows. When non-professional legislators that suffer from a lack of material and symbolic resources must cope with a regulator that might challenge the later stages of the policy-making process, due to its low de facto independence from those being regulated, they will have strong incentives to include ex-ante this agency in policy making for obtaining relevant information and in order to overcome any possible conflict or resistance during the implementation process. Given the above mentioned result, we can also conclude that agencies are actually influential in substantial policy-making processes and do not simply perform a political function of legitimisation. However, the ultimate empirical validation of the causal relations identified above will imply a further step, that is, a qualitative and systematic study of sequences of causal mechanisms influencing the role of each participating actor in the course of the political processes, such as the 'process tracing' analysis (George and Bennett 2005).

Conclusion

Formally independent regulatory agencies (IRAs), together with their regulatory competencies of rule-making, monitoring, adjudication, and sanctioning, often participate in policy making, from policy formulation to implementation. In fact, IRAs, due to their broad competencies, vast resources, and acquaintance with the regulated sector are likely to initiate new pieces of legislation, offer expertise to parliaments and governments, and ensure the implementation of the new laws. They are thus expected to hold a key role in lawmaking. Yet IRAs have hardly been the target of systematic policy analyses, possibly for the reason that it is difficult to assess and compare their role in cross-sectoral and cross-national comparisons.

This chapter focused on the assessment and examination of IRAs' political influence in policy making. Specifically, six decision-making processes were studied in three small corporatist European countries – The Netherlands, Sweden, and Switzerland – and two policy domains – finance and competition, related to the development of a crucial piece of legislation in the range of competencies of the related IRA in the years 2000-2006. A structural approach is combined with a reputational approach, drawing from both survey and documental information about the participation and weight of each actor in the course of the decision-making process under investigation, in order to calculate the degrees of centrality of IRAs in the course of lawmaking. The theoretical expectations were then tested with a two-step qualitative comparative analysis (Schneider and Wagemann 2006).

The analysis shows two crucial empirical findings. First, in line with the first hypothesis, IRAs are highly central in the course of each political decision-making process under scrutiny. As the actor-process-event schemes (Serdült and Hirschi 2004) clearly illustrate, not only are agencies crucial in the implementation phase, but also they actively participate in the whole process, especially in agenda-setting and pre-parliamentary discussions. Second, following the qualitative comparative analysis, a combination of conditions that is jointly sufficient to explain the maximal centrality of agencies in policy making is identified, confirming Hypotheses 3 and 5: the effect of the non-professionalisation of the legislature and scarce de facto independence of the IRA in charge from those being regulated. Moreover, the high de facto independence from political decision makers is a necessary condition for the outcome. This is the case of the Swiss Federal Banking Commission in the course of the revision of the stock exchanges act of 2006 and the Swiss Competition Commission during the revision of the act on cartels of 2003. In addition, it should be noted that Hypothesis 2, on the role of the politico-administrative culture, and Hypothesis 4, on the distinction between sector-specific and general regulation, are not supported by the results.

From this empirical chapter, we can derive three main insights. To begin with, IRAs are the most central actor in policy making related to their area of competence, more than expert commissions, organised interest representatives, and ordinary agencies subordinated to the ministerial level. This point corroborates the arguments about the rise of an age of 'regulocracy' (Levi-Faur 2005a) and 'agencification' (Christensen and Lægreid 2005). Yet the influential role of agencies in lawmaking epitomises the ambivalence of the concepts of regulatory state and regulatory capitalism. The term 'regulation' does not only connote the shift from state's interventionism to the decline of public authority in favour of market freedom, which would imply at best mere steering functions. It also illustrates the proliferation of a relatively new type of public body that endorses new regulatory functions to promote stricter, more transparent and more formalised rules, that should constrain the markets and sustain the so-called public interest (whatever this notion is defined by the political decision makers), representing thus an expansion of public authority.

At the same time, the centrality of IRAs in lawmaking, both from the point of view of their structural participation and their reputational weight, suggests that the activity of formally independent regulators is not limited to the execution of the delegated *regulatory* competencies (i.e. market supervision and technical regulatory functions). Interestingly, it shows that they are also developing a key *political* role and may exert significant political power in practice. They hold distinctive lawmaking functions, being particularly influential in agenda-setting and when preparing the drafts of the new bills. At the end of the day, the distinction between the political arena and the supposedly depoliticised, technocratic activity of specialised bodies offering technical expertise appears to be blurred.

Finally, it appears that the level of de facto independence – the distinctive feature of IRAs – may affect their centrality in policy making, in combination with other variables. On the one hand, the analysis suggests that the level of de facto independence from elected politicians is positively related to the need for including IRAs in policy making for problem-solving reasons, while their de facto independence from regulatees modifies the structure of incentives for including them strategically in policy making, in order to avoid any possible implementation failure. On the other hand, external factors, such as the professionalisation of the legislature, can alter the influence of IRAs in the course of lawmaking processes, by shaping their policy relevance for political decision-makers.

The conditions of generalisation of these results require a short comment. In fact, the relative centrality of IRAs could (also) be conditional on the structure of the decision-making process under investigation, which was purposely kept constant in the present comparison. Nonetheless, it is plausible that the causal connections identified above will hold independently of the type of political system and political economy, because they do not seem contingent on specific features of the selected countries and sectors. In fact, the relation between agencies' de facto independence and their centrality in policy making constitutes a 'meso-level effect' that is mostly due to organisational-level variables, under ceteris paribus conditions (Ricart *et al.* 2004). However, in this regard, further in-depth research is welcome, especially concerning the mechanisms underlying the causal relations identified above.

chapter five | the media coverage of agencies (part iii)

Summary

Independent regulatory agencies (IRAs), besides the expected benefits in terms of credibility and efficiency, are said to bring about a 'democratic deficit', following their statutory separateness from democratic institutions. Consequently, a 'multi-pronged system of control' is required. This chapter focuses on a specific component of this system, that is, the media. The goal is to determine whether media coverage of IRAs meets the necessary prerequisites to be considered a potential 'accountability forum' for regulators. The results of a comparison of two contrasted cases – the British and Swiss competition commissions – mostly support the expectations, since they show that media coverage of IRAs corresponds to that of the most relevant policy issues and follows the regulatory cycle. Furthermore, a systematic bias in media coverage can be excluded.

Introduction

IRAs epitomise a mode of governance in line with the observation that 'the real work of running democracies is now carried out by the unelected' (Vibert 2007). This apparent imbalance between power and responsibility led to the identification of a 'democratic deficit' in the European regulatory state (Majone 1999; Roberts 2001; Majone 2002; Follesdal and Hix 2006). Whereas the diagnosis of the intensity of this deficit may vary, it has been observed that governments can delegate regulatory authority to independent regulators, but not their democratic legitimacy, leading to a 'net loss' of democratic legitimacy for the political system (Majone 1999, 2001b, 2005; Maggetti 2009b, 2010).

In response to these considerations, it was argued that 'majoritarian standards' of legitimacy are not appropriate for independent regulators (Majone 2002). Their legitimacy should instead be appreciated with reference to alternative standards, especially through the revivification of the concept of 'accountability'. Majone points repeatedly to the need for a 'multi-pronged system of controls' to keep regulatory bodies accountable (Majone 1996b, 2002). This system consists of a variety of control mechanisms, such as (1) specification of clear and narrow objectives; (2) oversight by governmental and parliamentary committees; (3) procedural requirements like hearings and reporting duties; (4) judicial review; (5) professionalism and peer review; and (6) transparency and public participation. Academic research has focused so far on the first four points, which refer to traditional accountability arrangements between bureaucracy and other branches of the state (Schedler 1999; Mulgan 2000, 2003; Lodge 2004; Verschuere *et al.* 2006; Busuioc 2009), and, to a lesser extent, to the fifth mechanism, which is distinctive of independent bodies (Maggetti and Gilardi 2010). Conversely, the last solution has been either neglected or dismissed as scarcely relevant, because direct public participation in regulatory governance is considered empirically negligible and even normatively undesirable (Sosay 2006). In particular, it is believed that the participation of an increased heterogeneous number of actors would undermine the decision-making capacity of IRAs, i.e. their raison d'être (Majone 1999).

The goal of this chapter is to examine another, indirect, possible venue for securing transparency and responsiveness in regard to independent regulators, that is, their media coverage (Arnold 2004; Voltmer 2010). In this context, a specific question is explored: can the media help to hold independent regulators accountable, in line with the observation that 'in many countries, the media are fast gaining power as informal forums for political accountability' (Bovens 2007)? The next two sections discuss the relevance of media scrutiny for the accountability of regulators and, respectively, present some exploratory expectations about the frequency and tone of media coverage. Then, these expectations are operationalised for two contrasted cases: the British and Swiss competition commissions. The empirical analysis and conclusions follow. The main findings indicate that the media coverage of agencies corresponds to that of the most relevant policy issues and follows approximately the regulatory cycle. Furthermore, a systematic negative or positive bias in media coverage can be excluded.

Accountability and the Media

Thomas Jefferson, in the spirit of the first amendment to the US' Constitution, notoriously stated that

> the functionaries of every government have propensities to command at will the liberty and property of their constituents. There is no safe deposit for these but with the people themselves, nor can they be safe with them without information. Where the press is free, and every man able to read, all is safe.

> (Thomas Jefferson to Charles Yancey, 1816.)

In this vein, recent studies have shown that mass media are 'by far the most important' source of information about officials' performance (Arnold 2004), representing a 'necessary condition' for the existence of democratic government (Dahl 1989) and a precondition for accountability (Coglianese and Howard 1998; Lee 1999; Besley and Burgess 2001; Besley *et al.* 2002; Voltmer 2010). The media can play a key role in enabling citizens – who have imperfect information about government activities – to monitor the actions of ministers and civil servants, leading to government that is more accountable and responsive to its citizens (Besley and Burgess 2001; Besley *et al.* 2002; Besley and Prat 2006) and rendering elected politicians more accountable (Roberts 2002; Strömberg 2004; Louw 2005; Snyder and Strömberg 2008). Ideally, free media are expected to act as the societal institution that 'contributes to public accountability without being under the control to any other actor' (Fox 2000), that is, following a relatively endogenous logic stemming from market incentives and journalistic goals (Besley and Prat 2006). In particular, active and persistent media coverage encourages the formation of an informed public opinion (O'Donnell 1998), while press criticism and support are considered crucial for obtaining justifications from governments and civil service (Meyer 2004). The media could theoretically provide an 'accountability forum' (Bovens 2007) that is particularly suitable for IRAs, constituting 'one element of a complex accountability system' (Hodge and Coghill 2007), which would not hinder their independence (Majone 1996b, 2002).

Accountability means that an actor who is in a position of responsibility in relationship to the interests of another actor is required to *give an account* of the conduct of his duties, while the second actor can either *reward or sanction* the former (Schedler 1999; Castiglione 2006). Bovens underlines the fact that accountability should be conceptualised as a social relationship between an actor and its 'accountability forum', which can be an individual or collective actor through whom the first actor is held accountable (Bovens 2007). Following Bovens, in many countries, the media are fast gaining power as informal forums for political accountability (Bovens 2007). The media might constitute a particularly relevant accountability forum for IRAs for two reasons. First, public communication is a requisite for the accountability of political institutions (Sarcinelli 1987; Dahl 1989), which is particularly important when policy making takes place behind closed doors and scarce democratic responsiveness exists (Voltmer and Eilders 2003). In fact, the media do guide opinion formation and perception (de Vreese *et al.* 2006), especially when they cover issues that are overly technical or with which individuals are less familiar (Zaller 1992; Vogel 1996; Bryant and Zillmann 2002). This is the case of independent regulators, whereby citizens derive most of what they know about the issues from the media, and in turn the media might help to 'extend' the accountability of these bodies (Scott 2000a).

Second, the media represent a venue for policymakers for the appraisal of regulatory outcomes, performing a 'fire-alarm' function (McCubbins *et al.* 1987). Because the political principals suffer from a structural informational disadvantage *vis-à-vis* independent regulatory agencies, they must rely on external sources of information to monitor whether the agency is acting according to the predefined notion of the 'public interest' before eventually deciding to engage in costly political-oversight activities (Hopenhayn and Lohmann 1996). As such, media coverage constitutes an important 'linkage mechanism' between regulatory agencies and policy-makers (Waterman *et al.* 1998; Waterman and Rouse 1999; Carpenter 2002b), by playing a key role in communicating policy ideas and framing issues (Coglianese and Howard 1998). At the same time, the media affect the setting of the political agenda (Walgrave *et al.* 2008), given that decision-makers, for instrumental reasons, look for regulatory policies that reflect so-called public opinion (Stimson *et al.* 1994).

Therefore, the accountability of IRAs in front of the media can be examined by operationalising the two components of the definition outlined above: on the one hand, (1) the extent to which the media give an account of IRAs' conduct can be measured with the amount of media coverage with reference to the official goals of delegation, that is, the expected credibility of regulators associated with their supposed independence and the aspiration of enhancing decision-making efficiency thanks to their technical expertise (Majone 1994b, 1996a, 1997a, b; Gilardi 2002b; Moran 2002; Thatcher 2002a, b, c; Elgie and McMenamin 2005; Levi-Faur 2005a). Policy credibility is the expectation that an announced policy will be properly carried out (Drazen and Masson 1994) in order to create credible policy commitments *vis-à-vis* stakeholders (e.g. foreign investors), consumers, and citizens (Shepsle 1991). It is considered a crucial condition for solving the time-inconsistency problem related to the political cycle (Kydland and Prescott 1977; Barro and Gordon 1983). Decision-making efficiency refers to the resource-saving implementation of predetermined goals (Blühdorn 2006). That is, it involves reducing decision-making costs by taking advantage of agencies' expertise, while avoiding the enactment of policies that are different from those preferred by the political decision-makers (Epstein and O'Halloran 1999; Bendor *et al.* 2001; Majone 2001c)[1]. On the other hand, (2) the positive or negative tone of media coverage relating to agencies' credibility and efficiency can be considered an important symbolic sanction or reward, both of which have crucial consequences on their activeness, effectiveness and prospect for survival. In fact, 'not only performance but also the perceived appearance of performance [...] challenges the organisation's legitimacy and potential survival' (Lodge 2002). The tone of the media's coverage is particularly important from a reputational perspective. On the one hand, the media represent a point of view that is socially relevant for building a reputation of credibility; that is, a point of view that is relevant when regulatees, stakeholders and the public at large believe in the proper implementation of the announced policies and make choices based upon these expectations (Brabazon 2000). By analogy, in business management literature it is widely accepted that media-provided information affects the credibility of firms and, consequently, investors' behaviour, influencing such performances as price rate and stock turnover (Pollock and Rindova 2003). In fact, the media constitute a crucial element of the process of contagion that proceeds from the level of

---

1. The explanatory power of these normative arguments is limited, as there is cumulative evidence supporting the relevance of non-functional factors for the establishment of independent regulators, drawing from organisational theory and sociological institutionalism (Gilardi 2005b; Christensen and Yesilkagit 2006a). In particular, emulative processes and strategies for coping with political uncertainty and blame shifting are frequently highlighted (Thatcher and Stone Sweet 2002; Gilardi 2005b; Christensen and Yesilkagit 2006b; Gilardi 2008). However, the official goals of delegation in terms of credibility and efficiency represent a relevant analytical benchmark when, instead of examining why agencies are created, the focus is on the consequences of delegating public authority to IRAs, such as in the present research study. These official goals are further relevant because, from a new institutional perspective, although created following dynamics of symbolic diffusion, once in place, agencies are expected to 'take on a life of their own' (Pollack 1996), and exert also a direct impact on regulatory practices (Christensen and Lægreid 2003).

individual cognition to the level of social propagation and back to that of individual cognition, transmitting the image of the corporation through an informal network and eventually affecting its credibility (Balboni 2008). On the other hand, the tone of the media's evaluation of efficiency is crucial for IRAs. The media provide a forum for debate and dissemination of information, recording evaluations, reducing information asymmetry, and influencing the opinion of stakeholders by reputational mechanisms (Deephouse 2000), while organisational reputation is an essential property of regulators that largely influences the effectiveness of their actions (i.e. the factual delivery of their intended outcomes) (Blühdorn 2006). Specifically, a reputation for efficiency allows agencies to build networks and coalitions, exert political influence, increase their room for maneuvering *vis-à-vis* elected politicians, and reinforce their position before those being regulated (Carpenter 2001b; Carpenter 2001a). In addition, it is instrumental in gaining support from interest groups concerned with regulatory reforms (Krause and Douglas 2005).

Expectations about the Media Accountability of Agencies

It has been noted that political communication is increasingly 'mediated': political actors depend on the mass media to reach and mobilise citizens (Manin 1996), and citizens ever more frequently form their political opinions based on what they learn from the news media (Swanson and Mancini 1996; Gerber 1999; Hallin and Mancini 2004). Furthermore, it has been observed that the media can act as a partially autonomous actor that shapes political institutions and informs the public with growing independence from governments, parties and interest groups (Mazzoleni and Schulz 1999; Kepplinger 2002; Strömbäck and Esser 2009). However, one should recognise that the media is not necessarily impartial when evaluating agencies' functioning. On the one hand, politicians and representatives of organised groups can try to use the media strategically to convey their points of view. On the other hand, they also follow their commercial and/or ideological goals. Therefore, the media are neither neutral evaluators reflecting reality nor mere channels of communication for political actors (Strömbäck and Esser 2009). They are indeed involved in the process of constructing reality, and impose their views on the story (Swanson 1981; Mazzoleni 1987; Altheide and Snow 1988). In addition, media are selective, that is, media do not cover everything that political actors do, but do focus on those issues that have 'the most direct impact on the public' (Coglianese and Howard 1998), and on 'important and interesting news' (Cook 1998). Whether the media can however provide the minimal conditions to render IRAs accountable – notwithstanding the above mentioned shortcomings and variations in the institutional settings, political-administrative factors, varieties of media systems and agencies characteristics – constitutes the main empirical question of this chapter, similarly to previous research on the media coverage of the U.S. Congress (Arnold 2004). Nonetheless, the actual influence of the media on public opinion, politicians and regulators is beyond the scope of this piece of research, which is limited to the exploration of the subsistence of minimal prerequisites for considering the media as a potential accountability forum for IRAs.

As anticipated in the previous section, the first component of media accountability corresponds to evidence of regular media scrutiny of IRAs with reference to their official goals, credibility and efficiency, consistently with the ideal account of media as watchdogs of the political process (Besley *et al.* 2002; Curran 2005). However, establishing an absolute benchmark for the level of media coverage would be arbitrary. Instead, it can be appraised with the following three indications, which are in line with previous research on media accountability (Arnold 2004; Voltmer 2010): (1) the average frequency of news regarding IRAs' credibility and efficiency should be roughly comparable to that of other politically relevant issues; (2) given the growing role of independent regulators, the frequency of media coverage, at aggregated level, should follow a positive trend; and (3) media attention is expected to follow the regulatory cycle: news are expected to peak around events that are relevant for the investigated IRAs, such as the opening of a new important inquiry or the publication of the annual report.

The other component of accountability is even trickier to detect. The solution adopted in this chapter is to consider that media do apply symbolic sanctions and rewards when they consistently employ a negative or positive tone in news stories that have an evaluative focus regarding the credibility and efficiency of IRAs. Three minimal expectations regarding the tone of media evaluation can be mentioned: (4) the evaluation of agencies' *credibility* should vary across cases and not be systematically conditioned by a positive bias, which could stem from the widespread perception of the independent regulator as a 'taken for granted' organisational model and 'socially valued' solution for creating credible commitments (Gilardi 2005b); (5) while it has been observed that political news that explicitly evaluates performance is typically negative in tone (Kepplinger and Weißbecker 1991; Lee 1999; Clark 2005), the consistent evaluation of agencies' *efficiency* requires media to avoid an unconditional negative bias; and (6) since the media are simultaneously the most important channel of communication for agencies and its most attentive observer (Coglianese and Howard 1998; Lee 1999; Besley and Burgess 2001; Besley *et al.* 2002; Voltmer 2010), the media coverage is expected to frame IRAs' credibility and efficiency as typical issues of general interest, and thus focus on the topics that are considered relevant for the public. Therefore, the main hypothesis of this chapter can be formulated as follows.

H 3.1   The media can function as an 'accountability forum' for independent regulatory agencies.

In addition, as a subsidiary hypothesis, one can expect that the media evaluations of credibility and efficiency go together, or, at least, that the two properties are not a priori incompatible, following the two functional logics of delegation to IRAs (Majone 2001a).

H 3.2   IRAs can be evaluated as credible and efficient at the same time.

Methodology

Case Selection and the Logic of the Comparison

Following the idea that 'one strategy for explanation [...] would be to select administrative systems that differ most and, from the research into those systems, develop propositions that appear to hold true regardless of the vast differences that may exist among the research locales' (Peters 2004), this examination of media coverage aims to explore two cases for which IRAs share a medium-high level of factual independence from politicians (Maggetti 2007) – given that effective delegation is a necessary precondition for the analysis – but that ideally diverge in the other macro- and meso-conditions that might influence the media evaluation of agencies. The aforementioned expectations can be validated or dismissed by comparing two cases that are situated at the two extremes on a continuum of the expected media evaluation of credibility and efficiency: a 'most likely' and a 'least likely' case (Gerring 2007a, b). This way, it possible to examine whether the media can function as an accountability forum despite variations in political-administrative factors, institutional settings, media systems and agencies' characteristics. The application of this research design also permits drawing a conclusion based on a counterfactual case-oriented logic. For instance, if a theory is disconfirmed even for the 'most likely' case, this can be considered a strong argument against that theory. Similarly, when a theory is confirmed even for the 'least-likely' case, it means that this theory deserves further attention and consideration (Gerring 2004, 2007a; Seawright and Gerring 2008).

According to this logic, two IRAs are selected: the British Competition Commission (CC) and the Swiss Competition Commission (ComCo), both established at the beginning of 2000 with the official purpose of promoting 'non-majoritarian' regulatory governance (Wilks and Bartle 2002; Maggetti *et al.* 2011). Competition policy is a politically salient regulatory issue for electorally sensitive politicians (Elgie and McMenamin 2005), when the functionalist logic of delegation is strong (Christensen and Yesilkagit 2006), for which media coverage of credibility and efficiency should be particularly accurate. In addition, media coverage is examined for a commensurable period of time that is sufficiently long to avoid any potential bias due to contingent phenomena: the years 2006 and 2007[2]. It is worth stressing that the decisive argument for selecting this timeframe is reminiscent of the regulatory issues under investigation in the two countries. A similar big issue was examined in both cases: high concentration in the grocery market, which also represents a topic that is ideologically quite neutral on the left-right divide. Specifically, the selected media reported the following issues (as percentages): in the United Kingdom (UK), grocery markets (39 per cent), aviation regulation (17 per cent), TV media plurality (16 per cent), home credit

---

2.   This choice seems reasonable as Arnold's landmark study of the media accountability of the U.S. congress also comprises two years (Arnold 2004).

markets (8 per cent), book chains (6 per cent), payment protection insurance (3 per cent), price controls on business banks (2 per cent), store cards (2 per cent), the telephone directories market (2 per cent), and others (5 per cent); in Switzerland, grocery markets (41 per cent), book markets (9 per cent), import/export (9 per cent), liberalisation of the electricity sector (6 per cent), vertical cartels (6 per cent), credit cards (3 per cent), liberalisation of the postal service (3 per cent), telecommunications (3 per cent), the Zurich airport (3 per cent), and others (17 per cent). No particular crisis event occurred during this time period. Two particular features of this study shall be mentioned. First, this contribution does not deal with the reception, political impact or organisational reactions to media evaluation. Second, IRAs examined in this article are among the most media-savvy regulators in Western Europe, whilst the contribution of media coverage to their accountability is plausibly inferior for IRAs that work far from the media's spotlights. Therefore, the scope of the analysis is purposely limited to the media coverage of powerful, independent, mediatised regulators in Western Europe, which are the most important IRAs and those for which this type of accountability could be particularly relevant. The rest of this section shows how the British CC and the Swiss ComCo represent, respectively, a 'most likely' and 'least likely' case in terms of the outcomes of media evaluation in the population of Western European IRAs.

UK and Switzerland

To begin, these two IRAs are embedded in political-administrative systems that are exceedingly dissimilar (see Figure 5.1). Despite some recent trends toward the devolution of political competencies, the British political system is considered the ideal type of majoritarian polity (Dunleavy and Margetts 2001). The electoral system provides each major political party the opportunity to contend for governmental positions, with no need for grand coalitions. Once a candidate is in office, there are few political and institutional checks and balances. Therefore, the government relies on its majority to pass its legislative programmes and to make and implement decisions (Norris 2001; Armingeon 2002). The Anglo-Saxon style of public administration traditionally emphasises management rather than legalism in the performance of public tasks, a contractualist and market-oriented logic, and a career-based professionalised civil-service system (Peters 2004). The new public management (NPM) reforms implied both the reinforcement of market-oriented structures and the creation of quangos, semi-public organisations, and semi-autonomous agencies responsible for operational management (Hood *et al.* 2001). At the same time, a tendency emerged toward the centralisation of control and the use of performance assessment and oversight procedures (Knill 1998; Moran 2003).

Conversely, the Swiss political system typically follows a consensual model, traditionally showing a multi-party concordance government. The decision-making process is open, inclusive, and strongly shaped by the pre-parliamentary phase, in which expert committees play a crucial role and political parties, interest groups, and cantons are extensively consulted by the federal administration (Papadopoulos 2008). The participation of organised interests in policy formulation and collective negotiations is institutionalised, according to neo-corporatist logic (Armingeon 2002; Katzenstein 2003). According to the federal structure and the related principle of subsidiarity, political competencies are entrusted to the lowest possible level, especially regarding implementation (Braun 2003). In addition to this vertical dimension, the fragmentation of the system is increased horizontally by frequent reliance upon non-professional administrators, extra-parliamentary commissions, and quasi-state organisations (Varone 2007). The NPM was introduced to impose a greater degree of responsibility and to evaluate the results of public actions. However, it produced contradictory injunctions to civil servants, resulting in an increased 'institutional selfishness and one-purpose specialisation' that produced even greater fragmentation, less cooperation, and poorer coordination (Emery and Giauque 2004; Widmer and Neuenschwander 2004).

Besides these structural differences, it is important to deal with those meso-level variables that might have a direct impact on the media evaluation of agencies to operationalise the comparison of a 'most likely' and a 'least likely' case. The conditions that follow will systematically predict a better media evaluation of the British CC, in terms of credibility and/or efficiency, compared to the Swiss ComCo. First, the British CC could enjoy a more positive coverage, as it is formally more independent than the Swiss ComCo (Gilardi 2008). Second, the UK is a member of the European Union (EU), which is said to have a positive impact on agencies' activism through the promotion of a strong regulatory approach to sustain the economic integration and the common market (Majone 1996a). On the contrary, because it operates in a non-member state, the Swiss ComCo receives at best only indirect support from the EU. Third, the use of ex-post mechanisms to monitor and evaluate the quality of regulatory outcomes, such as oversight control tools and the application of procedures of regulatory impact assessment, might improve the agencies' media evaluation for regulatory efficiency. These instruments are consistently adopted in the UK, while they remain comparatively underdeveloped for Swiss IRAs (Widmer and Neuenschwander 2004; Radaelli and De Francesco 2007).

Fourth, the British CC is considered one of the world's leading antitrust authorities (GCR 2006; Wilks 2007). Furthermore, its analytical skills and capacities are highly rated by peer agencies, experts, and stakeholders, according to the survey enquiries of the Global Competition Review (five out of five stars). This might enhance its media evaluation for both credibility and efficiency. Conversely, the Swiss ComCo is relatively poorly rated (three out of five stars). Moreover, international experts frequently criticise it for its supposed lack of effectiveness (OECD 2005). Fifth, the type of political economy may also have an impact on the institutional appropriateness of the action of regulators (Hall and Soskice 2001). Again, the media evaluation for credibility and efficiency should be higher for the British regulator, given that the CC operates within a liberal market economy. Instead, the Swiss ComCo has the task of regulating a coordinated market economy, for which the internal market is traditionally strongly cartelised.

This situation could to lead interest groups and private actors that hassle the new wave of regulation-for-competition to challenge the regulatory activity of the competition commission by undermining its reputation.

Sixth, the structure of the media field might influence media perceptions of credibility and efficiency. Media industry concentration appears to be higher in Switzerland, producing incentives for the national media to be more critical toward ComCo, since the press industry might feel threatened by the regulator (Doyle 2002). On the contrary, in the UK, the press market is larger and more pluralist, segmented, and quite dynamic. Since there are fewer pressures for regulatory interventions, one can exclude any enduring bias against the CC for this reason. Finally, unlike ComCo, the CC has a strong and active department of press communication and public relations, plausibly doing its best to enhance agencies' media evaluations of credibility and efficiency. In general the human and financial resources of the British CC are significantly higher than those of the Swiss ComCo (Maggetti 2007). All these factors increase the chances that the former agency will perform better than the latter in terms of media evaluation of credibility and efficiency.

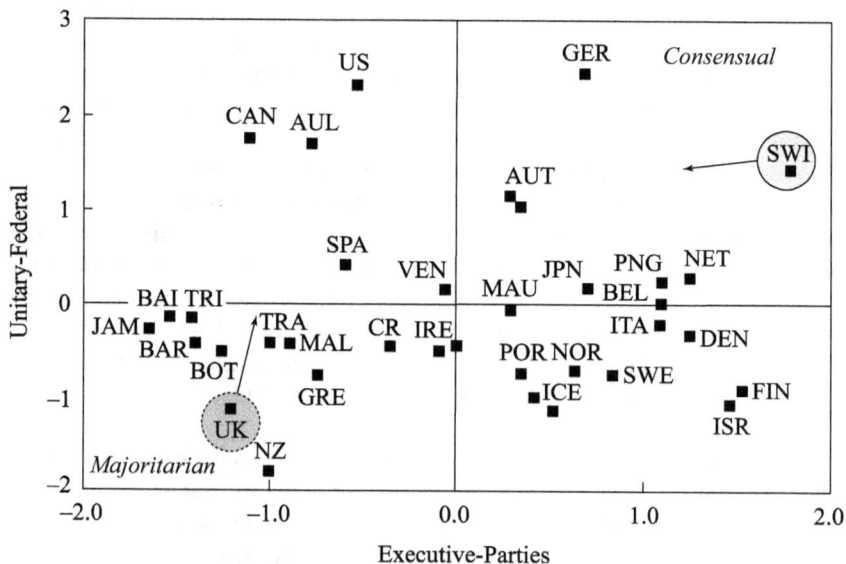

Figure 5.1: Typology of democracies (adapted from Lijphart 1999)

The Assessment of Media Evaluation

The empirical analysis zooms in on the so-called quality press. Quality newspapers are indeed considered crucial because they influence other media, thus directly or indirectly impacting the public (Coglianese and Howard 1998). It is widely recognised that the elite press reaches a much larger segment of the public by determining issues and perspectives for the news coverage of all types of media (Kepplinger *et al.* 2004). In addition, the perceived quality of information determines the magnitude of its effect on the prior beliefs of readers (Gentzkow and Shapiro 2006). Editorials and commentaries are particularly important in shaping the symbolic environment, although they are unfortunately quite neglected in media coverage studies (Voltmer and Eilders 2003). In fact, they become more and more essential as they respond to the people's need for orientation (Voltmer 1998), especially concerning 'non-obtrusive' issues such as the action of regulatory agencies that cannot be experienced in everyday life (Lang and Lang 1984). Moreover, editorials are the articles in which the media's own positions are most openly and legitimately expressed (Eilders 2000, 2002). Therefore, a focus on editorials, commentaries, and interviews would allow for the examination of press articles that include an explicit evaluation of the agency in a transparent and direct manner. To investigate how the media evaluate independent regulatory agencies and their regulatory action, a measure of 'media favourableness' will be created. For each newspaper, each article that mentions the investigated agency corresponded to an observation, and it was preliminarily coded as an editorial ('e'), comment ('c'), or interview ('i'). In addition, the day of the publication was recorded. News items in which the agency was marginally cited and ordinary articles in which the journalist referred to the agency without any judgement or comment were excluded from the sample. Then, each article was considered according to the explicit evaluation of two distinct elements that represents the 'official goals' of delegation: the credibility and the efficiency of the related agency (Majone 1996b, 2000; Franchino 2002; Gilardi 2002b; Braun and Gilardi 2006).

Each element was evaluated using four criteria: (1) autonomy from politicians, (2) predictability of decisions, (3) status of board members, and (4) autonomy from regulatees, with regard to credibility; and (1) public-good orientation, (2) uniqueness of the solution, (3) organisational capability, and (4) cost-benefit gains, with regard to efficiency. These criteria referred to a number of empirical measurements of organisational reputation that were derived and adapted from the literature dealing with organisational credibility and efficiency (Peters *et al.* 1997; Brunetti *et al.* 1998; Blinder 1999; Deephouse 2000; Maeda and Miyahara 2003; Blühdorn 2006; de Jonge *et al.* 2007; Kim *et al.* 2007; Radaelli and De Francesco 2007). Accordingly, each criterion can be considered as 'constitutive' of the related element (Goertz 2006b).

Further, the code for each single criterion was assigned on a three-point scale by considering whether the article explicitly referred to that criterion in a positive, negative, or neutral tone (i.e. no evaluation present; not all editorials were clearly evaluative; some were characterised by a neutral and diagnostic tone). A positive reference to one criterion was coded a '1'; a negative evaluation was coded a '-1'; and a neutral evaluation was coded a '0'. In turn, each element was nominally evaluated as positive, negative, or neutral according to the positive, negative, or neutral value of the sum of the four criteria defining that element. Following this approach, an article that positively evaluates IRAs' autonomy from politicians constitutes an instance of positive evaluation of credibility. More than one indicator can be simultaneously present in a news article. The coding procedure is consistent across newspapers. This information can be summarised by calculating 'c', the coefficient of media favourableness (Deephouse 2000). According to Deephouse, 'c' measures the relative proportion of favourable to unfavourable articles while controlling for the overall volume of articles. Consistent with prior research, each article is given equal weight in the measure. The formula for calculating 'c' is:

$$c = \begin{cases} (f^2 - fu)/(total)^2, & \text{if } f > u; \\ 0, & \text{if } f = u; \\ (fu - u^2)/(total)^2, & \text{if } u > f; \end{cases}$$

Where f = number of favourable recording units for an agency in a given time period; u = number of unfavourable recording units for the agency in that time period; and total = the total number of recording units for the agency in that time period. The range of this variable is -1 to 1, where 1 indicates all favourable coverage, -1 indicates all unfavourable coverage, and 0 indicates a balance between the two over the time period.

Empirical Analysis

The dataset encompasses all editorial articles, comments, and interviews in the daily broadsheet newspapers on the national competition commissions, during the years 2006–2007. The selected newspapers represent the so-called quality press, as usually defined in Switzerland and the UK.

Data

Case 1: UK (325 articles): *The Daily Telegraph* (63 articles), *The Financial Times* (70 articles), *The Guardian* (62 articles), *The Independent* (64 articles), *The Times* (66 articles).

Case 2: Switzerland (214 articles): *24 Heures* (11 articles), *Basler Zeitung* (28 articles), *Der Bund* (23 articles), *Neue Zuercher Zeitung* (54 articles), *Tages Anzeiger* (55 articles), *Le Temps* (31 articles), *Tribune de Genève* (12 articles).

Prior to the analysis, the consistency of the coding procedure was examined through the recoding of a random sample of articles by another researcher to establish intercoder reliability with Krippendorff's Alpha (Krippendorff 2004), using the SPSS macro developed by Hayes (Hayes and Krippendorff 2007). Then, a principal component analysis (PCA) was used to explore the structure of the dataset and to examine whether the aforementioned four criteria were adequate for measuring credibility and efficiency. These preliminary analyses are reported in the following two sections.

Reliability

When data are generated by (trained) human observers who systematically record or transcribe textual, pictorial, or audible material and make some kind of judgement in suitable terms for analysis, intersubjectively-valid measurement is not possible without the test of the reliability of collected data. The assessment of the reproducibility of the code is the strongest and most feasible kind of reliability test in content analysis – while the standard tests of 'stability' and 'accuracy' are less important in this context (Scott 1955; Lombard *et al.* 2002; Krippendorff 2004; Hayes and Krippendorff 2007; Krippendorff and Bock 2009). In content analysis, reproducibility is often conceptualised through the level of 'intercoder reliability', measuring 'the extent to which the different judges tend to assign the same rating to each object' (Krippendorff 2004). In other terms, it assesses the reproducibility of the coding, that is, the degree to which the coding process can be replicated by different analysts, working independent of each other, when applying the same recording instructions to the same observations. It is worth noting that a tension exists between choosing comprehensive but non-reproducible interpretations and superficial or oversimplified but very reliable text analysis (for instance generated through computer applications) (Krippendorff 2004). The middle path is a properly conceptualised measure with a satisfactory (but not necessarily perfect) level of intercoder reliability.

The Krippendorff's alpha is the most general agreement measure with appropriate reliability interpretations in content analysis (Hayes and Krippendorff 2007). The basic idea is to ensure that data do not deviate too much from perfect intercoder agreement (and *not* that they do not deviate from chance). Concretely, the alpha algorithm 'counts pairs of categories or scale points that observers have assigned to individual units, treating observers as freely permutable and being unaffected by their numbers' (Hayes and Krippendorff 2007). Measures of agreement are possible for nominal, ordinal, interval, and ratio data, rendering the reliabilities for such data fully comparable across different metrics. Approximations assumptions are avoided, and, instead, the distribution of alpha is bootstrapped from the given reliability data. So, the alpha scale defines two points: 1.000 for perfect reliability and 0.000 for the absence of reliability (as if categories or scale points were statistically unrelated to the units they describe). K-Alpha follows a quite demanding test of reliability, because data coding is considered reliable not simply when the null hypothesis that agreement occurs by chance can be rejected with statistical confidence, but when data are ensured not to deviate too much from perfect agreement. According to Krippendorff, there is no set answer to what is a good level of reliability (Krippendorff 2004). A level of 0.7 means that at least 70 per cent of the data are perfectly coded to a degree better than chance. This level is probably not 'beyond reasonable doubt' when the life of someone is directly affected, such as in court proceedings or in some medical tests. But it can be considered good for most types of content analyses, especially for social science research. Accordingly, the benchmark value for the minimum satisfactory level of intercoder reliability is 0.667, while a value of 0.800 or above indicates a very reliable measurement.

The first step of the procedure is the definition of a random sample of observations to be recoded by an independent analyst. Ideally, the recoding of the whole dataset would be desirable. However, it is hardly feasible because of the unavoidable constraints of time and resources. Thus, the sample must be representative of the population whose reliability is in question (Krippendorff 2004). According to the suggestions of Krippendorff (2004: 234-40), when the coding procedure involves the appraisal of values on three equally probable categories (as here), the sample size should be the following. For a minimum accepted alpha of 0.667, the required sample size is 34 at a level of significance of 0.050, and 68 at a level of significance of 0.010. For a minimum accepted alpha of 0.800, the required sample size is 59 at a level of significance of 0.050, and 117 at a level of significance of 0.010.

In the present case, after the main coding procedure executed by myself, a sample was given to another analyst (a sociologist working for another research institute) for recoding, by carefully following the written instructions, but being not aware of the purpose of the research, so as to independently measure the level of intercoder reliability. Following the aforementioned guidelines, I decided to maximise the sample size. I took 30 random observations for each case and for each one of the two variables. I obtained a total of 120 observations to be recoded, producing thus 120 pairs of judgements (120 by the principal coder and 120 recoded by the independent analyst), whose alpha level of agreement is representative of the population (at least) at 95 per cent significance level (see Tables 5.1 and 5.2). Once the recoding procedure was accomplished, I applied the SPSS macro developed by Hayes to calculate the Krippendorff's alpha, using the following formula (Hayes and Krippendorff 2007):

KALPHA judges = obsa obsb/level = 1/detail = 1/boot = 5000.

This means that I compared the agreement between the two pairs of judgements (obsa and obsb), treating data as nominal (for improving the robustness of the measurement), and allowing the software 5000 bootstraps. The result is a satisfactory level of intercoder reliability that is representative of the population at 95 per cent:

KALPHA: = 0.7194

Table 5.1: Sample of the coding of the British CC

Country	New.	Date	N°	Credibility		Efficiency	
				Coding	Recoding	Coding	Recoding
uk	ThG	21.12.2007	2	0	0	-1	-1
uk	ThG	3.11.2007	3	0	0	0	1
uk	ThG	2.11.2007	4	0	0	1	1
uk	ThG	1.11.2007	5	0	0	-1	-1
uk	ThG	1.11.2007	6	0	-1	0	-1
uk	ThG	1.11.2007	7	0	0	-1	-1
uk	ThI	8.12.2007	8	0	0	0	0
uk	ThI	8.12.2007	9	0	0	-1	-1
uk	ThI	4.12.2007	10	0	1	0	0
uk	ThI	8.11.2007	11	0	0	1	1
uk	ThI	1.11.2007	12	0	0	0	-1
uk	ThI	1.11.2007	13	0	0	0	0
uk	ThI	1.11.2007	14	0	0	1	1
uk	ThT	10.12.2007	15	0	0	-1	-1
uk	ThT	29.11.2007	16	0	0	1	1
uk	ThT	4.11.2007	17	1	1	0	1
uk	ThT	4.11.2007	18	0	0	-1	-1
uk	ThT	4.11.2007	19	0	0	0	0
uk	ThT	1.11.2007	20	0	1	-1	-1
uk	ThT	1.11.2007	21	0	0	0	0
uk	FiT	22.12.2007	22	0	0	-1	-1
uk	FiT	21.12.2007	23	0	0	1	1
uk	FiT	17.11.2007	24	0	0	0	-1
uk	FiT	3.11.2007	25	0	1	-1	-1
uk	DaT	27.12.2007	26	0	0	0	0
uk	DaT	27.12.2007	27	0	0	0	-1
uk	DaT	21.12.2007	28	0	0	0	0
uk	DaT	11.11.2007	29	0	0	-1	-1
uk	DaT	4.11.2007	30	0	0	-1	-1

Table 5.2: Sample of the coding of the Swiss ComCo

Country	New.	Date	N°	Credibility		Efficiency	
				Coding	Recoding	Coding	Recoding
ch	24H	15.9.2007	1	0	0	1	1
ch	Baz	28.11.2007	2	0	0	-1	-1
ch	Baz	27.11.2007	3	0	0	0	0
ch	Baz	23.11.2007	4	0	0	-1	-1
ch	Baz	8.9.2007	5	0	0	-1	-1
ch	Bun	28.11.2007	6	0	0	-1	-1
ch	Bun	27.11.2007	7	0	0	0	0
ch	Bun	27.11.2007	8	0	0	-1	-1
ch	Bun	10.9.2007	9	-1	-1	-1	-1
ch	LeT	7.12.2007	10	-1	0	0	-1
ch	LeT	27.11.2007	11	0	1	-1	0
ch	LeT	7.11.2007	12	0	0	1	1
ch	LeT	20.10.2007	13	0	0	0	0
ch	LeT	19.10.2007	14	0	-1	-1	-1
ch	LeT	27.9.2007	15	-1	-1	-1	-1
ch	LeT	10.9.2007	16	0	0	-1	-1
ch	LeT	7.9.2007	17	0	0	0	0
ch	NZZ	7.12.2007	18	0	0	0	0
ch	NZZ	28.11.2007	19	0	0	0	-1
ch	NZZ	27.11.2007	20	0	0	1	1
ch	NZZ	27.11.2007	21	0	0	0	0
ch	NZZ	7.11.2007	22	0	0	-1	-1
ch	NZZ	24.10.2007	23	0	0	-1	-1
ch	NZZ	9.9.2007	24	0	0	0	-1
ch	NZZ	6.9.2007	25	0	0	1	1
ch	Tag	12.12.2007	26	0	0	-1	-1
ch	Tag	17.11.2007	27	0	0	0	0
ch	Tag	7.11.2007	28	0	0	0	0
ch	Tag	18.10.2007	29	-1	-1	-1	0
ch	TrG	28.11.2007	30	0	0	0	0

Principal components

Principal component analysis is a statistical technique employed for identifying clusters of variables. Here, this technique is used to explore the structure of the dataset, and subordinately for examining whether the previously mentioned four criteria are adequate for the measurement of credibility and efficiency. The SPSS package is employed. Preliminarily, please note that criteria are assumed to constitute different conceptual facets of credibility or efficiency; therefore they are not expected to be necessarily consistent with a linear relationship. In other words, they should not be considered as indicators of the same thing. Principal component analysis reveals which variables (here: the selected criteria for evaluating agencies' reputation) are loaded to a factor, which represents a classification axis (here: being possibly consistent with the reputation for credibility or efficiency) (Field 2005). The principal component matrix can be rotated for improving interpretation, so as to maximise the loading of variables to each factor. In this paper, orthogonal rotation is adopted (varimax), because factors are theoretically assumed to be unrelated. According to Kaiser's criterion of retaining factors with eigenvalues greater than 1, four factors are extracted (Kaiser 1970). Finally, the benchmark value that is retained for displaying factor loadings that represent substantive values is 0.4, so as commonly assumed (Stevens 2002). Results indicate that the selected criteria cluster relatively well into two broad dimensions, with reference to credibility and, respectively, efficiency (see Table 5.3 and Figure 5.2). To be precise, in line with theoretical assumptions, two groups of variables for credibility and one for efficiency are identified, while another group displays mixed results (see Table 5.4).

Specifically, the first group that refers to credibility includes the criteria of autonomy from the political decision-makers and from the regulatees. The other includes the predictability of decisions and policies. The distinction between these two groups is theoretically meaningful, because they represent two diverse facets constituting the concept of credibility. The group related to agencies' efficiency consists of the uniqueness of the solution and cost-benefit gains. The last group also refers mainly to efficiency, as it comprises the criteria of public good – oriented action and agencies' capability (in addition to the status of board members). To sum up, it appears that the selected criteria, although being as expected fundamentally unrelated, tend to cluster meaningfully into groups that should correspond to the dimensions of credibility or efficiency. Moreover, interestingly, some subcomponents emerge from the analysis, such as the level of perceived autonomy.

Table 5.3: Principal component matrix

Criteria	Label	Extraction
1. Autonomy from elected politicians	CRED1	0.707
2. Predictability of decisions and policies	CRED2	0.974
3. Status of board members	CRED3	0.402
4. Autonomy *vis-à-vis* the regulatees	CRED4	0.722
1. Public good–oriented action	EFFIC1	0.412
2. Uniqueness of the solution	EFFIC2	0.563
3. Capability (competencies, expertise, fin./ hum. resources)	EFFIC3	0.394
4. Cost-benefit gains	EFFIC4	0.459

Extraction Method: Principal Component Analysis.

Table 5.4: Rotated component matrix

	Label	Component			
		1	**2**	**3**	**4**
1. Autonomy from elected politicians	CRED1	0.839			
2. Predictability	CRED2				0.987
3. Status of board members	CRED3		0.624		
4. Autonomy *vis-à-vis* the regulatees	CRED4	0.843			
1. Public good–oriented action	EFFIC1		0.620		
2. Uniqueness of the solution	EFFIC2			0.731	
3. Capability (comp., expertise, fin./hum. res.)	EFFIC3		0.566		
4. Cost-benefit gains	EFFIC4			0.655	

Extraction Method: Principal Component Analysis.
Rotation Method: Varimax with Kaiser Normalisation.
Rotation converged in 4 iterations.

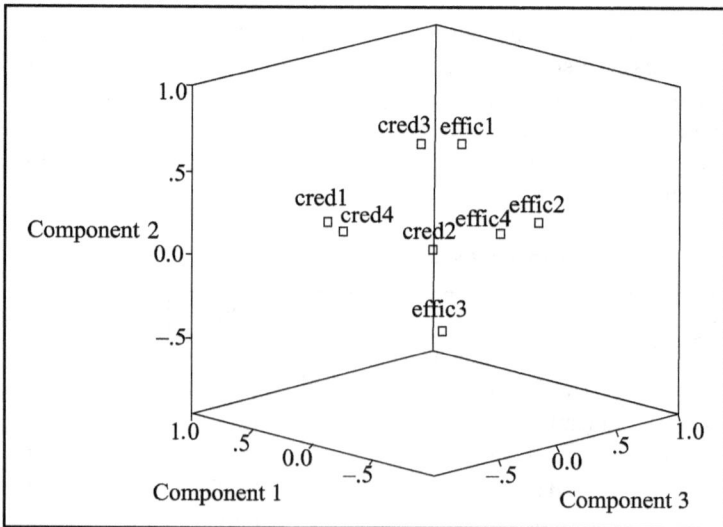

Figure 5.2: Component plot in rotated space

Results

The empirical analysis focused on six issues, in accordance with the theoretical expectations outlined above, which correspond to the minimal prerequisites to consider the media as a potential accountability forum for IRAs. The first three items illustrate to what extent do the media *give an account* of agencies' regulatory actions; the other three indicate the positive or negative tone of media coverage as a form of symbolic *reward or sanction*. The systematic study of a 'most likely' and a 'least likely' case as regards news coverage – the British and Swiss competition commissions – shall permit to enhance the analytical leverage of the comparison and explore the cross-case validity of prospects regarding agencies' media accountability.

1) *Frequency in Comparison with Other Issues.* Calculations based on data from Pfetsch *et al.* permit illustrating the annual average number of editorial comments per newspaper regarding seven relevant policy issues: monetary politics, agriculture, immigration, troops deployment, retirement/pensions, education, European integration; that is, 12.04 for the UK and 7.25 for Switzerland (Pfetsch *et al.* 2004). In comparison, the average annual coverage of the UK competition commission corresponds to 21.70 editorial comments per newspaper, and, respectively, to 13.00 related to the Swiss competition commission. These averages represent levels comparable to those of the most salient policy issues, such as European integration.

2) *Trend.* There was an overall increase in the frequency of articles evaluating the two competition commissions under investigation: from 137 news items in 2006 to 188 in 2007 on the UK CC, and from 70 to 142 on the Swiss ComCo (see Figure 5.3). More precisely, the average quarterly growth of news coverage was 12.28 per cent in the UK and 20.36 per cent in Switzerland during the investigated time period. This trend is remarkable, in comparison with the activity of the media in the seven salient policy issues studied by Pfetsch *et al.*, which remained fairly constant over time (Pfetsch *et al.* 2004). When the type of articles is considered, it appears that, on average, from 2006 to 2007 the increase is 71 per cent for comments, 78 per cent for editorials and 32 per cent for interviews.

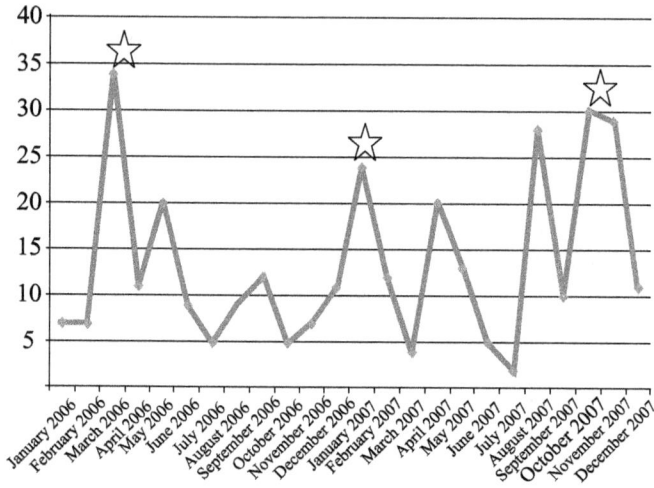

Media coverage in the UK

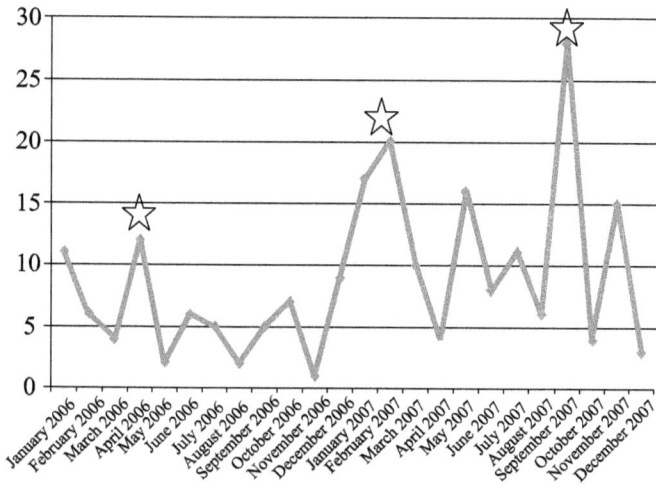

Media coverage in Switzerland

Figure 5.3: Trend of media coverage of the British CC and the Swiss ComCo

3) *Regulatory Cycle.* The trend in news coverage roughly follows the agencies' regulatory agenda, as it tended to cluster in relation to specific regulatory issues by peaking significantly near important events, such as the beginning of an investigation, a crucial decision, or the publication of the annual report. As indicated by the white stars in Figure 5.3, 13 articles were published in the UK when a full competition inquiry into the dominance of large British grocers was announced (10th March 2006). The publication of another 15 articles corresponded

to the unveiling of the initial findings of the CC's investigation on the grocery market (24th January 2007). Eighteen articles included a sensible CC report on the large supermarkets' dominance (1st November 2007). In Switzerland, meanwhile, 5 articles were published after ComCo's decision to sanction the country's leading telecommunications company for abusing its dominant position (11th April 2006). Nine articles were published prior to the disclosure of the initial position of the Swiss ComCo on an exceptional merger in the grocery market (17th February 2007). In addition, 13 articles reported and discussed the decision made by ComCo relative to that issue (5th September 2007). At the same time, the average tone was not decisively contingent upon specific events, but positive or negative evaluation of regulatory action by the investigated competition agencies followed comparable patterns across issues (when also controlling for newspaper type) (see Figure 5.4).

4) *Media Bias for Credibility*. The last row of Table 5.5 presents the coefficients of media favourableness[3]. According to media coverage, credibility was considered significantly more positive for the British CC (a coefficient of media favourableness of 0.48, or a differential between positive and negative cases of +5 percentage points) than for the Swiss ComCo (a coefficient of -0.74, or a differential of -8 per cent). As regards credibility, coefficients of media favourableness display absolute values that are distant from zero, indicating that media evaluations of agencies are consistent over news articles. In addition, Table 5.5 shows a good deal of 'neutral' articles, which is as expected according to the coding procedure.

5) *Media Bias for Efficiency*. The tone of the evaluations of the agencies' efficiency was almost identical in the UK and in Switzerland. In both cases, there were more negative articles than positive ones. The coefficient of media favourableness was -0.19 in the UK (-19 per cent) and -0.18 (-16 per cent) in Switzerland; therefore, the CC was evaluated slightly more negatively than the ComCo on this dimension (but both coefficients are quite close to zero). Figure 5.5 displays a scatterplot showing where the two IRAs are situated according to the mean values of their media evaluations of credibility and efficiency (the small bars represent the standard errors).[4] This scatterplot permits a comprehensive comparison of the media evaluation for the two agencies. As regards efficiency, the tone of media coverage is similar in both cases, and constantly negative; instead, credibility is positively evaluated for the British agency but negative in the Swiss case.

---

3. Excluding the 0 in order to improve the interpretation of results.

4. The mean values and 95 per cent confidence intervals of the differences are as follows: Credibility of the British CC: M = .0462; CI = .0163 to .0760. Efficiency of the British CC: M = -.1785; CI = -.2597 to -.0972. Credibility of the Swiss ComCo: M = -.0841; CI = -.1259 to -.0423. Efficiency of the Swiss ComCo: M = -.1636; CI = -.2644 to -.0627.

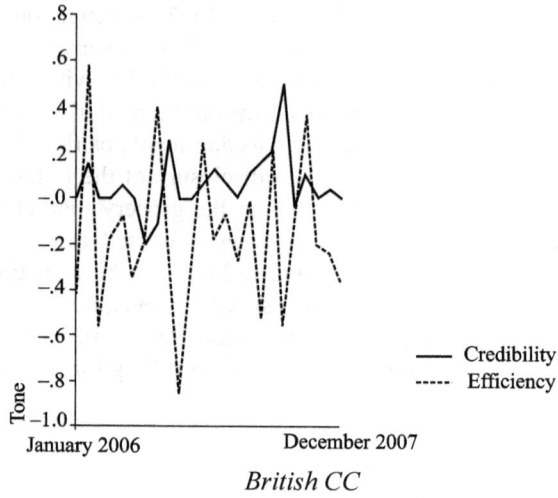

British CC

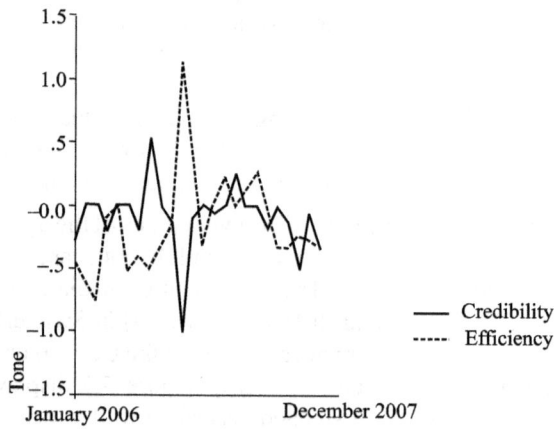

Swiss ComCo

Figure 5.4: Trend and tone of media coverage

Table 5.5: Media favourableness

	Credibility CC	Efficiency CC	Credibility ComCo	Efficiency ComCo
1	20	65	2	45
0	300	135	195	89
-1	5	125	20	80
c	0.48	-0.19	-0.74	-0.18

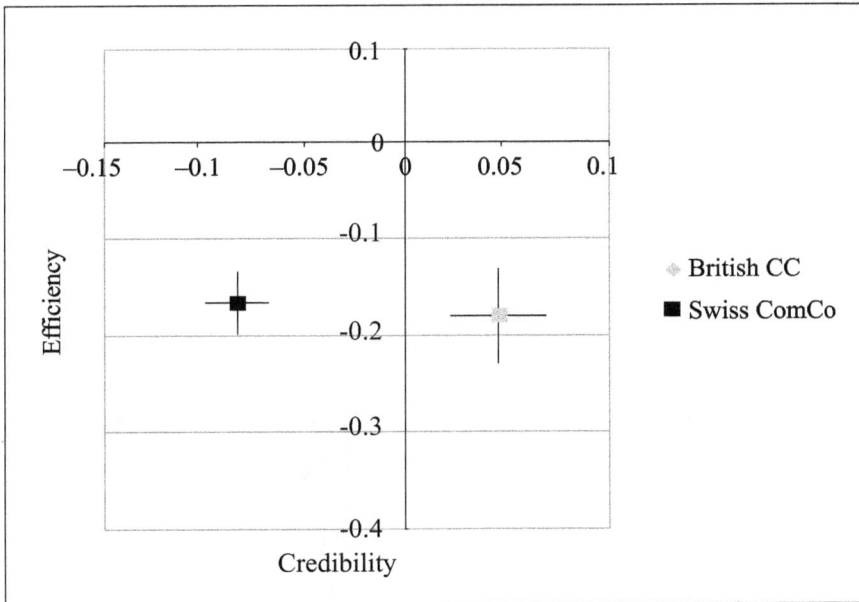

Figure 5.5: The tone of the media coverage of the British CC and the Swiss ComCo

6) Content. The element that received the most intensive media coverage by far was 'efficiency' in both cases. Among all articles referring to credibility or efficiency, 88 per cent evaluated the efficiency of the British CC, and 85 per cent evaluated the efficiency of the Swiss ComCo, respectively. Figure 5.6 illustrates the relevance of each criterion of the coding for the aggregated evaluation of credibility and efficiency, respectively. Concerning the British CC, the analysis shows that the positive evaluation of credibility is predominantly due to a perception of its being largely separated from politicians and organised interests. On the other hand, its negative reputation for efficiency stems largely from a harmful evaluation of cost-benefit gains. Pertaining to the Swiss ComCo, it appears that the negative evaluation of credibility is almost entirely due to the perception of its having scarce autonomy from those being regulated, whereas its perceived poor efficiency derives principally from a negative evaluation of organisational capabilities (i.e.

human and financial resources) and from the perception of low cost-benefit gains.

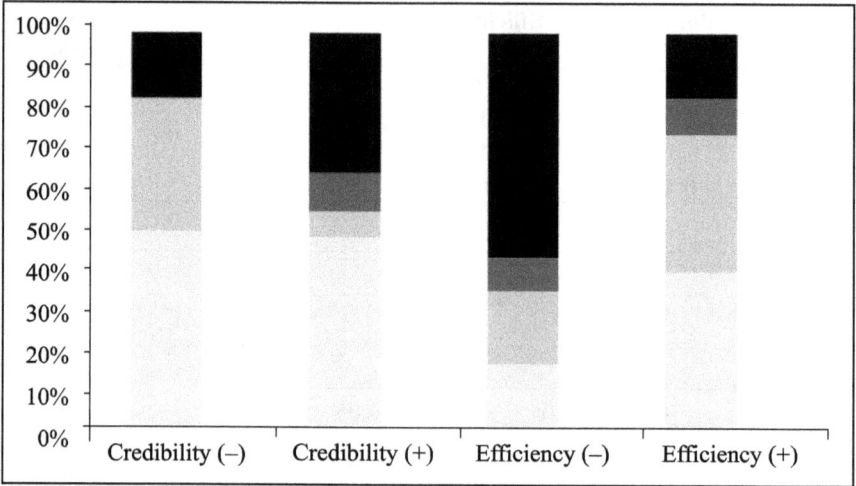

Credibility and efficiency in the UK

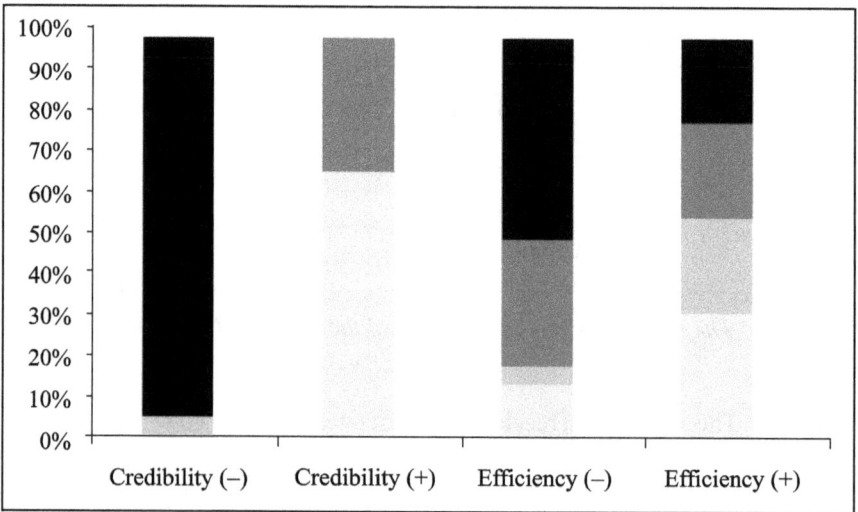

Credibility and efficiency in Switzerland

Credibility:
■ Autonomy from regulatees ■ Status of board members ▦ Predictability of decisions ░ Autonomy from politicians

Efficiency:
■ Cost-benefit gains ■ Organizational capability ▦ Uniqueness of the solution ░ Public-good orientation

Figure 5.6: The criteria for credibility and efficiency of the British CC and the Swiss ComCo

Discussion

The expectation that media can function as an 'accountability forum' (Bovens 2007) for IRAs finds considerable support in the cases of the British CC and the Swiss ComCo, confirming thus the main hypothesis of this chapter, that is, Hypothesis 3.1. To begin with, these agencies seem to be consistently scrutinised by the media (Schedler 1998), which *give account* of their regulatory activities quite regularly and consistently. (1) The coverage of the agencies in terms of the average annual number of editorial comments per newspaper is well above the average in both countries, in comparison with other relevant policy issues; and, (2) such coverage tends to increase over time. More importantly, (3) media coverage appears roughly in line with the regulatory cycle, with news peaks near crucial events for the IRAs under examination: the opening of new inquiries, the publication of the results of previous investigations, and key decisions such as important sanctions on the regulated industries.

Pertaining to the application of symbolic *rewards and sanctions*, results are also quite in line with our expectations. First, (4) a systematic positive bias for credibility can be dismissed, given that the British CC benefits from an excellent media evaluation of credibility, while the Swiss ComCo has a negative media evaluation of credibility. Similarly, (5) the existence of a negative bias as regards efficiency is improbable because, although persistently negative, the coefficients of media favourableness are quite close to zero, indicating a good balance between negative and positive evaluations. However, the fact that the average tone for efficiency is clearly negative, even for the 'most likely' case of the CC when one would expect a greater number of positive evaluations, is quite surprising and would deserve further investigation. Consequently, Hypothesis 3.2, the subsidiary expectation of this chapter, concerning the compatibility of (the media evaluations of) credibility and efficiency, is only partially corroborated. Finally, (6) the content of media coverage is largely in harmony with the topics that can be considered of general interest for the public: namely the 'autonomy' of agencies as regards credibility and their 'cost-benefit gains' as regards efficiency.

These results are not only relevant for the literature on regulatory governance, but they also indicate the analytical relevance of the concept of 'mediatisation' (Mazzoleni and Schulz 1999; Kepplinger 2002; Strömbäck and Esser 2009), according to which the media are becoming social institutions that operate according to their own logic and have an autonomous impact on political actors and political phenomena (Mazzoleni and Schulz 1999; Kepplinger 2002; Strömbäck and Esser 2009). Following this perspective, it seems that the growing importance of IRAs is recognised by the news media, which report IRAs' activity and mediate their communication, with increasing frequency and evaluating them according to the 'official goals' of delegation, in terms of credibility and efficiency, eventually making ordinary citizens potentially more aware of what IRAs do. Before concluding, it is fair to note that these findings are expected to account for cases presenting similar characteristics, that is, powerful, independent, mediatised regulators in Western Europe, and that they hold within the context of the quite limited research goal of this chapter, that is, the exploration of the role that media can play as a necessary but insufficient component of a 'multi-pronged' accountability system for independent regulatory agencies (Majone 2002).

Conclusion

The purpose of this chapter was to assess whether the media can function as an 'accountability forum' (Bovens 2007) for independent regulatory agencies (IRAs). To this aim, it explored the media's coverage of IRAs according to the official rationales that justified decisions to delegate public authority from governments to this type of non-majoritarian institutions: the enhancement of regulatory credibility and the improvement of decision-making efficiency. This approach is relevant not only because public communication is a requisite for the responsiveness of political institutions towards citizens but also because the media represent a venue for policymakers for the appraisal of regulatory outcomes. The two components of accountability – *to give an account* and *to reward and sanction* – are examined through comparison of a 'most likely' and a 'least likely' case, among Western European regulators (i.e. the British Competition Commission (CC) and the Swiss Competition Commission (ComCo), respectively). During the investigated period (2006–2007), media attention pertaining to the regulation of competition in both countries was primarily directed toward market concentration in the grocery sector. This quite exceptional situation permitted endogenising the possible effects of issue-specific conditions.

The main results can be summarised as follows: IRAs seem accountable to the media, given that the average annual coverage of the Swiss and UK competition commissions corresponds to the level of the most salient policy issues, and, in addition, follows a positive trend. What is more, media attention is approximately in line with the regulatory cycle of agencies. Concerning symbolic rewards and sanctions by the media, findings corroborate expectations concerning the tone of editorial comments. Evidence indeed confirms the absence of a systematic positive bias for credibility or a negative bias for efficiency when evaluating IRAs. Nevertheless, the case of the CC shows that even well endowed IRAs do not necessarily benefit from a positive media evaluation for efficiency. It is impossible at this stage to say whether this result stems from a misrepresentation of this particular dimension or whether it is connected to substantial underperformances of IRAs under scrutiny. However, if supported by further research, these results might defy the popular ambition of designing a structure of delegation that simultaneously enhances regulatory credibility through independence and decision-making efficiency through the simultaneous application of 'ex-ante', 'ex-post' or 'ongoing' control mechanisms. Furthermore, in line with other research studies, this chapter confirms that IRAs can be formally independent and yet be considered under control (Lægreid *et al.* 2008), with the application of the appropriate 'ex-post' accountability mechanisms (Busuioc 2009).

These exploratory findings are relevant not only for the burgeoning literature on the spread of regulatory capitalism and the functioning of IRAs (Levi-Faur

2006a, c; Gilardi 2008), but also for the discussion regarding the accountability of regulatory governance and the role of media in regulatory policy making, especially regarding the so-called democratic deficit of the regulatory state. This article offers both good and bad news to the proponents of media scrutiny as an alternative procedure to making independent regulators accountable and maybe enhance their legitimacy, following the inappropriateness of traditional forms of upward and downward accountability for institutions that lack input-legitimacy by design (Majone 1994a; Scott 2000a; Lodge 2004; Maggetti 2009b, 2010). On the one hand, the media can possibly act as a proper accountability forum that provides the public with consistent evaluations of agencies' work. On the other hand, whereas a positive media evaluation of credibility has proven to be attainable under specific conditions, the corresponding evaluation of efficiency seems chimerical for IRAs, even in the 'most likely' case, potentially compromising the reputation of (some) independent regulators in front of ordinary citizens.

chapter six | conclusive discussion

Regulation in practice: what we have learnt

Reframing the research questions

The current version of capitalism is said to correspond to the golden age of regulation. Following an apparent paradox, the ongoing dynamics of liberalisation, privatisation, decartelisation, internationalisation, and regional integration do not lead to the crumbling of the state, but they fostered instead a wave of regulatory growth, related to the new risks and new opportunities (Vogel 1996). Accordingly, since the 1980s, no government activity in OECD countries has grown faster than regulatory functions (Jacobs 1999). A new regulatory order is rising, which implies a new division of labour between state and society (Levi-Faur 2005a). The previous model of governance, relying on public ownership and public intervention, coupled with self-regulation by the private actors, is being gradually substituted by a more formalised, expert-based, transparent, and independently regulated model (Hollingsworth *et al.* 1994; Levi-Faur and Jordana 2005). This movement towards a new regulatory order is not linear, irreversible, or homogeneous, but it is increasingly pervasive across countries and sectors. Independent regulatory agencies (IRAs) represent the distinctive institutional feature of the regulatory state and regulatory capitalism (Gilardi 2005b).

In this book, I argued that the 'de facto independence' of IRAs constitutes the key variable for the study of regulatory governance after delegation. The starting point was a number of problem-driven empirical questions on the functioning of agencies. Do IRAs fulfil their mandates after the delegation of competencies? What shapes the implementation of formal independence? How do IRAs use their independence? What kind of relationship do they develop with their environment? Are they really independent in their routine or are they operating rather in the shadow of the administrative hierarchy? Are they deviating from the statutory prescriptions? Are they captured by the regulated industries? Who participates in the regulatory process? Which are the crucial political actors of the regulatory state? How far do agencies influence the policy-making process? Do IRAs improve decision making? Can they be held accountable?

A composite research design was then developed in order to investigate these research questions and test the related hypotheses, which entailed three distinct empirical analyses. (I) First, a novel approach was presented for conceptualising and assessing agencies' de facto independence in a systematic and comparable way. The relation between formal and de facto independence was investigated, showing that political, institutional, and organisational factors matter for explaining the variation of de facto independence beyond statutory prescriptions. (II) Second, the role of agencies in policy making was examined, with special attention to the consequences of de facto independence, so as to emphasise that agencies do not restrain themselves exclusively to the execution of regulatory functions. (III) The third empirical part of this book explored whether the news media meets the necessary prerequisites to be considered a potential 'accountability forum' for regulators, by means of the examination of the media coverage media of IRAs as regards their credibility and efficiency. Hypotheses are summarised in Tables 6.1 and 6.2 with the corresponding results of the empirical analysis.

Table 6.1: Summary of the hypotheses (1)

No.	Hypotheses	Result	
H 1.1	*High formal independence could be neither a necessary nor a sufficient condition for a high level of de facto independence from politicians.*	Supported	✓
H 1.2	*The combination of conditions that might give rise to high de facto independence from politicians is expected to be the old age of agencies and the presence of many veto players.*	Supported	✓
H 1.3	*A highly coordinated economy and sectoral path dependency will be two concomitant conditions for the low de facto independence of agencies from both the politicians and the regulatees.*	Not supported	×
H 1.4	*Intense participation of agencies in European networks and the organisational weakness of those being regulated are expected to lead to high de facto independence from the regulatees.*	Partially supported	~
H 1.5	*In cases of high de facto independence from the politicians, a 'footloose' agency could become scarcely independent vis-à-vis the regulatees.*	Supported	✓
H 2.1	*IRAs are expected to hold the most central role in the course of the political decision -making processes in their area of competence.*	Supported	✓
H 2.2	*The presence of a 'monocratic' system is expected to lead to the higher centrality of IRAs in policy making, unlike a dual model.*	Not supported	×

Table 6.2: Summary of the hypotheses (2)

No.	Hypotheses	Result	
H 2.3	*IRAs are expected to be highly central in policy making where the legislature is non-professionalised.*	Supported	✓
H 2.4	*Sector-specific expert-based IRAs are expected to play a very central role in policy making, unlike general regulators.*	Not supported	✗
H 2.5	*a) High de facto independent IRAs from the political decision makers should be central actors in policy making.* *b) Low de facto independent IRAs from the regulatees should be central actors in policy making.*	Supported	✓
H 3.1	*The media can function as accountability forum for IRAs*	Supported	✓
H 3.2	*Media can evaluate agencies as credible and efficient at the same time*	Partially	~

Main empirical findings

The main findings of the three empirical analyses presented in this book can be recapitulated as follows. The crucial point of part I is that high formal independence is neither a necessary nor a single sufficient condition for high de facto independence from political decision makers. The explanatory conditions leading to high de facto independence from politicians are the old age of the investigated agency and the presence of many veto players in the political system, the latter in combination with high formal independence. This means that the presence of multiple veto players enables the implementation of agencies' formal independence, as it becomes more difficult for divided principals to sway the regulatory action, while agencies may benefit from a process of autonomisation when ageing. In addition, the incorporation of agencies in regulatory networks appears to be a sufficient causal condition for their de facto independence from regulatees, when combined with low de facto independence from politicians. Networks plausibly offer a range of material and symbolic resources, empowering agencies in front of the regulated industries. At the same time, the relationship between an agency and those it regulates is influenced by the relationships it develops with the elected politicians. In other words, it appears that an agency cannot be a servant of two masters: if it is scarcely independent from politicians, it should be highly independent from those being regulated. Finally, and contrary to a number of expectations derived from the theory of agencies' life cycle, it seems that the old age might also support their independence *vis-à-vis* the regulatees.

Then, part II focused on the role of agencies in lawmaking, operationalising this concept with a measure of network centrality (representing IRAs' influence in policy making) that comprises structural and reputational features. The highest centrality of regulators is discovered where the professionalisation of the legislature is the lowest. The other condition that is jointly sufficient to explain the outcome of maximal agencies' centrality is the low level de facto independence from regulatees, and the related high de facto independence from political decision makers. Those agencies are plausibly perceived as credible veto players by the political decision makers. The underlying argument is that non-professional legislators (suffering from a lack of material and symbolic resources) that must cope with a regulator that might challenge the later stages of the policy-making process (due to its low de facto independence from those being regulated) have strong incentives to include this agency in policy making (if it has not been integrated yet). In that way, they can obtain relevant information, and they expect to avoid any possible implementation failure. The analysis reveals thus that the agencies' expertise capacity gives rise to the opportunity of exerting considerable political power in policy making, rather than restraining themselves to the mere technocratic execution of their regulatory functions.

Finally, part III explored the accountability of agencies, in terms of the media evaluation of their credibility and efficiency. The expectation that media can function as an 'accountability forum' for IRAs finds support in the cases of the British CC and the Swiss ComCo. To begin with, these agencies seem to be consistently scrutinised by the media, which give account of their regulatory activities quite regularly and consistently. Pertaining to the application of symbolic rewards and sanctions, results are also quite in line with our expectations. A systematic positive bias for credibility can be dismissed, and the existence of a negative bias as regards efficiency is improbable because, although persistently negative, the coefficients of media favourableness are quite close to zero, indicating a good balance between negative and positive evaluations. Finally, the content of media coverage is largely in harmony with the topics that can be considered of general interest for the public: namely the 'autonomy' of agencies as regards credibility and their 'cost-benefit gains' as regards efficiency.

Theoretical insights for the study of regulation

Part I demonstrated that formal independence is insufficient for explaining variations in IRAs' de facto independence. Therefore, more attention should be given to factors that consent the proper implementation of statutory prescriptions; otherwise the accountability structure could become unintelligible, and the separateness from representative institutions might become unjustified, making the democratic deficit even more problematical (Majone 1999), since the 'non-majoritarian standards of legitimacy' will be no longer supported (Majone 1998). Among the conditions leading to factual independence, it is worth emphasising that the embeddedness of domestic regulators into international networks reduces the risk of agency capture, while at the same time it might enable another, promising, form of accountability, that is, through 'peer pressures' and reputational mechanisms (Majone 1997b, 2000), ideally producing a situation where 'no one controls the agency [i.e. the agency is independent], yet the agency is under control [the agency is accountable]' (Moe 1985; Majone 1994a, 1996b). It also appears that actors other than the elected politicians, namely the representatives of the regulated sector, are able to mould agencies' de facto independence to some extent. This result supports the conceptualisation of IRAs as intermediary organisations (Braun 1993), where the three parties play complex cooperative and competitive regulatory games, instead of conceiving them as the mere agents of the political principals. Following this structure of interaction, agencies should be considered as involved in a double relationship with political decision makers and with those being regulated, whereby the two relations are mutually influencing. At the end of the day, factually independent agencies are those that are able to mediate between the (conflicting) interests of elected politicians and regulatees, by developing a 'functional antagonism', as shown by Dietmar Braun in the case of research policy (Braun 1997), which requires them to hold an equidistant position (in the Latin sense of *aequi* + *distare*), in order to manage the interdependence of politics and business in the name of the 'public interest'. Finally, the analysis shows that regulators are neither systematically under direct political control nor are they steadily captured by the regulated industries, thus challenging a crucial argument of the economic theory of regulation (Stigler 1971; Pelzman *et al.* 1989). Rather, they constitute a relatively new, autonomous and significant player in regulatory governance and regulatory capitalism (Levi-Faur 2005a; Levi-Faur and Jordana 2005), that, more often than not, enjoy a certain level of factual independence, while cumulating crucial competencies of rule-making, monitoring, sanctioning and adjudication.

Part II showed that IRAs are the most influent actor in lawmaking related to their area of competence, more than expert commissions, organised interest representatives, and ordinary agencies subordinated to the ministerial level. This point sustains the arguments about the rise of an age of 'regulocracy' (Levi-Faur 2005a) and 'agencification' (Christensen and Lægreid 2005), while also clarifying the apparent paradox inherent in the current use of the concepts of regulatory state and regulatory capitalism. To begin with, the term 'regulation' does not (only) connote the shift from state's interventionism to the decline of public authority, in favour of the 'negative' defence of market freedom. First and foremost, it refers to the wave of re-regulation after phenomena of liberalisation and privatisation (Johnson 2002), and the consequent proliferation of IRAs as a relatively new type of public body that endorses regulatory functions and promote stricter, more transparent and more formalised rules, that should constrain the markets and promote the 'public interest' (Jordana and Levi-Faur 2004; Jordana *et al.* 2007). At the same time, the evidence upholding IRAs' centrality in policy making suggests that the activity of formally independent regulators is not limited to the implementation of the delegated *regulatory* competencies (i.e. market supervision and technical regulatory functions), however important they are (Jacobs 1999). Very interestingly, it seems that IRAs are also developing a key *political* role, and may exert significant political power, extending their role as the 'third force' (Thatcher 2005a), not only in regulation but also in policy making. Specifically, they are noticed to hold distinctive lawmaking functions, beyond their implementation competencies, being particularly influential in agenda-setting and during draft preparation of the new bills. Hence, the distinction between the political arena and the supposedly depoliticised, technocratic activity of specialised bodies offering neutral, technical expertise appears to be blurred and artificial in practice. Depoliticisation looks like, rather than an objective condition, as a distinctive political strategy in the politics of regulatory governance (Burnham 2001; Flinders and Buller 2006). Above all, it appears that the level of de facto independence – the distinctive feature of IRAs – may affect their centrality in policy making, that is, their influence in the decision-making process, in combination with other variables. On the one hand, agencies' de facto independence from politicians is positively related to the technocratic, 'problem-solving' need for including IRAs in policy making, while their de facto independence from regulatees is likely to modify the structure of incentives for including them strategically in order to avoid any possible implementation failure. On the other hand, external factors, such as the professionalisation of the legislature, may alter the possible influence of IRAs in the course of the decision-making processes, by determining agencies' policy relevance and the expected legitimacy gains. This result reinvigorates the pertinence of the questions concerning the deployment of political power within the institutions and organisations of the regulatory state (Moe 2005), namely when considering that IRAs play a crucial role in policy making while being separated from democratic institutions, possibly increasing even more the political and societal concerns about the systemic 'net loss of legitimacy' and raising the fiduciary costs of delegation (Majone 2005).

Part III shows that the investigated IRAs seem accountable to the media. Therefore, in line with other research studies, this study confirms that IRAs can be formally independent and yet be considered under control (Lægreid et al. 2008), with the application of the appropriate 'ex-post' accountability mechanisms (Busuioc 2009). Nevertheless, the case of the British CC shows that even well endowed IRAs do not necessarily benefit from a positive media evaluation for efficiency. It appears that the proper implementation of the specific mode of delegation promoting IRAs' factual independence – through a fiduciary principle (Majone 2001a, c, 2005) – is appropriate to sustain their credibility, but hardly improves efficiency. This result might defy the popular ambition of designing a structure of delegation that simultaneously enhances regulatory credibility through independence and decision-making efficiency through the simultaneous application of 'ex-ante', 'ex-post' or 'ongoing' control mechanisms. Agencies' independence and bureaucratic control constitute thus two elements of a balance that is systemically unstable (Christensen and Lægreid 2007), reinforcing the claim that the quest for a middle way between these two poles can still be considered a crucial problem of regulatory policies (Braun 2002). Therefore, on the one hand, the media can possibly act as a proper accountability forum that provides the public with consistent evaluations of agencies' work. On the other hand, whereas a positive media evaluation of credibility has proven to be attainable under specific conditions, the corresponding evaluation of efficiency seems chimerical for IRAs, even in the 'most likely' case, potentially compromising the reputation of (some) independent regulators in front of ordinary citizens.

In that regard, it is worth noting that my findings concerning the effect of agencies' networks could offer a possible solution to reconcile these trade-offs, as networks could hypothetically promote a process of mutual adjustment leading to factual independence and credible/efficient regulation at the same time. On the one hand, agencies that perceive themselves as part of a formal or informal transnational network of regulators, sharing similar aims and problems, are more likely to resist external influences and conduct their regulatory action properly. Agencies' leaders have motivational incentives to maintain their reputation in the eyes of the other members of the network, to achieve international cooperation and avoid public blame (Majone 1997a). On the other hand, the embeddedness in networks is expected to supply agencies with expertise and information derived from other regulators, to give them potential allies in front of political decision makers, while also offering a range of technical and symbolic resources that should enhance their emancipation from the regulatees (Maggetti 2007). Therefore, regulatory networks may respond to the challenge of developing new, more adequate procedures for securing agencies' accountability, because they do not contradict the principle of IRAs' independence and at the same time they do not hinder high-quality regulation. Whether, to what extent and under which conditions this really happens, remains however an open empirical question.

Connecting the levels of analysis

Ontology and methodology

My hypotheses were formulated according to rational choice, sociological and historical institutionalist perspectives, applying the comprehensive theoretical framework elaborated in the introductory chapter. In part I, a number of integrated combinations of conditions were expected to lead to the different types of outcomes (i.e. high de facto independence from elected politicians, high de facto independence from regulatees, low de facto independence from elected politicians, and low de facto independence from regulatees), following the notion of complex causation (Ragin 1987, 2000). Hypothesis 1.1 and Hypothesis 1.5 refer to non-causal relationships portraying, respectively, the relationship between formal and de facto independence, and the relationship between de facto independence from elected politicians and de facto independence from regulatees. Hypothesis 1.2 mixes historical and rational institutionalisms by examining the joint effect of ageing and veto players. Hypothesis 1.3 combines historical and sociological explanatory factors, drawing from the varieties of capitalism approach and developing arguments in terms of sector-specific path dependence. Hypothesis 1.4 offers a rational – sociological account, looking at the effect of agencies' networks and organisational strength. Part II displays a specific focus on a smaller sample of agencies, implementing a specific 'effects-of-causes' approach (Mahoney and Goertz 2006). Therefore, a more inductive logic is adopted regarding the combination of complementary and competitive conditions, starting with a descriptive hypothesis (H 2.1) about the influence of agencies in policy making. Then, two remote factors are operationalised that should enable the occurrence of the outcome of agencies' maximal centrality: the appropriateness with a dual or monocratic politico-administrative system and the degree of professionalisation of the legislature. The former hypothesis (H 2.2) follows a sociological institutionalist logic, while the latter (H 2.3) goes along a more rational line of reasoning. Next, proximate explanations are examined. Hypothesis 2.4 refers to the relevance of sectoral patterns, according to an historical institutionalist argument. Hypothesis 2.5 offers two alternative sociological or rational explanations, depending from whether an efficiency-driven or legitimacy-driven behaviour is prevalent. Finally, Part III focuses on two distinct theoretical questions. Hypothesis 3.1 emphasises the role of the media when evaluating IRAs, with a sociological-organisational perspective. Hypothesis 3.2 adopts rational choice institutionalist arguments for describing the relationship between the media evaluation of agencies' credibility and efficiency.

Connecting the three new institutionalisms in a multi-layer explanatory model was possible by adopting a methodology that is not only appropriate for evaluating competing paradigms, but that in addition entails a configurational approach, in which the explanatory factors may be regarded as logically intertwined. This objective required in turn a framework that supports a view of causation that is equally *unified* (to treat the three new institutionalisms as complementary components of explanation) and *complex* (to keep the analytical levels distinct). The QCA analysis, its extension in terms of fuzzy-set, and the related analysis of necessary and sufficient conditions was the appropriate technique for this task (Ragin 1987, 2000; Rihoux 2006; Rihoux and Ragin 2008). Indeed, it has been possible to analyse cases as configurations, and to identify different combinations of causally relevant conditions. Then, instead of focusing on the symmetrical 'net effect' of independent variables, QCA permitted the examination of subset relationships, in order to discover the necessary and sufficient conditions for the outcome (Ragin 2005a, 2006b). The possibility of discovering complex patterns of causation implied, on the one hand, that much heuristic attention was given to discovery and diversity, assuming that it is possible, and even probable, that different causal paths may lead to the same outcome. On the other hand, each variable was considered valuable even as INUS (insufficient but necessary part of unnecessary but sufficient combination) or SUIN (sufficient but unnecessary part of an insufficient but necessary combination) condition (Mahoney 2007).

In this research study, the results of the application of the Fs/QCA, the two-step QCA and the comparative analysis of necessary and sufficient conditions support the 'abductive' complementarities of the three new institutionalisms and the convenience of combining them through a framework of analytical eclecticism (Sil 2000, 2004; Katzenstein and Sil 2005). This analytical perspective is not a priori committed to a specific theoretical perspective; it is ontologically relatively flexible; and problem-oriented. Therefore, a meta-theoretical synthesis is unnecessary and falls beyond the ambitions of this type of investigation. However, the moderate analytical eclecticism elaborated in the present research, based on three relatively compatible research traditions, offers a certain degree of coherence that permits to draw some more general insights.

Part I finds empirical support for the historical-rational institutional hypothesis (H 1.2) and, partly, for some sociological institutional insights (H 1.4). In turn, part II highlights the pertinence of combining rational (H 2.3) and sociological (H 2.5) factors. Finally, part III, again, illustrates the usefulness of examining rational and sociological explanations (H 3.1 and H 3.2). Therefore, it appears that the new three institutionalisms can be fruitfully connected, in the sense that historical institutionalism seems mainly useful for explaining the contextual causes enabling the possible occurrence of meso-level outcome variables (in this case, the causes of de facto independence), while sociological institutionalism is particularly relevant for studying the variation of meso or macro effects (here, the consequences of de facto independence). This means that, historical institutionalism seems more appropriate to a 'causes-of-effects' research design (such as in part I) (Mahoney and Goertz 2006), while sociological institutionalism corresponds better to a 'consequential and problem-oriented' approach (part II and III), which focuses, for instance, on 'how the existence of given institutions contributes to the emergence or avoidance of certain societal or economic problems' (Scharpf 2000b). Furthermore, in accordance with Lindenberg's method of decreasing abstraction, rational choice institutionalism can be integrated in both perspectives for operationalising the necessary connection with the actor's level, which is, at the end of the day, the actual source of action and change (Lindenberg 1992).

Towards a two-level model

The overall insights of the empirical parts I, II and III can bring into being a comprehensive, single model, configuring a two-level structure (Goertz and Mahoney 2005; Goertz 2006b). The basic level contains the main explanatory conditions and outcome variables (Goertz and Mahoney 2005). The former consist of IRAs' de facto independence from political decisions makers and IRAs' de facto independence from regulatees. Respectively, the outcomes are the centrality of IRAs in policy making and their media evaluation of credibility/efficiency. At the secondary level, we find variables that are less central to the core argument but still display a (indirect) causal connection to the main outcome variable (Goertz and Mahoney 2005). In other words, causal relationships exist between secondary-level variables and basic-level outcomes, mediated by the basic-level variables. Here, the combination of old age OR veto players AND formal independence leads to de facto independence from political decision makers. Old age OR networks AND de facto independence from political decision makers lead to de facto independence from regulatees. The secondary-level conditions, by contributing to the generation of more proximate causal conditions, constitute the remote causes of the outcomes at the basic level, while basic-level variables can be considered intermediary variables.

Regulation after the crisis

This is a very brief note on the future of the regulatory state after the financial crisis of 2008-2010, originated from the so-called US subprime mortgages crisis, and on the 'crisis of knowledge and ideas' it is producing (Hutter *et al.* 2008). The global crisis invokes a reassessment of the pertinence of the approach in terms of regulatory state – regulatory capitalism. Is a formalised, open, multi-level, and independently regulated model of regulatory governance still sustainable for the financial markets, and beyond? Or rather, will the financial turmoil imply the premature obsolescence of the new regulatory order, meaning that the regulatory state has actually failed and should be replaced by something else? The underlying question is whether are we moving towards a new form of 'regulatory statism'. On the one hand, the subprime crisis puts the spots on the failure of the devices for supervising the financial system, casting doubts on the capacity of the regulatory framework to prevent systemic crises; what is more, the main weaknesses emerged in the leading country in the development of the regulatory state, that is, the U.S.A, directly challenging the prudential supervision of the Treasury, the Federal Reserve, and the Securities Exchange Commission. On the other hand, the management of the disaster involved a series of massive measures of public intervention, to prevent the collapse of the system. As a result, not only the allocative efficiency of (financial) markets is severely put into question, but also the ambition of the (long-term) viability of a regulated capitalism becomes doubtful. Against the market-oriented politico-economic zeitgeist, governments promoted a colossal public rescue of the big financial players in many countries, through the offer of huge amounts of cash and even by the mean of a partial nationalisation of the companies of 'national interest' – reinvigorating a 'dirty word, designating a bad old past' (Miller 2008) – through a spectacular violation of the international accounting standards.

While acknowledging the systemic character of the crisis (Hutter *et al.* 2008; Nesvetailova and Palan 2008), it is useful to discuss its implications for regulatory governance, by provisionally treating the crisis as an epiphenomenon (and not as the consequence of inherent disequilibria). First of all, a number of regulatory failures can be identified, among which the most relevant for the present discussion are three: the insufficient supervision over the activities of some big banks and other financial institutions; the use of inadequate models for evaluating the systemic risks; and the lack of authoritative means for direct intervention (Chavagneux 2007, 2008b, c). To begin with, the regulators were materially unable to ensure the systematic supervision of the regulated industries. As a matter of fact, even the chairperson of one of the leading financial IRAs in Europe (the Financial Services Authority) admitted the fiasco of the previous 'light-touch' approach and asked for 'more resources and more personnel' (Turner 2009). The second point refers, for instance, to the questionable adoption of statistical models of historical probabilities based on relatively short time-series (generally fifteen years) for evaluating the future risk, and to the faulty assumption about the mutual independence of payment defaults, whereas the risk management would imply an extreme level of sophistication and technical skills (Moatti 2008). Finally, the crisis highlighted the need for more competencies of regulation, in order to control, among others, the activity of speculative hedge funds that introduced high volatility in the market, and the extensive use of financial derivatives. In this respect, the US supervision authorities are proposing to consent to the trade of derivatives only on so-called organised markets, where professional accountants would ensure the security of the transactions, under the direct supervision of independent regulators (Chavagneux 2008c). These regulatory failures draw attention to three main shortcomings of regulatory governance by (banking and financial services) IRAs: the amount of human and financial resources for enforcing effective supervision; the possible inadequacy of certain regulators' knowledge-based capacities; and, respectively, the (relatively) limited extent of the delegated competences of regulation beyond prudential supervision.

However, a number of elements would suggest that the diagnosis of these shortcomings will lead policy makers to reinforce regulatory governance, and not to challenge the present regulatory order with a paradigmatic change (Hall 1993; Sabatier 2007). First of all, one must bear in mind that these regulatory failures are located within the governance of the financial sector, and have limited consequences for other sector-specific agencies, which are usually regulating less deregulated domains. Concerning the financial sector, it appears that IRAs constitute, together with governments, the key players in the crisis (Hutter and Dodd 2008). Moreover, the public intervention is designed as merely temporary (Hutter and Dodd 2008). Finally, the solution to the problem is politically and societally framed in terms of 'more regulation' (Hofmann 2008; Lodge 2008; Miller 2008). In fact, one can observe that the immediate effect of the crisis is to support the trend towards re-regulation, in spite of self-regulation or deregulation.

For instance, in France two new public sector-specific agencies were created in the immediate aftermath of the crisis (Chavagneux 2008a). The first is the *Société de prise de participation de l'Etat*, to help the recapitalisation of the banks, by borrowing liquidity on the international financial markets. The second is the *Société de refinancement*, which was created to ensure the financing of short-term credit as a substitute of the interbank market. The Swiss case displays another interesting development. The two Swiss big banks, UBS and *Credit Suisse*, were severely knocked by the crisis. Namely, UBS was hit by the reverse of its highly risky investment activities in the USA It received a massive public help that amounts to a considerable percentage of its capitalisation, through a coordinated intervention of the Swiss government and the Swiss National Bank. The Swiss Federal Banking Commission remained passive for a long time, and was unable to predict and prevent the crisis. Its limited resources and scarce independence from regulated industries, especially from the big banks, were publicly blamed.[1]

---

1. David Gow, 'Switzerland unveils bank bail-out plan: UBS hit by "massive" outflows of clients' money', 'Bank's chief says markets in "panic mode"', *The Guardian*, 16 October 2008; Alan Cowell, 'Credit Suisse and UBS Get Funds', *The New York Times*, 16 October 2008; *The Economist*, 5 July 2008.

Meanwhile, a new, integrated regulator is being created (the *Finanzmarktaufsicht*, the Swiss Financial Market Supervisory Authority), in order to ensure the supervision of financial markets and insurances, which will benefit from more resources, a different organisational structure (consisting of a board, a general direction with decisional powers and an audit office) and a greater level of formal autonomy. Similarly, in the USA, the federal administration is proposing to give broader powers to the Securities Exchange Commission and to the Federal Reserve and to create new agencies to supervise hedge funds and all trading in financial derivatives, in order to impose tougher standards on big financial institutions, and to major non-bank financial firms (Geithner 2009). As a consequence, companies and financial instruments now unsupervised will be reregulated, fostering greater wide-ranging oversight also on credit rating agencies, mortgage brokers, and greater supervision of complex financial instruments (WGFR 2009). Finally, the European Parliament and the EU Commission gave new powers to the Committee of European Securities Regulators (CESR) (Wymeersch 2009), for instance in order to regulate and supervise rating agencies. At the same time, the de Larosière report suggested the creation of a European Systemic Risk Council, so as to collate and analyse issues and information relating to systemic risk and financial stability, and a new 'European System of Financial Supervisors', providing central co-ordination for regulators (but leaving day-to-day supervision to member states) (de Larosière *et al.* 2009). Correspondingly, the establishment of a new independent authority with regulatory powers has been proposed at European level, which would consist of 'a standard setter and overseer in the area of supervision, [that] would be involved, alongside central banks, in macro-prudential analysis' (whilst the primary responsibility for supervision would remain, again, at member state level) (Turner 2009).

At the end of the day, it appears that the regulatory state can also become interventionist; and that the regulation of the architecture and the practices of the banking and financial services is considered even more necessary, as the viability of self-regulated markets that were deemed to be naturally able to allocate efficiently resources and correctly evaluate the risks is being largely disconfirmed in practice (Grossman and Stiglitz 1980; Stiglitz 1982; Krugman 1992; Fligstein 2001; Rodrik 2002; Aglietta and Rebérioux 2004; Black 2008; Lodge 2008; Miller 2008). Therefore, the future of regulation, as a specific form of (public) governance, seems rosy, since (financial) regulatory institutions survived the crisis and they have been even reinforced and further legitimised, while at the same time the regulatory state is possibly coming of age, no longer constrained by the pure free-market ideology that shaped some stages of its early development (and eventually starting to address the questions of the effectiveness of regulators' independence and performance more seriously).

The virtues and perils and of independence

To conclude our discussion on the practice of regulation by independent regulatory agencies, a set of normative questions needs to be briefly addressed. At the end of the day, is de facto independence a good or a bad thing? To what extent and under which conditions are independent regulators beneficial or detrimental for democratic policy making? How do IRAs help or hinder policy making efficiency? Should decision-makers improve or reduce regulatory independence and how? After having analysed the causes of de facto independence and some of its consequences, it is possible to offer some tentative considerations. Now we know that regulatory agencies are mostly de facto independent from elected politicians, regardless of formal independence (with some variations); that they are important in lawmaking (the most independent, the most important); and that they are potentially accountable to media (but other control devices are needed).

These findings have normative implications for the political management of IRAs. In that regard, this section discusses the following points: (1) the need for aligning formal and de facto independence; (2) the functional antagonism between agencies, politicians and the regulatees; and (3) the balance between independence and accountability. The argument is at follows: IRAs' independence is not a priori good or bad, but their institutional design must be adequate and effective; IRAs can positively contribute to policy making as new powerful actors when they successfully develop and maintain a functional antagonism between politicians and the regulatees; finally, the most pressing question is how to keep regulators independent, accountable, credible and efficient in their day-to-day activity.

Adequacy of formal and de facto independence

One of the main empirical finding of this book is that the formal independence of agencies, as granted by statutory prescriptions, has a contingent impact, together with other conditions, but does not fully determine the level of de facto independence of IRAs. Factual independence is indeed shaped by a number of organisational and institutional factors. This result has important implications for the institutional design of IRAs. The argument has two steps.

First, policy-makers should select the adequate level of formal independence to be given to IRAs and to be inscribed in agencies' constitutions, according to the desired balance between agency's discretion and direct political control, by taking into account informal and contextual factors. The optimal level cannot be pre-defined once and for all, but it should be a matter of political debate, discussion and negotiation. This choice can be informed by some considerations. The adequacy of the level of independence firstly depends on the desired trade-off between credibility in front of external stakeholders and direct political accountability, in line with the characteristics of the regulated sector. Economic regulation typically requires higher independence from policymakers than social regulation (Gilardi 2008). In fact, in economic sectors such as utilities and finance, the main task of independent agencies is to promote regulation-for-competition by providing credible commitments that secure long-term policy consistency *vis-à-vis* customers and investors in the regulated industries (Drazen and Masson 1994; Brunetti *et al.* 1998). Conversely, social regulation – that concerns issues such as food safety, healthcare, pensions, environment – follows another, broader rationale than competition-oriented regulation, which is more concerned with welfare, health, quality control and consumer protection (Carpenter 2001b; Moran 2002). Such 'positive' regulation can be more controversial, as it has higher redistributive effects and entails more concentrated costs and benefits, for which a coordinated solution is more difficult and more demanding (Majone 1993a; Wincott 2003). As a consequence, in the case of social regulation, the political management of regulators requires higher accountability and increased 'bottom-up' participation, to overcome resistance and improve the implementation of regulatory policies, while economic regulation calls for more attention to the mechanisms that secure high de facto independence.

Furthermore, the design of independent regulators should depend on the institutional 'appropriateness' of the agency model for the target countries (March and Olsen 2004). It appears that contextual factors and path-dependent trajectories shape the functioning of public sector organisations that are adopted and implemented from the experience of other countries, following top-down and horizontal pressures – by the means of 'benchmarking', 'best practice', 'policy transfer', and 'lesson-drawing' (Radaelli 2004). For instance, institutional settings comprising an adversarial legal system, strong separation of powers and a system of checks-and-balances, like the USA, can quite easily accommodate powerful independent regulators, which constitute an 'at arm's length' branch of government that is consistent with their political-administrative culture (Levi-Faur 2005b; Van Waarden and Hildebrand 2009). On the contrary, in political systems based on consensual policy making, where trust and informal decision-making routines play a crucial role, the same level of independence from elected politicians could generate different results (Armingeon 2002). The example of the introduction of New Public Management in Norway showed that de-contextualised reforms promoting excessive formalisation and control mechanisms may disrupt a coherent institutional framework based on mutual trust and produce unnecessary conflicts and higher coordination costs (Fukuyama 1999; Bartle 2006; Christensen *et al.* 2008).

The second step is the alignment of formal and factual independence. Institutional engineering and the establishment of new public sector organisations always imply some unintended consequences (Pollitt and Bouckaert 2004). However, some safety measures can help minimising the risk of implementation problems. On the one hand, it is important to understand the role regulators will play in each political-administrative system, by recognising the 'functional equivalence' of organisations across countries and their 'institutional complementarities' within countries (Van Deth 1998). Therefore, political decision-makers should bear in mind the topography of the regulatory system, and be able to identify the 'political principal' and, respectively, the 'regulatees', that is, the relevant external actors to whom IRAs are expected to be related, as defined by their mandate.

In different institutional settings, functionally equivalent principals can be: the president, the government, one or more ministers, administrative offices, the parliament, parliamentary committees, or a specific oversight body. The target of regulation, which is affected by regulation, supervision and sanctions and rewards, may comprise: all economic actors, the industries operating in the sector, the licensed firms, liberal professionals, producers' associations, employees' associations, civil servants, stakeholders, consumers, and citizens. Next, the notion of 'institutional complementarities' is useful to stress the need for analysing institutions in a relational manner (Hall and Soskice 2001) and realise that IRAs' factual independence may also depend on the horizontal relationships that they develop with other public sector organisations. Regulators are indeed involved in a complex web of collaborative and competitive relationships with co-regulators, regional and local authorities, and tribunals, which may limit, or support, the effective independence of IRAs. To sum up, the alignment of formal and de facto independence requires the clarification of the structure of delegation concerning each regulator, in order to specify the systemic role of the investigated IRA and to qualify the nature of its linkages with the other relevant actors in the regulatory space.

On the other hand, in this book it has been suggested that some specific conditions influence de facto independence beyond formal prescriptions, for which special attention is needed. It appears that agencies are highly de facto independent from their principal when they are old and when the politicians have to cope with several veto players. To be precise, agencies may benefit from a process of autonomisation from the principal when ageing, due to the accumulation of material and symbolic resources in the course of repeated interactions with the regulated sector. This way, they acquire informational advantages in front of elected politicians and a unique acquaintance with those being regulated that enhance their emancipation from political control. At the same time, the presence of many veto players favours the independence of agencies, as it becomes more difficult for 'multiple principals' to coordinate themselves to sway the regulatory process, while the monitoring process also becomes more costly. Institutional veto points are constituted, for instance, by presidential vetoing prerogatives, the procedural requirements of parliamentary bicameralism, and the existence of federalist arrangements. Partisan veto players, that are populating these institutions, represent different configurations of political coalitions, whose agreement is necessary to make decisions (Tsebelis 2002).

Equally, the participation of agencies in transnational networks may support their independence from the regulatees, by offering them technical assistance and promoting learning, socialisation, and the diffusion of 'best practices'. By taking advantage of their position, network-embedded agencies can enhance their independence by relying on a transnational coalition supporting their regulatory policies, and providing the belief in their capacity (Carpenter 2001a, b). In addition, agencies' networks are said to sustain agencies' effective exercise of delegated competencies, while leaving wide discretionary power to independent regulatory agencies (Majone 2001b, 2002). Therefore, old agencies would require closer oversight to avoid excessive autonomisation from elected politicians, especially when the 'principal' must cope with many veto players, while transnational networks of regulators may help reducing the risk of capture by the regulated industries. Finally, it should be added that the relationship between an agency and the politicians and the relationship between an agency and those it regulates are mutually influential, suggesting that agencies cannot 'serve two masters'. The implications of this finding are discussed in the next section.

Agencies, politicians and the regulatees

It has been noted that agencies, besides elected politicians and the regulatees, represent a distinct set of actors, which accomplish their regulatory tasks quite effectively and autonomously (Thatcher 2002c, d). Two findings of this book permit to corroborate this argument and to qualify it. The first line of reasoning is as follows. Pertaining to their regulatory functions, effective IRAs are those that are able to successfully develop and maintain a 'functional antagonism' with their external actors (Braun 1993, 1997). Accordingly, factually independent agencies shall mediate between the conflicting interests of elected politicians and regulatees, and build up a situation where the two external actors are related through the IRAs but remain equally distant from them. When agencies develop this intermediary position, they can successfully manage the interdependence of politics and business in the name of the 'public interest'. Empirical research shows that functional antagonism is possible, but it configures a rather unstable equilibrium, which tends to oscillate permanently between the two opposite poles. In particular, agencies that are very independent from elected politicians cannot benefit from their political support *vis-à-vis* the regulated industries. These 'footloose' agencies are more prone to regulatory capture (Bernstein 1955, 1972). A number of conditions are helpful to counteract these tendencies, namely, as said, the support and coordination with other agencies, and, on the other hand, a complex, redundant system of ex-post controls increasing the legitimacy of regulators in front of the politicians and the regulated industries (this point will be dealt in detail in the last section).

Furthermore, given that IRAs have a key role in sector-specific lawmaking, they shall be considered as important political actors, too. Therefore, the development of functional antagonism is also desirable when agencies are involved in policy making at domestic, international and supranational level. This time, the risk is no longer to be captured by the regulatees, but that of political steering by the principal, beyond the official mandate, following the electoral agenda, in order to legitimise prior decisions through de-politicisation and technocratic rhetoric. Instead, agencies should be factually independent not only in the execution of their regulatory tasks, as stated in their constitutions, but they should also remain independent when they are integrated in lawmaking to provide expertise and offer policy advice, even though these activities do not follow the statutory competences of agencies. This time, functional antagonism can be favoured by another, complementary set of mechanisms, which comprises statutory prescriptions of formal independence and the presence of many veto points in the political system (or their functional equivalents). High formal independence consists of traditional arrangements concerning IRAs' board appointments and dismissals, their relationships with government and parliament, and their financial and organisational autonomy (Gilardi 2002a). These features are however insufficient to ensure factual independence from elected politicians. As discussed above, the presence of many veto points can contribute to guarantee adequate leeway to agencies. In fact, it appears that, as it is the case for ordinary bureaucracy, under 'multiple principals', agencies have wider discretion *vis-à-vis* elected officials (Wood and Petrovsky 2007), because the structure of agency incentives is blurred and there is a collective action problem for the principals (Gailmard 2009). The same holds for other institutional devices with similar effects of delegation, which counteract 'majoritarian' policy making, through the fragmentation of political power in the executive and the geographical partitioning of sovereignty, such as power sharing, federalism and devolution (Lijphart 1999).

Independence, accountability, credibility, efficiency

The main functional rationales for delegating public authority to IRAs, that is, the expected enhancement of regulatory credibility and efficiency, are expected to derive from their statutory separateness from elected politicians and organised interests (Majone 1993b, 2001b). Therefore, delegation to IRAs implies a 'net loss' of legitimacy for the political system, because the political 'principal' can transfer his powers to the independent delegate, but not his legitimacy; hence IRAs must rely on other – external – sources of legitimacy (Majone 2005). This situation implies two theoretical problems: the reconciliation of independence and accountability; and the concomitant pursuit of regulatory credibility and efficiency.

In this book, it was repeatedly argued that neither 'inputs-oriented legitimacy' nor traditional top-down (or 'downward') accountability and bottom-up (or 'upward') accountability are relevant for agencies that are formally independent by design. Instead, following Majone, the possible solution is a 'multi-pronged system of controls' to keep regulatory bodies accountable and yet independent (Majone 1996a, 2002). This system consists of a variety of control mechanisms, whose crucial elements are network embeddedness and media accountability. On the one hand, the emergence and ongoing consolidation of transnational networks of regulators could provide, 'as a more or less unintended by-product' (Majone 2000), incentives and means to agencies for the development of a system of mutual controls, ideally making the agencies horizontally accountable (Moe 2005). In addition, networks may provide regulators with additional dynamism, resources and expertise, and favour a process of policy diffusion, which is expected to follow rational and problem-solving orientations, eventually producing 'better' regulatory outputs. On the other hand, the media can function as an 'accountability forum' for IRAs, by scrutinising agencies with increasing attention and growing autonomy, and working as 'linkage mechanisms' for solving informational asymmetries *vis-à-vis* elected politicians and ordinary citizens.

However, the second problem, the extent to which regulatory credibility and efficiency can really coexist, constitutes an open question. According to a theoretical argument, there is a possible trade-off between IRAs' credibility and efficiency, because they entail two structures of delegation that appear hardly reconcilable in practice. On the one hand, in order to create credible commitments, we should expect agencies to be factually independent in the exercise of their powers. Indeed, the pre-condition for solving the policy time-inconsistency problem of regulation is a broad delegation of powers, following the fiduciary principle, derived from the framework of transaction-cost politics (Majone 2001; de Visscher *et al.*), which entails a substantial differentiation between the trustor and the trustee's preferences and behaviour. The need for credibility in the long term requires freedom from ex-ante, ongoing and also ex-post controls, implying the transfer of political property rights—i.e. specific policy competences—to independent regulators, while the key problems of agency theory—hidden action and hidden information—are no longer central (Majone 2001b). On the other hand, the implementation of efficient regulation should imply that the de facto independence of the agency be more restricted and constrained (Franchino 2002). In fact, in this case, the main problem is to avoid inefficient delegation and 'bureaucratic drift and slippage' (Epstein and O'Halloran 1999, Majone 2001). This means that the principal should be able to retain some formal and informal controls on agencies' behaviour (Calvert *et al.* 1989; Bendor *et al.* 2001) to minimise any possibility of agencies' 'shirking' (Pollack 2002, 2003). As a consequence, the concomitant pursuit of credibility and efficient seems puzzling and calls for new regulatory arrangements and innovative solutions.

Directions for further research

This book was designed in order to contribute to advance knowledge on the regulatory state and regulatory capitalism through the examination of the de facto independence of regulators and the consequences of agencification on policy-making and regulatory outcomes. The study of regulation in practice is, however, still in its infancy, as three limitations of this research study illustrate.

(1) To begin with, the question of the real performance of regulators is still very much undetermined, both conceptually and empirically. On the one hand, at conceptual level, we still lack an intersubjective standard for assessing and evaluating the quality of agencies' regulatory action from an outcome-oriented perspective. There is neither consensus on the type of regulatory result that should be considered primary (among, for instance, the quality of agencies' individual outputs, in the form of rules or decisions; their effects on the behaviour of the regulatees, such as the cases of infringement and litigation; and the macro-impact of regulation on the markets, or even on the whole society), nor on the specific goals that constitute the notion of IRAs' regulatory quality (either economic, or technical, social, political). On the other hand, empirical evidence continues to be mixed, partial and ambiguous. In particular, the problem of developing reliable measures of IRAs' performance remains methodologically unsolved, and with

existing data meaningful cross-cases comparisons are extremely difficult to execute.[2]

(2) In addition, in Chapters 4 and 5, I examined the consequences of agencification for policy making and for the media evaluation of credibility and efficiency. The focus on the de facto independence of IRAs justified this analytical decision. Nevertheless, in a next step, it would be interesting to bridge the gap with the literature on policy diffusion, illustrating how regulatory agencies operate in a context of interdependence, not only as regards their establishment, but also in the execution of their day-to-day regulatory action, namely by investigating the implications of the diffusion of 'best practices' for the regulatory process and regulatory outcomes, either framed as intended or unintended consequences. Specifically, one shall expect that the timing, the sequence and the mechanism of diffusion will crucially shape the consequences of regulatory governance. For instance, early adopters should perform better when one supposes that the implementation of regulatory reforms is an incremental phenomenon. But one may also suppose that the followers could avoid the negative experiences and adopt the most favourable innovations, if they are able to circumvent the take-for-grantedness of apparent 'best practices' that do not 'travel' across countries and/or sectors; and that processes of reflexive learning from successful experiences are plausibly expected to produce better results than dynamics of social emulation.

(3) Finally, a normative concern is becoming urgent, and even more following the recent trend towards 'more regulation', that is, the need to deal with the 'democratic deficit' of the regulatory state. Further research should investigate the conditions under which it is possible (or, respectively, impossible) to ensure the new forms of accountability, and, in turn, the legitimacy of regulatory governance by IRAs. Seeing that, as it was theoretically argued at the beginning of this dissertation and empirically supported later on, the traditional procedures for legitimising regulatory governance by IRAs are hardly sustainable in the long run, this enterprise calls for the elaboration of new forms of legitimacy and accountability, as component of a 'multi-pronged' accountability system, to complement and qualify their media scrutiny, as presented in Chapter 5. As anticipated, a promising venue for improving IRAs' legitimacy might stem from the creation and institutionalisation of networks of regulators. In fact, according to the empirical analysis in Chapter 3, it appears that regulatory networks could provide agencies with informational, technical, and symbolic resources, while they might also constitute potential devices for promoting a reciprocal control through horizontal interactions and the social valorisation of virtuous behaviour, without compromising their independence.

---

2. Though the current developments of the COBRA project seem very promising for the study of the performances of public sector organisations at large (see http://www.publicmanagement-cobra.org/).

appendix | the questionnaire to chapter 3

Introduction

The first part will ask you some general questions about the functioning of your agency and its relationships with other actors. In the second section we will ask questions about the dynamic and the composition of the management board of your agency. Finally, we are interested in the agency's rule-making process, namely by studying the 'regulations' (rules, ordinances, circulars, recommendations, communications, advices and so forth) issued by the agency, to which the supervised institutions (companies, firms, etc.) should conform.

1 --- questions --- first part (self-determination of preferences):

- What proportion of the current employees of the agency's secretariat have previously worked in the public administration?*
- What proportion of the current employees of the agency's secretariat have previously worked in the private sector?
- What proportion of the former employees of the agency's secretariat will work in the public administration in the future?
- What proportion of the former employees of the agency's secretariat will work in the private sector in the future?
- What proportion of the employees of the secretariat of the agency have accomplished internships in the public administration?
- What proportion of the employees of the secretariat of the agency have accomplished internships in the private sector?
- The agency asks for the support of the public administration for expertise purposes...

  _____

- The public administration asks for the support of the agency for expertise purposes...

  _____

- The agency asks for the support of the private sector for expertise purposes...

  Very infrequently or never   Very frequently

  _____

- The private sector asks for the support of the agency for expertise purposes...

  Very infrequently or never   Very frequently

- Meetings between the agency and the public administration are...

  Very infrequently or never   Very frequently

- Meetings between the agency and the representatives of the private sector are...

  Very infrequently or never   Very frequently

- To what extent can the government influence the budget of the agency?

  Not at all   Entirely

- To what extent can the parliament influence the budget of the agency?

  Not at all   Entirely

- To what extent can the public administration influence the budget of the agency?

- To what extent can the private sector influence the budget of the agency?

  Not at all   Entirely

- How far can the government determine the internal organisation of the agency?

  Not at all   Entirely

- How far can the parliament determine the internal organisation of the agency?

  Not at all   Entirely

- How far can the public administration determine the internal organisation of the agency?

Not at all   Entirely

- How far can the private sector determine the internal organisation of the agency?

Not at all   Entirely

- Generally speaking, do you consider budgetary resources of the agency...

Largely sufficient   Completely insufficient

- Generally speaking, do you consider human resources of the agency...

Largely sufficient   Completely insufficient

- Political parties play an important role when deciding who should become a member of the management board of the agency.

Strongly agree   Strongly disagree

- If yes, are the representatives of the political parties homogenously represented in the board?

Yes ☐   No ☐

- How are the powers distributed among the board members?

Equally distributed   Unequally distributed

- The departure of a member of the management board before the end of its mandate is:

Very rare   Very frequent

- The discussions of the board are generally:

Very conflicting   Very consensual

- The decisions of the board are in effect taken :

By a majority vote   By consensus   Other :

2 --- questions --- second part (self-determination of preferences):

- When has there been a replacement of the management board's director or chairperson of the agency in the last twenty years? More than one answer is possible.

☐ 1985	☐ 1992	☐ 1999
☐ 1986	☐ 1993	☐ 2000
☐ 1987	☐ 1994	☐ 2001
☐ 1988	☐ 1995	☐ 2002
☐ 1989	☐ 1996	☐ 2003
☐ 1990	☐ 1997	☐ 2004
☐ 1991	☐ 1998	☐ 2005

- At the moment, is the director of the board of the agency hired full time?

Yes ☐   No ☐

If not, which is the current occupation of the director (more than one answer is possible)?

☐ Public official
☐ Employee of the Secretariat of the agency
☐ Member of the Board of the agency
☐ Employee, executive or manager in the private sector
☐ Representative of a producer association
☐ Representative of a consumer association
☐ Liberal professional (lawyer etc.)
☐ Professor, researcher or other academic occupations
☐ Other :

If yes, which was the former occupation of the director (more than one answer is possible)?

☐ Public official
☐ Employee of the Secretariat of the agency
☐ Member of the Board of the agency
☐ Employee, executive or manager in the private sector
☐ Representative of a producer association
☐ Representative of a consumer association
☐ Liberal professional (lawyer etc.)
☐ Professor, researcher or other academic occupations
☐ Other :

- Are board members (except the director) full time hired?

  Yes ☐   No ☐

  If not, could you approximately distribute 100 percentage points among the following current occupations of the board members (more than one answer is possible)? For example, if roughly 1/2 of board members are professors, write '50' in the corresponding space.

☐	Public officials	%
☐	Employees of the Secretariat of the agency	%
☐	Employees, executives, managers in the private sector	%
☐	Representatives of producer associations	%
☐	Representatives of consumer associations	%
☐	Liberal professionals (lawyers etc.)	%
☐	Professors, researchers or other academic occupations	%
☐	Others :	%
	→ Total :	100%

If yes, could you approximately distribute 100 percentage points among the following former occupations of the board members (more than one answer is possible)? For example, if roughly 1/2 of board members were professors, write '50' in the corresponding space.

☐	Public officials	%
☐	Employees of the Secretariat of the agency	%
☐	Employees, executives, managers in the private sector	%
☐	Representatives of producer associations	%
☐	Representatives of consumer associations	%
☐	Liberal professionals (lawyers etc.)	%
☐	Professors, researchers or other academic occupations	%
☐	Others :	%
	→ Total :	100%

3 --- questions --- (autonomy of the activity of regulation):
Could you specify which are the main 'regulations' produced by the agency (if any)? *

1) Who inspired the basic principles of the 'regulations' that institutions your agency supervise should satisfy? More than one answer is possible. If possible, we would appreciate if you could specify who the actors are (names of the individuals or organisations).

	Participant	If possible, could you specify the actors?
☐	Agency secretariat	
☐	Agency manag. board	
☐	Government	
☐	Parliament	
☐	Public administration	
☐	Other indep. agencies	
☐	Producer associations	
☐	Consumer associations	
☐	Liberal professionals	
☐	Academic profession.	
☐	Audit companies	
☐	Supervised institutions	
☐	European Union	
☐	Others:...	
☐	No one	

2) Who worked out the draft of the 'regulations'? More than one answer is possible. If possible, we would appreciate if you could specify who the actors are (names of the individuals or organisations).

	Participant	If possible, could you specify the actors?
☐	Agency secretariat	
☐	Agency man- ag. board	
☐	Government	

☐	Parliament	
☐	Public administration	
☐	Other indep. agencies	
☐	Producer associations	
☐	Consumer as-sociations	
☐	Liberal professionals	
☐	Academic pro-fession.	
☐	Audit companies	
☐	Supervised in-stitutions	
☐	European Union	
☐	Others:..	
☐	No one	

3) Who was consulted during the draft preparation of the 'regulations'? More than one answer is possible. If possible, we would appreciate if you could specify who the actors are (names of the individuals or organisations).

	Participant	If possible, could you specify the actors?
☐	Agency secretariat	
☐	Agency manag. board	
☐	Government	
☐	Parliament	
☐	Public administration	
☐	Other indep. agencies	
☐	Producer associations	
☐	Consumer associations	
☐	Liberal professionals	
☐	Academic profession.	
☐	Audit companies	

☐	Supervised institutions	
☐	European Union	
☐	Others:..	
☐	No one	

4) Who decided the adoption of the 'regulations'? More than one answer is possible. If possible, we would appreciate if you could specify who the actors are (names of the individuals or organisations).

	Participant	If possible, could you specify the actors?
☐	Agency secretariat	
☐	Agency manag. board	
☐	Government	
☐	Parliament	
☐	Public administration	
☐	Other indep. agencies	
☐	Producer associations	
☐	Consumer associations	
☐	Liberal professionals	
☐	Academic profession.	
☐	Audit companies	
☐	Supervised institutions	
☐	European Union	
☐	Others:..	
☐	No one	

5) Who is monitoring the respect of the 'regulations' by the institutions that you supervise? More than one answer is possible. If possible, we would appreciate if you could specify who the actors are (names of the individuals or organisations).

	Participant	If possible, could you specify the actors?
☐	Agency secretariat	
☐	Agency manag. board	
☐	Government	
☐	Parliament	
☐	Public administration	
☐	Other indep. agencies	
☐	Producer associations	
☐	Consumer associations	
☐	Liberal professionals	
☐	Academic profession.	
☐	Audit companies	
☐	Supervised institutions	
☐	European Union	
☐	Others:..	
☐	No one	

6) Who can decide a sanction in case of non-respect of 'regulations' by the institutions you supervise? More than one answer is possible. If possible, we would appreciate if you could specify who the actors are (names of the individuals or organisations).

	Participant	If possible, could you specify the actors?
☐	Agency secretariat	
☐	Agency manag. board	
☐	Government	
☐	Parliament	
☐	Public administration	

☐	Other indep. agencies	
☐	Producer associations	
☐	Consumer associations	
☐	Liberal professionals	
☐	Academic profession.	
☐	Audit companies	
☐	Supervised institutions	
☐	European Union	
☐	Others:..	
☐	No one	

Additional remarks …
Details

Preliminary and control study	• Interviews:	- 6 Face-to-face semi-directive interviews - 10 Telephone and 25 electronic interviews
	• Documentation:	- Annual agencies reports - Agencies' web sites - Official documents (public administrations) - Official documents (parliamentary services)
Survey	• Targets:	- IRAs' chairpersons - Total = 20 (16)
	• Waves:	- 3 (non-anonymous, by mail and email)
	• Response rate:	- 80%
Aggregated outcomes data	• Maximum:	- Politicians = 6 ; Regulatees = 6
	• Minimum:	- Politicians = 2 ; Regulatees = 2
	• Mean:	- Politicians = 4.06 ; Regulatees = 4.56
	• Median:	- Politicians = 4 ; Regulatees = 5
	• Mode:	- Politicians = 4 ; Regulatees = 5

[*] In the first wave, the formulation was slightly different.

appendix | the questionnaire to chapter 4

Introduction

We are interested in studying the ___ act, which came into force on ___. We have some questions about the decision-making process concerning this legislative revision. Our focus is on the participants (please check the corresponding box). We would also appreciate if you could roughly approximate the weight of each actor during the corresponding phase of the process (please check a box on the seven-point scale). If possible, you could also specify the actors (names of persons or organisation). More than one answer is possible.

Questions:

1) Who inspired the basic principles of the new law?

	Participant	Approximate weight	If possible, please specify the actors
☐	Government	Low ☐-☐-☐-☐-☐-☐-☐ High	
☐	First Chamber	Low ☐-☐-☐-☐-☐-☐-☐ High	
☐	Second Chamber, if any	Low ☐-☐-☐-☐-☐-☐-☐ High	
☐	Parl. Committee FC	Low ☐-☐-☐-☐-☐-☐-☐ High	
☐	Parl. Committee SC, if any	Low ☐-☐-☐-☐-☐-☐-☐ High	
☐	Public administration	Low ☐-☐-☐-☐-☐-☐-☐ High	
☐	Independent agency	Low ☐-☐-☐-☐-☐-☐-☐ High	
☐	Other agencies or courts	Low ☐-☐-☐-☐-☐-☐-☐ High	
☐	Employers/producers associations	Low ☐-☐-☐-☐-☐-☐-☐ High	
☐	Consumer associations	Low ☐-☐-☐-☐-☐-☐-☐ High	
☐	Liberal professionals	Low ☐-☐-☐-☐-☐-☐-☐ High	
☐	Academic experts	Low ☐-☐-☐-☐-☐-☐-☐ High	
☐	Trade Union	Low ☐-☐-☐-☐-☐-☐-☐ High	
☐	Supervised institutions	Low ☐-☐-☐-☐-☐-☐-☐ High	

☐	European Union	Low ☐-☐-☐-☐-☐-☐-☐ High	
☐	Others:	Low ☐-☐-☐-☐-☐-☐-☐ High	
☐	Don't know/don't answer		

2) Who conducted preliminary investigations for the new law?

	Participant	Approximate weight	If possible, please specify the actors
☐	Government	Low ☐-☐-☐-☐-☐-☐-☐ High	
☐	First Chamber	Low ☐-☐-☐-☐-☐-☐-☐ High	
☐	Second Chamber, if any	Low ☐-☐-☐-☐-☐-☐-☐ High	
☐	Parl. Committee FC	Low ☐-☐-☐-☐-☐-☐-☐ High	
☐	Parl. Committee SC, if any	Low ☐-☐-☐-☐-☐-☐-☐ High	
☐	Public administration	Low ☐-☐-☐-☐-☐-☐-☐ High	
☐	Independent agency	Low ☐-☐-☐-☐-☐-☐-☐ High	
☐	Other agencies or courts	Low ☐-☐-☐-☐-☐-☐-☐ High	
☐	Employers/producers associations	Low ☐-☐-☐-☐-☐-☐-☐ High	
☐	Consumer associations	Low ☐-☐-☐-☐-☐-☐-☐ High	
☐	Liberal professionals	Low ☐-☐-☐-☐-☐-☐-☐ High	
☐	Academic experts	Low ☐-☐-☐-☐-☐-☐-☐ High	
☐	Trade Union	Low ☐-☐-☐-☐-☐-☐-☐ High	
☐	Supervised institutions	Low ☐-☐-☐-☐-☐-☐-☐ High	
☐	European Union	Low ☐-☐-☐-☐-☐-☐-☐ High	
☐	Others:	Low ☐-☐-☐-☐-☐-☐-☐ High	
☐	Don't know/don't answer		

3) Who worked out the draft of the new law?

	Participant	Approximate weight	If possible, please specify the actors
☐	Government	Low ☐-☐-☐-☐-☐-☐-☐ High	
☐	First Chamber	Low ☐-☐-☐-☐-☐-☐-☐ High	

	Participant	Approximate weight	If possible, please specify the actors
☐	Second Chamber, if any	Low ☐-☐-☐-☐-☐-☐-☐ High	
☐	Parl. Committee FC	Low ☐-☐-☐-☐-☐-☐-☐ High	
☐	Parl. Committee SC, if any	Low ☐-☐-☐-☐-☐-☐-☐ High	
☐	Public administration	Low ☐-☐-☐-☐-☐-☐-☐ High	
☐	Independent agency	Low ☐-☐-☐-☐-☐-☐-☐ High	
☐	Other agencies or courts	Low ☐-☐-☐-☐-☐-☐-☐ High	
☐	Employers/producers associations	Low ☐-☐-☐-☐-☐-☐-☐ High	
☐	Consumer associations	Low ☐-☐-☐-☐-☐-☐-☐ High	
☐	Liberal professionals	Low ☐-☐-☐-☐-☐-☐-☐ High	
☐	Academic experts	Low ☐-☐-☐-☐-☐-☐-☐ High	
☐	Trade Union	Low ☐-☐-☐-☐-☐-☐-☐ High	
☐	Supervised institutions	Low ☐-☐-☐-☐-☐-☐-☐ High	
☐	European Union	Low ☐-☐-☐-☐-☐-☐-☐ High	
☐	Others:	Low ☐-☐-☐-☐-☐-☐-☐ High	
☐	Don't know/don't answer		

4) Who was consulted during the draft preparation of the new law?

	Participant	Approximate weight	If possible, please specify the actors
☐	Government	Low ☐-☐-☐-☐-☐-☐-☐ High	
☐	First Chamber	Low ☐-☐-☐-☐-☐-☐-☐ High	
☐	Second Chamber, if any	Low ☐-☐-☐-☐-☐-☐-☐ High	
☐	Parl. Committee FC	Low ☐-☐-☐-☐-☐-☐-☐ High	
☐	Parl. Committee SC, if any	Low ☐-☐-☐-☐-☐-☐-☐ High	
☐	Public administration	Low ☐-☐-☐-☐-☐-☐-☐ High	
☐	Independent agency	Low ☐-☐-☐-☐-☐-☐-☐ High	
☐	Other agencies or courts	Low ☐-☐-☐-☐-☐-☐-☐ High	
☐	Employers/producers associations	Low ☐-☐-☐-☐-☐-☐-☐ High	
☐	Consumer associations	Low ☐-☐-☐-☐-☐-☐-☐ High	

☐	Liberal professionals	Low ☐-☐-☐-☐-☐-☐-☐ High	
☐	Academic experts	Low ☐-☐-☐-☐-☐-☐-☐ High	
☐	Trade Union	Low ☐-☐-☐-☐-☐-☐-☐ High	
☐	Supervised institutions	Low ☐-☐-☐-☐-☐-☐-☐ High	
☐	European Union	Low ☐-☐-☐-☐-☐-☐-☐ High	
☐	Others:	Low ☐-☐-☐-☐-☐-☐-☐ High	
☐	Don't know/don't answer		

5) Who modified the draft of the new law?

	Participant	Approximate weight	If possible, please specify the actors
☐	Government	Low ☐-☐-☐-☐-☐-☐-☐ High	
☐	First Chamber	Low ☐-☐-☐-☐-☐-☐-☐ High	
☐	Second Chamber, if any	Low ☐-☐-☐-☐-☐-☐-☐ High	
☐	Parl. Committee FC	Low ☐-☐-☐-☐-☐-☐-☐ High	
☐	Parl. Committee SC, if any	Low ☐-☐-☐-☐-☐-☐-☐ High	
☐	Public administration	Low ☐-☐-☐-☐-☐-☐-☐ High	
☐	Independent agency	Low ☐-☐-☐-☐-☐-☐-☐ High	
☐	Other agencies or courts	Low ☐-☐-☐-☐-☐-☐-☐ High	
☐	Employers/producers associations	Low ☐-☐-☐-☐-☐-☐-☐ High	
☐	Consumer associations	Low ☐-☐-☐-☐-☐-☐-☐ High	
☐	Liberal professionals	Low ☐-☐-☐-☐-☐-☐-☐ High	
☐	Academic experts	Low ☐-☐-☐-☐-☐-☐-☐ High	
☐	Trade Union	Low ☐-☐-☐-☐-☐-☐-☐ High	
☐	Supervised institutions	Low ☐-☐-☐-☐-☐-☐-☐ High	
☐	European Union	Low ☐-☐-☐-☐-☐-☐-☐ High	
☐	Others:	Low ☐-☐-☐-☐-☐-☐-☐ High	
☐	Don't know/don't answer		

6) Who decided the adoption of the new law?

	Participant	Approximate weight	If possible, please specify the actors
☐	Government	Low ☐-☐-☐-☐-☐-☐-☐ High	
☐	First Chamber	Low ☐-☐-☐-☐-☐-☐-☐ High	
☐	Second Chamber, if any	Low ☐-☐-☐-☐-☐-☐-☐ High	
☐	Parl. Committee FC	Low ☐-☐-☐-☐-☐-☐-☐ High	
☐	Parl. Committee SC, if any	Low ☐-☐-☐-☐-☐-☐-☐ High	
☐	Public administration	Low ☐-☐-☐-☐-☐-☐-☐ High	
☐	Independent agency	Low ☐-☐-☐-☐-☐-☐-☐ High	
☐	Other agencies or courts	Low ☐-☐-☐-☐-☐-☐-☐ High	
☐	Employers/producers associations	Low ☐-☐-☐-☐-☐-☐-☐ High	
☐	Consumer associations	Low ☐-☐-☐-☐-☐-☐-☐ High	
☐	Liberal professionals	Low ☐-☐-☐-☐-☐-☐-☐ High	
☐	Academic experts	Low ☐-☐-☐-☐-☐-☐-☐ High	
☐	Trade Union	Low ☐-☐-☐-☐-☐-☐-☐ High	
☐	Supervised institutions	Low ☐-☐-☐-☐-☐-☐-☐ High	
☐	European Union	Low ☐-☐-☐-☐-☐-☐-☐ High	
☐	Others:	Low ☐-☐-☐-☐-☐-☐-☐ High	
☐	Don't know/don't answer		

7) Who is monitoring the respect of the new law?

	Participant	Approximate weight	If possible, please specify the actors
☐	Government	Low ☐-☐-☐-☐-☐-☐-☐ High	
☐	First Chamber	Low ☐-☐-☐-☐-☐-☐-☐ High	
☐	Second Chamber, if any	Low ☐-☐-☐-☐-☐-☐-☐ High	
☐	Parl. Committee FC	Low ☐-☐-☐-☐-☐-☐-☐ High	
☐	Parl. Committee SC, if any	Low ☐-☐-☐-☐-☐-☐-☐ High	
☐	Public administration	Low ☐-☐-☐-☐-☐-☐-☐ High	

☐	Independent agency	Low ☐-☐-☐-☐-☐-☐ High	☐
☐	Other agencies or courts	Low ☐-☐-☐-☐-☐-☐ High	☐
☐	Employers/producers associations	Low ☐-☐-☐-☐-☐-☐ High	☐
☐	Consumer associations	Low ☐-☐-☐-☐-☐-☐ High	☐
☐	Liberal professionals	Low ☐-☐-☐-☐-☐-☐ High	☐
☐	Academic experts	Low ☐-☐-☐-☐-☐-☐ High	☐
☐	Trade Union	Low ☐-☐-☐-☐-☐-☐ High	☐
☐	Supervised institutions	Low ☐-☐-☐-☐-☐-☐ High	☐
☐	European Union	Low ☐-☐-☐-☐-☐-☐ High	☐
☐	Others:	Low ☐-☐-☐-☐-☐-☐ High	☐
☐	Don't know/don't answer		

8) Who can decide a sanction in case of non-respect of the new law?

	Participant	Approximate weight	If possible, please specify the actors
☐	Government	Low ☐-☐-☐-☐-☐-☐ High	☐
☐	First Chamber	Low ☐-☐-☐-☐-☐-☐ High	☐
☐	Second Chamber, if any	Low ☐-☐-☐-☐-☐-☐ High	☐
☐	Parl. Committee FC	Low ☐-☐-☐-☐-☐-☐ High	☐
☐	Parl. Committee SC, if any	Low ☐-☐-☐-☐-☐-☐ High	☐
☐	Public administration	Low ☐-☐-☐-☐-☐-☐ High	☐
☐	Independent agency	Low ☐-☐-☐-☐-☐-☐ High	☐
☐	Other agencies or courts	Low ☐-☐-☐-☐-☐-☐ High	☐
☐	Employers/producers associations	Low ☐-☐-☐-☐-☐-☐ High	☐
☐	Consumer associations	Low ☐-☐-☐-☐-☐-☐ High	☐
☐	Liberal professionals	Low ☐-☐-☐-☐-☐-☐ High	☐
☐	Academic experts	Low ☐-☐-☐-☐-☐-☐ High	☐
☐	Trade Union	Low ☐-☐-☐-☐-☐-☐ High	☐
☐	Supervised institutions	Low ☐-☐-☐-☐-☐-☐ High	☐

☐	European Union	Low ☐-☐-☐-☐-☐-☐-☐ High	
☐	Others:	Low ☐-☐-☐-☐-☐-☐-☐ High	
☐	Don't know/don't answer		

Additional questions

- Do you consider that I should contact any alternative important actor or interlocutor?
- Do you have any additional remarks?

The data matrices

Netbk standard matrix							
2	2	2	0	2	3	1	0
1	0	0	0	1	3	0	0
1	0	0	0	0	2	0	0
2	2	2	0	1	0	0	0
2	3	2	1	0	0	3	3
1	0	0	0	0	0	0	3
1	0	0	1	0	0	0	0
1	0	0	1	0	0	0	0
2	0	0	1	0	0	0	0
2	0	0	1	0	0	0	0
2	1	0	1	0	0	0	0

Netco standard matrix							
2	3	3	1	1	3	2	2
3	1	0	0	1	3	1	0
3	3	2	1	0	0	3	2
2	0	0	1	0	0	0	0
1	1	0	0	0	0	0	0
1	0	0	0	0	0	0	0
0	1	0	0	0	0	0	0
3	2	0	0	0	0	0	0
0	1	0	0	0	0	0	0
2	0	0	0	0	0	0	0

Swebk standard matrix							
0	1	2	1	1	1	1	0
0	0	0	0	1	3	0	0
0	0	0	1	2	0	1	0
0	0	0	1	1	1	3	3
0	0	0	1	1	0	1	1
0	0	0	1	2	0	0	0
0	0	0	1	0	0	0	0
0	0	0	1	0	0	0	0
0	0	0	1	0	0	0	0
0	0	0	1	0	0	0	0
0	0	0	1	2	0	0	0
1	0	0	1	1	0	0	0
2	3	2	1	0	0	0	0

Sweco standard matrix							
2	3	3	1	3	1	0	0
0	0	0	0	0	3	0	0
0	0	0	0	0	1	0	0
0	0	0	1	0	0	0	0
2	2	1	1	0	0	3	1
0	0	0	1	0	0	0	3
0	0	0	1	0	0	0	0
0	0	0	1	0	0	0	0
0	0	0	1	0	0	0	0
0	1	1	1	0	0	0	0
0	0	0	1	0	0	0	0
3	0	0	0	0	0	0	0
0	1	1	0	0	0	0	0

Swibk standard matrix							
0	0	1	1	2	2	0	0
0	0	0	1	2	3	0	0
0	0	0	0	0	1	0	0
0	0	2	1	2	0	0	0
3	3	3	1	2	0	3	2
2	1	0	1	0	0	2	1
0	0	0	1	0	0	0	0
0	0	0	1	0	0	0	0
0	0	0	1	0	0	0	0
0	0	0	1	0	0	0	0
0	0	2	1	2	0	2	0
1	0	0	0	0	0	0	0
3	2	0	0	0	0	0	0

Swico standard matrix							
2	2	1	1	2	1	1	1
1	0	1	1	3	3	0	0
2	0	1	1	2	2	0	0
1	2	3	1	1	1	0	0
3	3	3	1	2	1	3	3
1	1	0	1	1	0	1	3
1	0	0	1	1	0	1	0
1	1	1	1	1	0	1	0
1	0	0	0	1	0	0	0
2	1	1	1	1	0	0	0
1	0	0	1	0	0	1	0
1	0	0	1	0	0	0	0
1	0	0	1	0	0	0	0
1	1	0	1	0	0	0	0

Details

Preliminary and control study	• Interviews:	- 1 face-to-face semi-directive interview - 6 electronic interviews
	• Documentation:	- Agencies' annual reports - Agencies', public administrtion's, and parliaments' Websites - Drafts of the new pieces of legislation - Expert commissions' reports - Parliamentary debates - Specialised press articles - Agencies', public administration's, and parliaments' press releases
Survey	• Targets:	- Relevant IRAs services; civil servants in charge; chancellor, chairperson, members of the parliamentary comissions in charge - Total = 69 (42)
	• Waves:	3 (non-anonymous, by mail and email)
	• Response rate:	62%
Aggregated outcome data	• Maximum:	168
	• Minimum:	4
	• Mean:	36.68
	• Median:	30
	• Mode:	11

appendix | the data to chapter 5

United Kingdom – Competition Commission

Country	Newspaper	Date	Type	Credibility	Efficiency
uk	DaT	12.1.2006	c	0	-1
uk	DaT	25.1.2006	c	0	0
uk	FiT	25.1.2006	c	0	0
uk	FiT	25.1.2006	c	0	0
uk	ThI	25.1.2006	e	0	-1
uk	ThT	25.1.2006	c	0	0
uk	FiT	28.1.2006	c	0	-1
uk	ThT	13.2.2006	c	0	0
uk	FiT	14.2.2006	c	0	0
uk	FiT	16.2.2006	e	0	1
uk	ThI	16.2.2006	c	1	0
uk	ThT	16.2.2006	c	0	1
uk	ThG	25.2.2006	i	0	1
uk	ThT	25.2.2006	c	0	1
uk	ThT	5.3.2006	c	0	1
uk	ThG	8.3.2006	i	0	-1
uk	ThI	8.3.2006	c	0	0
uk	DaT	10.3.2006	c	0	-1
uk	DaT	10.3.2006	c	0	1
uk	FiT	10.3.2006	e	0	-1
uk	FiT	10.3.2006	e	0	-1
uk	FiT	10.3.2006	i	0	-1
uk	FiT	10.3.2006	i	0	-1
uk	FiT	10.3.2006	c	0	-1
uk	ThG	10.3.2006	c	0	0
uk	ThI	10.3.2006	c	0	1
uk	ThI	10.3.2006	e	0	-1
uk	ThT	10.3.2006	i	0	-1
uk	ThT	10.3.2006	c	0	0
uk	ThT	10.3.2006	i	0	1
uk	ThI	11.3.2006	e	0	-1
uk	DaT	12.3.2006	i	0	0
uk	DaT	12.3.2006	c	0	-1
uk	ThT	12.3.2006	i/c	0	-1

Country	Newspaper	Date	Type	Credibility	Efficiency
uk	ThT	12.3.2006	i	0	-1
uk	ThG	14.3.2006	c	0	-1
uk	ThI	14.3.2006	e	0	-1
uk	DaT	16.3.2006	i	0	-1
uk	FiT	16.3.2006	c	0	0
uk	ThT	16.3.2006	e	0	-1
uk	DaT	31.3.2006	i	0	0
uk	ThG	31.3.2006	c	0	-1
uk	ThI	31.3.2006	i	0	-1
uk	ThI	31.3.2006	i	0	-1
uk	ThI	31.3.2006	i	0	-1
uk	ThI	31.3.2006	i	0	0
uk	ThI	31.3.2006	c	0	-1
uk	ThI	31.3.2006	i	0	1
uk	ThG	1.4.2006	c	0	-1
uk	ThT	23.4.2006	c	0	-1
uk	ThT	24.4.2006	i	0	1
uk	DaT	25.4.2006	c	0	-1
uk	DaT	26.4.2006	i	0	1
uk	DaT	28.4.2006	c	0	-1
uk	FiT	28.4.2006	c	0	0
uk	ThG	28.4.2006	c	0	-1
uk	ThG	28.4.2006	i	0	0
uk	ThT	28.4.2006	c	0	1
uk	ThT	29.4.2006	c	0	0
uk	FiT	6.5.2006	c	0	-1
uk	DaT	10.5.2006	i	0	1
uk	DaT	10.5.2006	i	0	1
uk	DaT	10.5.2006	c	0	-1
uk	DaT	10.5.2006	c	0	1
uk	FiT	10.5.2006	c	0	1
uk	ThG	10.5.2006	c	0	-1
uk	ThI	10.5.2006	c	-1	0
uk	ThT	10.5.2006	c	0	0
uk	ThT	10.5.2006	c	0	-1

Country	Newspaper	Date	Type	Credibility	Efficiency
uk	FiT	11.5.2006	c	1	0
uk	ThI	11.5.2006	c	0	1
uk	FiT	12.5.2006	c	0	0
uk	FiT	16.5.2006	i	1	-1
uk	ThG	17.5.2006	c	0	-1
uk	DaT	23.5.2006	i	0	-1
uk	FiT	26.5.2006	c	0	0
uk	FiT	26.5.2006	e	0	1
uk	FiT	28.5.2006	c	0	0
uk	ThT	28.5.2006	i/c	0	-1
uk	ThI	1.6.2006	c	0	0
uk	DaT	10.6.2006	c	0	-1
uk	ThT	13.6.2006	i	0	0
uk	DaT	14.6.2006	e	0	-1
uk	FiT	14.6.2006	c	0	-1
uk	FiT	16.6.2006	i	0	0
uk	ThI	16.6.2006	c	0	1
uk	FiT	20.6.2006	i	0	-1
uk	DaT	26.6.2006	i	0	0
uk	FiT	3.7.2006	c	0	0
uk	DaT	4.7.2006	i	0	0
uk	ThG	4.7.2006	i	0	0
uk	DaT	16.7.2006	c	-1	0
uk	ThG	18.7.2006	c	0	-1
uk	DaT	10.8.2006	c	0	0
uk	FiT	12.8.2006	i	0	0
uk	ThI	12.8.2006	i	0	0
uk	ThI	12.8.2006	c	-1	0
uk	ThT	18.8.2006	i	0	1
uk	FiT	19.8.2006	i	0	0
uk	ThG	19.8.2006	i	0	0
uk	ThT	23.8.2006	i	0	1
uk	FiT	25.8.2006	i	0	1
uk	DaT	8.9.2006	i	0	0

Country	Newspaper	Date	Type	Credibility	Efficiency
uk	ThG	8.9.2006	i	0	-1
uk	ThI	8.9.2006	e	0	-1
uk	ThI	8.9.2006	c	0	0
uk	ThT	8.9.2006	i	0	0
uk	DaT	9.9.2006	c	0	0
uk	FiT	23.9.2006	c	0	0
uk	ThT	25.9.2006	c	1	0
uk	ThG	26.9.2006	c	0	0
uk	ThT	26.9.2006	i	1	0
uk	ThT	26.9.2006	c	1	0
uk	ThI	30.9.2006	i	0	0
uk	DaT	1.10.2006	i	0	0
uk	ThT	14.10.2006	i/c	0	-1
uk	DaT	15.10.2006	c	0	-1
uk	FiT	20.10.2006	c	0	-1
uk	ThI	20.10.2006	c	0	-1
uk	FiT	8.11.2006	c	0	0
uk	ThG	11.11.2006	i	0	-1
uk	DaT	19.11.2006	i	0	-1
uk	DaT	19.11.2006	c	0	0
uk	ThI	30.11.2006	c	0	-1
uk	ThI	30.11.2006	i	0	0
uk	ThT	30.11.2006	c	0	0
uk	ThG	1.12.2006	i	0	1
uk	ThI	1.12.2006	c	0	-1
uk	ThT	2.12.2006	i	0	0
uk	ThT	3.12.2006	i/c	0	1
uk	ThI	5.12.2006	e	0	0
uk	ThT	10.12.2006	c	0	0
uk	ThT	10.12.2006	i	0	1
uk	DaT	11.12.2006	c	0	0
uk	ThI	13.12.2006	e	1	0
uk	ThT	17.12.2006	i	0	0
uk	DaT	31.12.2006	c/i	0	0
uk	DaT	6.1.2007	c	0	-1

Country	Newspaper	Date	Type	Credibility	Efficiency
uk	DaT	7.1.2007	c	0	0
uk	ThG	20.1.2007	e	0	0
uk	DaT	23.1.2007	c	1	0
uk	ThG	23.1.2007	c	1	0
uk	DaT	24.1.2007	c	0	0
uk	DaT	24.1.2007	c	0	0
uk	FiT	24.1.2007	c	0	1
uk	FiT	24.1.2007	c	0	-1
uk	FiT	24.1.2007	i	0	0
uk	FiT	24.1.2007	i	0	0
uk	ThG	24.1.2007	i	0	-1
uk	ThG	24.1.2007	e	0	-1
uk	ThG	24.1.2007	c	0	-1
uk	ThI	24.1.2007	c	0	0
uk	ThI	24.1.2007	c	1	0
uk	ThI	24.1.2007	i	0	0
uk	ThI	24.1.2007	e	0	0
uk	ThT	24.1.2007	e	0	1
uk	ThT	24.1.2007	c	0	1
uk	ThG	25.1.2007	c	0	-1
uk	ThT	28.1.2007	c	0	0
uk	DaT	29.1.2007	c	0	0
uk	ThG	31.1.2007	c	0	-1
uk	ThG	7.2.2007	c	0	-1
uk	DaT	8.2.2007	i	0	-1
uk	DaT	8.2.2007	c	0	1
uk	FiT	8.2.2007	i	0	0
uk	ThG	8.2.2007	c	0	-1
uk	ThI	8.2.2007	i	0	0
uk	ThG	9.2.2007	c	0	-1
uk	ThT	9.2.2007	i	0	1
uk	ThT	18.2.2007	c	0	0
uk	ThI	20.2.2007	e	0	0
uk	FiT	27.2.2007	c	1	0
uk	ThI	27.2.2007	c	0	1
uk	ThG	1.3.2007	c	0	-1
uk	ThI	21.3.2007	c	0	-1
uk	ThG	31.3.2007	i	0	1
uk	ThT	31.3.2007	i	0	0
uk	DaT	1.4.2007	i	0	0

Country	Newspaper	Date	Type	Credibility	Efficiency
uk	ThT	1.4.2007	c	0	1
uk	ThT	1.4.2007	c	1	1
uk	FiT	2.4.2007	c	0	1
uk	DaT	3.4.2007	i	0	0
uk	ThI	3.4.2007	c	0	0
uk	FiT	5.4.2007	c	0	-1
uk	ThG	9.4.2007	c	1	-1
uk	FiT	11.4.2007	c	0	0
uk	ThG	11.4.2007	i	0	0
uk	ThT	11.4.2007	c	0	0
uk	DaT	12.4.2007	i	0	-1
uk	ThG	12.4.2007	i	0	-1
uk	ThI	12.4.2007	i	0	-1
uk	DaT	16.4.2007	i	0	1
uk	ThI	18.4.2007	i	0	1
uk	ThI	20.4.2007	e	-1	0
uk	DaT	26.4.2007	c	0	-1
uk	FiT	27.4.2007	i	0	0
uk	FiT	27.4.2007	c	1	0
uk	FiT	3.5.2007	c	0	0
uk	ThT	5.5.2007	c	0	-1
uk	ThT	5.5.2007	c/i	0	-1
uk	ThT	5.5.2007	c/i	0	-1
uk	DaT	6.5.2007	c	0	-1
uk	ThG	8.5.2007	i	1	0
uk	ThT	19.5.2007	c	0	-1
uk	FiT	25.5.2007	i	0	-1
uk	ThG	25.5.2007	i	0	0
uk	ThI	25.5.2007	c	1	-1
uk	ThI	25.5.2007	c	0	0
uk	ThT	25.5.2007	i	0	1
uk	ThG	28.5.2007	e	0	0
uk	FiT	11.6.2007	c	1	0
uk	FiT	15.6.2007	c	0	1
uk	FiT	22.6.2007	c	0	0

Country	Newspaper	Date	Type	Credibility	Efficiency
uk	ThG	22.6.2007	i	0	-1
uk	DaT	23.6.2007	i	0	1
uk	ThI	10.7.2007	c	0	-1
uk	ThG	16.7.2007	c	1	0
uk	FiT	4.8.2007	c	0	0
uk	ThT	4.8.2007	c	0	0
uk	ThI	7.8.2007	e	0	-1
uk	DaT	9.8.2007	c	0	1
uk	FiT	10.8.2007	c	0	0
uk	ThG	10.8.2007	c	0	0
uk	ThI	10.8.2007	c	0	-1
uk	ThT	10.8.2007	c	0	1
uk	ThT	10.8.2007	c	0	1
uk	ThT	12.8.2007	i	0	-1
uk	ThG	20.8.2007	e	0	0
uk	ThI	20.8.2007	c	0	0
uk	DaT	22.8.2007	i	0	1
uk	FiT	23.8.2007	i	0	0
uk	ThG	23.8.2007	c	-1	1
uk	DaT	24.8.2007	c	0	0
uk	FiT	24.8.2007	i	0	0
uk	FiT	24.8.2007	c	0	0
uk	FiT	24.8.2007	i	0	0
uk	ThG	24.8.2007	i	0	-1
uk	ThI	24.8.2007	c	0	-1
uk	ThI	24.8.2007	i	0	-1
uk	ThT	24.8.2007	i	0	-1
uk	ThT	24.8.2007	c	0	-1
uk	ThG	25.8.2007	e	0	-1
uk	DaT	29.8.2007	c	0	-1
uk	ThG	30.8.2007	i	0	-1
uk	ThI	31.8.2007	i	0	1
uk	ThG	8.9.2007	i	0	1
uk	FiT	14.9.2007	i	0	1

Country	Newspaper	Date	Type	Credibility	Efficiency
uk	ThT	16.9.2007	i	1	-1
uk	FiT	17.9.2007	i	0	0
uk	ThI	21.9.2007	c	0	1
uk	ThG	22.9.2007	c	0	1
uk	ThI	22.9.2007	c	0	0
uk	ThT	22.9.2007	c	0	0
uk	FiT	26.9.2007	i	0	1
uk	ThI	27.9.2007	i	0	-1
uk	ThI	1.10.2007	e	0	-1
uk	DaT	3.10.2007	c	0	-1
uk	DaT	3.10.2007	c	0	-1
uk	FiT	3.10.2007	c	0	0
uk	FiT	3.10.2007	c	0	1
uk	ThG	3.10.2007	c	0	1
uk	ThG	3.10.2007	e	0	0
uk	ThI	3.10.2007	c	0	-1
uk	ThT	3.10.2007	c	0	0
uk	ThT	3.10.2007	c	0	1
uk	DaT	4.10.2007	c	0	-1
uk	FiT	4.10.2007	i	0	1
uk	FiT	4.10.2007	c	0	0
uk	ThG	4.10.2007	i	0	1
uk	ThG	4.10.2007	c	0	-1
uk	ThG	4.10.2007	c	0	0
uk	ThG	4.10.2007	i	0	-1
uk	ThI	4.10.2007	c	0	1
uk	ThT	4.10.2007	i	0	-1
uk	ThI	5.10.2007	c	0	-1
uk	ThT	7.10.2007	c	0	0
uk	ThG	8.10.2007	c	0	-1
uk	ThG	8.10.2007	e	0	0
uk	ThI	12.10.2007	c	0	-1
uk	FiT	19.10.2007	e	0	1
uk	DaT	20.10.2007	e	0	-1

Country	Newspaper	Date	Type	Credibility	Efficiency
uk	ThG	29.10.2007	c	0	0
uk	DaT	31.10.2007	e	0	1
uk	FiT	31.10.2007	i	0	-1
uk	ThT	31.10.2007	i	0	1
uk	DaT	1.11.2007	c	0	0
uk	DaT	1.11.2007	i	0	0
uk	DaT	1.11.2007	c	0	0
uk	DaT	1.11.2007	c/i	0	-1
uk	FiT	1.11.2007	c	0	-1
uk	FiT	1.11.2007	e	0	1
uk	FiT	1.11.2007	c	0	0
uk	FiT	1.11.2007	i	0	-1
uk	FiT	1.11.2007	i	0	-1
uk	ThG	1.11.2007	i	0	-1
uk	ThG	1.11.2007	e	0	-1
uk	ThG	1.11.2007	c	0	-1
uk	ThG	1.11.2007	c	0	0
uk	ThI	1.11.2007	c	0	1
uk	ThI	1.11.2007	i	0	-1
uk	ThI	1.11.2007	c	0	0
uk	ThT	1.11.2007	i	0	-1
uk	ThT	1.11.2007	c	0	0
uk	ThG	2.11.2007	i	0	-1
uk	FiT	3.11.2007	c	0	0
uk	ThG	3.11.2007	i	0	1
uk	DaT	4.11.2007	c	0	0
uk	ThT	4.11.2007	c	0	0
uk	ThT	4.11.2007	c	0	1
uk	ThT	4.11.2007	i	0	-1
uk	ThI	8.11.2007	c	0	1
uk	DaT	11.11.2007	c	1	0
uk	FiT	17.11.2007	c	0	-1
uk	ThT	29.11.2007	c	0	0
uk	ThI	4.12.2007	i	0	-1

Country	Newspaper	Date	Type	Credibility	Efficiency
uk	ThI	8.12.2007	c	0	0
uk	ThI	8.12.2007	e	0	-1
uk	ThT	10.12.2007	i	0	1
uk	DaT	21.12.2007	c	0	0
uk	FiT	21.12.2007	e	0	-1
uk	ThG	21.12.2007	c	0	0
uk	ThG	21.12.2007	e	0	0
uk	FiT	22.12.2007	i	0	0
uk	DaT	27.12.2007	i	0	-1
uk	DaT	27.12.2007	i	0	-1

Switzerland – Competition Commission

Country	Newspaper	Date	Type	Credibility	Efficiency
ch	Tag	7.1.2006	c	0	-1
ch	Tag	7.1.2006	e	0	-1
ch	NZZ	8.1.2006	c	0	-1
ch	Tag	10.1.2006	i/c	-1	-1
ch	Tag	10.1.2006	c	-1	0
ch	Tag	11.1.2006	i/c	0	-1
ch	Tag	13.1.2006	i	0	0
ch	NZZ	14.1.2006	i	0	0
ch	Tag	14.1.2006	i	-1	-1
ch	NZZ	22.1.2006	c	0	0
ch	Tag	31.1.2006	i/c	0	1
ch	NZZ	8.2.2006	c	0	-1
ch	NZZ	10.2.2006	c	0	-1
ch	Tag	15.2.2006	i	0	0
ch	NZZ	17.2.2006	c	0	0
ch	NZZ	25.2.2006	c	0	-1
ch	LeT	28.2.2006	c	0	-1
ch	Baz	2.3.2006	c	0	-1
ch	Bun	31.3.2006	c	0	0
ch	NZZ	31.3.2006	c	0	-1
ch	Tag	31.3.2006	c	0	-1

Country	Newspaper	Date	Type	Credibility	Efficiency
ch	Tag	1.4.2006	c	0	-1
ch	Baz	5.4.2006	e	-1	-1
ch	NZZ	5.4.2006	c	0	-1
ch	Tag	5.4.2006	c	0	0
ch	LeT	5.4.2006	e	0	-1
ch	Baz	11.4.2006	c	0	1
ch	Bun	11.4.2006	c	-1	1
ch	NZZ	11.4.2006	c	0	1
ch	NZZ	11.4.2006	e	0	-1
ch	Tag	11.4.2006	c	0	0
ch	NZZ	16.4.2006	c	-1	1
ch	Baz	27.4.2006	c	0	0
ch	Bun	6.5.2006	c	0	0
ch	LeT	23.5.2006	c	0	0
ch	Bun	10.6.2006	c	0	0
ch	Tag	10.6.2006	c	0	-1
ch	Bun	12.6.2006	c	0	0
ch	NZZ	20.6.2006	c	0	-1
ch	NZZ	20.6.2006	i	0	-1
ch	NZZ	30.6.2006	c	0	0
ch	Tag	1.7.2006	c	0	0
ch	NZZ	5.7.2006	c	-1	-1
ch	Tag	8.7.2006	i	0	-1
ch	Tag	11.7.2006	e	0	0
ch	Baz	12.7.2006	c	0	0
ch	Tag	12.7.2006	C	0	0
ch	LeT	3.8.2006	i	1	0
ch	LeT	5.8.2006	c	0	-1
ch	LeT	12.9.2006	c	0	-1
ch	Bun	14.9.2006	c	0	0
ch	Baz	15.9.2006	c/i	0	-1
ch	NZZ	21.9.2006	c	0	1
ch	LeT	23.9.2006	i	0	-1
ch	NZZ	4.10.2006	c	0	0

Country	Newspaper	Date	Type	Credibility	Efficiency
ch	Bun	6.10.2006	c	0	0
ch	Tag	6.10.2006	c	0	0
ch	Tag	7.10.2006	c	0	-1
ch	NZZ	12.10.2006	c	-1	0
ch	NZZ	22.10.2006	i	0	1
ch	Tag	27.10.2006	c	0	-1
ch	TrG	7.11.2006	c	0	0
ch	24H	8.11.2006	c	0	-1
ch	Baz	11.11.2006	c	-1	-1
ch	Tag	11.11.2006	c	0	0
ch	24H	24.11.2006	i	0	1
ch	NZZ	26.11.2006	c	0	1
ch	Tag	28.11.2006	i	0	1
ch	NZZ	29.11.2006	c	0	0
ch	Tag	29.11.2006	e	0	1
ch	24H	23.12.2006	c	-1	0
ch	Tag	3.1.2007	i	0	-1
ch	24H	9.1.2007	i	0	-1
ch	Baz	9.1.2007	c	0	0
ch	Tag	9.1.2007	c	0	0
ch	Tag	12.1.2007	c	0	0
ch	Tag	12.1.2007	c	0	-1
ch	Baz	13.1.2007	c	0	0
ch	LeT	13.1.2007	c	0	-1
ch	LeT	13.1.2007	e	0	-1
ch	TrG	13.1.2007	e	0	-1
ch	TrG	13.1.2007	c	0	0
ch	Baz	15.1.2007	c	0	1
ch	Baz	15.1.2007	e	0	0
ch	Bun	15.1.2007	c	0	1
ch	NZZ	16.1.2007	c	0	0
ch	LeT	16.1.2007	c	0	-1
ch	Baz	20.1.2007	c	0	0
ch	Baz	1.2.2007	c	0	0

Country	Newspaper	Date	Type	Credibility	Efficiency
ch	24H	10.2.2007	c	0	1
ch	NZZ	10.2.2007	c	0	0
ch	TrG	10.2.2007	c	0	1
ch	Tag	13.2.2007	c	0	-1
ch	Tag	13.2.2007	i	0	-1
ch	LeT	16.2.2007	c	0	-1
ch	24H	17.2.2007	c	0	1
ch	Baz	17.2.2007	c	0	1
ch	Bun	17.2.2007	e	0	1
ch	NZZ	17.2.2007	e	0	-1
ch	NZZ	17.2.2007	c	0	1
ch	Tag	17.2.2007	c	0	1
ch	Tag	17.2.2007	c	0	1
ch	TrG	17.2.2007	e	0	-1
ch	TrG	17.2.2007	i	0	0
ch	NZZ	18.2.2007	c	-1	-1
ch	LeT	23.2.2007	c	0	1
ch	LeT	24.2.2007	i	0	-1
ch	LeT	24.2.2007	c	0	-1
ch	NZZ	2.3.2007	c	0	1
ch	Tag	3.3.2007	c	0	0
ch	NZZ	4.3.2007	c	0	0
ch	NZZ	7.3.2007	c	0	0
ch	Tag	17.3.2007	i	0	-1
ch	Tag	17.3.2007	i	0	-1
ch	Tag	20.3.2007	c	0	1
ch	24H	21.3.2007	c	0	1
ch	TrG	21.3.2007	c	0	1
ch	NZZ	23.3.2007	c	0	0
ch	Tag	27.3.2007	c	0	0
ch	LeT	7.4.2007	i	1	0
ch	LeT	23.4.2007	c	0	-1
ch	24H	24.4.2007	i	0	0
ch	Tag	30.4.2007	c	0	1

Country	Newspaper	Date	Type	Credibility	Efficiency
ch	NZZ	3.5.2007	c	0	0
ch	Tag	7.5.2007	c	0	1
ch	24H	12.5.2007	c	0	-1
ch	Baz	12.5.2007	c	0	0
ch	Baz	12.5.2007	c	0	0
ch	Bun	12.5.2007	c	0	-1
ch	NZZ	12.5.2007	c	0	1
ch	Tag	12.5.2007	c	0	1
ch	LeT	12.5.2007	e	0	0
ch	TrG	12.5.2007	i	0	1
ch	Bun	26.5.2007	c	0	0
ch	Baz	30.5.2007	c	0	-1
ch	Bun	30.5.2007	c	0	0
ch	NZZ	30.5.2007	c	0	1
ch	NZZ	30.5.2007	c	0	0
ch	Tag	30.5.2007	c	0	0
ch	Tag	2.6.2007	c	0	1
ch	Tag	2.6.2007	i	0	0
ch	LeT	8.6.2007	i	0	0
ch	LeT	11.6.2007	i	0	1
ch	NZZ	16.6.2007	c	0	0
ch	Baz	22.6.2007	c	0	1
ch	Tag	22.6.2007	i	0	0
ch	Tag	30.6.2007	c/i	0	-1
ch	NZZ	7.7.2007	c	0	0
ch	NZZ	7.7.2007	c	0	0
ch	Tag	7.7.2007	c	0	0
ch	NZZ	20.7.2007	c	0	1
ch	Tag	20.7.2007	c	0	1
ch	24H	23.7.2007	c	-1	-1
ch	TrG	23.7.2007	c	-1	-1
ch	TrG	23.7.2007	e	0	-1
ch	Baz	27.7.2007	c	0	1
ch	NZZ	27.7.2007	c	0	0

Country	Newspaper	Date	Type	Credibility	Efficiency
ch	Tag	27.7.2007	c	0	0
ch	Bun	22.8.2007	c	0	0
ch	Tag	22.8.2007	c	0	1
ch	Bun	23.8.2007	c	0	0
ch	Bun	23.8.2007	c	0	-1
ch	Bun	23.8.2007	c	0	-1
ch	NZZ	28.8.2007	c	0	-1
ch	NZZ	1.9.2007	c	0	1
ch	NZZ	2.9.2007	c	0	0
ch	Baz	3.9.2007	c	0	0
ch	Bun	3.9.2007	c	0	0
ch	LeT	4.9.2007	c	0	0
ch	LeT	4.9.2007	c	-1	0
ch	Baz	5.9.2007	c	0	0
ch	Baz	5.9.2007	c	0	0
ch	Bun	5.9.2007	e	0	-1
ch	Bun	5.9.2007	c/i	0	-1
ch	NZZ	5.9.2007	c	0	0
ch	NZZ	5.9.2007	c	0	0
ch	NZZ	5.9.2007	c	-1	0
ch	Tag	5.9.2007	c	0	1
ch	Tag	5.9.2007	i	0	-1
ch	LeT	5.9.2007	c	0	0
ch	LeT	5.9.2007	e	-1	-1
ch	TrG	5.9.2007	e	0	-1
ch	Baz	6.9.2007	i	0	-1
ch	Baz	6.9.2007	c/i	0	-1
ch	NZZ	6.9.2007	i	0	1
ch	LeT	7.9.2007	c	0	-1
ch	Baz	8.9.2007	e	0	0
ch	NZZ	9.9.2007	c	0	-1
ch	Bun	10.9.2007	i	0	-1
ch	LeT	10.9.2007	i	0	-1
ch	24H	15.9.2007	i	0	0

Country	Newspaper	Date	Type	Credibility	Efficiency
ch	LeT	27.9.2007	c	0	-1
ch	Tag	18.10.2007	c	-1	-1
ch	LeT	19.10.2007	c	-1	0
ch	LeT	20.10.2007	i	0	-1
ch	NZZ	24.10.2007	c	0	1
ch	NZZ	7.11.2007	c/i	0	0
ch	Tag	7.11.2007	i	0	-1
ch	LeT	7.11.2007	c	-1	-1
ch	Tag	17.11.2007	c	0	-1
ch	Baz	23.11.2007	c	0	0
ch	Baz	27.11.2007	c	0	0
ch	Bun	27.11.2007	e	0	0
ch	Bun	27.11.2007	c	0	1
ch	NZZ	27.11.2007	c	0	0
ch	NZZ	27.11.2007	c	0	-1
ch	LeT	27.11.2007	c	0	-1
ch	Baz	28.11.2007	c	0	0
ch	Bun	28.11.2007	c	0	1
ch	NZZ	28.11.2007	c	0	-1
ch	TrG	28.11.2007	c	0	0
ch	NZZ	7.12.2007	c	0	0
ch	LeT	7.12.2007	c	-1	-1
ch	Tag	12.12.2007	c	0	0

| bibliography

Abbott, K. and Snidal, D. (2003) 'Hard and soft law in international governance', *International Organization*, 54, 421–56.

Adam, S. and Kriesi, H. (2007) 'The Network Approach', in P. A. Sabatier (ed.) *Theories of the Policy Process*, Boulder: Westview Press.

Aglietta, M. and Rebérioux, A. (2004) *Dérives Du Capitalisme Financier*, Paris: Albin Michel.

Alesina, A. and Summers, L. (1993) 'Central bank independence and macroeconomic performance: some comparative evidence', *Journal of Money, Credit and Banking*, 25: 151–62.

Allardt, E. (1990) 'Challenges for comparative social research', *Acta Sociologica*, 33: 183.

Altheide, D. L. and Snow, R. P. (1988) 'Toward a theory of mediation', *Communication Yearbook*, 11: 223.

Andeweg, R. B. and Irwin, G. A. (2005) *Governance and Politics of the Netherlands*, 2nd edn, New York: Palgrave Macmillan.

Armingeon, K. (2002) 'The effects of negotiation democracy: a comparative analysis', *European Journal of Political Research*, 41: 81–105.

Arnold, R. (2004) *Congress, the Press, and Political Accountability*, Princeton, N.J.: Princeton University Press.

Austin, M. T. and Milner, H. V. (2001) 'Strategies of European standardization', *Journal of European Public Policy*, 8: 411–31.

Baccaro, L. (2003) 'What is alive and what is dead in the theory of corporatism', *British Journal of Industrial Relations*, 41: 683–706.

Bachrach, P. and Baratz, M. (1994) 'Decisions and nondecisions: an analytical framework', *Power: Critical Concepts*, 2: 95–110.

— (1962) 'Two faces of power', *American Political Science Review*, 56: 947–52.

Bade, R. and Parkin, M. (1982) *Central Bank Laws and Monetary Policy*, Ontario: University of Western Ontario Press.

Baker, A. (2005) 'The Three-Dimensional Governance of Macroeconomic Policy in Advanced Capitalist World', in A. Baker, D. Hudson and R. Woodward (eds) *Governing Financial Globalization: International political economy and multi-level governance*, Oxon: Routledge, pp. 102–29.

Balboni, B. (2008) 'Perceived Corporate Credibility as the Emergent Property of Corporate Reputation's Transmission Process', *MPRA Paper*, (7944), 1–9, accessed at http://mpra.ub.uni-muenchen.de/7944/ on 10 September 2010.

Baldwin, R., Scott, C. and Hood, C. (1998) *A Reader on Regulation*, New York: Oxford University Press.

Barber, B. R. (2004) *Strong Democracy: Participatory politics for a new age*,

Berkeley: University of California Press.

Barro, R. and Gordon, D. (1983) 'Rules, discretion and reputation in a model of monetary policy', *Journal of Monetary Economics*, 12: 101–21.

Bartle, I. (2006) 'Europeans outside the EU: telecommunications and electricity reform in Norway and Switzerland', *Governance*, 19: 407–36.

Bates, R. H., Greif, A., Levi, M. and Rosenthal, J.-L. (1998) *Analytic Narratives*, Princeton, N.J.: Princeton University Press.

Bawn, K. (1995) 'Political control versus expertise: Congressional choices about administrative procedures', *American Political Science Review*, 89: 62–73.

Bendor, J., Glazer, A. and Hammond, T. (2001) 'Theories of delegation', *Annual Review of Political Science*, 4: 235–69.

Bennett, A. and Elman, C. (2006) 'Qualitative research: recent developments in case study methods', *Annual Review of Political Science*, 9: 455–76.

Berg-Schlosser, D. (2003) 'Comment on Welzel, Inglehart & Klingemann's "The Theory of Human Development: a cross-cultural analysis"',*European Journal of Political Research*, 42: 381–86.

Berger, P. L. and Luckmann, T. (1966) *The Social Construction of Reality: A treatise in the sociology of knowledge*, Garden City, New York: Anchor Books.

Bernstein, M. H. (1955) *Regulating Business by Independent Commission*, Princeton, N.J.: Princeton University Press.

— (1972) *The Government as Regulator*, Philadelphia: American Academy of Political and Social Science.

— (1977) *Regulating Business by Independent Commission*, Westport, Conn.: Greenwood Press.

Besley, T. and Burgess, R. (2001) 'Political agency, government responsiveness and the role of the media', *European Economic Review*, 45: 629–40.

Besley, T., Burgess, R. and Prat, A. (2002) 'Mass media and political accountability', in T.W. Bank (ed.) *The Right to Tell: The role of mass media in economic development*, Washington: WBI, pp. 45–60.

Besley, T. and Prat, A. (2006) 'Handcuffs for the grabbing hand? Media capture and government accountability', *The American Economic Review*, 96: 720–36.

Black, J. (2008) 'The death of credit, – and principles based regulation?', *Risk & Regulation*, Financial Crisis Special, 8.

Blinder, A. S. (1999) 'Central bank credibility: why do we care? How do we build it?', *The American Economic Review*, 90: 1421–31.

Blühdorn, I. (2006) 'Democracy, Efficiency, Futurity: Contested Objectives of Societal Modernization', in I. Bluehdorn and U. Jun (eds) *Economic Efficiency - Democratic Renewal: Contested modernization in Britain and Germany*, Lanham, Maryland: Lexington Press.

Blyth, M. (2006) 'Great punctuations: prediction, randomness, and the evolution of comparative political science', *American Political Science Review*, 100: 493–98.

Boer, A., van Engers, T. and Winkels, R. (2003) *Using Ontologies for Comparing and Harmonizing Legislation*, New York: Association for Computing Machinery.

Borgatti, S. P., Everett, M. G. and Freeman, L. C. (2002) *Ucinet for Windows: Software for social network analysis*, Harward: Analytic Technologies.

Börzel, T. A. and Risse, T. (2000) 'When Europe hits home: Europeanization and domestic change', *European Integration online Papers (EIoP)*, 4: 1–20.

Bouckaert, G. and Verhoest, K. (1999) 'A Comparative Perspective on Decentralisation as a Context for Contracting in the Public Sector: Practice and Theory', in Y. Fortin (ed.) *La Contractualisation Dans Le Secteur Public Des Pays Industrialisés Depuis 1980*, Paris: L'Harmattan, pp. 199–239.

Bovens, M. (2007) 'Analysing and assessing accountability: a conceptual framework', *European Law Journal*, 13: 447.

Brabazon, T. (2000) *Behavioural Finance: A new sunrise or a false dawn?*, University of Limerick, Department of Accountancy: University College Dublin, pp. 1–8.

Braithwaite, J. and Drahos, P. (2000) *Global Business Regulation*, Cambridge: Cambridge University Press.

Braumoeller, B. F. and Goertz, G. (2000) 'The methodology of necessary conditions', *American Journal of Political Science*, 44: 844–58.

Braun, D. (1993) 'Who governs intermediary agencies? Principal-Agent Relations in research policy-making', *Journal of Public Policy*, 13: 135–62.

— (1997) *Die Politische Steuerung Der Wissenschaft. Ein Beitrag Zum "Kooperativen Staat"*, Frankfurt/New York: Campus Verlag.

— (2002) 'Debate: state intervention and delegation to Independent Regulatory Agencies', *Swiss Political Science Review*, 8: 93–6.

— (2003) 'Dezentraler und unitarischer Foderalismus. Die Schweiz und Deutschland im Vergleich', *Swiss Political Science Review*, 9 (1): 57–90.

Braun, D. and Gilardi, F. (2006) *Delegation in Contemporary Democracies*, Abingdon, Oxon; New York: Routledge.

Breton, A. and Fraschini, A. (2003) 'The ndependence of the Italian Constitutional Court', *Constitutional Political Economy*, 14: 319–33.

Brudney, J. L. and Hebert, F. T. (1987) 'State agencies and their environments: examining the influence of important external actors', *Journal of Politics*, 49: 186–206.

Brunetti, A., Kisunko, G. and Weder, B. (1998) 'Credibility of rules and economic growth: evidence from a worldwide survey of the private sector', *The World Bank Economic Review*, 12: 353–84.

Bryant, J. and Zillmann, D. (2002) *Media Effects: Advances in theory and research*, Mahwah, N.J.: L. Erlbaum.

Buchanan, J. M., Tullock, G. and Rowley, C. K. (2004) *The Calculus of Consent: Logical foundations of constitutional democracy*, Indianapolis, IN: Liberty Fund.

Burnham, P. (2001) 'New Labour and the politics of depoliticisation', *British*

Journal of Politics and International Relations, 3: 127–49.

Busuioc, M. (2009) 'Accountability, control and independence: the case of European agencies', *European Law Journal*, 15: 599–615.

Calvert, R. L., McCubbins, M. D. and Weingast, B. R. (1989) 'A theory of political control and agency discretion', *American Journal of Political Science*, 33: 558–661.

Carpenter, D. (2002a) 'The political foundations of bureaucratic autonomy: a response to Kernell', *Studies in American Political Development*, 15: 113–22.

—   1996) 'Adaptive signal processing, hierarchy, and budgetary control in federal regulation', *American Political Science Review*, 90: 283–302.

—   (2001a) 'State building through reputation building: coalitions of esteem and program innovation in the national postal system, 1883–1913', *Studies in American Political Development*, 14: 121–55.

—   (2001b) *The Forging of Bureaucratic Autonomy: Reputations, networks, and policy innovation in executive agencies, 1862–1928*, Princeton, N.J.: Princeton University Press.

—   (2002b) 'Groups, the media, agency waiting costs, and FDA drug approval', *American Journal of Political Science*, 46: 490–505.

Castiglione, D. (2006) 'Accountability', in M. Bevir (ed.) *Encyclopedia of Governance*, London: Sage, pp. 1–7.

Chavagneux, C. (2007) *Les Dernières Heures Du Libéralisme: Mort D'une Idéologie*, Paris: Perrin.

—   (2008a) 'Comment fonctionnent les plans de sauvetage? L'example Français', *Alternatives Economiques*, 274: 55.

—   (2008b) 'Les dix chantiers de la régulation financière', *Alternatives Economiques*, 274: 61–2.

—   (2008c) 'Six principes pour réguler la finance mondiale', *Alternatives Economiques*, 271: 40–4.

Christensen, J. G. (2001) 'Bureaucratic Autonomy as a Political Asset' in B. G. Peters and J. Pierre (eds) *Politicians, Bureaucrats and Administrative Reform,* London: Routledge.

Christensen, J. G. and Yesilkagit, K. (2006a) 'Delegation and Specialization in Regulatory Administration: A Comparative Analysis of Denmark, Sweden and the Netherlands', in T. Christensen and P. Lægreid (eds) *Autonomy and Regulation: Coping with agencies in the modern state*, Cheltenham: Edward Elgar.

—   (2006b) 'Political Responsiveness and Credibility in Regulatory Administration', in T. Christensen and P. Lægreid (eds) *Autonomy and Regulation: Coping with agencies in the modern state*, Cheltenham: Edward Elgar, pp. 203–234.

Christensen, T. and Lægreid, P. (2001) *New Public Management: The transformation of ideas and practice*, Aldershot: Ashgate.

—   (2002) 'New Public Management-Undermining Political Control', in T. Christensen and P. Lægreid (eds) *New Public Management: The transformation of ideas and practice*, Aldershot: Ashgate, pp. 93–120.

— (2003) 'Administrative reform policy: the challenges of turning symbols into practice', *Public Organization Review*, 3: 3–27.

— (2005) *Agencification and Regulatory Reforms*, Stanford University.

— (2007) 'Regulatory agencies - the challenges of balancing agency autonomy and political control', *Governance*, 20: 499–520.

Christensen, T., Lie, A. and Lægreid, P. (2008) 'Beyond new public management: agencification and regulatory reform in Norway', *Financial Accountability & Management*, 24: 15–30.

Clark, M. (2005) *Scandalous! The electoral effects of valence issues in Western Europe, 1976–1998*, paper presented at the Annual Meeting of the Midwest Political Science Association, Chicago 2005.

Coen, D. (2005) 'Managing the political life cycle of regulation in the UK and German telecommunication sectors', *Annals of Public and Cooperative Economics*, 76: 59–84.

Coen, D. and Héritier, A. (2005) *Refining Regulatory Regimes: Utilities in Europe*, Cheltenham: Edward Elgar.

Coen, D. and Thatcher, M. (2005) 'The new governance of markets and non-majoritarian regulators', *Governance: An international journal of policy, administration, and institutions*, 18: 329–46.

— (2006) *Network Governance and Delegation: European networks of regulatory agencies*, Working Paper, London.

— (2007) 'Network governance and multi-level delegation: European networks of regulatory agencies', *Journal of Public Policy*, 28: 49–71.

— (2008) 'The emergence of networks of European regulators', *Journal of Public Policy*, 27.

Coglianese, C. and Howard, M. (1998) 'Getting the message out: regulatory policy and the press', *Politics*, 3: 39–55.

Coleman, J. S. (1990) *Foundations of Social Theory*, Cambridge, Mass. and London: Harvard University Press.

Collier, D. and Mahon, J. E. J. (1993) 'Conceptual "stretching" revisited: adapting categories in comparative analysis', *The American Political Science Review*, 87: 845 - 55.

Colomer, J. M. (2002) *Political Institutions in Europe*, London: Routledge.

— (1996) *Political Institutions in Europe*, London: Routledge.

Compston, H. (1994) 'Union participation in economic policy-making in Austria, Switzerland, the Netherlands, Belgium and Ireland, 1970–1992', *West European Politics*, 17: 123–45.

Conway, P. and Nicoletti, G. (2006) 'Product market regulation in non-manufacturing sectors in OECD countries: measurement and highlights', *OECD Economics Department Working Paper*.

Cook, P. (2004) *Leading Issues in Competition, Regulation, and Development*, Cheltenham: Edward Elgar.

Cook, T. (1998) *Governing with the News: The news media as a political institution*, Chicago: University of Chicago Press.

Copeland, G. W. and Patterson, S. C. (1994) *Parliaments in the Modern World: Changing institutions*, Ann Arbor: University of Michigan Press.

Costanza, R. (1992) *Ecological Economics: The science and management of sustainability*, New York: Columbia University Press.

Cronqvist, L. (2007) *Tosmana - Tool for Small-N Analysis* (version 1.3.2), Trier, Internet: http:www.tosmana.net

Crouch, C. and Streeck, W. (1997) *Political Economy of Modern Capitalism: Mapping convergence and diversity*, London; Thousand Oaks, Calif.: Sage.

Cukierman, A., Webb, S. and Neyapti, B. (1992) 'Measuring the independence of central banks and its effects on policy outcomes', *World Bank Economic Review*, 6: 353–98.

Curran, J. (2005) 'What Democracy Requires of the Media', in Overholser, G. and Jamieson, K. (eds) *The Press*, New York: Oxford University Press.

Dahl, R. A. (1989) *Democracy and its Critics*, New Haven: Yale University Press.

Dalton, R. J. (2004) *Democratic Challenges, Democratic Choices: The erosion of political support in advanced industrial democracies*, Oxford; New York: Oxford University Press.

de Jonge, J., van Trijp, H., Jan Renes, R. and Frewer, L. (2007) 'Understanding consumer confidence in the safety of food: its two-dimensional structure and determinants', *An International Journal,* 27: 729–40.

de Larosière, J., Balcerowicz, L., Issing, L., Masera, R., McCarthy, C., Nyberg, L., Pérez, J. and Ruding, O. (2009) *The High-Level Group of Financial Supervision in the EU Report*, Brussels: The de Larosière Group.

de Visscher, C., Maiscocq, O. and Varone, F. (2007) 'The Lamfalussy Reform in the EU securities markets: fiduciary relationships, policy effectiveness and balance of power', *Journal of Public Policy,* 28 (01): 19–47.

de Vreese, C. H., Banducci, S. A., Semetko, H. A. and Boomgaarden, H. G. (2006) 'The news coverage of the 2004 European Parliamentary election campaign in 25 countries', *European Union Politics*, 7: 477–504.

Deeg, R. and Jackson, G. (2007) 'Towards a more dynamic theory of capitalist variety', *Socio-Economic Review*, 5: 149–79.

Deephouse, D. L. (2000) 'Media reputation as a strategic resource: an integration of mass communication and resource-based theories', *Journal of Management*, 26: 1091–112.

Diani, M. (2003) '"Leaders" or brokers? Positions and Influence in Social Movement Networks', in M. Diani, and D. McAdam (eds) *Social Movements and Networks : Relational approaches to collective action*, Oxford; New York: Oxford University Press, pp. xix, 348.

DiMaggio, P. and Powell, W. W. (1991) *The New Institutionalism in Organizational Analysis*, Chicago: University of Chicago Press.

—— (1983) 'The iron cage revisited: institutional isomorphism and collective rationality in organizational fields', *American Sociological Review*, 48: 147–60.

Dolowitz, D. and Marsh, D. (1996) 'Who learns what from whom: a review of the policy transfer literature', *Political Studies*, 44: 343–57.

— (2000) 'Learning from abroad: the role of policy transfer in contemporary policy-making', *An International Journal of Policy and Administration*, 13: 5–23.

Downs, A. (1967) *Inside Bureaucracy*, Boston: Little/Brown.

Doyle, G. (2002) *Media Ownership: The economics and politics of convergence and concentration in the UK and European media*, Thousand Oaks: Sage.

Drazen, A. and Masson, P. (1994) 'Credibility of policies versus credibility of policymakers', *Quarterly Journal of Economics*, 109: 735–54.

Dunleavy, P. and Margetts, H. (2001) 'From majoritarian to pluralist democracy?: Electoral reform in Britain since 1997', *Journal of Theoretical Politics*, 13: 295–319.

Ebbinghaus, B. and Hassel, A. (1999) 'The role of tripartite concertation in the reform of the welfare state', *Transfer*, 5: 64–81.

— (2000) 'Striking deals: concertation in the reform of continental European welfare states', *Journal of European Public Policy*, 7: 44–62.

Eberlein, B. (2003) 'Formal and informal governance in single market regulation', in T. Christiansen and S. Piattoni (eds) *Informal Governance in the European Union*, Cheltenham: Edward Elgar, pp. 150–72.

Eberlein, B. and Grande, E. (2005) 'Beyond delegation: transnational regulatory regimes and the EU regulatory state', *Journal of European Public Policy*, 12: 89–112.

Eberlein, B. and Newman, A. L. (2008) 'Escaping the international governance dilemma? Incorporated transgovernmental networks in the European Union', *Governance*, 21: 25–52.

Eckstein, H. (1998) 'Unfinished business: reflections on the scope of comparative politics', *Comparative Political Studies*, 31: 505–34.

Egan, M. (1998) 'Regulatory strategies, delegation and European Market integration', *Journal of European Public Policy*, 5: 485–506.

Egeberg, M. (1999) 'The impact of bureaucratic structure on policy making', *Public Administration*, 77: 155–70.

Eilders, C. (2000) 'Media as political actors? Issue focusing and selective emphasis in the German quality press', *German Politics*, 9: 181–206.

— (2002) 'Conflict and consonance in media opinion: political positions of five German quality newspapers', *European Journal of Communication*, 17: 25–63.

Elgie, R. and McMenamin, I. (2005) 'Credible commitment, political uncertainty or policy complexity? Explaining variations in the independence of non-majoritarian institutions in France', *British Journal of Political Science*, 35: 531–48.

Emery, Y. and Giauque, D. (2004) *Paradoxes De La Gestion Publique*, Paris: L'Harmattan.

Epstein, D. and O'Halloran, S. (1996) 'Divided government and the design of administrative procedures: a formal model and empirical test', *Journal of Politics*, 58: 373–97.

—   (1999) *Delegating Powers: A transaction cost politics approach to policy making under separate powers*, Cambridge, U.K.; New York: Cambridge University Press.

Everett, M. G. and Borgatti, S. P. (2005) 'Extending Centrality', in P. J. Carrington, J. Scott and S. Wasserman (eds) *Models and Methods in Social Network Analysis*, Cambridge: Cambridge University Press, pp. 57–76.

Falkner, G., Treib, O. and Hartlapp, M. (2004) Europeanization of social partnership in smaller European democracies? *European Journal of Industrial Relations* 10:3.

Feintuck, M. (2004) '*The Public Interest' In Regulation*, Oxford: Oxford University Press.

Field, A. P. (2005) *Discovering Statistics Using Spss: (and Sex, Drugs and Rock 'N' Roll)*, 2nd edn, London; Thousand Oaks: Sage Publications.

Fligstein, N. (2001) *The Architecture of Markets: An economic sociology of twenty-first century capitalist societies*, Princeton N.J.; Oxford: Princeton University Press.

Flinders, M. and Buller, J. (2006) 'Depolitization, Democracy and Arena Shifting', in T. Christensen and P. Lægreid (eds) *Autonomy and Regulation: Coping with agencies in the modern state*, Cheltenham: Edward Elgar.

Follesdal, A. and Hix, S. (2006) 'Why there is a democratic deficit in the EU: a response to Majone and Moravcsik', *Journal of Common Market Studies*, 44: 533–62.

Fox, J. (2000) *Civil Society and Political Accountability: Propositions for discussion,* South Bend, USA: University of Notre Dame.

Franchino, F. (2002) 'Efficiency or credibility? Testing the two logics of delegation to the European Commission', *Journal of European Public Policy*, 9: 677–94.

Francis, J. (1993) *The Politics of Regulation, a Comparative Perspective*, Oxford: Blackwell.

Friedberg, E. (1997) *Le Pouvoir et La Règle: Dynamiques de L'action Organisée*, Paris: Editions du Seuil.

Fukuyama, F. (1999) *Social Capital and Civil Society*, Accessed at http://www.imf.org/external/pubs/ft/seminar/1999/reforms/fukuyama.htm on 10 September 2010.

Gailmard, S. (2009) 'Multiple principals and oversight of bureaucratic policy-making', *Journal of Theoretical Politics*, 21: 161.

GCR (2006) 'The 2006 handbook of competition enforcement agencies', *Global Competition Review*, Special Report.

Gehring, T. (2004) 'The consequences of delegation to independent agencies: separation of powers, discursive governance and the regulation of telecommunications in Germany', *European Journal of Political Research*, 43: 677–98.

Geithner, T. (2009) Treasury Secretary, Tim Geithner, Opening Statement presented at Senate Banking Committee Hearing, Washington, February 2009.

Gemici, K. (2008) 'Karl Polanyi and the antinomies of embeddedness', *Socio-Economic Review*, 6: 5–33.

Gentzkow, M. and Shapiro, J. M. (2006) 'Media bias and reputation', *Journal of Political Economy*, 114: 280–316.

George, A. L. and Bennett, A. (2005) *Case Studies and Theory Development in the Social Sciences*, Cambridge, MA: MIT Press.

Gerber, B. J. and Teske, P. (2000) 'Regulatory policymaking in the American States: a review of theories and evidence', *Political Research Quarterly*, 53: 849–86.

Gerber, E. (1999) *The Populist Paradox: Interest group influence and the promise of direct legislation*, Princeton: Princeton University Press.

Gerring, J. (2001) *Social Science Methodology: A criterial framework*, Cambridge; New York: Cambridge University Press.

— (2004) 'What is a case study and what is it good for?', *American Political Science Review*, 98: 341–54.

— (2007a) *Case Study Research: Principles and practices*, Cambridge: Cambridge University Press.

— (2007b) 'Is there a (viable) crucial-case method?', *Comparative Political Studies*, 40: 231.

Giddens, A. (1986) *The Constitution of Society: Outline of the theory of structuration*, Cambridge: Polity Press.

Giddens, A. and Turner, J. H. (1987) *Social Theory Today*, Stanford, Calif.: Stanford University Press.

Gilardi, F. (2002a) 'Delegation to independent regulatory agencies: insights from Rational Choice Institutionalism', *Swiss Political Science Review*, 8: 96–102.

— (2002b) 'Policy credibility and delegation to independent regulatory agencies: A comparative empirical analysis', *Journal of European Public Policy*, 9: 873–93.

— (2005a) 'The formal independence of regulators: a comparison of 17 countries and 7 Sectors', *Swiss Political Science Review*, 11: 139–67.

— (2005b) 'The institutional foundations of regulatory capitalism: the diffusion of independent regulatory agencies in Western Europe', *The Annals of the American Academy of Political and Social Science*, 598: 84-101.

— (2007) 'The same, but different: central banks, regulatory agencies, and the politics of delegation to independent authorities', *Comparative European Politics*, 5: 303–27.

— (2008) *Delegation in the Regulatory State : Independent Regulatory Agencies in Western Europe*, Northampton, MA: Edward Elgar.

Goertz, G. (2003) 'Assessing the importance of necessary or sufficient conditions in fuzzy-set social science', WP2003–7, accessed at www.compasss.org/wp.htm on 10 September 2010.

— (2006a) 'Assessing the trivialness, relevance, and relative importance of necessary or sufficient conditions in social science', *Studies in*

Comparative International Development (SCID), 41: 88–109.

— (2006b) *Social Science Concepts: A User's Guide*, Princeton: Princeton University Press.

Goertz, G. and Mahoney, J. (2005) 'Two-level theories and fuzzy-set analysis', *Sociological Methods & Research*, 33: 497–538.

Goodin, R. E. (1996) *The Theory of Institutional Design*, Cambridge; New York: Cambridge University Press.

Goodin, R. E. and Klingemann, H.-D. (1996) 'Political science: the discipline', in R. E. Goodin and H.-D. Klingemann (eds) *A New Handbook of Political Science*, Oxford: Oxford University Press, pp. 3–49.

Goodsell, C. T. and Gayo, C. C. (1970) 'Appointive control of federal regulatory commissions', *Administrative Law Review*, 23: 291–324.

Grilli, V., Masciandro, D. and Tabellini, G. (1991) 'Institutions and policies. political and monetary institutions and public financial policies in the industrial countries', *Economic Policy*, 6: 342–92.

Grossman, S. J. and Stiglitz, J. (1980) 'On the impossibility of informationally efficient markets', *The American Economic Review*, 70: 393–408.

Haas, P. M. (1992) 'Introduction: epistemic communities and international policy coordination', *International Organization*, 46: 1–35.

Hall, P. A. (1993) 'Policy paradigms, social learning, and the state: the case of economic policymaking in Britain', *Comparative Politics*, 25: 275–96.

— (2003) 'Aligning Ontology and Methodology in Comparative Research', in J. Mahoney and D. Rueschmeyer (eds) *Comparative Historical Analysis in the Social Science*, Cambridge: Cambridge University Press, pp. 373–404.

Hall, P. A. and Gingerich, D. W. (2004) 'Varieties of capitalism and institutional complementarities in the macroeconomy: an empirical analysis', *MPIfG Discussion Paper*, 04.

Hall, P. A. and Soskice, D. W. (2001) *Varieties of Capitalism : The institutional foundations of comparative advantage*, Oxford; New York: Oxford University Press.

Hall, P. A. and Taylor, R. C. R. (1996) 'Political Science and the three new Institutionalisms', *Political Studies*, 44: 936–57.

Hallin, D. and Mancini, P. (2004) *Comparing Media Systems: Three models of media and politics*, Cambridge: Cambridge University Press.

Hamilton, A. and Madison, J. (1788) 'The Federalist No. 51: The structure of the government must furnish the proper checks and balances between the differ-ent departments', *Selected Federalist Papers*, 120–122.

Hammond, T. H. and Knott, J. H. (1996) 'Who controls the bureaucracy?: Presidential power, Congressional dominance, legal constraints, and bureaucratic autonomy in a model of multi-institutional policy-making', *Journal of Law, Economics, and Organization*, 12: 119–66.

Häusermann, S., Mach, A. and Papadopoulos, Y. (2004) 'From corporatism to partisan politics: social policy making under strain in Switzerland', *Swiss Political Science Review*, 10: 33–59.

Hayes, A. F. and Krippendorff, K. (2007) 'Answering the call for a standard reliability measure for coding data', *Communication Methods and Measures*, 1: 77–89.

Héritier, A. (1997) 'Policy-making by subterfuge: interest accommodation, innovation and substitute democratic legitimation in Europe- perspectives from distinctive policy areas', *Journal of European Public Policy*, 4: 171–89.

Héritier, A. and Eckert, S. (2008) 'New modes of governance in the shadow of hierarchy: self-regulation by industry in Europe', *Journal of Public Policy*, 28: 113–38.

Héritier, A., Kerwer, D., Knill, C., Lehmkuhl, D., Teutsch, M. and Douillet, A. C. (2001) *Differential Europe: The European Union impact on national policymaking*, Lanham: Rowman and Littlefield.

Hirschman, A. O. (1997) 'Against parsimony: three easy ways of complicating some categories of economic discourse', *Frontier Issues in Economic Thought*, 3: 184–87.

Hodge, G. A. and Coghill, K. (2007) 'Accountability in the privatized state', *Governance*, 20: 675–702.

Hofmann, J. (2008) 'Cyclic dreams of a strong state', *Risk & Regulation*, Financial Crisis Special, 9.

Hollingsworth, J. R., Schmitter, P. C. and Streeck, W. (1994) *Capitalism, Sectors, Institutions, and Performance*, New York; Oxford: Oxford University Press.

Hood, C., Rothstein, H. and Baldwin, R. (2001) *The Government of Risk: Understanding risk regulation regimes*, Oxford: Oxford University Press.

Hopenhayn, H. and Lohmann, S. (1996) 'Fire-alarm signals and the political oversight of regulatory agencies', *Journal of Law, Economics, and Organization*, 12: 196–213.

Howlett, M. and Ramesh, M. (2003) *Studying Public Policy: Policy cycles and policy subsystems*, Toronto; New York: Oxford University Press.

Huber, J. D. and Shipan, C. R. (2002) *Deliberate Discretion: The institutional foundations of bureaucratic autonomy*, Cambridge; New York: Cambridge University Press.

Huber, J. D., Shipan, C. R. and Pfahler, M. (2001) 'Legislatures and statutory control of bureaucracy', *American Journal of Political Science*, 45: 330–45.

Hutter, B. and Dodd, N. (2008) 'Social systems failure? Trust and the credit crunch', *Risk & Regulation*, Financial Crisis Special, 4–5.

Hutter, B., Lodge, M., Miller, P. and Power, M. (2008) 'Carr on crisis', *Risk & Regulation*, Financial Crisis Special, 3.

Immergut, E. M. (1998) 'The theoretical core of the New Institutionalism', *Politics & Society*, 26: 5–34.

IOSCO (2002) *Principles of Auditor Independence and the Role of Corporate Governance in Auditor's Independence*, International Organization of Securities Commissions.

Jachtenfuchs, M. (2006) 'Deepening and widening', *Journal of European Public Policy*, 9: 650–657.

Jackson, G. (2005) 'Employee representation in the board compared: a fuzzy sets analysis of corporate governance, unionism, and political institutions', *Industrielle Beziehungen*, 12: 1–28.

Jacobs, S. (1999) *The Second Generation of Regulatory Reforms*, Washington, D.C.: IMF.

James, O. (2000) 'Regulation inside government: public interest justifications and regulatory failures', *Public Administration*, 78: 327–43.

Jayasuriya, K. (1999) 'Globalization, law, and the transformation of sovereignty: the emergence of global regulatory governance', *Indiana Journal of Global Legal Studies*, 6: 425–55.

Jefferson, T. (1816) *Thomas Jefferson to Charles Yancey,* ME 14: 384.

Johnson, C. (2002) 'Democratic transition in the Balkans: Romania's Hungarian and Bulgaria's Turkish Minority (1989–99)', *Nationalism and Ethnic Politics*, 8: 1-28.

Jordana, J. and Levi-Faur, D. (2004) *The Politics of Regulation: Institutions and regulatory reforms for the age of governance*, Cheltenham; Northampton, MA: Edward Elgar.

Jordana, J., Levi-Faur, D. and Fernandez, X. (2007) *The Global Diffusion of Regulatory Agencies: Institutional emulation and the restructuring of modern bureaucracy*, paper presented at IV ECPR General Conference, Pisa, Italy, September 2007.

Kahn, A. E. (1988) *The Economics of Regulation: Principles and institutions*, Cambridge, Mass.: MIT Press.

Kaiser, H. F. (1970) 'A second generation little jiffy', *Psychometrika*, 35: 401–15.

Katzenstein, P. J. (1985) *Small States in World Markets: Industrial policy in Europe*, Ithaca, N.Y.: Cornell University Press.

—— (1996) *Cultural Norms and National Security: Police and military in postwar Japan*, Ithaca, NY: Cornell University Press.

—— (2003) 'Small states and small states revisited', *New Political Economy*, 8: 9–30.

Katzenstein, P. and Okawara, N. (2001) 'Japan, Asian-Pacific security, and the case for analytical eclecticism', *International Security*, 26: 153–85.

Katzenstein, P. and Sil, R. (2005) 'What Is Analytic Eclecticism and Why Do We Need It? A Pragmatist Perspective on Problems and Mechanisms in the Study of World Politics', paper presented at the Annual Meeting of the American Political Science Association, Washington, DC, September 2005.

Kemp, R. and Rotmans, J. (2005) 'The Management of the Co-Evolution of Technical, Environmental and Social Systems', in M. Weber and J. Hemmelskamp (eds) *Towards Environmental Innovation Systems*, Heidelberg/New York: Springer Verlag, pp. 33–55.

Kepplinger, H. (2002) 'Mediatization of politics: theory and data', *Journal of Communication*, 52: 972–86.

Kepplinger, H. M., Donsbach, W., Brosius, H. B. and Staab, J. F. (2004) 'Media tone and public opinion: a longitudinal study of media coverage and public opinion on Chancellor Kohl', *International Journal of Public Opinion Research*, 1: 326–42.

Kepplinger, H. M. and Weißbecker, H. (1991) 'Negativität Als Nachrichtenideologie', *Publizistik*, 36: 330–42.

Khalil, E. L. (1995) 'Organizations versus institutions', *Journal of Institutional and Theoretical Economics*, 151: 445–66.

Kiewiet, D. R. and McCubbins, M. D. (1991) *The Logic of Delegation: Congressional parties and the appropriations process*, Chicago: University Of Chicago Press.

Kim, J. N., Bach, S. B. and Clelland, I. J. (2007) 'Symbolic or behavioral management? Corporate reputation in high-emission industries', *Corporate Reputation Review*, 10: 77–98.

Knill, C. (1998) 'European policies: the impact of national administrative traditions', *Journal of Public Policy*, 18: 1–28.

Knoepfel, P., Nahrath, S. and Varone, F. (2007) 'Institutional Regimes for Natural Resources: An Innovative Theoretical Framework for Sustainability', in P. Knoepfel, (ed.) *Environmental Policy Analyses: Learning from the past for the future - 25 years of research*, Berlin: Springer, pp. 455–506.

Knoke, D. (1990) *Political Networks: The structural perspective*, Cambridge ; New York: Cambridge University Press.

Kohler-Koch, B. (2002) 'European networks and ideas: changing national policies?', *European Integration online Papers (EIoP)*, 6(6), accessed at http://eiop.or.at/eiop/texte/2002–006a.htm on 10 September 2010.

Krause, G. A. and Douglas, J. W. (2005) 'Institutional design versus reputational effects on bureaucratic performance: evidence from US Government Macroeconomic and Fiscal Projections', *Journal of Public Administration Research and Theory*, 15: 281–306.

Kriesi, H. (1994) *Les Démocraties Occidentales: Une Approche Comparée*, Paris: Economica.

— (1995) *Le Système Politique Suisse*, Paris: Economica.

— (2001) 'The federal parliament: the limits of institutional reform', *West European Politics*, 24: 59–76.

Krippendorff, K. (2004) *Content Analysis: An introduction to its methodology*, 2nd edn, Thousand Oaks, Calif.: Sage.

Krippendorff, K. and Bock, M. A. (2009) *The Content Analysis Reader*, Thousand Oaks: Sage Publications.

Krugman, P. (1992) 'Exchange rates in a currency band: a sketch of the new approach', in P. Krugman and M. Miller (eds) *Exchange Rate Targets and Currency Bands*, Cambridge; New York: Cambridge University Press, pp. 9–14.

Kydland, F. and Prescott, E. (1977) 'Rules rather than discretion: the inconsistency on optimal plans', *Journal of Political Economy*, 85: 473–91.

Lægreid, P., Roness, P. G. and Rubecksen, K. (2006a) 'Autonomy and Control in the Norwegian Civil Service: Does Agency Form Matter?', in T. Christensen and P. Lægreid (eds) *Autonomy and Regulation: Coping with agencies in the modern state*, Cheltenham: Edward Elgar.

— (2006b) 'Performance management in practice: the Norwegian way', *Financial Accountability & Management*, 22: 251–70.

— (2008) 'Controlling regulatory agencies', *Scandinavian Political Studies*, 31: 1–26.

Lang, G. E. and Lang, K. (1984) *Politics and Television Re-Viewed*, Beverly Hills, Calif.: Sage Publications.

Lee, M. (1999) 'Reporters and bureaucrats: public relations counter-strategies by public administrators in an era of media disinterest in government', *Public Relations Review*, 25: 451–63.

Lehmbruch, G. and Schmitter, P. C. (1982) *Patterns of Corporatist Policy-Making*, London; Beverly Hills, Calif.: Sage Publications.

Levi, M. (1997) 'A Model, a Method, and a Map: Rational Choice in Comparative and Historical Analysis', in M. I. Lichbach and A. S. Zuckerman (eds) *Comparative Politics: Rationality, Culture and Structure*, Cambridge: Cambridge University Press, pp. 19–41.

Levi-Faur, D. (2005a) 'The global diffusion of regulatory capitalism', *The Annals of the American Academy of Political and Social Science*, 598: 12–32.

— (2005b) 'The political economy of legal globalization: juridification, adversarial legalism, and responsive regulation: a comment', *International Organization*, 59: 451–62.

— (2006a) 'Regulatory capitalism: the dynamics of change beyond telecoms and electricity', *Governance*, 19: 497–525.

— (2006b) 'Varieties of regulatory capitalism: getting the most out of the comparative method', *Governance*, 19: 367–82.

— (2006c) 'Varieties of regulatory capitalism: sectors and nations in the making of a new global order', *Governance*, 19: 363–66.

Levi-Faur, D. and Jordana, J. (2005) 'The making of a new regulatory order', *The Annals of the American Academy of Political and Social Science*, 598: 6–9.

Lijphart, A. (1984) *Democracies: Patterns of majoritarian and consensus government in twenty-one countries*, New Haven and London: Yale University Press.

— (1999) *Patterns of Democracy: Government forms and performance in thirty-six countries*, New Haven: Yale University Press.

Lindenberg, S. (1992) 'The Method of Decreasing Abstraction', in J. Coleman and T. J. Fararo (eds) *Rational Choice Theory: Advocacy and critique*, Newbury Park, CA: Sage, pp. 3–20.

Lindvall, J. and Rothstein, B. (2006) 'Sweden: the fall of the strong state', *Scandinavian Political Studies*, 29: 47–63.

Lodge, M. (2002) 'The wrong type of regulation? Regulatory failure and the railways in Britain and Germany', *Journal of Public Policy*, 22: 271–97.

— (2004) 'Accountability and Transparency in Regulation: Critiques,

Doctrines and Instruments', in J. Jordana and D. Levi-Faur (eds) *The Politics of Regulation*, Cheltenham: Edward Elgar.

— (2008) 'Towards a new age of regulation?', *Risk & Regulation*, Financial Crisis Special, 11–12.

Lombard, M., Snyder-Duch, J. and Bracken, C. C. (2002) 'Content analysis in mass communication: assessment and reporting of intercoder reliability', *Human Communication Research*, 28: 587–604.

Louw, P. E. (2005) *The Media and Political Process*, London: Sage Publications.

Lowi, T. J. (1969) *The End of Liberalism: Ideology, policy, and the crisis of public authority*, New York: WW Norton.

Lukes, S. (1974) *Power: A radical view*, Basingstoke: Palgrave Macmillan.

Maeda, Y. and Miyahara, M. (2003) 'Determinants of trust in industry, government, and citizen's groups in Japan', *Corporate Reputation Review*, 10: 303–10.

Maggetti, M. (2007) 'De facto independence after delegation: a fuzzy-set analysis', *Regulation & Governance*, 1: 271–94.

— (2009a) 'Are Regulatory Agencies Delivering What They Promise?', in P. Lægreid and K. Verhoest (eds) *Governance of Public Sector Organizations: Autonomy, control and performance*, Basingstoke: Palgrave MacMillan.

— (2009b) 'Delegated Authority: Legitimizing Independent Regulatory Agencies', in I. Blühdorn (ed.) *In Search of Legitimacy: Policy making in Europe and the challenge of societal complexity*, Opladen/Farmington Hills, MI: Barbara Budrich.

— (2009c) 'The role of Independent Regulatory Agencies in policy-making: a comparative analysis', *Journal of European Public Policy*, 16: 445–65.

— (2010) 'Legitimacy and accountability of Independent Regulatory Agencies: a critical review', *Living Reviews in Democracy*, 2: 1–9.

Maggetti, M., Afonso, A. and Fontana, M. C. (2011) 'The More It Changes, the More It Stays the Same?', in C. Trampusch and A. Mach (eds) *Switzerland in Europe*, Oxon: Routledge, p. 205.

Maggetti, M. and Gilardi, F. (2010) 'Establishing regulatory networks and the diffusion of best practices', *Network Industries Quarterly*, 12: 10–13.

— (2011) 'The policy-making structure of European regulatory networks and the domestic adoption of standards', *Journal of European Public Policy*, 18(6): 830–847.

Mahoney, J. (2007) 'Qualitative methodology and comparative politics', *Comparative Political Studies*, 40: 122–44.

— (2008) 'Toward a unified theory of causality', *Comparative Political Studies*, 41: 412.

Mahoney, J. and Goertz, G. (2004) 'The possibility principle: choosing negative cases in comparative research', *American Political Science Review*, 98: 653–69.

(2006) 'A tale of two cultures: contrasting quantitative and qualitative research', *Political Analysis*, 14: 227–49.

Mahoney, J. and Rueschemeyer, D. (2003) *Comparative Historical Analysis in* the *Social Sciences*, Cambridge; New York: Cambridge University Press.

Majone, G. (1993a) 'The European Community between social policy and social regulation', *Journal of Common Market Studies*, 31: 153–70.

— (1993b) 'The European Community: an independent fourth branch of government?', European University Institute SPS Working Papers; 1993/09.

— (1994a) *Independence Vs. Accountability?: Non-majoritarian institutions and democratic government in Europe*, European University Institute, SPS Working Papers; 1994/09.

— (1994b) 'The rise of the regulatory state in Europe', *West European Politics*, 17: 77–101.

— (1996a) *Regulating Europe*, London; New York: Routledge.

— (1996b) 'Temporal consistency and policy credibility: why democracies need non-majoritarian institutions', *EUI Working Paper SPS*, 96.

— (1997a) 'From the positive to the regulatory state: causes and consequences of changes in the mode of governance', *Journal of Public Policy*, 17: 139–67.

— (1997b) 'The agency model: the growth of regulation and regulatory institutions in the European Union', *European Institute of Public Administration, EIPASCOPE* 3: 1–6.

— (1998) 'Europe's "democratic deficit": The question of standards', *European Law Journal* 4 (1): 5–28.

— (1999) 'The regulatory state and its legitimacy problems', *West European Politics*, 22: 1–24.

— (2000) 'The credibility crisis of community regulation', *Journal of Common Market Studies*, 38: 273–302.

— (2001a) 'Nonmajoritarian institutions and the limits of democratic governance: a political transaction-cost approach', *Journal of Institutional and Theoretical Economics*, 157: 57–78.

— (2001b) 'Regulatory Legitimacy in the United States and the European Union', in K. Nicolaidis and R. Howse (eds) *The Federal Vision: Legitimacy and levels of governance in the United States and the European Union*, Oxford: Oxford University Press.

— (2001c) 'Two logics of delegation: agency and fiduciary relations in EU governance', *European Union Politics*, 2: 103–22.

— (2002) 'Europe's "democratic deficit": the question of standards', *European Law Journal*, 4: 5–28.

— (2005) 'Delegation of Powers and the Fiduciary Principle', paper presented at CONNEX workshop, Paris, May 2005.

Manin, B. (1996) *Principes Du Gouvernement Représentatif*, Paris: Flammarion.

— (1997) *The Principles of Representative Government*, Cambridge: Cambridge University Press.

Maravall, J. M. and Przeworski, A. (2003) *Democracy and the Rule of Law*, Cambridge: Cambridge University Press.

March, J. G. and Olsen, J. P. (1984) 'The New Institutionalism: organizational factors in political life', *American Political Science Review*, 78: 734–49.

— (1989) *Rediscovering Institutions: The organizational basis of politics*, New York; London: The Free Press, Macmillan.

— (2004) 'The logic of appropriateness', *ARENA Working Papers*, 04: 1–28.

— (2005) 'Elaborating the "New Institutionalism"', *ARENA Working Papers*, 11.

March, J. G. and Simon, H. A. (1958) *Organizations*, New York: Wiley.

Marsh, D. and Stoker, G. (1995) *Theory and Methods in Political Science*, London: Macmillan Press.

Martimort, D. (1999) 'The life cycle of regulatory agencies: dynamic capture and transaction cost', *The Review of Economic Studies Limited*, 66: 920947.

Mattli, W. and Büthe, T. (2003) 'Setting international standards', *World Politics*, 56: 1–42.

— (2005) 'Accountability in accounting? The politics of private rule-making in the public interest', *Governance*, 18: 399–429.

Mayntz, R. and Scharpf, F. W. (1995) 'Der Ansatz Des Akteurzentrierten Institutionalismus', in R. Mayntz and F. W. Scharpf (eds) *Steuerung Und Selbstorganisation in Staatsnahen Sektoren*, Frankfurt: Campus, pp. 39–72.

Mazzoleni, G. (1987) 'Media logic and party logic in campaign coverage: the Italian General Election of 1983', *European Journal of Communication*, 2: 81–103.

Mazzoleni, G. and Schulz, W. (1999) '" Mediatization" of politics: a challenge for democracy?', *Political Communication*, 16: 247–61.

McCubbins, M. D., Noll, R. G. and Weingast, B. R. (1987) 'Administrative procedures as instruments of political control', *Journal of Law, Economics, and Organization*, 3: 243–77.

McGowan, F. and Wallace, H. (1996) 'Towards a European regulatory state', *Journal of European Public Policy*, 3: 560–76.

McLean, I. and Foster, C. (1992) 'The political economy of regulation: interests, ideology, voters, and the UK Regulation of Railways Act 1844', *Public Administration*, 70: 313–31.

Meyer, C. (2004) 'The hard side of soft policy co-ordination in EMU: the impact of peer pressure on publicized opinion in the cases of Germany and Ireland', *Journal of European Public Policy*, 11: 814–31.

Meyer, J. W. and Rowan, B. (1977) 'Institutionalized organizations: formal structure as myth and ceremony', *American Journal of Sociology*, 83: 340–63.

Miller, P. (2008) 'When markets and models fail: rethinking risk, regulation and the state', *Risk & Regulation*, Financial Crisis Special, 6–7.

Mitnick, B. M. (1980) *The Political Economy of Regulation: Creating, designing, and removing regulatory forms*, New York: Columbia University Press.

Moatti, S. (2008) 'La Machine À Dettes', *Alternatives Economiques*, 274: 48–52.

Moe, T. M. (1985) 'Control and feedback in economic regulation: the case of the

NLRB', *American Political Science Review*, 79:1094–116.

— (2005) 'Power and political institutions', *Perspectives on Politics*, 3: 215–33.

Moran, M. (2002) 'Review article: understanding the regulatory state', *British Journal of Political Science*, 32: 391–413.

— (2003) *The British Regulatory State: High modernism and hyper-innovation*, Oxford; New York: Oxford University Press.

Mulgan, R. (2000) 'Accountability: an ever-expanding concept?', *Public Administration*, 78: 555–73.

— (2003) *Holding Power to Account: Accountability in modern democracies*, Basingstoke: Palgrave Macmillan.

Nesvetailova, A. and Palan, R. (2008) 'A very North Atlantic credit crunch: geopolitical implications of the global liquidity crisis', *Journal of International Affairs*, 62: 165–86.

Nordlinger, E. A. (1981) *On the Autonomy of the Democratic State*, Cambridge, Mass.: Harvard University Press.

Norris, P. (2001) 'The twilight of Westminster? Electoral reform and its consequences', *Political Studies*, 49: 877–900.

North, D. C. (1990) *Institutions, Institutional Change, and Economic Performance*, Cambridge; New York: Cambridge University Press.

— (1998) 'Economic performance through time', *International Agricultural Development*, 3: 78–89.

O'Donnell, G. (1998) 'Horizontal accountability in new democracies', *Journal of Democracy*, 9: 112–26.

OECD (2004) *Principes De Gouvernement D'entreprise De L'ocde*, OECD, pp. 70–72.

— (2003) *Public Sector Modernization: Changing organizations*, Paris: OECD/PUMA.

— (2005) 'Switzerland - the role of competition policy in regulatory reform', *OECD Reviews of Regulatory Reform*.

Olsen, J. P. (2001) 'Garbage cans, New Institutionalism, and the study of politics', *American Political Science Review*, 95: 191–98.

Olson, M. (1971) *The Logic of Collective Action; Public goods and the theory of groups*, Cambridge, Mass.: Harvard University Press.

— (1982) *The Rise and Decline of Nations: Economic growth, stagflation, and social rigidities*, New Haven: Yale University Press.

Olson, M. K. (1995) 'Regulatory agency discretion among competing industries: inside the FDA', *Journal of Law, Economics, and Organization*, 11: 379–405.

Ostrom, E. (1986) 'An agenda for the study of institutions', *Public Choice*, 48: 3–25.

— (1991) 'Rational Choice Theory and institutional analysis: toward complementarity', *The American Political Science Review*, 85: 237–43.

Papadopoulos, Y. (1997) *Les Processus De Décision Fédéraux En Suisse*, Paris: Harmattan.

—   (2003) 'Cooperative forms of governance: problems of democratic accountability in complex environments', *European Journal of Political Research*, 43: 473–501.

—   (2008) 'Europeanization? Two logics of change of policy-making patterns in Switzerland', *Journal of Comparative Policy Analysis*, 10: 255–78.

Papadopoulos, Y. and Benz, A. (2006) *Governance and Democracy: Comparing national, European and international experiences*, Abingdon, Oxfordshire; N.Y.:Routledge.

Pedersen, L. H. (2006) 'Transfer and transformation in processes of Europeanization', *European Journal of Political Research*, 455: 985–1021.

Pelzman, S., Levine, M. E. and Noll, R. G. (1989) 'The economic theory of regulation after a decade of deregulation', *Brookings Papers on Economic Activity: Microeconomics*, 1989, 1–59.

Perry, J. L. (1993) 'Strategic human resource management', *Review of Public Personnel Administration*, 13: 59–71.

Persson, T., Roland, G. and Tabellini, G. (1997) 'Separation of powers and political accountability', *The Quarterly Journal of Economics*, 112: 1163–202.

Peters, B. G. (1990) 'The necessity and difficulty of comparison in public administration', *Asian Journal of Public Administration*, 12: 3–28.

—   (1998) *Comparative Politics: Theory and methods*, Houndsmills: Macmillan Press Ltd.

—   (2001) *The Politics of Bureaucracy*, London: Routledge.

—   (2004) 'Administrative Traditions and the Anglo-American Democracies', in J. Halligan (ed.) *Civil Service Systems in Anglo-American Countries*, Cheltenham: Edward Elgar.

—   (2005) *Institutional Theory in Political Science: The 'New Institutionalism'*, London: Continuum.

Peters, R. G., Covello, V. T. and McCallum, D. B. (1997) 'The determinants of trust and credibility in environmental risk communication: an empirical study', *Risk Analysis*, 17: 43–54.

Petiteville, F. and Smith, A. (2006) 'Analyser Les Politiques Publiques Internationales', *Revue Francaise de Science Politique*, 56: 357–66.

Pfetsch, B., Adam, S., Berkel, B. and Medrano, J. (2004) 'The voice of the media in European public sphere: comparative analysis of newspaper editorials', *Berlin: Wissenschaftszentrum für Sozialforschung*.

Pierre, J. (1993) 'Legitimacy, institutional change, and the politics of public administration in Sweden', *International Political Science Review/Revue internationale de science politique*, 14: 387–401.

—   (2004) 'Politicization of the Swedish civil service: a necessary evil - or just evil?', in B. G. Peters and J. Pierre (eds) *Politicization of the Civil Service in Comparative Perspective*, London: Routledge.

—   (2000) 'Increasing returns, path dependence, and the study of politics', *The American Political Science Review*, 94: 251–67.

—   (2004) *Politics in Time: History, institutions, and social analysis*, Princeton: Princeton University Press.

Pierson, P. and Skocpol, T. (2002) 'Historical Institutionalism in contemporary political science', in I. Katznelson and H. V. Milner (eds) *Political Science: The state of the discipline*, New York and Washington, DC: Norton and the American Political Science Association, pp. 1–31.

Polanyi, K. (1983) *La Grande Transformation: Aux Origines Politiques et Économiques De Notre Temps*, Paris: Gallimard.

Pollack, M. A. (1996) 'The New Institutionalism and EC governance: the promise and limits of institutional analysis', *Governance*, 9: 429–58.

—   (2002) 'Learning from the Americanists (again): theory and method in the study of delegation', *West European Politics*, 25: 200–19.

—   (2003) 'Delegation, agency, and agenda setting in the European Community', *International Organization*, 51: 99–134.

Pollitt, C. and Bouckaert, G. (2004) *Public Management Reform: A comparative analysis*, Oxford: Oxford University Press.

Pollitt, C., Tablot, C., Caufield, J. and Smullen, A. (2004) *Agencies: How governments do things through semi-autonomous organizations*, New York: Palgrave Macmillan.

Pollock, T. G. and Rindova, V. P. (2003) 'Media legitimation effects in the market for initial public offerings', *Academy of Management Journal*, 46: 631–42.

Popper, K. R. (2002) *The Logic of Scientific Discovery*, London: Routledge.

Posner, R. A. (1974) 'Theories of economic regulation', *The Bell Journal of Economics and Management*, 5: 335.

Power, M. (1997) *The Audit Society: Rituals of verification*, Oxford: Oxford University Press.

Przeworski, A. (2007) 'Is the science of comparative politics possible', in C. Boix and S. Stokes (eds) *Oxford Handbook of Comparative Politics*, Oxford; New York: Oxford University Press.

Przeworski, A. and Teune, H. (1970) *The Logic of Comparative Social Inquiry*, New York: Wiley-Interscience.

Radaelli, C. M. (2000a) 'Policy transfer in the European Union: institutional isomorphism as a source of legitimacy', *An International Journal of Policy and Administration*, 13: 25–43.

—   (2000b) 'Public policy comes of age', *Journal of European Public Policy*, 7: 130–35.

—   (2000c) 'Whither Europeanization? Concept stretching and substantive change', *European Integration online Papers (EIoP)*, 4(8), pp. 1–28, accessed at http://eiop.or.at/eiop/texte/2000–008a.htm on 10 September 2010.

—   (2004) 'The diffusion of regulatory impact analysis - best practice or lesson-drawing?', *European Journal of Political Research*, 43: 723–47.

—   (2005) 'Diffusion without convergence: how political context shapes the adoption of regulatory impact assessment', *Journal of European Public*

Policy, 12: 924–43.

Radaelli, C. M. and De Francesco, F. (2007) *Regulatory Quality in Europe: Concepts, measures and policy processes*, Manchester: Manchester University Press.

Rae, D. W. and Taylor, M. (1970) *The Analysis of Political Cleavages*, New Haven; London: Yale University Press.

Ragin, C. C. (1987) *The Comparative Method: Moving beyond qualitative and quantitative strategies*, Berkeley: University of California Press.

— (1994) *Constructing Social Research: The unity and diversity of method*, Thousand Oaks, Calif.: Pine Forge Press.

— (2000) *Fuzzy-Set Social Science*, Chicago: University Of Chicago Press.

— (2005a) 'Core versus tangential assumptions in comparative research', *Studies in Comparative International Development (SCID)*, 40: 33–8.

— (2005b) *From Fuzzy Sets to Crisp Truth Tables*, Tucson: University of Arizona.

— (2006a) 'Set relations in social research: evaluating their consistency and coverage', *Political Analysis*, 14: 291–310.

— (2006b) 'The limitations of net-effects thinking', in B. Rihoux and H. Grimm (eds) *Innovative Comparative Methods for Policy Analysis*, New York: Springer, pp. 13–41.

— (2008a) 'Fuzzy sets: calibration versus measurement', in J. Box-Steffensmeier, H. E. Brady and D. Collier (eds) *The Oxford Handbook of Political Methodology*, Oxford: Oxford University Press.

— (2008b) *Redesigning Social Inquiry: Fuzzy sets and beyond*, Chicago: University Of Chicago Press.

Ragin, C. C., Drass, K. A. and Davey, S. (2006) *Fuzzy-Set/Qualitative Comparative Analysis 2.0*, Tucson, Arizona, Department of Sociology, University of Arizona.

Ragin, C. C. and Giesel, H. (2006) 'User's guide: fuzzy-set/qualitative comparative analysis', *Department of Sociology, University of Arizona*, 18, p. 2006, accessed on 10 December 2010.

Ricart, E. J., Enright, M. J., Ghemawat, P., Hart, S. L. and Khanna, T. (2004) 'New frontiers in international strategy', *Journal of International Business Studies*, 35: 175–201.

Richardson, J. (2000) 'Government, interest groups and policy change', *Political Studies*, 48: 1006–25.

Rihoux, B. (2006) 'Qualitative Comparative Analysis (Qca) and related systematic comparative methods: recent advances and remaining challenges for social science research', *International Sociology*, 21: 679–706.

Rihoux, B. and Ragin, C. (2008) *Configurational Comparative Analysis*, Thousand Oaks, CA and London: Sage Publications.

Riker, W. H. (1982) *Liberalism against Populism: A confrontation between the theory of democracy and the theory of social choice*, San Francisco: W.H. Freeman.

Roberts, A. (2001) 'Structural pluralism and the right to information', *University of Toronto Law Journal*, 51: 243–71.

Roberts, N. C. (2002) 'Keeping public officials accountable through dialogue: resolving the accountability paradox', *Public Administration Review*, 62: 658–69.

Rodrik, D. (2002) *After Neoliberalism, What?*, Washington, D.C: New Rules for Global Finance Coalition, pp. 1–12.

Rogoff, K. (1985) 'The optimal degree of commitment to an intermediate monetary target', *Quarterly Journal of Economics*, 100: 1169–89.

Rogowski, R. (1987) 'Political cleavages and changing exposure to trade', *American Political Science Review*, 81: 1121–37.

Rose, R. and Mackenzie, W. J. M. (1991) 'Comparing forms of comparative analysis', *Political Studies*, 39: 446–62.

Ruffieux, R. (1975) 'The political influence of senior civil servants in Switzerland', in M. Dogan (ed.) *The Mandarins of Western Europe: The Political Role of Top Civil Servants*, New York: Sage.

Sabatier, P. A. (2007) *Theories of Policy Process*, Boulder, Colo.: Westview Press.

Sabel, C. and Zeitlin, J. (2010) *Experimentalist Governance in the European Union: Towards a new architecture*, Oxford: Oxford University Press.

Sarcinelli, U. (1987) *Symbolische Politik: Zur Bedeutung Symbolischen Handelns in Der Wahlkampfkommunikation Der Bundesrepublik Deutschland*, Opladen: Westdeutscher Verlag.

Sartori, G. (1970) 'Concept misformation in comparative politics', *The American Political Science Review*, 64: 1033–53.

— (1991) 'Comparing and miscomparing', *Journal of Theoretical Politics*, 3: 243–57.

Scharpf, F. W. (2000a) *Gouverner L'europe*, Paris: Presses de Sciences Po.

— (1997) *Games Real Actors Play: Actor-centered institutionalism in policy research*, Boulder, Colo.: Westview Press.

— (2000b) 'Institutions in comparative policy research', *Comparative Political Studies*, 33: 762–90.

Schedler, A. (1998) 'What is democratic consolidation?', *Journal of Democracy*, 9: 91–107.

— (1999) 'Conceptualizing Accountability', in A. Schedler, L. Diamond and M. F. Plattner (eds) *The Self-Restraining State: Power and accountability in new democracies*, Boulder, Colorado: Lynne Rienner Publishers, pp. 13–28.

Schmidt, V. A. (2006) *Give Peace a Chance: Reconciling four (not three) New Institutionalism*, paper presented at the Annual Meeting of the American Political Science Association, Philadelphia, 2006.

Schmitter, P. and Grote, J. (1997) 'The corporatist Sisyphus: past, present and future', *EUI Working Paper SPS*, 97: 1–22.

Schmitter, P. C. and Lehmbruch, G. (1979) *Trends toward Corporatist Intermediation*, Beverly Hills; London: Sage Publications.

Schneider, C. Q. and Wagemann, C. (2003) 'Improving inference with a 'two-step' approach: theory and limited diversity in Fs/Qca', *EUI Working Paper SPS*, 7.

— (2006) 'Reducing complexity in Qualitative Comparative Analysis (Qca): remote and proximate factors and the consolidation of democracy', *European Journal of Political Research*, 45: 751–86.

Schneider, V. (2003) *Regulatory Governance and the Modern Organizational State: The place of regulation in contemporary state theory*, paper presented at Workshop on the Politics of Regulation, Universitat Pompeu Fabra, Barcelona, 2003.

Schnyder, G. (2008) 'Revisiting the party paradox of finance capitalism: evidence from Switzerland, Sweden and the Netherlands', *Centre for Business Research, University of Cambridge, Working Paper*, 372: 1–32.

Sciarini, P. (2002) 'La Formulation De La Décision', in U. Klöti, P. Knoepfel, H. Kriesi, W. Linder and Y. Papadopolos (eds) *Handbuch Der Schweizer Politik - Manuel De La Politique Suisse*, Zürich: NZZ Verlag.

Sciarini, P., Nicolet, S. and Fischer, A. (2002) 'L'impact de L'internationalisation Sur Les Processus De Décision en Suisse: Une Analyse Quantitative Des Actes Législatifs 1995–1999', *Swiss Political Science Review*, 8: 1–34.

Scott, C. (2000a) 'Accountability in the regulatory state', *Journal of Law and Society*, 27: 38–60.

Scott, J. (2000b) *Social Network Analysis: A handbook*, 2nd edn, London; Thousands Oaks, Calif.: Sage Publications.

Scott, W. A. (1955) 'Reliability of content analysis: the case of nominal scale coding', *Public Opinion Quarterly*, 19: 321–25.

Scott, W. R. (2001) *Institutions and Organizations*, Thousand Oaks Calif.; London: Sage.

Searle, J. R. (2005) 'What is an institution?', *Journal of Institutional Economics*, 1: 1–22.

Seawright, J. and Gerring, J. (2008) 'Case selection techniques in case study research: a menu of qualitative and quantitative options', *Political Research Quarterly*, 61: 294.

Serdült, U. and Hirschi, C. (2004) 'From process to structure: developing a reliable and valid tool for policy network comparison', *Swiss Political Science Review*, 10: 137–55.

Serdült, U., Vögeli, C., Hirschi, C. and Widmer, T. (2005) *Apes - Actor-Process-Event Scheme*, Zurich, Switzerland, IPZ, University of Zurich.

Shepsle, K. A. (1991) 'Discretion, institutions, and the problem of government commitment', in P. Bourdieu and J. Coleman (eds) *Social Theory for a Changing Society*, Boulder; New York: Westview Press; Russell Sage Foundation, pp. 245–65.

— (1995) 'Studying institutions: some lessons from the Rational Choice approach', in J. Farr, J. S. Dryzek, and S. T. Leonard (eds) *Political Science in History: Research programs and political traditions*, Cambridge; New York: Cambridge University Press, pp. 276–95.

Siaroff, A. (2003) 'Varieties of parliamentarianism in the advanced industrial democracies', *International Political Science Review*, 24: 445–64.

Sil, R. (2000) 'The foundations of eclecticism: the epistemological status of agency, culture, and structure in social theory', *Journal of Theoretical Politics*, 12: 353–87.

— (2004) 'Problems Chasing Methods or Methods Chasing Problems? Research Communities, Constrained Pluralism, and the Role of Eclecticism', in I. Shapiro, R. M. Smith and T. E. Masoud (eds) *Problems and Methods in the Study of Politics*, Cambridge: Cambridge University Press.

Skocpol, T. and Fiorina, M. P. (1999) *Civic Engagement in American Democracy*, Washington, D.C.; New York: Brookings Institution Press; Russell Sage Foundation.

Slaughter, A. (2004) *A New World Order*, Princeton: Princeton University Press.

Smithson, M. and Verkuilen, J. (2006) *Fuzzy Set Theory: Applications in the social sciences*, Thousand Oaks, CA: Sage.

Snyder, J. M. and Strömberg, D. 'Press coverage and political accountability', *Journal of Political Economy*, 118: 355–408.

Snyder, S. K. and Weingast, B. R. (2000) 'The American system of shared powers: the President, Congress, and the Nlrb', *Journal of Law, Economics, and Organization*, 16: 269–305.

Sørensen, E. (2002) 'Democratic theory and network governance', *Administrative Theory & Praxis*, 24: 693–720.

Sørensen, E. and Torfing, J. (2003) 'Network politics, political capital, and democracy', *International Journal of Public Administration*, 26: 609–34.

Sosay, G. (2006) 'Consequences of Legitimizing Independent Regulatory Agencies in Contemporary Democracies. Theoretical Scenarios', in D. Braun and F. Gilardi (eds) *Delegation in Contemporary Democracies*, Abingdon, Oxon; New York: Routledge, pp. 171–90.

Spence, D. B. (1997) 'Agency policy making and political control: modeling away the delegation problem', *Journal of Public Administration Research and Theory*, 2: 199–219.

Spiller, P. T. (1998) 'Regulatory agencies and the courts', in P. Newman (ed.) *The New Palgrave Dictionary of Economics and the Law*, London Macmillan, pp. 263–66.

— (1990) 'Politicians, interest groups, and regulators: a Multiple-Principals Agency Theory of Regulation, or "let them be bribed"', *The Journal of Law and Economics*, 33: 65–81.

Steinmo, S., Thelen, K. A. and Longstreth, F. (1992) *Structuring Politics: Historical Institutionalism in comparative analysis*, Cambridge; New York: Cambridge University Press.

Stern, J. (1997) 'What makes an independent regulator independent?', *Business Strategy Review*, 8: 67–74.

Stern, J. and Holder, S. (1999) 'Regulatory governance: criteria for assessing the performance of regulatory systems an application to infrastructure industries in the developing countries of Asia', *Utilities Policy*, 8: 33–50.

Stevens, J. (2002) *Applied Multivariate Statistics for the Social Sciences*, 4th edn, Mahwah, N.J.: Lawrence Erlbaum Associates.

Stigler, G. J. (1971) 'The Theory of economic regulation', *The Bell Journal of Economics and Management Science*, 2: 3–21.

Stiglitz, J. (1982) 'Ownership, Control and Efficient Markets: Some Paradoxes in the Theory of Capital Markets',in J. R. Nelson and K. D. Boyer (eds) *Economic Regulation: Essays in Honor of James R. Nelson*, Michigan State University Graduate School of Business, pp. 311–41.

Stimson, J. A., MacKuen, M. B. and Erikson, R. S. (1994) 'Opinion and policy: a global view', *PS: Political Science and Politics*, 27: 29–34.

Streeck, W. and Thelen, K. A. (2005) *Beyond Continuity: Institutional change in advanced political economies*, Oxford; New York: Oxford University Press.

Strom, K., Bergman, T. and Müller, W. C. (2003) *Delegation and Accountability in Parliamentary Democracies*, Oxford; New York: Oxford University Press.

Strömbäck, J. and Esser, F. (2009) 'Shaping Politics: Mediatization and Media Interventionism', in *Mediatization: Concept, changes, consequences.* New York: Peter Lang, 205–23.

Strömberg, D. (2004) 'Mass media competition, political competition, and public policy', *The Review of Economic Studies*, 71: 265.

Svensson, T. and Oberg, P. O. (2002) 'Labour market organisations' participation in Swedish public policy-making', *Scandinavian Political Studies*, 25: 295–315.

Swanson, D. and Mancini, P. (1996) *Politics, Media, and Modern Democracy: An international study of innovations in electoral campaigning and their consequences*, Westport: Praeger Publishers.

Swanson, D. L. (1981) 'A Constructivist Approach', in D. D. Nimmo and K. R. Sanders, (eds) *Handbook of Political Communication*, Beverly Hills; London: Sage Publications, pp. 169–91.

Thatcher, M. (2002a) 'Analysing Independent Regulatory Agencies in Western Europe: functional pressures mediated by context', *Swiss Political Science Review*, 8: 103–10.

— (2002b) 'Analysing regulatory reform in Europe', *Journal of European Public Policy*, 9: 859–72.

— (2002c) 'Delegation to Independent Regulatory Agencies: pressures, functions and contextual mediation', *West European Politics*, 25: 125–47.

— (2002d) 'Regulation after delegation: Independent Regulatory Agencies in Europe', *Journal of European Public Policy*, 9: 954–72.

— (2005a) 'The third force? Independent Regulatory Agencies and elected politicians in Europe', *Governance*, 18: 347–73.

— (2005b) 'Varieties of capitalism in an internationalized world', *Comparative Political Studies*, 37: 751–80.

Thatcher, M. and Stone Sweet, A. (2002) 'Theory and practice of delegation to non-majoritarian institutions', *West European Politics*, 25: 1–22.

Thelen, K. (1999) 'Historical Institutionalism in comparative politics', *Annual Reviews in Political Science*, 2: 369–404.

Tilly, C. (1975) *The Formation of National States in Western Europe*, Princeton: Princeton University Press.

— (2006) 'How and Why History Matters', in R. E. Goodin and C. Tilly (eds) *The Oxford Handbook of Contextual Political Analysis*, Oxford: Oxford University Press.

Tsebelis, G. (2002) *Veto Players: How political institutions work*, Princeton: Russel Sage Foundation/ Princeton University Press.

Turner, A. (2009) *The Turner Review: A regulatory response to the global financial crisis,* London: The Financial Services Authority.

Van Deth, J. W. (1998) 'Equivalence in comparative political research', *Comparative Politics: The problem of equivalence*, 6: 1.

van Waarden, F. and Drahos, M. (2002) 'Courts and (epistemic) communities in the convergence of competition policies', *Journal of European Public Policy*, 9: 913–34.

Van Waarden, F. and Hildebrand, Y. (2009) 'From corporatism to lawyocracy? On liberralization and juridification', *Regulation & Governance*, 3: 259–86.

Varone, F. (2007) 'The Federal Administration', in U. Klöti, P. Knoepfel, H. Kriesi, W. Linder, Y. Papadopoulos and P. Sciarini (eds) *Handbook of Swiss Politics*, Zürich: Neue Zürcher Zeitung Publishing, pp. 282–308.

Verhoest, K. (2005) 'Effects of autonomy, performance contracting, and competition on the performance of a public agency: a case study', *Policy Studies Journal*, 33: 235–58.

Verhoest, K., Peters, G. B., Bouckaert, G. and Verschuere, B. (2004) 'The study of organisational autonomy: a conceptual review', *Public Administration and Development*, 24: 101–18.

Verschuere, B., Verhoest, K., Meyers, F. and Peters, B. G. (2006) 'Accountability and Accountability Arrangements in Public Agencies', in T. Christensen and P. Lægreid (eds) *Autonomy and Regulation: Coping with agencies in the modern state*, Cheltenham: Edward Elgar.

Vibert, F. (2007) *The Rise of the Unelected: Democracy and the new separation of powers*, Cambridge: Cambridge University Press.

Vogel, D. (1986) *National Styles of Regulation: Environmental policy in Great Britain and the United States*, Ithaca; London: Cornell University Press.

Vogel, S. K. (1996) *Freer Markets, More Rules: Regulatory reform in advanced industrial countries*, Ithaca, N.Y.: Cornell University Press.

Voltmer, K. (1998) *Medienqualität Und Demokratie: Eine Empirische Analyse Publizistischer Informations-Und Orientierungsleistungen in Der Wahlkampfkommunikation*, Baden-Baden: Nomos.

— (2010) 'The Media, Government Accountability, and Citizen Engagement', in P. Norris (ed.) *Public Sentinel: News media and governance reform*, Washington: World Bank, p. 395.

Voltmer, K. and Eilders, C. (2003) 'The Media Agenda: The Marginalization and Domestication of Europe', in K. Dyson and K. H. Goetz (eds) *Germany,*

Europe and the Politics of Constraint, Oxford: Oxford University Press, pp. 173–97.

Walgrave, S., Soroka, S. and Nuytemans, M. (2008) 'The mass media's political agenda-setting power', *Comparative Political Studies*, 41: 814.

Waterman, R. W. and Rouse, A. (1999) 'The determinants of the perceptions of political control of the bureaucracy and the venues of influence', *Journal of Public Administration Research and Theory*, 9: 527–69.

Waterman, R. W., Rouse, A. and Wright, R. (1998) 'The venues of influence: a new theory of political control of the bureaucracy', *Journal of Public Administration Research and Theory*, 8: 13–38.

Weingast, B. R. (1984) 'The Congressional-Bureaucratic system: a Principal Agent Perspective (with applications to the Sec)', *Public Choice*, 44: 147–91.

Weingast, B. R. and Katznelson, I. (2007) *Preferences and Situations: Intersections between Historical and Rational Choice Institutionalism*, New York: Russel Sage Foundation.

Weingast, B. R. and Moran, M. J. (1983) 'Bureaucratic discretion or Congressional control? Regulatory policymaking by the Federal Trade Commission', *The Journal of Political Economy*, 91: 765–800.

Werle, R. (2001) 'Institutional aspects of standardization', *Journal of European Public Policy*, 8: 392–410.

WGFR (2009) *Financial Reform: A framework for financial stability*, Washington, Working Group on Financial Reform, The Group of Thirty.

Whitford, A. B. (2005) 'The pursuit of political control by multiple principals', *Journal of Politics*, 6: 28–49.

Widmer, T. and Neuenschwander, P. (2004) 'Embedding evaluation in the Swiss Federal Administration: purpose, institutional design and utilization', *Evaluation*, 1: 388–409.

Wilks, S. (2005) 'Agency escape: decentralization or dominance of the European Commission in the modernization of competition policy?', *Governance*, 1: 431–52.

— (2007) 'Agencies, networks, discourses and the trajectory of European competition enforcement', *European Competitionc Journal*, 3: 437–64.

Wilks, S. and Bartle, I. (2002) 'The unanticipated consequences of creating independent competition agencies', *West European Politics*, 25: 148–72.

Williamson, O. E. (1985) *The Economic Institutions of Capitalism: Firms*, New York; London: The Free Press; Collier Macmillan.

— (1993) 'Transaction cost economics and organization theory', *Industrial and Corporate Change*, 2: 107–56.

Wilson, J. Q. (1980) *The Politics of Regulation*, New York: Basic Books.

— (1989) *Bureaucracy: What government agencies do and why they do it*, New York: Basic Books.

Wincott, D. (2003) 'Beyond social regulation? New instruments and/or a new agenda for social policy at Lisbon?', *Public Administration*, 81: 533–53.

Wittgenstein, L. (1958) *Philosophical Investigations*, Oxford Blackwell.

Wood, B. D. and Petrovsky, N. (2007) 'Multiple Principals and Political Control of the Bureaucracy', paper presented at the Annual Meeting of the Southern Political Science Association, New Orleans, 2007.

Wood, B. D. and Waterman, R. W. (1991) 'The dynamics of political control of the bureaucracy', *American Political Science Review*, 85: 801–28.

Wymeersch, E. (2009) *Preparing for the Future*, Paris: Committee of European Securities Regulators.

Yesilkagit, K. and Van Thiel, S. (2008) *Venues of Influence and Regulatory Agencies*, Utrecht: ECPR Standing Group Regulatory Governance.

Zadeh, L. A. (1965) 'Fuzzy Sets', *Information and Control*, 8: 338–53.

Zaller, J. (1992) *The Nature and Origins of Mass Opinion*, Cambridge; New-York: Cambridge University Press.

| index

Abbott, K. 12
accountability, concept of 143, 166
  see also under IRAs; media
Actor-Process-Event-Scheme (APES)
  101, 104, 119–21, 123, 124, 125,
  126, 139
Adam, S. 121
agencification 4, 7, 8, 9, 12
  consequences of 9
  global level and 12–13
  see also IRAs; regulatory governance
Aglietta, M. 180
Alesina, A. 37, 66
Allardt, E. 111
Altheide, D. L. 145
Andeweg, R. B. 113, 114, 121
Armingeon, K. 113, 148, 149, 182
Arnold, R. 142, 145, 146, 147 n.2
Austin, M. T. 13
Austria
  IRAs study *51, 56, 62, 76, 77*
  *Rundfunk und Telekom Regulier-
  ungs* (RTR) *51,* 55, 83–4, 90, 95
autonomy, study of 35–40
  conceptions of 35–7
    'actual autonomy' 37
    internal/external 36
    organisational 35, 36
  independence, notion of and 36–7
  see also IRAs 'de facto indepen-
  dence' study; media

Baccaro, L. 112 n.2
Bachrach, P. 67, 70, 102
Bade, R. 37
Baker, A. 19

Balboni, B. 145
Baldwin, R. 7, 19
banking and finance IRAs 1, 179, 180,
  181–2
  central banks 37, 44
    independence, study of 37, 52,
    66, 99, 101, 114–40
  regulatory competencies of 101–2,
    115, 179
  2008–2010 crisis 178–80
Baratz, M. 67, 70, 102
Barber, B. R. 20
Barro, R. 66, 144
Bartle, I. 17, 42, 43, 103, 147, 182
Basler Zeitung 152
Bates, R. H. 25
Bawn, K. 102
Belgium
  *Commission Bancaire, Financière
  et des Assurances 51,* 52, 78, 86,
  95
  IRAs study *51, 56, 57, 76, 77*
Bendor, J. 42, 105, 144, 186
Bennett, A. 40, 138
Benz, A. 19, 113
Berg-Schlosser, D. 27, 32
Berger, P. L. 23, 106
Bernstein, M. H. 14, 50, 105, 184
Besley, T. 142, 143, 146
Black, J. 180
Blinder, A. S. 151
Blühdorn, I. 34 n.1, 144, 145, 151
Blyth, M. 25, 26
Bock, M. A. 153
Boer, A. 111
Borgatti, S. P. 120, 123
Börzel, T. A. 106

Bouckaert, G. 17, 36, 103, 182
Bovens, M. 22, 143, 165, 166
Brabazon, T. 144
Braithwaite, J. 16
Braumoeller, B. F. 92
Braun, D. ix, 34, 39, 42, 49, 50, 99, 149, 151, 173, 174, 184
Breton, A. 66, 68
Brudney, J. L. 69
Brunetti, A. 151, 182
Bryant, J. 143
Buchanan, J. M. 66
Buller, J. 19, 174
Burgess, R. 142, 146
Burnham, P. 174
Busuioc, M. 142, 166
Büthe, T. 13

Calvert, R. L. 15, 35, 102, 103, 105, 186
capitalism
    models of 45
        coordinated market economies (CMEs) 45–6
        liberal market economies (LMEs) 45, 46
    regulatory activity and 1, 4, 5, 169
    'varieties of capitalism' approach (VoC) 45, 53, 175
    see also regulatory capitalism
capture theory 2, 4, 14, 39, 42, 48–50, 66
Carpenter, D. 9, 35, 47–8, 67, 105, 143, 145, 182, 183
Castiglione, D. ix, 143
Chavagneux, C. 178, 179
Christensen, J. G. x, 16, 103, 113, 144 n.1, 147
Christensen, T. x, 4, 7, 16–17, 21, 22, 103, 139, 144 n.1, 173, 174, 182
Clark, M. 146
COBRA project 187n.2
Coen, D. 13, 21, 44, 48, 101, 103
Coghill, K. 143
Coglianese, C. 142, 143, 145, 146, 151

Coleman, J. S. 27, 32
Collier, D. 111
Colomer, J. M. 114, 121
Committee of European Securities Regulators (CESR) 13, 48, 180
Compston, H. 113
Conway, P. 53
Cook, P. 12
Cook, T. 145
Copeland, G. W. 114
corporatism 112–13
Costanza, R. 19
Council of European Energy Regulators (CEER) 48
Cronqvist, L. 53
Crouch, C. 45
Cukierman, A. 37, 66
Curran, J. 146

Dahl, R. A. 142, 143
Daily Telegraph, The 152
Dalton, R. J. 42
De Francesco, F. 17, 149, 151
de Jonge, J. 151
de Larosière, J. 180
de Visscher, C. 186
de Vreese, C. H. 143
Deeg, R. 46
Deephouse, D. L. 145, 151, 152
democracy
    consensus democracy and 112, 113
    'deficit' in 18, 141
    legitimacy and 18–19
    Madisonian model of 18
    see also regulatory governance
Der Bund 152
deregulation 7, 12, 15, 179
    game theory and 15
Diani, M. 121
DiMaggio, P. 11, 102, 106
Dodd, N. 179
Dolowitz, D. 111
Douglas, J. W. 145
Downs, A. 42
Doyle, G. 150

Drahos, P. 16, 67, 69
Drazen, A. 144, 182
Dunleavy, P. 148

Ebbinghaus, B. 112
Eberlein, B. 13, 21, 48
Economist, The 179 n.1
Eckert, S. 108
Eckstein, H. 26
Egan, M. 42
Egeberg, M. 16, 42, 67, 106
Eilders, C. 143, 151
Elgie, R. 144, 147
Elman, C.13, 40
Emery, Y. 149
Epstein, D. 45, 102, 105, 144, 186
Esser, F. 145, 165
European Commission 10, 13, 21, 180
    network governance and 13–14, 48
    subsidiarity, principle of 10
European National Competition
    authorities (ECN) 48
European Parliament (EP) 13, 180
European Platform of Regulatory
    Authorities 13
European Regulators Group 13
European Union (EU) 10
    financial crisis (2008–2010)
        response to 180
    regulation in 10, 13, 149
        competition law and 124
        IRA networks 48, 55, 124
Everett, M. G. 120

Flkner, G. 112 n.2
Feintuck, M. 15
Fernandez, X. 12
Field, A. P.
Financial Services Authority 178
Financial Times, The 152
Finland
    IRAs study *51, 56, 58, 76, 77*
    Rahoitustarkastus *51,* 79, 86–7, 97
Fiorina, M. P. 47
Fligstein, N. 180

Flinders, M. 19, 174
Follesdal, A. 141
Foster, C. 15
Fox, J. 143
France
    IRAs study 21, 39
    2008–10 financial crisis, response
        to 179
Franchino, F. 151, 186
Francis, J. 15
Fraschini, A. 66, 68
Friedberg, E. 42
Fukuyama, F. 182

Gailmard, S. 185
Gayo, C. C. 68
GCR 149
Gehring, T. 103
Geithner, T. 180
Gemici, K. 45
Gentzkow, M. 151
George, A. L. 138
Gerber, B. J. 105, 145
Germany
    Bundesanstalt für Finanzdienstleis-
        tungaufsicht *51,* 52, 55, 78–9, 86,
        95, 97
    financial system in 45–6
    IRAs study 21, 39, *51, 56, 57, 76,
        77*
Gerring, J. 29, 147
Giauque, D. 149
Giddens, A. 23
Giesel, H. 92
Gilardi, F. ix, 1, 8, 11, 14, 18, 33, 37,
        44, 51–2, 99, 101, 114, 142, 144,
        146, 149, 151, 167, 169, 181, 185,
        index 51–2, *54*
Gingerich, D. 45, 53
Global Competition Review 149
Goertz, G. 70, 92, 111, 137, 151, 176,
        177
Goodin, R. E. 15, 26
Goodsell, C. T. 68
Gordon, D. 66, 144

Grande, E. 13, 21
Grilli, V. 37, 66
Grossman, S. J. 180
Grote, J. 112
Guardian, The 152, 179 n.1

Haas, P. M. 48, 67, 69, 107
Habermas, J. 20
Hall, P. A. 3, 24, 29, 45, 53, 149, 183
Hallin, D. 145
Hamilton, A. 18
Hammond, T. H. 102, 105
Hassel, A. 112
Häusermann, S. x, 112 n.2, 113
Hayes, A. F. 153, 154
    SPSS macro 152
Hebert, F. T. 69
Héritier, A. 10, 13, 48, 108
Hildebrand, Y. 182
Hirschi, C. 119, 139
Hirschman, A. O. 26, 27
Hix, S. 141
Hodge, G. A. 143
Hofmann, J. 179
Holder, S. 20, 42
Hollingsworth, J. R. 169
Hood, C. 7, 16, 103, 148
Hopenhayn, H. 143
Howard, M. 142, 143, 145, 146, 151
Howlett, M. 70, 111, 120
Huber, J. D. 15, 35, 102, 103, 107
Hutter, B. 178, 179

IMF (International Monetary Fund)
    125
Immergut, E. M. 24
independence 7, 36–40
    formal and de facto 4, 30, 33, 37,
        38–9, 114
    organisational 36–7
    political and economic 37
    see also IRAs, 'de facto indepen-
        dence' study
Independent, The 152
Independent Regulators Group (IRG) 48

institutionalism
    historical 3, 24, 25, 26, 27, 31, 41,
        43, 47, 175, 176
    'new institutionalisms' 3, 11, 23,
        144 n.1, 176, 177
    approaches/types of 3, 24–5
    research use of 24–7, 176–7
    rational choice 3, 24, 25, 27, 31,
        44, 45, 46–7, 106, 108, 175, 176,
        177
    sociological 3, 24, 25–6, 27, 31, 45,
        46, 106, 108, 144 n.1, 175, 176,
        177
    see also rational choice theory
institutions 23–4, 106
    definitions of 23
    'logic of appropriateness' argument
        106, 138
    organisations and 23–4
international political economy (IPE)
    12
international relations (IR) 12
IOSCO (International Organisation of
    Securities Commissions) 66, 69,
    125
IRAs (independent regulatory agen-
    cies)
    accountability and 1, 2, 4, 9, 18,
        19–22, 30, 34, 98, 141, 169, 172,
        181, 185, 187
        future research and 172–3, 181,
            187
        media coverage and 2, 3, 4, 5,
            21, 31, 141, 142–3, 166–7
        'multi-pronged system of
            control' and 141–2, 185, 187
        see also under IRAs, 'de facto
            independence' study
    cross-country comparisons 46, 47,
        96, 103, 138, 182, 187
    definition of 8
    delegation to 14, 15–16, 17, 18, 21,
        33, 34, 102–3, 105, 146, 174,
        185
    democratic legitimacy and 34,

102, 174, 185, 187
political justification for 108
diffusion, patterns of 9, 11–12, 13,
183, 185, 187
democratic legitimacy of 1, 9,
18–19, 20–1, 34, 50, 98, 172,
187
'democratic deficit' arguments
141, 172
procedural accountability and
19–21
independence of 35–40, 42–3, 169,
172–3, 181, 183, 184–5
de facto independence 37, 38–9,
40, 42–3, 44–5, 47, 50, 108,
114, 169, 174, 181, 186
effectiveness and 33–4, 37,
39–40, 186
formal/informal structures and
37, 42, 183
politicians, relationships with
43–4, 66–8, 174, 184
regulatees and 4, 37, 38, 39, 40,
68–69, 175, 184
see also IRAs, 'de facto independence' study
intermediary position of 49, 66, 97,
98, 99, 173, 184
functional antagonism and 181,
184
media, role of see media, IRAs and
network-embedded agencies 47–9,
99, 171, 172, 175, 183–4, 185,
187
regulation effectiveness and 175
policy-making, role in 4, 5, 22, 30,
31, 101–4, 105, 106, 138, 140,
169, 173, 181, 184
centrality variations of 103–4,
105, 108, 140, 171, 173
functional antagonism, importance of 184
research and 105
regulatory functioning of 7–8, 29,
43–4, 101–2, 138–9, 173

'capture', problem of 50, 172,
184
economic regulation and 181–2
performance measures and 186–7
research and 21, 186–7
social regulation and 182
'revolving door' phenomena and
39, 40
Western European 8–9, 11, 101–2,
103
see also banking and finance IRAs;
regulatory governance
IRAs, 'de facto independence' study
analytic framework of 2–4, 23–8,
29–32, 40–50, 109–12, 175–7
case selection 50–2, 109, 110,
112–15
hypotheses 41–50, 105–9, 170–1,
175
new institutionalisms, use of in
176–7
QCA and fuzzy-set analysis 28,
29, 40–1, 52, 91–6, 98, 101,
104, 109, 110, 135, 136, 137,
176
questionnaires, examples of
189–205
use of term 'de facto independence 40
formal independence, relationship
with 33, 34, 37, 40, 42, 55, 98,
115, 169–70, 170, 181
life cycles of agencies and 33, 53,
97, 171
main findings, summary of 4, 33,
98–9 , 171–2
future research directions 186–7
normative implications of 181–6
media as 'accountability forum'
study 141–167, 170, 171, 172,
174
case studies 141, 147–50
hypotheses 146–7, 165, 176
media coverage analysis and
143–4, 146, 159, 160, 165–7

'media favourability' as measure
    in 151, 161, *163*, 165, 172
policy credibility and efficiency
    analysis 143–5, 146, 147,
    151, 157, 161, 163, *164,*
    166–7, 170, *171,* 172, 174–5,
    187
reliability testing and 153–6
results 159–64, 166–7, *171*
technical expertise and 144, 172
tone of coverage and 145, 146,
    151–2, 159, 161, *162, 163,*
    166
see also under Switzerland;
    United Kingdom
networks of agencies, participation
    in 33, 47, 55, *56,* 97, 98, 99, 171
policy-making study, centrality of
    role in 101–40, 170, 171–2, 174,
    176
    APES, use of 101, 104, 119–21,
        123, 125, 139
    case selection 110–15, 139
    monocratic systems and 106–7,
        113, 135, 138, *170,* 176
    hypotheses 105–9, 114, *171,* 176
    sector-specific and general
        regulation 108, 113, 114,
        138, 139, *170,* 175
    results analysis 135–40, *171*
    see also under The Netherlands;
        Sweden; Switzerland
politicians, relationship with 37,
    38, 39, 41, 43, 44, 46, 55, 66, 71,
    72, 110, 114, *115,* 137, 171, 172,
    174, 184
    indicators used 66–8
    survey results 74, *75, 76,* 78–85,
        93, *94, 95,* 96, 97, 98, 99,
        115, 140, *170, 171*
regulatees, relationship with 4, 37,
    38, 39, 40, 41, 43, 44, 46, 48–9,
    50, 55, *56,* 66, 71, *73,* 101, 110,
    115, 137, 171, 172, 174, 184
    indicators used 68

survey results 74, *75, 77,* 86–91,
    96–7, 98, 99, 101, *115, 170,*
    171
'revolving door' indicator and 66,
    67, 68, 74 n.14, 78, 79, 81, 82,
    83, 85, 86, 87, 88, 89, 90, 91
veto players, effect of 33, 41, 44–5,
    56, 95, 98, 99, 109, 138, *170,*
    171, 175, 183
Western European countries
    comparison 33, 34, 98
Irwin, G. A. 113, 114, 121
Italy 21
    Autorità per le Garanzie nelle
        Comunicazioni 51, 84, 90, 95
    IRAs study *51, 56, 63, 76, 77*

Jachtenfuchs, M. 26
Jackson, G. 46, 92
Jacobs, S. 1, 169, 173
James, O. x, 7, 49
Jayasuriya, K. 12
Jefferson, T. 142
Johnson, C. 173
Jordana, J. 7, 8, 12, 14, 16, 22, 33,
    101, 169, 173

Kahn, A. E. 43
Kaiser, H. F. 157, *158*
Katzenstein, P. 26, 27, 112, 149, 176
Katznelson, I. 25
Kemp, R. 19
Kepplinger, H. 146, 151, 165
Khalil, E. L. 23
Kiewiet, D. R. 102, 105
Kim, J. N. 151
Klingemann, H. -D. 26
Knill, C. 148
Knoepfel, P. 19
Knoke, D. 121
Knott, J. H. 102, 105
Kohler-Koch, B. 13
Krause, G. A. 145
Kriesi, H. 112, 113, 114, 121
Krippendorff, K. 152, 153–4

alpha measure 152–4
Krugman, P. 180
Kydland, F. 144

Lægreid, P. x, 4, 7, 16–17, 21, 22, 36, 38, 103, 139, 144 n.1, 166, 173, 174
Lang, G. E. 151
Lang, K. 151
Le Temps 152
Lee, M. 142, 146
Lehmbruch, G. 25, 112, 113
Levi, M. 25, 27
Levi-Faur, D. ix, 1, 4, 7, 8, 12, 14, 16, 22, 33, 47, 101, 139, 144, 166, 169, 173, 182
Lijphart, A. 113, *150*, 185
Lindenberg, S. 177
Lindvall, J. 113
Lodge, M. 18, 20, 142, 144, 167, 179, 180
Lohmann, S. 143
Lombard, M. 153
Louw, P. E. 142
Lowi, T. J. 102
Luckmann, T. 23, 106
Lukes, S. 70

McCubbins, M. D. 102, 105, 143
McGowan, F. 17, 103
Mach, A. 112 n.2
Mackenzie, W. J. M. 110
McLean, I. 15
McMenamin, I. 144, 147
Madison, J. 18
Maeda, Y. 151
Maggetti, M. 14, 48, 50 n.7, 108, 114, 136, 137, 141, 142, 147, 150, 167, 175,
Mahon, J. E. J. 111
Mahoney, J. 4, 26, 70, 92 n.18, 109, 176, 177
Majone, G. 10, 13, 15, 18, 19, 20, 21, 22, 34, 38, 48, 98, 99, 101, 103, 105, 107, 141, 142, 143, 144, 146, 149, 151, 166, 167, 172, 173, 174,

175, 182, 183, 185, 186
Mancini, P. 145
Manin, B. 18, 145
Maravall, J. M. 18
March, J. G. 23, 25, 27, 42, 106, 182
Margetts, H. 148
Marsh, D. 22, 111
Martimort, D. 43
Masson, P. 144, 182
Mattli, W. 13
Mayntz, R. 24
Mazzoleni, G. 145, 165
media
    accountability, political and 142–5, 166, 167
    'fire-alarm' function of 143
    freedom of 142–3
    information, political and 145
        reality construction and 145
    IRA accountability, role in 2–3, 4, 21, 141, 142–6, 165–7, 172, 174–5, 181, 185
        'accountability forum' and 22, 31, 141, 143, 165, 166, 167, 172, 185
        policy credibility and 143–5, 146, 166, 167, 172, 174–5
        see also study under IRAs de facto independence study
    opinion formation, role in 143, 145
    quality press, influence of 151
        editorials, comments and interviews 151, 152
Meyer, C. 143
Meyer, J. W. 42
Miller, P. 13, 178, 179
Milner, H. V. 13
Mitnick, B. M. 14
Miyahara, M. 151
Moatti, S. 178
mobilisation, political 145
Moe, T. M. 5, 13, 21, 35, 99, 102, 173, 174, 185
Montesquieu, C.-L. de S. 18
Moran, M. 9, 10, 11, 15, 102, 103,

105, 144, 148, 182
Mulgan, R. 142

Nesvetailova, A. 178
Netherlands, The
    Autoriteit Financiële Markten
        (AFM) *51,* 55, 79–80, 87, 115,
        119, 123, 124
    civil service in 113, 114
    consensus democracy, as 112, 113
    decision-making process in 113–14
    IRA policy-making study *51,* 55,
        56, 58, 60, 63, 76, 77, 101, 112,
        113, 121, 123, 124, 139
        banking and finance regulation
            115–16, *119,* 124, *125, 129,*
            135, 136
        EU centrality and 124
        competition regulation 117, *119,*
            124, *125, 130, 135, 136*
    IRA politician/regulatee indepen-
        dence study *51,* 55, *56, 58, 60,*
        63, 76, 77
    Nederlandse Mededingingsauto-
        riteit (NMa) *51,* 81, 88, 97, *115,*
        117, *119, 123,* 124
    Onafhankelijke Post en Telecommu-
        nicatie Autoritei 51, 55, 84, 90–1
Neue Zuercher Zeitung 152
Neuenschwander, P. 149
new public management (NPM) 11,
    33, 148, 182
New York Times 179 n.1
Newman, A. L. 13
Nicoletti, G. 53
Nordlinger, E. A. 38
Norris, P. 148
North, D. C. 23, 47, 107
Norway
    IRAs study *51, 56, 60, 64, 76, 77*
    Konkurransetilsynet 51, 82, 88, 95
    New Public Management, introduc-
        tion of 182
    Post- Og Teletilsynet 51, 85, 91

O'Donnell, G. 143
O'Halloran, S. 144, 186
Oberg, P. O. 113
OECD 8, 66, 69, 149
    agencies, level of expenditure and 8
    principles of 'good governance' 69
    regulatory activity in 1, 169
Okawara, N. 27
Olsen, J. P. 23, 25, 26, 27, 106, 111,
    182
Olson, M. 20, 43, 49
Olson, M. K. 69
opinion, political 143, 144, 145
    see also media
Ostrom, E. 25, 107

Palan, R. 178
Papadopoulos, Y. ix, 18, 19, 66, 108,
    112, 113, 121, 149
Parkin, M. 37
Patterson, S. C. 114
Pedersen, L. H. 39 n.3
Pelzman, S. 4, 14, 15, 49, 66, 99, 173
Perry, J. L. 69
Persson, T. 18
Peters, B. G. 16, 23, 24, 66, 103, 105,
    106, 110, 121, 147, 148
Peters, R. G. 151
Petiteville, F. 111
Petrovsky, N. 185
Pfetsch, B. 159
Pierre, J. 113
Pierson, P. 25, 43, 47, 107
Polanyi, K. 45
Pollack, M. A. 108, 144, 186
Pollitt, C. 8, 16, 17, 36, 103, 182
Pollock, T. G. 144
Popper, K. R. 70
Posner, R. A. 49
Powell, W. W. 11, 106
Power, M. 7
Prat, A. 142, 143
Prescott, E. 144
principal component analysis (PCA)
    153, 156–7, *158*

privatisation 1, 7, 12, 169, 172
Przeworski, A. 18, 109, 112

Qualitative Comparative Analysis
    (QCA) 28, 29, 40–1, 52, 71 n.13,
    91–6, 101, 104, 109, 110, 111, 123
    n.14, 135, 136, 137, 138, 176
    fuzzy-set analysis and 40–1, 52
        n.11, 91, n.15, 92, 93, 98, 176

Radaelli, C. M. ix, 7, 17, 53, 111, 149,
    151, 182
Rae, D. W. 112
Ragin, C. C. 3, 28, 40, 44, 50 n.7, 52,
    91 n.15, 92, 93, 94, 104, 109, 114,
    135, 175, 176
Ramesh, M. 70, 111, 120
rational choice theory 25, 48–9
    bureaucratic autonomy, study of 35
    economic theory of regulation (ET)
        and 14–15
    rational choice institutionalism 3,
        24–5, 26, 27, 31, 45, 46, 106,
        108, 175, 176, 177
Rebérioux, A. 180
regulation 7, 173
    agencification and 7, 9, 12, 103
    definitions of 7, 10, 139, 173
    economic theory of (ET) 14–15, 99,
        173
    public and private interests theories
        and 14–15
    sector-specific and general 108
    'three forces' in 39, 173
regulatory capitalism 29, 30, 166, 169,
    173, 186
    financial crisis (2008–2010), effect
        on 178
    globalisation, effect on 12, 16, 33
        mechanisms driving 16, 169
    see also IRAs; regulatory gover-
        nance
regulatory governance 7, 8, 12, 16, 17,
    99, 169, 174, 180
    banking and financial services
        179–80
        shortcomings with 179
    competition policy and 147
    democratic legitimacy and 18,
        19–20, 34, 141–2, 172, 187
        'majoritarian standards' of 141
    depoliticisation in 174
    financial crisis of 2008–10, effect
        on 178–80
        regulatory failures and 178–9
    future of 178–80
    institutional design and 15–16, 181,
        182
    IRAs and 1, 7, 9, 11, 17, 29, 33,
        169, 172–4, 181–6
        democratic deficit and 18, 141,
            172, 187
        incentives for delegation to 11,
            33
        independence, effectiveness of
            33–4, 39–40, 42, 169, 172–3,
            183, 186
        policy-making, role of in 101–4,
            169, 173–4
        technical expertise of 33, 97,
            102, 174
        unintended consequences of 17,
            33–4, 103, 182
        see also IRAs; IRAs 'de facto'
            independence study
    media coverage, role in transpar-
        ency 142, 143–6, 174
        as 'linkage mechanism' 143
        'mediatisation', concept of 22,
            165
        see also media
    NPM (new public management)
        and 33
    policy diffusion and 185, 187
    research, future directions of 186–7
'regulocracy' 4, 139, 173
Ricart, E. J. 140
Richardson, J. 103
Rihoux, B. 3–4, 28, 41, 93 n.20, 104,
    176

Riker, W. H. 18
Rindova, V. P. 144
Risse, T. 106
Roberts, A. 141
Roberts, N. C. 142
Rodrik, D. 180
Rogoff, K. 36
Rogowski, R. 112
Rose, R. 110
Rothstein, B. 113
Rotmans, J. 19
Rouse, A. 143
Rowan, B. 42
Rueschemeyer, D. 26
Ruffieux, R. 113

Sabatier, P. A. 179
Sabel, C. 13
Sarcinelli, U. 143
Sartori, G. 36, 53, 111
Scharpf, F. W. 19, 24–5
Schedler, A. 142, 143, 165
Schmidt, V. A. 26
Schmitter, P. 25, 112, 113
Schneider, C. Q. 41, 104, 110, 135–6,
    139
Schneider, V. 25
Schnyder, G. 112
Schulz, W. 145, 165
Sciarini, P. 121
Scott, C. 143, 167
Scott, J. 18, 120
Scott, W. A. 153
Scott, W. R. 24
Searle, J. R. 23
Seawright, J. 147
Serdült, U. 119, 123, 139
Shapiro, J. M. 151
Shepsle, K. A. 107, 144
Shipan, C. R. 15, 35, 102, 103, 107
Siaroff, A. 112
Sil, R. 26, 27, 176
Skocpol, T. 43, 47, 107
Simon, H. A. 42
Slaughter, A. 13

Smith, A. 111
Smithson, M. 28, 40
Snidal, D. 12
Snow, R. P. 145
Snyder, J. M. 142
Snyder, S. K. 15
Sørensen, E. 102
Sosay, G. 20, 142
Soskice, D. W. 53, 149, 183
Spence, D. B. 18, 105
Spiller, P. T. 15, 69, 105
Steinmo, S. 27
Stern, J. 20, 42
Stevens, J. 157
Stigler, G. J. 4, 14, 42, 49, 66, 99, 173
Stiglitz, J. 180
Stimson, J. A. 143
Stoker, G. 22
Streeck, W. 45
Strom, K. 18, 34
Strömbäck, J. 145, 165
Strömberg, D. 142
Stone Sweet, A. 8, 21, 66, 68, 108, 144
    n.1
Summers, L. 37, 66
Svensson, D. 113
Swanson, D. L. 145
Sweden
    civil service/public administration
        in 8, 113, 114
    consensus democracy, as 112, 113
    decision-making process in 113, 114
    Finansinspektionen 51, 80, 87, 97,
        115, 116, *123*, 124
    IRA policy-making study *51, 55,
        56, 59, 61, 64, 76, 77*, 101, 112,
        113, 121, 139
        banking and finance regulation
            116, *119*, 124–5, *127, 131,
            135, 136*
        competition regulation 117–18,
            119, 124–5, *127, 132, 135,
            136*
    IRA politician/regulatee indepen-
        dence study *51*, 55, *56, 59, 61,*

64, 76, 77
Konkurrensverhet (KKV) *51,* 82,
    89, 95, *115, 119,* 123, 124
Sweden Post & Telestyrelsen (PTS)
    51, 53, 85, 91
Switzerland
    banking crisis 2008–2012, response
        to 179–80
    civil service/public administration
        in 113, 114, 149
    consensus democracy, as 112, 113,
        149
    Credit Suisse 179
    decision-making process in 113,
        114, 138, 148–9
        new public management reforms
            149
    Economiesuisse 125
    Eidgenössische Bankenkommission
        51, 55, *56,* 81, 88, *115,* 116–17,
        119, 123, 125, 139
    Federal Banking Commission 179
    Finanzmarktaufsicht 180
    IRA policy-making study *51, 59,*
        61, 76, 77, 101, 112, 113, 121,
        125, 138, 139
        competition/cartel regulation
            118, *119,* 125, *134, 135, 136,*
            139
        finance and stock exchange
            regulation 116–17, *119, 133,*
            135, 136
    IRA politician/regulatee indepen-
        dence study *51, 56, 59, 61, 76,*
        77
    media as 'accountability forum'
        study 141, 142, 147
        survey data 218–24
        Swiss Comco, media evaluation
            of 147, 149, 159, *156,*
            159–67, 172
    media industry in 150
        policy issues study 148
    SECO (State secretariat for eco-
        nomic affairs) 125

Swiss Competition Commission
    (ComCo) *51*, 82–3, 89, *115,* 116,
    119, 123, 125, 139, 147, 149,
    150, *156*
UBS bank 179
Wettbewerbskommission (WeKo)
    see Switzerland, Swiss Competi-
    tion Commission

Tages Anzeiger 152
Taylor, M. 3, 24, 112
Teske, P. 105
Teune, H. 109, 111
Thatcher, M. 8, 13, 21, 37, 39, 40, 42,
    43, 45, 48, 66, 68, 101, 103, 105,
    108, 114, 144, 173, 184
Thelen, K. A. 11, 26, 43, 45, 107
Tilly, C. 43
Times, The 152
Torfing, J. 102
Tribune de Genève 152
Tsebelis, G. 44, 45, 53, 109, 183
Turner, A. 178, 180
Turner, J. H. 23
24 Heures 152

UCINET 120, 123
United Kingdom
    civil service, agencification of 8
    Competition Commission (CC) *51,*
        83, 89–90, 118, 141, 142, 147,
        149, 152, 159, 166, 172, 174,
        209
        survey data 209–18
        media relations and 150, 174
        rating of 149
        see also U.K., media as 'account-
            ability forum' study
    EU, impact of 149
    IRAs study 21, 39, *51, 56, 62, 76,*
        77
    majoritarianism in 148
    media as 'accountability forum'
        study 141, 142, 147
        British CC, media evaluation

of 147, 148, 149–50, *152, 159–67*
media industry in 150
  policy issues study 147–8
privatisation and 11
state regulation in 10–11, 148
  IRA delegation and 21, 42–3, 148
  new public management reforms (NPM) and 148
welfare state in 11
United States
  as a liberal market economy (LME) 46
  bureaucracy, study of 35
  Constitution of 142
  Federal Reserve 178, 180
  financial crisis (2008–2012), response to 178, 180
  media, role in Congress study 145, 147 n.2
  New Deal 9
  policy making in 102–3, 182
  postal system 47–8
  Progressive Movement 9
  regulatory capitalism in 182
    origins of 9–10, 15
  Securities Exchange Commission 178, 180

Van Deth, J. W. 182
Van Thiel, S. 37
van Waarden, F. 67, 69, 182
Varone, F. 114, 149
Verhoest, K. x, 21, 35, 36
Verkuilen, J. 28, 40
Verschuere, B. 8, 36, 142
Vibert, F. 141
Vogel, S. K. 1, 7, 9, 16, 143, 169
Voltmer, K. 142, 143, 146, 151

Wagemann, C. x, 104, 110, 135–6, 139
Walgrave, S. 143
Wallace, H. 17, 103
Waterman, R. W. 68, 143

Weingast, B. R. 15, 25, 102, 105
Weißbecker, H. 146
Werle, R. 13
WGFR 180
Whitford, A. B. 45
Widmer, T. 149
Wilks, S. x, 13, 17, 42, 43, 48, 103, 147, 149
Williamson, O. E. 42
Wilson, J. Q. 22, 67
Wincott, D. 182
Wittgenstein, L. 42
Wood, B. D. 68, 185
Wymeersch, E. 180

Yancey, C. 142
Yesilkagit, K. 16, 37, 103, 113, 144 n.1, 147

Zadeh, L. A. 92 n.17
Zaller, J. 143
Zeitlin, J. 13
Zillmann, D. 143